The Daily Battle

for a

Normal Life

A Memoir

My sincere appreciation
Gay 7/2/19

LORETTE GAY

Contents

Preface 7
The Reasons 9

1. Childhood 13
2. Belligerence and Belief 23
3. Irresistible Nature 29
4. Trust 35
5. Reverse Life 42
6. Déjà Vu 48
7. Teenage-hood 51
8. The Mystery 62
9. Why Now? 69
10. Deception 74
11. Turbulent Adolescence 81
12. Vacation 87
13. Ineluctable Deaths 96
14. Meeting Sam 106
15. Engagement 110
16. The Return 115
17. The Third Pregnancy 119
18. The Aftermath 125
19. Emotional Distress 131
20. An Unceremonious Goodbye 135
21. Unaccustomed Life 139
22. Another Beginning 144
23. The Grotesque Irony of Fate 150
24. Full House 157
25. An Alley through Sicknesses 160

26. The First Treatment 167
27. What's Next? 180
28. Life Goes On 192
29. The Mistaken Intruder 199
30. Repossession 205
31. The Second Treatment 211
32. Deprivation 220
33. Ravaged by Dementia 224
34. Valentine's Day 230
35. Death, My Enemy 236
36. Another Invisible Disorder 248
37. The Third Treatment 257
38. Too Much to Handle 269
39. My Misery Is Mine 273
40. The Scare 280
41. Confirmation 285
42. The Catastrophic Day 292
43. More Ailments 299
44. Side Effects 309
45. Insane Behavior 321
46. Imminent Departure 328
47. Understanding Chronic Disease 341
48. The Walk-In 347
49. Grace 360
50. The Precious Call 365
51. Find Happiness Again 373
52. The Heavy Secret 382
53. An Unpredictable Life 395
54. Lifetime Friendship 401

Acknowledgements 405

Preface

THIS BOOK IS DEDICATED to the millions of people who, like me, suffer in silence from chronic health conditions and problematic life issues. We might sometimes think that in life, we choose our fates, or that life is a matter of selecting what we want. Unfortunately, this isn't always the case. Our consequence on earth has nothing to do with what we desire. Ostensibly, we are who we are and who we were created to be.

This is the story of a woman who has been tormented from the time she was born. Despite all the harshness she's encountered on her path, she is still living with a soul full of faith. This is a valuable story about how experience has made her who she is—appreciative of and observant to things that might seem meaningless to others but are precious to her. This life hasn't always been a walk in the Catherine de Medici flowering gardens. Mostly, it's been a walk in the rain, a walk through a storm, a walk in the pitch-dark. This is a story of a spirit searching for light as it tries to escape from terrible, scary passages of arrant darkness. This is a factual story of pain hiding behind the mask of normality, the story of a woman hiding in plain sight, and the story of her daily battle for a normal life.

The Reasons

I'M FIFTY-EIGHT GOING RAPIDLY on fifty-nine. Time flies too quickly after you reach middle age, which doesn't seem fair. Descending from the mountaintop of middle age should go as slowly as climbing up did, but instead, it seems that we run down even faster to the bottom. It leaves us with no time to recharge our adulthood batteries.

Aging scares the hell out of me, even more than all the diseases inside me do. My children know it too. Every time I feel depressed, one of them always asks me if the natural, biological process of getting old is the cause of my depression.

"No, sunshine," I tell him, "the world with all its inconveniences is just depressing, that's all. When you reach my age, you'll understand."

The tale of my life that I'm about to narrate isn't unique. Millions of people like me are moving through life the same way as I am at this very moment, living with similar health problems and family issues. As simple it might look in some people's eyes, it's very complicated and burdensome for me. My life is a bizarre, unordinary life. I've gone through so many periodical issues that I've had to name them. I call them "dancing the tango in life's war." Whenever I'm sliding to the dark side of the road, I dance to return to the base. This helps me reboot my self-confidence every time something tries to plunder my life away.

What I have learned from my life is interesting and noteworthy, I think, despite the trials I have encountered on my path, one after another. Therefore, I decided to keep a diary about my journey. What I'm going to tell you is only half the story. Like everybody else, I keep part of myself a secret. I keep the other half in my story cache, which I won't reveal in this book.

I was motivated to come out of my dungeon and open my door to the public for three reasons. First, I'm scared about my tomorrows—what might happen to me overnight when I'm alone in my house. I wait with my heart in my mouth. Second, I fight against so many things. Emotionally, I'm losing ground, I feel weak, and I have little control over myself. Third, I don't want to lose my battle with life, and any defeat can deplete my chances of survival. I'm conscious of my sicknesses, but nobody else is. It's my secret. Anyway, who would give a damn about it if I told them? Everyone has their own problems.

On the outside, I look fine. I must look the way I look so I can glory in the knowledge that I'm a winner, despite my despair. My mind works hard to keep me company, even at this very moment. This refuge too might leave me someday, might scrupulously run away from this busy head of mine.

God is only my witness. I feel strange in my skin and wonder, "Am I getting worse?" Come what may, I vow to myself to keep fighting against my tumultuous illnesses until death. Isn't life normally a quotidian battle to survive? We fight to successfully reach our goals. Each of us have different prospects in life, and for me, life has always been a struggle to survive. "Smile," "laugh," and "faith" are the watchwords that keep me going forward.

"View of Olivia childhood house"

1

Childhood

My name is Marie Rosette, but people call me Olivia, the name that was given to me at birth by a midwife, a Canadian nun, in commemoration that I was the first baby she delivered in Haiti. Her name was Sister Olivia, and she gave me her own name like I was her own daughter. My mother legally registered me as Marie Rosette Robert. Not too many people are aware of my real name, but from that moment forward, everyone, including my mother, called me Olivia. My mother likely forgot about her right to use the name on my birth certificate because she called me Oli from that day forward.

Was it out of respect for the nun who delivered me? I don't know, but the ecclesiastical sister's name will stay with me forever.

At the moment of my birth, Marie Rosette became nonexistent. The genuine me stopped existing at the very onset of my life, and a counterfeit me took her place. Later on, when I started going to school, the matter of my name became more complicated, and later, when I changed my last name in marriage, Marie Rosette Robert—a woman whom I never met—was utterly obliterated. As you can see, my life was set before me by the muses and the power on high the moment I exhaled my first crybaby breath on earth.

I was born in a small town, Roche-a-Bateau, which is situated in the south of Haiti. One side of this tiny village is positioned on the Caribbean Sea, and the other side is surrounded with mountains—a beautiful, peaceful piece of green land. The panorama is a spectacular from all angles. When I lived there, the population was about two thousand, so everyone knew everybody else. It was very cozy, admirable, and inviting, made even more picturesque and impressive by its smattering of little houses topped with sheets of aluminum or palm leaves, depending on the resident's financial capacity. The abodes were surrounded by wild gardens. All sorts of uncultivated flowers, disorderly plants, and weeds grew around these tiny houses. From above, the town looked like a bowl of kale salad with tomatoes, yellow peppers, and a few slices of almond scattered here and there.

Lush verdure comprised most of the landscape. Grass and wild vegetation sprouted between the stones, gravel, and flat rocks that comprised the narrow streets, which offered just enough space for one person to find the entranceway of each dwelling. The smell of the greenery was like allspice dampened by aromatic ylang-ylang oil. Imposing trees, including ylang-ylang, lined the streets and had done so for centuries (or decennials, who knows?), making the landscape even more unique and lugubrious, especially at night.

At that time in history, Roche-a-Bateau hardly saw any private cars or buses on its dusty streets, or *terre battue*, as we say in French. There were specific days to travel—only three times a week—when people waited at a designated place for a single bus. If you got lucky, you might get a seat (likely only reasonably big enough for a small child, so you had to squeeze), and the trip might take three to four hours, depending on the weather and where you were going. If there was rain, the mud made it difficult for the bus to go at a normal speed. The same bus picked up people from different towns, meaning that the bus stopped and started regularly. That said, travel was uncommon for the people of Roche-a-Bateau. We didn't easily leave home to go to the cities unless it was absolutely necessary. When possible, we made bus reservations and paid ahead to guarantee our seats, lest we wait on standby in the hot, dusty streets for hours.

When I lived there, none of the families possessed cars. We were free of that kind of expense and pollution. There was no electricity, no television, and no telephones except for a public payphone in the gendarmes' barracks. No one had a refrigerator, and water was sourced from the stream in calabash containers. Calabash is a large, coarse species of gourd, similar to a pumpkin. To make a water container, the inside of the gourd was removed, cleaned, and dried. After the water was carried from the stream, it was stored at home in a clay ceramic vase called a *cruche,* which kept it fresh even when the weather was extremely hot.

For entertainment, children like me read book after book, went to church, and hung out with friends, but the latter wasn't permitted to me by my grandparents. My three aunts were my only friends, and that was that. My maternal grandparents believed that home was where I belonged, not hanging out with untrustworthy kids, even though they were friends with their parents. They preferred to send me to an old woman's house to keep her company rather than let me be with kids my own age. She was a good friend of my mother's and didn't have any children of her own, so she treated me like I was hers. She had a bakery and would give me bags of cookies, which was the main reason I liked to go there.

It was at her house where I had my first bad taste of life. I was five years old, running into her house, when I missed a step on the porch. I fell down onto the glossy gray concrete and split open my chin, blood gushing out. That fall gave me long, ugly gash under my chin. Fortunately, none of my bottom teeth were broken, but I still have a big scar as a souvenir, which has since grown hair.

A very powerful river separated Roche-a-Bateau from the other village in the south. The water came from the mountains and streamed into the ocean. During the rainfall season, the river flooded, and the villages were submerged in water, destroying houses and roads and killing many people and animals. However, this didn't stop the residents from rebuilding in the same place every year, hoping that one day, the watercourse would forget its route.

During the summer, this dangerous river looked crystal clear, paved with stones of many colors. It served as a self-service laundry and a bathhouse for both children and adults. I could only go to the river under my aunts' supervision. The beach wasn't far away either, not even three miles from where I lived. It wasn't really a beach but a place where fishermen sold their catches, unclothed children played and splashed in the water, and half-naked adults swam for recreation. Because my grandparents didn't allow me to stray far from home, I never put my feet in the seawater, but I watched it closely. I told myself that as soon as I was old enough, my first adult decision would be to have a taste of the vast, exuberant sea. It's part of the wonderful gifts that God generously gave to us at creation, and for the sake of God, it has remained available to us to this day, free to the public.

My grandparents and my aunts were too cautious to let me have fun in the water for fear that something bad would happen to me. "The sea waves are too dangerous," they said to me again and again. "They don't distinguish between an innocent child and an adult. The power of the surf can drive you away to the deep side of the ocean. However, we know that you are our little girl, and we are here to protect you, Oli. You can do this when your mother comes on vacation with us."

Like many grandparents, they had the uncanny ability to say things so sweetly and softly that I took what they said as the absolute truth. Later in my life, I understood that my grandparents had a responsibility when they cared for me. My mother left me with them as my guardians, so they intended to do the job well. Plus I wasn't completely alone; I had three aunts, living in the same house, who were only slightly older than I was and who loved me very much. Still, there were things that I couldn't say to or do with my aunties that I could with a friend my own age, out of respect for them.

I had to use my imagination to create something to do so that I didn't get bored. That is how I started staring at the birds, talking to them. I found them to be so beautiful and lovely to watch. I fed them with cornmeal, millet, or whatever grain I could find. The fun didn't stop there; I also captured butterflies with an empty jar and ran after animals of any sort, like cats and dogs. I also played with my fabric baby doll, which didn't resemble anything on earth. The doll was made with brown fabric and had two black buttons for eyes, black threads for hair, and a fine embroidered line for the mouth. I thought it was pretty nicely made until I went overseas and saw the white porcelain dolls that were common there, which I owned later.

Tita, my mother, was even more protective of me than my grandparents were. When she was around, I didn't even go near the river. She uttered to me with her lovely voice, "Oli, even I myself... even I don't go to the ocean. One moment of inattention, and you can drown in the water. The waves are too high for you, so you are better off at home." She paused and then continued. "Do you know how many children have disappeared in the water? A lot. You're too young to understand. When you get older, I'll make it a priority to go with you to the beach."

That never happened. Instead, I'm the one that took her to the beach after I got married.

In a big plastic washbasin (served as a pool) outside the house, she firmly ordered the little boy who lived with us as a domestic maid (without pay) to fill it up with water. She then told me that I can splash water all over the cement terrace for my enjoyment, and she laughed with pride at my gestures.

My mother, to convince me that she was right in keeping me away from other young people and to show me how much she loved and cared about me, would say, "Oli, you are the only matchstick I have in the box. If it burns out, there will be no other one."

Behind her back, my grandmother would pantomime with her eyes, trying to tell me not say that I'd been to the river. I knew that and wasn't going to jeopardize the fun I had when I went out with my aunties by telling my mother. Being around grownups so often gave me an adult mind. Having been raised by my aunts, my grandfather, and my grandmother and hearing their adult conversations made me a professional in things that other children didn't know yet. I would never make that mistake by telling her that.

I could do nothing other than assent to my mother's apprehensions and rules. As a child, it would be a defamation to dispute an adult's decision. Now, when I look back on my childhood, I think that I had a very simple life with lots exposure to nature and lots of worth values. I was very much protected by my family, which I couldn't understand at the time.

That said, I should've had opportunities to experience what other children did. I should've had the freedom to do some stuff by myself. I talked to my costudents in class, but as soon I left school, they were not my pals. I couldn't even stop in the streets to socialize with anyone. I didn't have any friends until I turned nine and met Irma, who lived in the north side of Haiti. I saw her once every two or three years. My family managed to acclimate me to their world, enough for me to be satisfied with what I had. I missed a great deal in my infancy, but I enjoyed life in other ways later.

When I became a mother, I better understood their worry and insistence on fortification. I was anxious all the time as my children were growing up. When they went to the pool or drove a car, I always speculated that dreadful things would happen to them. Even though they're all adults now, I'm still concerned about their well-being. I don't show my worries too much because I don't want them to experience what I experienced in my youth. Motherhood comes with unchangeable concerns and worries that will always be inside of me as part of my daily, emotional existence.

When I was a child, we had a house servant named Ti-Dimanche, meaning "Little Sunday." I guess he was born on a Sunday, so his parents gave him that name. He was about two years older than I was. He did most of the domestic duties in our house. In compensation, my family provided him with food, clothes, and a roof over his head. In a way, his parents had given him away, and he became an adopted child-maid. It's difficult to understand this process if you are unfamiliar with it, but it is common in my country. This type of service trade is very normal for the average family. He never rested during the day for fear of punishment. From dawn to sunset, he was up and going. His first task in the morning was always to make coffee for my grandparents before they began working on the farm—coffee that he wasn't allowed to taste. He wouldn't dare. He would have been in deep shit!

Normally, children in my country don't drink strong coffee, but they do drink "make-believe coffee." I called it "sweet dirty water." The recipe is to add more water to already-processed coffee grounds. The first batch is for the adults, and the second batch, which is boiled from the same grounds, is reused to make children's coffee. It doesn't taste like coffee, just hot brown water. Sometimes they mixed it with boiled cow's milk and plenty of sugar and served it with bread as breakfast.

THE DAILY BATTLE FOR A NORMAL LIFE

Ti-Dimanche didn't get to enjoy such things, he had his bread without coffee, make-believe or otherwise. It seemed to be fine with him—at least he was eating. He didn't go to school during the day like other children of his age did. He was too busy cleaning the house, filling containers with fresh water from the river, and going to the grocery store with a list that my grandmother had verbally inculcated into his head before leaving. He needed to remember everything on the list and report back to her on the price of each product. No cent could be missing, and no error was acceptable. As I think about it now, I realize that it was a big mission to fulfill every day for such a young person. He was very smart to remember it all.

Most maids in the city went to school at night depending on their workloads and the agreeability of their employers. Few didn't go to school at all. They were called *hoi polloi*, and according to social rules, they didn't need to be educated. They didn't even need to learn how to sign their names because they used their fingerprints instead. My grandfather taught Ti-Dimanche at night. Ti-Dimanche had to be vigorously sharp because he got a beating each time he answered something wrong. He stood in front of my grandfather for about two hours every evening to receive his lessons. If his eyes ever closed from tiredness because he'd taken a long, hard journey that day, or simply because it was past bedtime for children of his age, my grandfather pulled his ears to awaken him. He was supposed to do well in his studies—not only for his own sake but for ours too. It was a family tradition to believe that we are all born intelligent and to stay intelligent. There was no escaping this; we were all supposed to be clever, even our servant. This made life even harder for Ti-Dimanche because he didn't have time during the day to open his abecedarian book and study his lessons. It saddens me to think about him now. They expected far too much from that nipper.

These were not the only punishments inflicted on Ti-Dimanche. When he stole something (which I don't call stealing—hunger was inevitably the reason for his actions), he was punished like a grown-up thief would be. It was terrible. The boy, empty-bellied, would fetch a piece of bread or coconut. Because my grandparents hadn't offered it to him specifically, he'd be deemed a thief. If I'd done the exact same thing, it would've been absolutely normal. I assisted in his punishments so many times, which left me aghast and unable to sleep at night. As a ten-year-old, I couldn't understand the sadistic spirit that got into my family's brain and made them treat that boy like a slave—the same family that showed me so much affection.

This was 1965. We were freed from slavery in 1804. It appalls me that we inflicted slavery onto someone else with the same antagonism that our ancestors were subjected to. This thought has kept me company for a long time. To this day, when I watch a slavery movie, I cry not only because it saddens me but because it reminds me of my Ti-Dimanche and my teenage years. I pray and ask for forgiveness like I was at fault. When Ti-Dimanche was tortured by my relatives, I didn't say anything. I just watched, thinking that it was the way it supposed to be. After the beatings, they would often make him dance for their amusement. That's the most disgusting part of it. Even animals don't treat their kind like that. The boy was a genius; he composed his own song and witheringly danced to it with a scornful smile, as if to say, "You're the criminal, not me."

Later in my life, I figured out that almost all aristocratic Haitian families at that point in history saw the lower class as the proletariat, and many treated their servants with the same cruelty. Aristocracy is a French heritage that positions nobility above all others. Haitian people often don't need to have money in the bank to feel "upper class." Rather superiority is seen as an inner characteristic. After I left Roche-a-Bateau for high school, I never saw Ti-Dimanche again. I can't say if he's still alive, but I never stop thinking about him with sorrow and helplessness.

My mother was always an absentee in my life. I called my grandmother "Manman," meaning "Mother," and my grandfather "Papa." My aunts raised me as if I was their sister, not their niece. They liked to sing, and so did I, so we often sung harmonies together. We loved music and knew all the romantic Haitian and French songs (*chansonette Francaises*). We were very romantic, dramatic, and artistic at the same time. My aunts were very engaged in the local church chorus and in the town band. At night, for recreation or for quick digestion, we would sing all kinds of songs like cicada birds. We sat outside on the veranda and gave free concerts to our neighbors and the passersby. Our goal was to sing lullaby songs, expecting, as a mother does, to cradle her baby to sleep. We thought that we could bring tranquility and peace of mind to the population. We wanted to soothe people. We thought our songs could smooth their sorrows and help the sick have a relaxing night.

At the same time, singing created a sort of program to fill our empty nights. When we began, people used to compliment us the next day and thank us for serenading them, but as the years passed, they got so used to it that they rarely bothered to say anything to us at all. It was a beautiful time when we could go out, leaving all the doors wide open without any concern. We mostly sang during the full moon because there was no electricity, so the moon was our light. The dark wasn't nearly as inspirational. The resonance of our voices carried throughout the entire town. We lived on the hill, and at night, it got so quiet that you could hear everything, even from far away. We observed the moon going under the translucent clouds and changed our rhythms as the moonlight changed. We started our serenade early in the evenings, always afraid of bad spirits that might be roaming around. Before midnight, we had to be in bed to ensure that the bad spirits passed us by.

I had the good fortune of being utterly spoiled by my mother's family. I was the first grandchild and niece. My three aunts were very young, the last children from a family of ten, and my mother was the second-born child. Growing up around them made me feel like I was a small-fry with a mature brain. One of my aunts played the guitar, and my uncle played piano. He worked as a school principal in another town, and he conducted the church chorus on the piano and pipe organ. Occasionally, I sang at church with my aunties. I was definitely a grown-up in a child's body. I always loved music. It's in my blood, but I was too lazy to take music lessons. Once I decided to have proper piano lessons, but I became sick soon after they started and never continued. I guess that I have no genes in my DNA for playing instruments, but I could sing. Lately, I have made singing part of my life again. No matter how I feel—bad or good—I use my voice to express the crosses I bear, my moments of weakness, and my happiness to boost my stamina. I cannot physically work without music, not at a workplace or at home. Even at my age, I still remember all the old songs from my youth and try to stay updated on new music, especially American music. The joy it gives me is inexplicable. It's difficult for me to pray, so I sing religious songs instead. San Augustin once said, "Singing is like praying twice." It really does give me the courage I need to do any task. I can tell for sure that I'm sick when no song will come from my mouth.

2

Belligerence and Belief

I DIDN'T GO TO kindergarten. We didn't have that kind of school in Haiti. My aunts were my first teachers. When I was six, my grandmother registered me for primary school under the name Olivia Cassis, my informal first name and my grandfather's last name. Supposedly, the school didn't require that I use my father's last name and the first name given to me by my mother—the name on my birth certificate—but my family was so mad at my father and his family that whoever registered me for school completely changed my identity—my first and last name were wrong.

Legally, Olivia Cassis wasn't me at all. As I mentioned before, since my birth, everybody called me Olivia. Our entire town was corrupted in that case, like a gang's affair. No one ever said anything about it. They had great respect for my family. Maybe they didn't want to interfere in our business, or maybe they thought they were supporting my mother's family with their muteness. But the school administration officials knew my mother very well, so why did they too accept my fake name?

What is the mission of religious people in an underdeveloped country like mine? To instruct and to educate the people. They knew that my name would be a problem for me in the future, but they let it pass anyway. Because we didn't have social security numbers, only our names count. People in the town were afraid of my grandmother's funky character, so that might be the reason they never piped up about it. She was a well-known person in the community, and so they accepted everything she dictated them to do. Innocently, I didn't see the problem with having the same last name as my aunts because we were already like sisters. I never called them anything other than their own names. What did I know? A child of that age knows nothing about marital laws.

So the nuns and teachers just went about their normal business without paying notice to my grandmother's decision to register me under an informal name. If they knew of her motives, they didn't say anything about it, nor did anyone else. If I had been a celebrity's child, I would assume that she did it to protect me and keep me anonymous, but I'm not. She was a mad, uncontrollable woman who couldn't set her anger down. Unbelievably, my grandmother enthused me with her strong personality and her standing for carrying out what she deemed right. I have a stoical ego like hers too. Despite everything, I admire her, as she does me.

The real me never existed. I was invisible. All my diplomas are under the name Olivia Cassis. I have carried this with me for a long period of my life. When I got married, I made it sure that I gave the court officer my real name because they needed to put exactly what was written on my birth certificate. After that, I went back to calling myself Oli or Olivia, and my husband did too. The real me is a nonexistent creature. My last name has since changed to his, and I still carry a first name that was given to me wrongfully. My marriage certificate shows a different name than the one everybody calls me. I never corrected it; I'm so used to being Olivia, and I never liked the name my mother gave me. *So I have a double life*, I thought. *So what?* I can only laugh at it.

There was a period in my young life when I was constantly sick. I caught everything in the air. In my little town, there was no hospital or doctor, only a clinic administered by nuns from Canada. Sister Olivia was likely a nurse practitioner, so we went to see her when we had health issues. She always knew exactly what to give me for each sickness. There was no pharmacy, no prescriptions. Medications were administered directly at the clinic in brown envelopes. The name of the medicines was never provided. The rationale, I assume, was that the majority of the population was analphabetic, so what would we do with the names of the drugs? Most of us didn't know how to read, and we certainly didn't have the internet to look anything up. We could have it as proof, but to prove what? As a matter of fact, most of the patients weren't even able to follow the verbal instructions given to them before leaving the clinic.

Thinking about it today makes me laugh. I wonder how much we should have trusted the missionaries. But there was no other choice for medical care, and there were no malpractice laws. Maybe sometimes she prescribed the wrong medication, or her assistant give us the wrong dosage—who cares? How could we tell if the medication was wrong when we didn't even know the name of the malady we suffered from? To whom could we complain? There was no bureau for that kind of law. We could either take the medications that were given to us at the clinic, or we could stay sick. Should we stay sick? No way!

"Help yourself, and heaven will help you." That's what the Bible says, so it's preferable to seek health. We are talking about trust and naivety here, but miracles happen for believers. In our town, there was no alternative means of getting care—no second nurse to compare her diagnoses with. She was God for some and the angel of the death for others, depending the length of your destiny.

Occasionally, once a month or so, a doctor came in from the big city to consult people afflicted with the flu, infections, malaria, fevers, or other little things. If someone had cancer or a stroke or died overnight from cardiac arrest, we assumed that he or she was sold to the devil. Besides, we didn't know the names of these illnesses, so we couldn't concern ourselves with them. When the doctor came, the line to see him could get very long. Not everybody could be seen, but if you were from a well-known family, you would definitely get seen and likely without waiting. Like everywhere else, the power of the rich over the poor was radical in my country. We were greenhorn about killer diseases, but we were also so grateful to have someone helping us. That was enough for us. This might seem like a bittersweet life to some, but it meant simplicity to us.

When Sister Olivia couldn't cure someone, people consulted a priest of voodoo to buy back their souls from Satan. It was a second resource. Other nations thought (and probably still do) that our national religion was only voodoo because most of us, regardless of our faith (e.g., Catholics, Baptists, Adventists, Witnesses of Jehovah) went to voodoo temples seeking cures. I suppose that we probably did it because of our ignorance; we didn't know much about medical illnesses. Of course, I can't fully attribute this medieval tradition to ignorance. For centuries, voodoo was prominent in other countries as well. For example, Faust, the unhappy German protagonist, was believed to have sold his soul to the devil for earthly happiness. For centuries, gifted people have been able to cure patients with herbal medicines, even if they didn't fully understand the scientific basis of their remedies. Ironically, when we go to a voodoo priest, sometimes the search for health is deeply demonic, not merely curative. It still looks largely the way it did during primitive times.

This was around 1960, when medicine wasn't practiced widely in Haiti. Most of us were fervent Christians who also believed strongly in voodoo. We believed that God would not murder his children, so it had to be bad spirits who abruptly took lives away. Some also thought that to fight a bad spirit, you needed the help of another bad spirit. Despite all of this, there was still a minority of people who preferred to die than go to a voodoo doctor. My family wasn't exempt from this. Although we were strong Catholics, to save anyone in the family, my grandparents would blindly devote themselves to the voodoo.

As I grew up, the curse of my destiny followed me everywhere. At five years old, I became very sick with a high fever and for a long time didn't respond to Sister Olivia's medicines. My grandparents called the Catholic priest to give me the last sacrament, thinking that I was going to die. However, my grandmother had a second thought; she wasn't going to let my life expire so soon. She promised my mother that she would take care of me, so she was willing to do anything to save me from the devil's curse. She was the type of woman who didn't give up easily on anything. In fact, she was convinced that our neighbor had cursed me and was the reason for my malady. Our neighbor had the bad reputation of killing children with black magic and transforming them into fish to sell. Our house was the three away from hers. In her seafood market, the fish were bigger than usual, which turned most people's heads. She had a Mephistopheles reputation; rumor had it that she was a witch. No one understood that perhaps the fishermen had just reserved the big ones for her, per her request. No way—that size? It surely had to be dead children! Ironically, kids who suffer from malnutrition die out of the blue every day! How can you remove that belief in the minds of an illiterate population? It may seem awkward to understand, but we believed in malefic superstition. Everybody was afraid of our elderly neighbor. People alleged that she was a cannibal and a sorcerer (or *lougarou,* in Creole), which made everybody who bought her salted fish cannibals as well. Despite people's fears, she stayed in business.

Desperately, my grandmother took me into her arms, grabbed a sharpened machete, and went to the neighbor's house. She commanded that the woman treat me with the same devilish spells she cast on me. She gave me a cup of tea and rubbed my little body with an unction—all kinds of herbs infused in oil. In religious rites, we anoint our bodies with oil for divine treatments, so I speculate she was doing the same. I guess she didn't pay any mind to my grandmother's accusations and was more interested in helping me than in causing me harm. In my parents' view, as well as some other families and friends, this gesture confirmed that she was the cause of my sickness to begin with; the next day, I woke up fine. The fever went down, and I was able to open my eyes and eat. I don't think my grandparents saw our neighbor as a good, spiritual lady who could cure diseases but as a witch who almost killed me. I don't even know what was wrong with me, and nobody else knows either, but what I know for sure is that the old lady was cleverer than the nurse was; she knew exactly what kinds of plants and oils could cure what I had. I'm more grateful to her than suspicious. I never asked too much about it, but my grandparents wouldn't tell me anyway because they didn't have the answer. Plus I wouldn't dare ask too many questions, which wasn't permitted.

To avoid insolent behavior from their children, adults instilled in us that it was better to forget the past and continuously live merrily in the present. In addition, they taught us the adage "The less we know, the less regret we accumulate inside." The more often I heard that story, the less I accepted it as true. My mother always bragged about the horrific fairy tale of my near-death experience and how brave her mother was to take such a risk to save my life. The queerest part is that we youngsters believed that all old women and men were *lougarous* with the exception of our own family members. A few years later, our elderly neighbor left town for the big city after another family publicly accused her of the same crime. There wasn't enough evidence to find her guilty, of course, but she couldn't rid herself of the reputation as a killer of children.

3

Irresistible Nature

SOMETIMES, WHEN MY AUNTS talked among themselves and I was too young to be included, life got really boring. I let myself becoming friends with nature. At seven, I became fascinated by the sublime blue water that majestically stood in front of me all the time, looking at me with its gray-silver eyes. The more my parents didn't want me to go into that water, the more I became obsessed with it. On occasion, when there wasn't school, I woke at dawn, right after my grandparents left to go to the farm, and sat on the front porch to wait for sunrise. I would stay there for hours, my breath taken away by the contemplation of this powerful, constant immensity. Moreover, I thought that the sky was a lot like me: always waiting for the sun or the rain. I loved the folkloric, picturesque scene—the beautiful paintings that paraded in front of me when the sun rose. I didn't have television; truth be told, I didn't even know that TV existed. The sky was my telecasting screen. The sun rose discreetly and luminously like a fireball between the ocean and the blue sky to express a jovial "good morning" to both of them, the ocean and the firmament. As the hours passed, many changes occurred in the atmosphere. Variations of colors artistically designed the ocean and the sky. I had to hold my heart lest it explode in jubilation at the magnificent mystery of nature. I found myself in that raptured position many times. I was irresistibly engaged in the recrudescence of the sunrise.

I thought that our house was at the same level as the sea because it perched on the top of a mountain, facing the ocean. Also, it appeared to me that there was no line that separated the ocean from the firmament. They seemed happily blended together, like a gigantic mass of liquid. From noon to the decline of the day, the manifestation of incandescent sunlight on the brilliant water dappled the wavelengths with bright, gleaming light, so bright that I had difficulty watching it. The silvery stripes flashed in my eyes with persistence. Sometimes, after staring at the water for hours, I experienced double vision, my mind and my eyes working together in a confused juncture. Around 2:00 p.m., the glares from the sun became very imposing, almost impossible to stare at anymore. The sky, surrounded by transparent light, turned light gray, and slow-moving clouds overpowered the sea with pallid white, blue, gray, and silver. All day, different scenes played out on the surface of the water. I became so intimate with these scenes that most of the time, I forgot to eat until one of my aunts called me in, which I considered to be a disturbance. At dusk, the sun slowly disappeared from the horizon, leaving spectacular, reflective lines of dazzling orange and soft red. These colors bordered the ocean—the sun's liaison with the sky. Inexplicably, the same way it appeared in the morning, the sun gradually sank into the saltwater and spread into harmony. Foremost to uttermost, a day came and departed, leaving no trace except for the marks and memories in my mind.

At night, the sea was either a dark mass when the moon was absent, or a phosphorescent, quiescent surface, reckoning with the lunar satellite. From where I sat on the porch, I didn't realize how large the sea was. Everything appeared quiet, tranquil, and inviting. Nearby, the waves were not as smooth as they looked when I sat on the porch. Beyond my vantage point, the sea was a giant, monstrous, transparent, and untrustworthy body of water. The enraged empire waves roared, greenish and translucent—maybe evidence of seagrass at the bottom—peacefully tempering the white sand.

As I see it, this is similar to a person's life; every day is a mystery, a surprise, a different day than the one before it. It all depends on your perception. I don't completely understand why my parents didn't let me go into the sea, but I partially think they were right.

When I got older and was lucky enough to pass by the ocean with my aunts, it looked devilish, far from being as friendly as I thought it was. The sea water can be so unpredictable, just like life itself, which led me to think that they might have been right to have overawed me. Whether we like it or not, nature reflects quotidian life.

Jimmy Dean said, "I can't change the direction of the wind, but I can adjust my sails to always reach my destination." I couldn't go to the ocean or the river and was restricted from accessing so many things, so I made nature my friend. Despite my restraining order to stop watching the sun all the time (the glare would damage my eyes, my grandparents said), I never got tired of watching it shine over the water. I always loved the view; each day came with something different for me to enjoy. To this day, I like most of the things that others might find ordinary, especially in the emancipated universe that does not follow any rule on earth. I love it because it allows me to envision having that kind of opulence and dream about how I would feel if I could have that kind of freedom. Everything in nature comes and goes as it pleases. The shade of a dark cloud passing leaves space for the bright sun afterward. It's beautiful, an elixir for my soul. I was possessed by nature. With an open mouth and dazing eyes, I let myself enjoy these moments of admiration and communion with the natural world that I wished would never end.

During the full moon, I remember seeing multitudes of sparkly specks, like vivid silver clusters, jumping against the unruffled, limpid surface of the ocean. It seemed to me that the radiant stars in the sky were doubled. They formed a spiritual union with one another to dance on the serene water. As far of my vision could go, on a clear, moonlit night, I saw no joint separating the sky from the sea, which made me believe that the sky was one with the ocean, blended together in a microcosmic structure. At night, the water gave the appearance of tranquility, which added more confusion into my young mind. The languid sea awarded me with the impression that the ocean was tired from the events of the day and needed rest to prepare itself for the next day. At nighttime, during the full moon, I thought the stars danced on the magical water. How could it be? All I could see was the bounded, unexplainable unison among them.

That thought filled up my mind so much that I couldn't resist asking for an explanation. My grandfather, in his charming language, tried giving me an intelligent answer. He said, "The stars on the ocean are not stars, Oli, but a myriad of fishes that God has sent us to replace those that the fishermen caught today, so we'll never be without seafood. We are very blessed. He's taking care of us day after day in many ways. That is why we should never worry about tomorrow. Put everything in His hands. The Lord knows what he is doing and won't let us down. He will always provide." He went on: "Imagine if overnight, God didn't multiply everything in the universe, like Jesus did with the five little fishes and the water he turned into wine at the Canaan marriage. The ocean would go empty, the plants wouldn't grow, the animals would go extinct, and there wouldn't be you and me. There would be no birth to replace the dead. Our father in heaven is always working for our well-being."

This was the kind of confidence my grandfather had in the power of God, which made him composed in every circumstance. I didn't know precisely the meaning of his words, but they sounded fine and sweet to me. I didn't care about tomorrow, just about the image that was right in front of me. He repeated these words every night with a "Father in heaven" prayer before he slept. I now conclude that this was probably his way of hiding the fact that he was worried. He preferred to give an impression of certitude and assure us that he knew that God would always supply. His certainty about primeval things made him appear to be free from stress, calm, and at ease all the time. I always saw him as a sage or a wise man, unbounded by the distress the rest of us go through every day.

What else could I do all day other than play with my friend, nature! There were no children my age to talk to or play with. When there was no school, I had to find a passion, and nature was the one I picked, observing the elements around me. There was no forest nearby where I could walk, and I was kept captive in a 100×120 square-foot yard. I didn't often get to go to the farm either, so I paid attention to everything in my immediate surroundings. I attended to every little detail in the firmament.

THE DAILY BATTLE FOR A NORMAL LIFE

As I spied on my friend, nature, I discovered more elements that needed attention. The battles in nature soon became my favorite. I found out that the sky and the ocean were not always sympathetic to each other or to my credence. Like a bird staring at a worm before swallowing it, the sky, sun, and ocean also engaged in controversy, which mesmerized me. I couldn't escape from my obsessive observations, which in retrospect seem to be so enigmatically in contradiction with my ritual vision. All three changed to sudden squalor in relation to one another. The sun disappeared, as if leaving the sky and ocean to have their argument. Ominously, as if a flashlight had turned on under the thick dark-gray clouds, a veiled anonymity enveloped the ocean. The thundered intonation of the hullabaloo resounded like a notice from the sky to the people of earth. We knew that this obscurity would swathe not only the surface of the sea but also our town in heavy rainstorm. Life operates much like the weather does; if we know where to look for it, there is always a sign to let us know what is going on within our anatomy. Sometimes, we are just too inattentive to pay mind to it.

My irrational, compulsive inclination to be with Mother Nature didn't stop there. Some days, I watched with euphoria as the half circle of a rainbow enlightened the sky, and the ocean hurriedly became lighter and lighter, dissipating behind the delineation between two extraordinary creations. What else could I do but relish this new program on nature's television screen? People always told me that rainbows had seven colors in them, but I could only ever count five. By the time I identified five stripes of color, the rainbow was already fading away, leaving no vestige. Maybe that's why rainbows remain a mystery to people. It looked like a colorful bridge connecting the sky to the ocean, as if letting an invisible specter pass over and collapse into the ocean. I remember that rainbows dominated my thoughts so much that they appeared to walk right beside me as I walked—the same rainbow in every direction. And then it vanished. After the rain, or by a fluke, I would see it. There was no waiting for it or expecting it. Miraculously and rapidly, it showed off to tell us that we would have nice weather. Some religions believe that the rainbow signified the union between God and us, but I'm not sure if that is the explanation I would assign to that paradox.

On principle, I avoided pointing my finger at rainbows, frightened that they might bite me. This was a nonsensical anecdote my grandparents told me, and I believed them. I never knew why they invented that nonsense philosophy, but I was devoted, in my cowardice, to complying with it. My grandmother's word, likewise, was that I shouldn't be watching the rainbow because it meant that a goddess was having her shower in the ocean. So out of respect for her modesty, I never watched the whole evolution of a rainbow. When I talked about this to other children at school, everybody told me that they'd heard similar speeches. Every culture has their own trust in regard to enigmas.

Later, when a few chronic diseases invaded my body, my experiences with nature helped me stay strong and positive about my physical structure. I embraced a fervent relationship with my body. I thought, any abnormality or change shouldn't cause worry but rather should just be taken into consideration. Our body is the sky, the sun, and the ocean combined into one—our personal sphere. We need to pay devoted attention to it in order to make our time on earth more efficient and pleasant. In nature, things change rapidly. A sunny day rapidly spirals into a storm, and so does the body. Sometimes, we can shift from being healthy to being unwell without any warning signs.

I'm on the defensive toward my ailments not because I have a fear of death but because I'm afraid of suffering and the psychological marks my death might leave on my loved ones if I go too soon. This doesn't mean that I believe that when the deadline of our time on earth has expired, we can request for an extension. No. Rather I want to do the maximum to protect my body and get my soul ready for my inevitable ending. When you think about it, why should anyone be scared of death? One day, we will all fade like flowers, and that is the ultimate fact of life.

4

Trust

BETWEEN THE AGES OF eight and ten, I was sexually attacked by an employee of my grandparents—someone who my family trusted enough to let spend time with me. What they didn't know was that he was a faker. He wasn't the man he pretended to be. I became his target, and his presence in my family's house—six days a week, and sometimes seven—exasperated me. Supposedly, when he wasn't working on the farm, he had the green light to play with me. He did play, but what kind of game did he choose? He wasn't a babysitter but a child molester on the watch, always looking for an occasion to be alone with me. The opportunist is always searching for the opportune moment for onslaught.

That said, "babysitter" is an ironic description of the man because he would make me sit on his lap so that he could masturbate. I'm sure that in his sick mind, he was disillusioned, thinking that he was doing it with an imaginary person of his own age and simply using my little body for the sensation. I could feel his private part getting big under my dress, and I could feel and hear his scraping exhalations from his odorous, open mouth. At this period in time, girls wore dresses more often than pants, which made it easier for him. The first and the second time he molested me, I didn't know what he was doing or that it was inappropriate and wrong. The third time, he started touching me to help him reach his insane fantasy faster, which made me even more uncomfortable. I started thinking that what he was doing had to be bad because it made me feel so intolerably upset and frightened. I didn't want to play this kind of "game." I didn't want to sit on his lap anymore.

I tried to avoid him as much as possible, but he still got his hands on me, grabbing me and hoisting me up onto his shoulders—even in front of my grandparents—as if he was doing nothing wrong. He seemed so at ease about all of it, but it wasn't easy for me. I was suffocated by his abominable, sneaky, dishonest behavior. I hid my tears so that no one would ask me what was wrong. I couldn't tell my grandparents because I was too scared of the consequences. I now know my grandmother well enough to know that she wouldn't have hesitated to do what was best for me: remove him forever from my presence and tell no one about it. She was a woman with a strong and unafraid character. I know now also that if he had disappeared, nobody would have searched for him. He didn't seem to have any family. I know now that if I'd told my grandmother, she would've killed him, especially because he'd so significantly betrayed her trust. I now know that it could've ended there. I could've been free from his wicked face.

But at the time, I didn't know those things. In reality, I just didn't say anything. I was scared…scared of him? His presence in the house became an embarrassment for me. I couldn't even look at him. I searched for the words to try to tell my family what he'd done to me, but I could never say it aloud. I can't say why I stayed silent. Even now, after so many years of thinking about the past, I still can't find a rational motive for my muteness. I reckon that I was far too intimidated by the elders to discuss something so serious with them. I wouldn't have even known how to start such a taboo conversation.

He never attempted to rape me, so in my young mind, I thought that was reason enough to keep silent. I prayed and prayed that one day he would be mature enough to understand that I was only a little girl and that he should leave me alone. Despite my daily prayers, his brain couldn't be cured from the devilish sickness. He was too far gone to realize that he was living within a psychoactive hallucination. Why me? I thought. Couldn't he find somebody his own age?

When I saw him coming, I ran into the house where other eyes could see me, but he knew what he was doing. My grandparents had a little house in the backyard where they stored farm products. I don't remember why I was there—probably playing—and he found me. That was the third time he molested me. The worst was that when I played outside, I could often hear my grandmother instructing him to go check on me. I always had to drop what I was doing and rush inside for safety. I frantically scrambled into my own house to avoid his presence. Like a cat after a mouse, he was after me. I didn't do anything wrong, but I became the runner—excluding myself when he was around. I couldn't face him. I felt sick to my stomach just looking at him. Apparently, he was taking pleasure in what he was doing: tracking me and waiting for the right moment to attack. Even as I grew up, I remained afraid of him. I was revolted by what he had done and was scared that he was still searching for me to attack again. I wondered, would pleasure from a little girl sitting on his lap always suffice for him, or was he waiting for me to get older so that he could rape me? I wondered, was this normal? Did this happen to other girls my age, or was it just me? I had no way to answer these questions because I couldn't talk to anyone about it. It was all far too gross to tell even a best friend, and besides, I didn't have one.

That was a hard time in my life. I was an obedient girl, letting him use my innocence for his own perverted pleasure and never saying anything. Still now, at this very moment, when I think about it, I feel like I need to throw up. I could've raised my voice for everybody to hear so that they could've come to my rescue, but I didn't. I could've let my family members see me weeping so that they would ask what was paining me, but I didn't. Like I said, I don't know exactly why I stayed silent, and I don't dare try to offer an explanation, even now. I blame it on my childishness. Even though I deeply deplored my own silence, I never broke it. At that age and at that time, I obeyed my abuser like he was my master and thought that speaking up about it would spell punishment from my grandparents.

I was a little child, so everyone put me on their laps. It was normal. I could never have predicted that somebody would abuse that position. When men or women came over—relatives or not—I'd sit on their laps without a problem; that's just what little kids did. Miserable creature—miserable prick! He took advantage of my innocence. He was a human-beast. He is probably dead by now, but I can never forget him. I try to, and some days I'm able to, but not always. I always tell people that "forgiveness clears the mind's obscurity." I preach this like a religious teaching, but I still haven't mastered practicing it. I haven't yet reached the highest level. Even all these years later, I still find myself fuming over what he did to me.

His name was Toto, and he worked for my family as a farmer—a shabby, befouled man in his late twenties. To my family, he is the sweetest thing on earth, always ready to help in any circumstance. He was loved for his loyalty and his reputation as a handyman who was always up to any task. Perchance, he was with them before I was even born. I'm not sure about that. However, to me, he was the biggest asshole I ever encountered in my life. His foxlike manners made him sly and manipulative, and he tricked my family into thinking that he was a perfect gentleman, if not a little sundry. When he held me in front of my family, like any grown-up would hold any child, he looked respectable on the outside. But I felt disgusting and nauseated. I could smell his sweat and feel the strain that constantly avoiding him was imposing on me. He told me imaginary stories too, and everybody laughed as if he was a wonderful caretaker.

His job at the farm was to take care of the horses, cows, pigs, donkeys, and goats. We had all kinds of animals, including chicken and turkeys. Imagine the smell—his body fluids mixing with the farmyard filth and air. When he came home after work in the afternoon to eat, it was detestable. If my aunts were helping around the house, and my grandmother was elsewhere cooking, he would discreetly harass me, knowing he was away from their eyes. Most of my grandparents' farmers come to my parents' house after work to eat a plate of hot food, drink *tafia*, a sort of cheap rum, and play cards or dominos. It was traditional that an employing family offer their employees this kind of hospitality to thank them for their hard work from dawn to three in the afternoon. Toto was the only one who ever volunteered to watch me playing in the backyard. Everybody else was too preoccupied to see what was going on. He had permission from my grandparents to play with me anywhere in the house and outside.

I didn't know what to do. The more I aged, the more I panicked, thinking that one of these days, it would fall upon me to end my suffering. I couldn't bear the stress anymore. But how? Poisoning his *tafia*? That seemed like a good idea. But with what? Rat poison, I figured, because it was easy to find. We always kept it at home in case of infestations of rats and mice, which ate the produce we intended to sell. Often, my grandfather buried many dead rodents in the mornings. Perhaps that is why I'm so unfriendly to rats and all animals of the same aggregation, even now. I didn't want Toto to die in my parents' house. Then how? *This has to end*, I thought to myself resolutely. There was no other way to get out of the situation. Nobody was going to open another door for me. I was turning ten soon, so I had to come up with a plan. I decided that I would ask him to go somewhere with me, taking my chances in order to get him out of the house. I would procure a cheap drink, mix it with the poison, and give it to him. But it wasn't that simple. First and foremost, my grandparents never let me stray farther than the backyard.

My brain went wacko. I thought I'd better get a move on it. My mind raced with terrible thoughts: what happens if before I can serve him the deadly booze, he forces me to have real sex with him? The mind of a child runs faster than an adult brain does, for sure. I ruminated one possibility after another, my mind preoccupied with searching for solutions. I needed to plan this carefully, I thought. Perhaps he would know what I was up to and would make me drink the poison before raping me. I decided against it; even if he died too, it wasn't a good plan because nobody would ever find out what happened to us, and his horrible deeds would remain a secret. They might even assume that it was suicide that did both of us in. Nevertheless, I didn't want to be my own murderer and go down in history as the girl who scrupulously arranged to end someone's life but instead got herself killed. As the proverb says, "What you wish for your stepmother can happen to your mother."

The plan changed and changed until there was no plan. The more I thought about my maniac plan, the more I realized that I didn't have the heart for it. It's monstrous, I realized, a bitter and heinous deed that would poison my soul. I decided that I didn't want to carry that sin for the rest of my life. But then I thought about the Bible verse that says, "You may kill in self-defense." I used to read a lot, especially books or verses in the Bible that make sense to me. That seemed like a reasonable justification to me. I had two people speaking in my mind; the first one wanted me to find a way to eliminate him, and the second said, "No, Oli, don't do it." In the end, I guess the second person was stronger because I resisted the urge to kill him. At the time, I didn't know that premeditated murder was a crime worse than self-defense against an attack. Of course, I was too young to know about these regulations. All I knew for sure was that I couldn't do it. If I had been a born criminal, I would've found a faster way to kill him. But even then, I had too much respect for life. To this day, I'm prolife and against capital punishment.

My little mind didn't know what else to do other than keep the abuse secret. It was hell to always be hiding—six days a week and sometimes more. Even on Sundays, when he had time off, hunger stormed in his stomach, and he showed up at the house looking for a free meal. My resolution faltered. I realized that I could never kill the man. It would be an evildoing, and I would become like him—a damnable child. *I believe in Almighty God*, I thought. The only alternative was to pray and to tell Tita when she came for vacation. I planned on telling her everything—the whole saga of the abuse and my suffering. Even though she was a stranger to me, I looked forward to being able to talk to someone about it.

I prayed to the Lord at night to elucidate the truth and to assist me in my battle—to help me search for the right words and prepare me for that strange, embarrassing conversation. When I turned ten, God finally heard my prayers. Like my grandfather used to say, "The Lord always finds a way to resolve our problems if you believe in him. He's our Father and our Savior, so always talk to him first." It turned out to be true. At last, I had a chance to escape from his grasp. My mother and I were leaving Haiti and moving to Canada. Thanks to God for hearing my prayers and solving my quandary! I didn't have to resort to committing a crime—hoo-ha! I didn't have to struggle anymore and didn't even have to tell my mother. As usual my mother was always on the running away home. Out of the blue, she found a job as housekeeper in Canada. Even earlier than we predicted, Tita came to pick me up, and we moved to Port-au-Prince to start the immigration process. I was so relieved that the nightmare was coming to an end at last.

In 2014, I tried to tell this story to my living two aunts, who are living in Canada. They didn't take it seriously, stating that he was homosexual. I don't know if they didn't believe me or if they just didn't want to talk about it. Maybe that was why he was so trusted among them—they never wanted to look too closely. I now realize that homosexuality could, in part, explain why he never went further with his sexual abuse; the touch sufficed him. All he needed for self-pleasure was to come in contact with something, and that something was me. Was it a temporary stage of erotic sexuality, wherein the sense of touch alone could satisfy his sexual desire? What to think about that? I heard that he had a child. Could he have been a psychopathic bisexual? Would he have hurt me even more if I hadn't left town? Perhaps not—perhaps he only needed the touch of skin to fulfil his perverted desires. To this day, I puzzle over these questions. I still cannot determine what in his mind provoked him to molest me—I'm just guessing. What I have realized is that life is built according to our fate. I never heard Tita talking about leaving the country before that precarious moment in my life—and then *bam*! At that very moment, as I stood at the edge of the cliff and was seriously considering resorting to criminality, a miracle happened that freed me from the monster.

I pity men like him who have this kind of sickness. Is it all right for men to sexually oppress women—especially little girls who don't know anything about monsters with human faces? No. Is it all right for men to degrade women as objects? No. Do they think that women don't have hearts and feelings? Where is God at these moments of abuse? Is he absent like the parents are? Why do men chase women like kids chasing butterflies to store in a jar for their entertainment? Why can't they see us as their mothers who give them life, regardless of who we are? Women meritoriously deserve respect.

5

Reverse Life

IN CANADA, LIFE WAS so different. My mother let me play with the other children my age, and I did so without fear. Everybody knew my mother and me. Even going to school was fun—no retaining lessons by heart, less homework to do, and there was even gym class—and snow! I forgot about my past hardships very quickly, like other children of my age would unconsciously do, I presume. My real name on my mother's passport wasn't brought up by the school administration because all my reports had been sent directly from Haiti to my new school. Thus, I continued my schooling under the same illegal name. The Canadian nuns in Roche-a-Bateau and the Canadians nun in Epiphany trusted each other. I wasn't any the wiser and certainly didn't care. All I knew was that life was good. Living in Canada was like a different existence. The only similarity between my old home and my new one was nature: the trees, the verdure, and the air. Everything in nature looked the same during the summer. The other three seasons were spectacular for me, especially when the leaves changed colors in fall.

We were the only black family in the little town of Epiphany, which is near Montreal. That was 1965. Tita and I were unique among the majority-white citizenry. At school, the other children were amazed by the color of my skin, which they had never seen up close before. I was the princess of Egypt, encircled by lots curious people who were eager to find out if my chocolate skin was real. Some people with narrow minds thought that I'd never had a shower, thus explaining the brownness of my body. Some abstained from socializing with me, afraid that they might catch something unhygienic. I heard this all the time, especially from babies who were around a year old. "Why doesn't she have a bath?" they asked their mothers. "That's why her skin looks dirty, isn't it?"

I was used to Canadian nuns and missionaries in Haiti. I found the white people to be normal and pretty. It wasn't a shock for me to be around them. Blue eyes, green eyes, darker eyes—they were all beautiful. Where I came from, we paid little attention to these types of differences because regardless of the lighting of your skin, we're all Haitians, period. I didn't care about any of it—I was just happy to play with children, mindless of what they said about me. I'd never had friends my own age before and had never played in my backyard or on the school grounds with someone like me. I was deliriously happy. I couldn't believe that it was me, outside of my house, playing like a normal kid with these white dudes! Despite their exculpated, biased remarks, I never felt hurt in any way. They didn't see me for my race but as myself—a kid like them who happened to be a contrasting color. That's the beauty with children; they don't see racial heterogeneity unless their parents talk about it at home.

I was innocent in that matter too. I never heard the world "discrimination." When someone said something prejudicial to me, I just laughed like an idiot because I had no clue what they meant. My peers' parents seemed to be all right too. Some of them even sent their daughters to school with cookies and fruit for me. After school, I often stayed with my good friend, Marielle Papineau, to play at her house. I thought that I had beautiful hair—not too coarse and not too soft either, just perfect mix, like a couple's procreation. But Lord, theirs was very fluffy and feathery, like touching a bird. I thought that it was really beautiful. I didn't dare touch their hair because I was aghast by its softness; it was too beautiful and too fragile, and I was afraid I might mess it up. My mother loved to braid my hair in two parts, which resembled a hairstyle that the white girls often donned—two braids tied with ribbons. The white children loved me for who I was and often treated me like a big doll who was there for their delectation. They would touch me without hesitation; I was there inasmuch as a toy to play with as I was their peer. I didn't see the issue with this at the time. Within this conviction, I didn't have any problems with my race or color. Little did I know, that part of Canada hadn't even been emancipated yet.

My friend's father was a policeman. He conducted traffic in the mornings, always standing at the same place with white gloves and an impeccable uniform. He was very sophisticated. As soon he saw me, he stopped all the cars, raising his right hand toward the sky to let me cross the street. I thought, *How great that he gives me precedence over all these car drivers!* I felt powerful, like a queen. I didn't know the inner workings of traffic circulation in countries like this one, which was way more advanced than where I came from. After many years, of course, I found out that it was a normal process for school children and that he wasn't giving me special treatment at all. I don't think my mother knew that either, because she didn't tell me otherwise. "Oli, they love you, my child," she said.

At Christmastime, my mother's boss, Mrs. Ratel, did a lot of cooking. I didn't usually like her tasteless cooking, which was devoid of spices. She cooked with solemnness, as if it were a grave duty to make special food for her husband, her daughter France, and us. The house was well-decorated in green and red for the season. The contrast with the dark cherry furniture and the scintillating lights made it even more festive. Days before the holiday, I could smell a mixture of wood burning in the brick chimney and the fresh pine trees. Intermittently, I could capture this air with a deep inhalation and closed eyes. On the morning of the twenty-fourth of December, Mrs. Ratel fetched the wild pheasants, which they'd hunted in November in Quebec and frozen, and rested them in a big bowl on the kitchen table. The boiling of the bird utterly ruined the sweet scent. An odor similar to that of garbage overran the house. It was pollution covering the natural air that I breathed with pleasure before. It spoiled everything.

On Christmas Eve, everyone sat down to eat around the round cherry wood table, which was covered with a white, green, and red tablecloth. I sat in the middle of Tita and France. Next to her were her father and mother. The chimney flashed with sparkles and clicks as the wood burned. We sat listening to it, well-dressed and awaiting the feast. Nevertheless, I was just there because I had to be. I was thinking *When will this meal be over?* and *What will Santa give me this year?* I was so anxious. The soup was soon served, and from the first sip, I felt like I had to puke. Suddenly, I felt like I couldn't drink the soup anymore, which was made from the broiling water of the wild pheasant. There was nothing more in it, just the broth, which was served with fresh bread and butter. I ate lots of bread to help me cope with that soup. I placed a piece of bread on my tongue and then poured soup onto it like a sponge, which helped me swallow it. But my strategy soon stopped working. I felt nauseated. I was heaving, my head and chest going forcefully front and back, my right hand covering my mouth. I tasted saltwater in my mouth as my body tried to regurgitate the disgusting broth. Tita understood what was happening. She whispered to me that I wouldn't dare vomit at the table and to control myself. But I'd reached my limit. I couldn't hold it any longer. Suddenly, everything in my stomach splashed onto the table—a culmination of the horrible smells that had filled the house all day and the horrible broth I'd been forced to eat.

I felt relieved to have emptied my aching stomach, but I was so embarrassed. Not to mention terrified of the scolding my mother would rebuke me with afterward. France, seeing what I had done, wanted to imitate me, which made the whole scene even more uncouth. She was four years old, so everything was a game for her. Tita felt prestigiously abashed by my indocile behavior. She held my chest without a smile, pulled me from the table, and grabbed a wet towel to clean my face in order to ease my mortifying discomfort. She went back to clean the table, changed the tablecloth, and rearranged the servers with Mrs. Ratel. I was sent to my bedroom for the night. On another day, I wouldn't have considered this to be a punishment, but on that day—Christmas Eve—it was a severe one, especially because I was guilty of nothing. The strong smell of the bird made me sick. That's all.

After midnight, France ran up the steps to my room, excited show me her gifts from Santa. However, I was sad and full of regret, so I couldn't share her happiness. I just wanted to be left alone to wait for daylight, when I would get my belated gifts. I didn't sleep and neither did France, but not for the same reason; she played with her dolls until her mother showed up at the doorstep close to dawn and ordered her to go to her bedroom. Sunrise genteelly gleamed into the room, but everybody was still sleeping. I figured that I was already awake, so I might as well go downstairs. I sat impatiently on the floor facing the tree, which had a few wrapped boxes under it. My mother soon came downstairs but didn't say a word to me until Mrs. Ratel appeared to give me my presents. I received a very nice doll that looked like a real white baby, half-plastic and half-fabric, plus lots of other Barbie dolls. I was delighted that I could remove or turn their heads and legs without damaging them. Soon, I forgot everything that'd happened the night before. My mother cooked, I ate, and I had a good Christmas Day.

Nearly two years after we landed in Canada, we had to go back to Haiti to file for permanent residence. My mother decided, however, that she didn't want to go back to Canada because of the cold weather. I suppose that was her main reason, but I also suspected that the work in the house and the boutique were too much for her. She paid for my room and all my supplies, and I couldn't help her with her duties. That was one of the Ratels' rules; I was a child, so I was their pensioner, not their employee. It was forbidden for me to execute any duties around the house, and my mother wouldn't have let me help her, anyway. The Ratels treated me exactly like they treated their own daughter, France. They were very good people who took us with them on their trips and outings, including the 1967 Expo. There, we visited the Haiti pavilion, and my mother was so happy to finally talk to a few Haitians.

Instead of returning to Canada, Tita moved to northern Haiti to work and left me with her parents again. I regretted this because I liked living in Canada so much. I could be a Haitian Canadian in lieu of being a Haitian American, no problem, but that wasn't in the cards. Tita never expressed a desire to go back there, even for vacation. Since then, I have often traveled to Canada to visit a few of my family members who fled to Montreal to build their lives. These days, much of my close family lives there: aunts, native Canadian cousins, etc. I don't regret anything because I believe that it was meant to be like that. The city of Epiphany, where we lived for that year and a half, was just one stop on my trajectory, or perhaps it was merely the answer to my prayers during the period in my life when I lived in constant fear of sexual abuse. It was an escape hatch for me, which wasn't meant to last forever. For my mother as well, Epiphany was just a step in her life. I never heard her talk about it or saw her writing to anyone she knew there, but I can't be sure if she did or not. All I knew was that I really missed my friends and the freedom I tasted there for the first time.

6

Déjà Vu

One of my aunts got married to a man who had first been my friend. I met him at a dance competition for children. I won, and he was one of the judges. I invited him home. He was from the big city, Cayes, south of Haiti, and he'd come to our village to treat people with malaria. An amorous dalliance developed between him and my oldest aunt. While I was in Canada, they got married. I was happy for them and remembered that my aunt had promised me that I could be her first child's godmother. She got pregnant, and I thought, *I'll be back just in time!* And I was. I became the female baptism sponsor for Clara, along with my grandfather, who became her godfather. My grandfather, who I called father and whose last name I wore for almost a quarter of my life, became her male baptism sponsor as well.

I was twelve years old at the time. I'd returned from overseas with a lot of beautiful new clothes, and my face was blossoming into an adult's. Every young boy's eyes were on me. It made me crazy. My aunts were members of a jazz club, and a boy, Saul, was the singer there. One day, while my aunts were out and I was home alone, Saul tried to force himself on me. *This time it won't be the same*, I thought. I was ready to fight back. I wasn't a child anymore, and my consciousness had developed pretty well on that subject. He shoved me onto the canape. I bit him very hard and told him that if he didn't stop, I would tell my grandmother. I knew he would get served justice; my grandparents would file a deposition to have him arrested for a sex crime. He wouldn't go to jail because of his notable family and because only men held the judicature, most of whom inevitably thought that women were nothing but sex objects and servants. But at least his reputation would be tarnished around the community and he would be known by all as a sex offender.

He automatically stopped and never tried to abuse me again, but he continued to let me know, on many occasions, that he would always love me. That was fine with me. I could live with that. He was very intelligent and handsome, and he came from a nice family, but he'd attacked me before declaring himself, which made him a brute and an aggressor in my eyes. Anyway, I didn't want to have any kind of affair with him. My two years in a foreign country and traveling for vacation to so many places that were more developed than Roche-a-Bateau—even the places where my mother went to work—made me believe that I was too advanced for the people in my town. I was awash in pretense from Tita that my world had no limit. She taught me well during the time we spent together in Canada. "You're a princess," she told me, "and can be married to anyone you want. The world is yours to explore, so don't ever think that any kind of man is too high or too good for you, Oli."

I liked hearing that. I learned early on that you need to take what you can get from your parents—learn what they have to teach you and ignore the rest. What she didn't teach me was love, something with which she didn't make any connection. I never heard "I love you" from her mouth. Deep down, however, I always knew that she loved me more than she loved herself, and let's be serious, the word "love" is used mostly by men when they are flirting with women. I believe that after marriage, it is gone from their mouths forever. It's more of a courtesan word. Parents with old-time values feel ashamed and weak to use it with their children.

Saul stayed friends with my aunts but not with me. I told my two aunts about the abuse, but again, they opted to avoid the conversation. They didn't say anything to me—no antipathy, no animosity. They were likely immune and indifferent to it, and they refused to engage in this sort of conversation with me. Why? Did they feel culpable because they'd let it happen on their watch, or they were still under the impression that victims are to be blamed in instances of sexual abuse?

7

Teenage-hood

As I approached my thirteenth birthday, my mother moved me to the big city, Cayes, so that I could go to middle school. I lived at the sisters' pension house, which was a kind of foster home run by the church. In my hometown, we only had elementary school, which I completed in Epiphany, Canada, so I had to go elsewhere to complete my education. The nuns' pension house was like a college campus; if your parents didn't reside in the city, you could still stay there to go to school. My mother paid every month for my lodging, school, and food. Life in middle school was stressful and sometimes unpleasant. Twenty-one children from multiple towns lived there together. A Latin phrase describes the experience well: *homo homini lupus* (man is a wolf to man). From the beginning, the other students showed me that I wasn't welcome there because I was the only one who'd traveled overseas. You would think this would help me succeed in social situations but no way! I was deemed a snob, spoiled child, and jealousy, competition, and lies were rampant among us. They would complain to the Catholic nuns about things I didn't do. Even though the nuns knew their lies about me weren't true, almost all the other girls had set their minds on evicting me, which made my life hard. What's new with teenagers?

Almost every week, I was reprimanded by the religious. I wasn't a kiss-ass either. My luck—I couldn't find myself a friend, even in my own country. Even the more-timid children who didn't interfere in people's business didn't give a damn about my torment. This triteness wasn't new for me. It was déjà vu. This was typical for me, and I didn't care a flake. I thought, if they wanted to see things like that, so be it. I wasn't raised with any children in my life, so it didn't bother me at all. I became closer to the Canadian nuns, which made many of the other girls even more enraged. That gave me real pleasure, and I wanted to provoke them. Despite it all, I was afflicted by more punishments than the other girls were because I had a big mouth and I was around a bunch of liars.

One day, the nuns took us to the beach—a very beautiful beach with white sand named Gelee. They said we could go miles into the ocean before it got too deep. We were very excited and happy to go out for pleasure instead of for school or church. It was a very hot day. The brightness of the sun warmed our heads. When we got out of the water, the sun dried our swimming clothes so fast, and the heat made it impossible to breathe, so we stayed in the water. We had so much fun in the ocean that we forgot our animosities. We got along well, showing each other that we could swim and performing all kinds of stupid acrobatics and aerobics in the water. Inadvertently and spontaneously, we forgot about our disputes and had a great time. For me, it was double satisfaction: enjoyment and fulfillment. I was finally in the saltwater that I'd always dreamed of in my childhood.

I tried to swim like the others, but I was very amateur at it. I plunged into the water at the same time another girl did, and her foot hit me very hard in the right ear. I lost consciousness. The waves were very high and furious. I don't know exactly what happened, and I don't know how long I stayed under the water, but I was lucky that somebody pulled me out and laid my carcass on the immaculate beach. After I came to, they told me that I could've drowned and that it was a miracle that I didn't. I bled a lot from the ear onto the pure sand. When I regained conscious, I was momentarily confused. I heard people calling my name very distantly, and it seemed like bees were buzzing in my ears. It was very difficult for me to stay focused. We didn't have mobile phones to call for an ambulance, and we'd walked to the beach. I remember wondering how I could possibly get to the hospital. I was wordless. I could hear and I can think, but my mind was confused and wouldn't let me speak. I didn't know what'd happened to me or what might be left of me afterward. A world of confusion invaded my soul, and then I lost consciousness again. I can't recall what happened after that. I know that they rushed me to the hospital, but my ailment was simply a broken pinna cartilage canal. Thank goodness, nothing was severely affected, and I was very much alive. I remember that I couldn't hear well for a while. I thought that I would be partly deaf in the future, but things healed very well, and I grew up without any hearing abnormalities.

This pension house was directed by nuns from Canada who were responsible for many children. They taught us the best pedagogy. We were at their mercy and had to adhere to their very strict regulations. Lord, have mercy! We were twenty-one students in two lengthy bedrooms, or as we called them, *dortoir*, or dormitories, which had only one bathroom per room. We each had a bed (that was even smaller than twin bed) and a table lamp with two drawers. The closet was a long, linen sectional separated by a piece of wood with each pensioner's name on the door. We each had a wide four-foot-long space where we hung our uniforms. The rest of our clothing stayed in our luggage, which we stored under our bed. What else did we need? We spent the majority of our time wearing uniforms—every school day and for mass on Sunday. Every morning, the bell rang at 5:00 a.m. to give us enough time to get ready for the thirty-minute mass at 6:00 a.m. We were instructed to not stay too long in the shower because the water was limited and because ten or eleven of us shared the bathroom at one time. After mass, we were instructed to be in the cafeteria at 6:35 a.m. for breakfast and to leave for school at 7:00 a.m. We arrived at the school building at 7:50 a.m. sharp. We followed the same rules at night, except there was no chapel service. According to the ad hoc policies of that place, we had to finish all our homework before supper, which was always at the same time, 6:30 p.m. If you missed it, you went hungry for the night. Everybody was in bed at exactly 9:00 p.m., when the lights were turned off. We were allowed continue our studies in our bedroom before bedtime.

When I couldn't sleep, I snuck out to the adoration room with a book hidden under my missal so that I could pretend to be praying if

Mother Superior caught me there. I always felt like sleeping too much was a waste of time for young people, so I preferred to feed my brain with a good story instead. My travels and previous schooling gave me advantages, and I was largely ahead of my friends in that regard. On Saturdays, we still had to wake up early, at 7:00 a.m., to clean our little space and hand-wash our personal laundry, such as our undergarments. Our uniforms were washed and ironed each week by staff members so that we always looked immaculate. We were not allowed to make a mess of our uniforms. It was considered sacrilege if we weren't perfectly tidy and clean, crisp as the sacred priest's cassock. We represented their community, *Villa la Madone,* they said, and they wanted us to look impeccable, especially when we went out.

There weren't ever significant changes in the cafeteria menu. We always knew what we'd be eating a week in advance. On Fridays, however, our evening meals were a little different than usual. One week, they served cooked okra with beef. Okra is a very gummy, sticky kind of vegetable, and it vastly outnumbered the meat in that dish. I could hardly find any meat in it at all and couldn't eat the okra. Just looking at the texture of it on my plate over white rice made me want to puke. But the nuns were very dictatorial. They told us what to do, and we wouldn't dare disobey. I had to eat that wild food, like it or not. As a rebel child, I refused to have this disgusting meal. I went without dinner that day. That was fine with me. I thought it was over, but I paid for my sacrifice eight days after. They had to make an example of me in case other girls decided to do the same. As punishment, I was forced to eat the okra dish the next week. They had frozen the leftovers, and a week later, they warmed it up and gave it to me. The other students were having a pink tomato spaghetti with some ham in it. It was imperative to eat what they gave you, but to obey wasn't in my nature, and neither was it one of my qualifications. To get the humiliation over with, I ate all of it, which made me sick to my stomach, and I ran to the bathroom after. They made me swallow all that food just to maintain their reputation of being tough and all-knowing. All the other students ate theirs, they said, so why not me? The funny thing is that I came to love okra later in my life when my mother cooked it for me.

The nuns certainly wanted the best for us, but their allegiance to proving to our parents that they'd done a perfect job turned the pension house into children's prison. It's hard when you are that age to be restrained in so many things. I stayed for a year. After complaining to my mother about the okra incident, she placed me with a local family instead—friends of hers who I didn't know before. I knew that it would be tough, but I had to make the best of it if I didn't want to go back to the pension house. I learned that there is always something good we can learn from hardship. I learned that if you want to be a strong leader, you have to stick to what you believe. I believed that the nuns were using dictatorial power over us and didn't want to stay with them for another year. That was the right decision for me in many ways, and I'm grateful that God and my mother listened to me.

October approached, and it was time to go back to school. I packed my bags for another stage of life. The new family I lived with was okay at first. They took me in because they were in need of the additional monthly income, so they made it as comfortable for me as possible. It was a small house with three rooms in total: two bedrooms and a big hall for the living and dining rooms. The tiny kitchen was outside. I didn't have a room to myself. In the evening, their living room became my bedroom. I never had any privacy and could never sleep or rest during the day because of the foot traffic in and out of the house. The living room was linked to the outside kitchen. A fold-out bed was my sole piece of furniture at night. I cannot remember where I hung my clothes, but that's not important. Given what I went through the year before, I didn't want to make it difficult for them to keep me. I didn't want to go back to the religious pension house, so I was determined to make it work. I wasn't concerned about superfluous comforts, just the essential things—that was all that mattered to me for the moment. I wasn't under the tyranny of the religious dictators, so the minimal comfort I had in my new home soothed me perfectly. I had more freedom too, except that I wasn't allowed to stay out late at night. I had no problem with this; after all, I wasn't used to liberty. For a while, I was generally happy there.

However, the master of the house, Mr. E. S., soon began to play with my mind, offering me rides on his bicycle and teaching me how to ride it myself. I realize now that he knew what he wanted from the moment I arrived at his home. Innocently, I wasn't prepared for the possibility that he might think I could be his mistress. I thought that his kindness was his normal character that he extended to everybody, and I was too young to understand the reason why he paid so much attention to me. He even called me Oli, like my mother and my grandparents did. One night, while I was in the deepest depths of sleep, he came to my bed, stark naked, and leaned down shamelessly in front of me, one of his legs already on my bed. I thought that I was dreaming, but soon I realized the reality of situation. His yellowish teeth glanced at me in the dark. His face was close to my face as if he was preparing to kiss me—the pervert! Suddenly, I became very aware of what was actually happening to me. I screamed, but he rapidly put his hand over my mouth. I never anticipated that in that small, open living room, where every night I had to push away chairs to make space for my bed, the man who'd been entrusted with my care would be so demonically possessed to sexually assault me.

Quivering like a dog's tail in the obscurity of that tiny space, I was shocked and furious. I liked to read all kinds of monster books, and suddenly, I was face-to-face with one. His phiz was the face of a behemoth bent over me. I looked at him, incapable of saying a word. With his right hand still covering my mouth, he whispered in my left ear to stop screeching. "Please don't scream again, I'm leaving," he said, and then on his tiptoes, he left. He didn't persist, afraid to wake up his family. Clandestinely, he returned to his bedroom and wife. I was scared. This man was the father of a girl and a boy—did he not think that the same might occur to his daughter one day? How could he like that? I couldn't sleep anymore. I wouldn't ever be able to close my eyes at night again, I thought. How would I be capable of looking at this man in the morning and in the coming days? Should I leave? Go where? I had two months of school left. *What am I going to do?* I wondered.

Like the brain of a computer, a lot of thoughts were swirling inside of mine. I blamed my mother for placing me there. I was angry at all the men on earth. I was only fourteen, and I'd already experienced abuse from three molesters. Every night, I was on the *qui-vive* (lookout) for that man. I was waiting for him to return, more equipped to accomplish his perverted goal. Next time, I thought, I would shriek so loudly that the neighbors would wake up and discover what kind of predator was living near their children. The main door to the house was just a few steps from my fold-out bed, and so I left it unlocked for the rest of the time that I stayed there so I could easily open it if I saw him coming. I didn't fear outsiders, only that corrupted insider. Fortunately, he never tried this again, but he kept harassing me verbally and with gestures and face-making anytime his family wasn't around. The man was uncontrollably, extremely possessed by the devil.

I speculate that everybody has a guardian angel. Mine was present that night. I woke up before he could hurt me any more than he did. If my archangel hadn't been safeguarding me that night, that horrible man would have had the time to lay down completely over my body. I don't know if I would've been able-bodied enough to fight under that muscled, ready-to-do-it, old man. The smell of cigarettes on his hand stayed in my nostrils for days. I couldn't get rid of that repugnant odor. To this day, I don't know how I didn't wake anybody else up that night when I screamed. The house was quite small. The two children were very little, but at least, I thought, his wife must've heard my loud screech. Did she know that her husband had uncontrollable sexual perversities? Did she condone what he wanted to do to me? Why did she not ask me what happened the next morning? Why did she not inquire about why I'd screamed at the top of my lungs in the middle of the night? A few days after, he had the nerve to tell me, without shame, that I'd almost awoken his wife that night. That made me sure that she'd had heard my yelling. I felt more embarrassed than he was. I don't know where my troubled spirit came from—he should've been the one who felt ashamed, not me, but it was the complete opposite. Feeling disgraced, with my head down, I avoided looking at him. What kind of creature makes a young girl believe that she did something wrong after being abused?

"It's your fault," he said later. "You're too pretty, Oli." What kind of monster-animal was he? He was completely insane! The biggest antagonist of humanity, the devil, entered his body and took over of his soul. Even though he never tried to abuse me again, he harassed me incessantly during the two months before school ended.

"You are so beautiful, Oli," he said to me when nobody else was around. "My Lord, you look like an angel."

Shh, man! I thought. His stupid compliments made me fume and always reminded me of that night. If I was truly an angel to him, he would've felt obligated to respect me. I repeatedly said to myself, "Be patient and try your best to stay away from him so you can survive these two long months." I didn't have a good friend who I could go play with and talk to on Saturdays and after church on Sundays. I stayed home most of the time, and it was a very difficult task. Days felt like months, and months felt like years. This adversity was even worse than the abuse I encountered at my grandparents' house. His wife was a sweet lady despite her ignorance of my tragedy, but he was evil personified. When it came down to it, the fact that the wife never mentioned anything about that night made her untrustworthy to me. My mother had trusted them enough to put me in their house, assuming that I would be in safe hands, but he tried to rape me. What an unreasonable trust my mother had in him! He wasn't my father, so how could Tita be so doe-eyed to rely on him for something so important? Of course, mischievous goblins don't have a specific face; they aren't marked with Satan's stamp on their foreheads. Often, their malice, debauchery, and corruption lays below the surface. This man's friendship with my mother didn't change because I never said anything to my mother. Above all, he was a man, and just like all the others, when he saw female, the clairvoyant, positive, kind side of his brain stopped functioning. She thought that he would not do any harm to me, that he would protect me as if I was his own daughter. A poor state of mind! You were bloody wrong, Mother. He was a man, after all.

My mother didn't have too many experiences with the male gender. As far as I know, after my father, she never had another man in her life, and so she didn't get the chance to find out that some of them are viperous. However, she was scared of giving me a stepfather for these reasons. I'm so grateful to her, and I thank her a lot for her sacrifice in this regard. Likely, any man she remarried would act like my father did to her, keeping mistresses and such. Because she largely recused herself from men, she forgot that they are monsters in so many ways and everywhere. Every day, young girls and women battle with pathetic men to retain their innocence. All females will likely been thrown into lion's dens to be sacrificed at one point in their lives. I can't be sure, but if I had to guess, I'd say that only 5 percent of men are respectful humans. And even that 5 percent I'm not so sure about. A man is a man, period.

When it comes to sex, men don't know what is wrong and what is right. Even when they need to urinate in the morning, they think that it's sex that they need. I never said anything to Tita about the abuse I endured there, nor did I speak of it to anyone else. I only wanted to leave that horrible place. I was so angry at my mother. She could keep her friendship with him, I thought. I didn't care about that. In fact, I even enjoyed my muteness toward her. Let her have her foolishness, trusting this humbug man while he laughs at her silliness. "Who knows?" I thought. "Maybe he will attack her the same way he attacked me, and then she will find out what I went through!" That is cynical thinking, I realize that, but it was the only way I could get revenge for her absenteeism. At that time, I really meant it. I had run from a cool rain at the religious pension house, but I'd jumped into a boiling river. Life is the way it is—a hard candy that you may think is sweet enough to bite but which can also break your teeth. To quote the film *Forrest Gump*: "Life is like a box of chocolates. You never know what you're gonna get."

The man who abused me had a hidden life. He was an example of man's hypocrisy, man's double face. He was dye in the wool of the Catholic religion. He went to Sacred Heart Church every Sunday like a good Christian, but more than likely, his goal wasn't to worship but to seek new young girls to prey on. I nevertheless was able to forgive him. The older you are, the more things like these incidents hurt. Religion doesn't make a person good or bad. They are what they are. Plausibly, by going to church every Sunday, he was seeking redemption, repentance from God, or simply forgetfulness that he was a son of Satan.

I cannot rebuke all men for being the same in evildoing. There are those who still value and conserve the tenets of the past. For example, some men go directly to a woman's parents to ask for the hand of their daughter in marriage. One such man in my life was named T-Al. He was around the age of my father when he formally went to my mother to ask for her blessing to marry me. He never said anything to me at all, and when he came over, he talked to my aunts, who were closer to his age. I was sixteen and had never even had a boyfriend. I couldn't fathom that his visits to the house might be for me. What would I even say to a grown man like him? I recall that he used to devour me with his eyes. As my mother said to me later, he came with papers detailing his worth to brag about his riches. He said that if she accepted his offer (I call it that—an "offer"), I wouldn't be deprived of anything. Yeah, moron, except my teenage-hood and freedom! My mother denied his request, telling him that I was too young to get married. By telling him that, she was just trying to be polite. He probably thought that he could manipulate her into agreeing, that she was a myrmidon and would be persuaded by his wealth. He was wrong; mother had bigger better fish to fry for me, and she had higher expectations for her only child. Believe me, I passed on all kinds of male gimmickry and tricks. For me, his interest in me was another type of perversion. Why he didn't look for someone his own age? Why me? Was he still living in one of those countries where parents sold their girls to old men? I could see that he liked young girls, but I'd never heard anything bad about his sexual behavior. So who was he? A male chauvinist who believed that women were worth nothing. I'm certain that if my father had been alive, he would've gone to him instead of my mother to seek my hand in marriage. He retained the belief that men should have power over women. He thought we were still living in an era when females could be treated like belongings without consequences.

Men are sick in many different ways. This one tried to show my mother all his worth. He promised that he'd be able to take care of me, that I wouldn't have to worry about anything. Didn't he know what "anything" meant for a girl of my age? It meant being in a golden cage without anything for oneself—the end of my life before it even started. I'm sure he perceived me as a child, not a woman, a thing that would be easy for him to manipulate. He was a destroyer of women's freedom to choose who they want for a spouse. He wanted someone who wouldn't be able to stand up to him—someone who would accept all his ill will. He was an arrogant man who believed that money could buy everything, even the "love of a little girl." We need to stop these kinds of people, those who think that everything is permitted to them because they have money. Wake up! Girls and women are not things or artifices, and we deserve respect and dignity. Even though this one made his approach in the formal way, relying on an ancient and oft-forgotten tradition that is supposed to imply respect—his intentions weren't respectful at all. Being made into a sexual object even once hurts for lifetime, and it hurts even more when people around you ignore it or don't believe the truth when you speak it.

8

The Mystery

WHEN YOU LIVE IN Satan's house, you give him the right to persecute you. There is no proof that I was bedeviled by Mr. E. S. I don't believe too much in superstition—and I know that we have a tendency to appropriate bad things to evil and good ones to God—but some facts appear too flagrant for me to ignore. The following is a story of something puzzling that happened to me there, in the two months before I left that confounding home. It's real, not science fiction, and it might be difficult to believe.

    I said that I wouldn't ever fall asleep in that house again, but with time, my body got tired of staying awake. Finally, I slumbered. As a Girl Scout, I had to go to mass every morning at 5:30 a.m. with my group. One morning, I heard my alarm ringing, which was set for 5:00 a.m. I looked at it with casualness and made an effort to wake up, get dressed in my uniform, leave the house, and walk to Sacred Heart Church, which wasn't too far away. Usually, at this time of the day, the street was already full of little merchants, students going to church like I was, and other people strolling about, starting their days. That morning, however, the street was empty, but I was all by myself and I didn't pay attention to the desertedness around me.

    The church had a clock similar to Big Ben in London but much smaller. With my missal and rosary in my hand, I kept on going until suddenly I heard the clock strike only once. I shuddered. I stopped.

As I stood for a moment looking at the clock above the church's roof, a cold breeze hit me like an opened refrigerator door. The air pushed me back. No dog, cat, or human being was in the street except for me. It was one o'clock in the morning! *What the heck am I doing here at this hour?* I asked myself. I walked home, removed my uniform, and looked at the little clock, which not too long ago had awoken me. It read 1:15 a.m., meaning that when I'd woken up, it'd been 12:30, thirty minutes after midnight. The house was completely dark and silent. Gently, I went back to bed and fell asleep, forgetting about what had just happened as well as my vow to stay awake.

I wrote off this accident as incidental and innocuous—an odd flub on my part that had little consequence—and so I never told anyone about it. It didn't have any important meaning for me. Four weeks later, however, I received a letter from my mother, who was living 400 or 430 kilometers away from me, inquiring about the incident. She asked me what I'd been doing in the street so early in the morning. Her friend, Mrs. A., had written her a letter to tell her that she'd saved my life that night. I was puzzled. Had I been in danger that night? Mrs. A. saved me from what? Where were she? How did she know?

I didn't say anything about it to anybody, and Mr. and Mrs. E. S. didn't seem to be aware of my leaving in the middle of the night. It was a mystery! I thought about it for a while but eventually forget about it again. However, when I went on vacation in the summer to visit my mother, I decided to find out how Mrs. A. had known so much about this incident and what she allegedly saved me from. I asked my mother.

Tita looked at me straight in the eyes. "Olivia," she said. She paused, trying to be kind. "Oli, my child, there are things in this world that are too old for you to understand. You're here today because of her, and I'm so grateful."

I still didn't understand. "I remember that I was the only one in the street," I said. "I didn't see her, and there was no way that she shouldn't been behind or around me."

"Well, she has the ability to be invisible to your eyes. Don't ask me for more information, because I don't know. I just know that the devil exists and is around all of us in this world." She stopped talking and shook her head for a few seconds. I could see that she had more to say but was restraining herself, as to not confused me more. "She told me to give you this tea," she added after a few breaths, "and I'm going to make it now. I already bought all the ingredients."

I drank the tea. It was a regular tea that tasted slightly bittersweet and a little salty. There were no side effects, and in my view, nothing about changed. Had someone been trying to kidnap me or take possession of my soul that night? Was Mrs. A. part of a demoniac group, or she was there by chance? I had my missal and my rosary in my hands, so shouldn't they give some credit to my belief in God? All these questions remain unanswered to this day. Believe it or not, this really happened to me in 1969, in Cayes, Haiti, at the intersection of Jet Cine, or Grand Rue, a crossroads of five streets. This isn't a fiction but a fact. Do I believe that something bad really happened to me that night? That a spirit entered my body, or tried to? Probably yes, probably no. Was Mr. E. S. behind all of it as revenge? Perhaps. In my country, everything is possible. My mother trusted that lady and made me drink that tea that could've killed me. God bless her naivety. I could see in her face that she was afraid and desperate enough about that night to give me this potion to swallow without hesitation. Maybe she weighed her options and decided that the tea was less likely to kill me than the devil was.

In that same year, 1969, my aunt moved to the big city with her husband and daughter. Her husband was originally from the city; like I said before, he was only in our little town for work, and that's when he met my aunt. His contract with the company had been terminated, so he returned home. Their house wasn't far from my school, so I decided that I wanted to live there—to continue my gypsy life of moving from place to place.

I didn't have a room of my own and slept on a big couch. I didn't care, though, because she was my sister-aunt. Her house was a little bigger. Only once, I alluded to my family about what'd happened to me in a goofy manner, but nobody paid any mind to what I was trying to tell them. A little disconcerted by their blankness, I mumbled that I was raised as a grown person, and now that I was old enough to take care of my own business, I wouldn't bother disclosing my hush-hush secrets to them anymore. So I shut my mouth, relinquished to reserving my story for myself. Once again, I carried my secret underground. I moved on, carving my pathway toward another chapter in my life. The three attempts of rape that I survived would be my secret. Who would believe that I'd experienced these instants of violence in my life? So I moved to my aunt's house—a whole new environment. I have to leave all these hardships behind. Living with her again was like going back to the old times: we sang together, she combed my hair, we laughed, and she called me *ma comere Oli*. *Comere* is the traditional name you receive from a mother when you're the godmother of her child.

    I know that lot of you will criticize me for waiting so long to talk about these three instances in my life. First, it's embarrassing, and second, I've taught myself to forget about all of it. Third, when you're young, you rarely think about the past because you're too busy with the present and looking forward to a better future. Voluntary, I let go of the memories of these unpleasant incidents. To tell the truth, I never forgot about them completely, but I forced myself to live a normal life regardless of these ghosts. The past wasn't my priority, and so instead, I focused on the future. I wanted to move on in a positive way. I thought that low, pitiful people shouldn't affect my future even though they hurt me in the past. In reality, I wasn't raped by any of them, but the fact is that they each tried to. They abused and disrespected me, and they diminished and took advantage of me. My third vulture was about twenty years older than I was. He tried to take away my purity in his own wife's house. I don't know if there is another word to call these men other than "animals." I worked very hard to let it all go, freeing my soul from the hate I had for these four men, including my father, who had abandoned me. That said, even now, I have a blockage within me that prevents me from showing much love and respect to men in general.

    I have to emphasize that there are multiple ways for a man to abuse a woman, namely verbal assault, obstruction of sexual rights, and sexual harassment and abuse. All are very common. We perceive verbal abuse as saying bad, ugly words, but some sweet ones, which are often employed incessantly by men to attain a goal are as well verbal abuse. Some women may take those words as compliments, and some may not. Men have the inclination to label women at first sight. As soon as a man meets me, he might begin calling me sweetie, honey, sweetheart, baby, babe, love, etc., and this is a kind of derangement in and of itself. This implies that his intentions might not be kind or pure. Once, when I was visiting a new doctor for the first time, he said, "Sit down, sweetie," as soon as I entered. He was from Puerto Rico, a different culture, so maybe for him, the pet name was simply part of his bedside manner—a kind way to sympathize with his elderly Spanish patients. Regardless, I didn't find it professional at all. I look at him haggardly, to the point at which he asked if something was bothering me. If you prick me you, you wouldn't find blood because of my anger. I felt like he was trying to diminish me with a demeanor of superiority. I was sixty. I was old enough to be his big sister, and I was a married woman. He didn't know me at all—where did he get off calling me "sweetie?" In the street, it was always the same scenario: strangers rushing to my side just to tell me that I'm "hot." Who are you to know so much about me? I don't recall seeing you before!

Another man, every time we saw each other, he always kissed me on the chin because we were friends, but on multiple occasions, he's tried to kiss me on the mouth. I've had to spontaneously turn my face. It's a fight. I've tried to ignore the gesture, thinking that he might think nothing of it, but this man was persistent. I had to gently stop him. I had to escape it many times and began wondering how long I could put up with the battle. He didn't give up easily. Finally, I decided to shake his hand instead, to make him understand that I would not be his prey. I understand that sometimes when you're attracted to someone, you might attempt to kiss them once, to take your chances, but how long do you keep trying? This is when it becomes sexual harassment. I have been harassed many times by men who could clearly see that I wasn't interested. They're unscrupulous swindlers. Women are always walking on our tiptoes as to not awaken any man's sexual avidity. We're constantly trying not being too nice to a man, because he might take it as an invitation to hop into bed with us.

Workplaces too can be the worst places for a woman. Every day comes with some kind of verbal assault. "Your husband is a lucky one." "You look sensational." "You're hot today." Sure, they're great compliments, but it's the delivery and the context that makes the difference between kindness and harassment. You're sniffing while telling me that I'm beautiful, and you're eating me with your piercing eyes. Not to mention the fact that we are in a professional environment where we are supposed to be equal. They're just words, sure, but words have meaning, and sometimes, they're used for violence and sexuality. "Nothing ventured, nothing gained," sure—complimenting a woman is a chance that men might take to find out if their attraction is reciprocated—but there is an appropriate way to do this. There is an appropriate time and place and an inappropriate time and place. Men often plead that they're trying to be gentlemanly, when in reality, they are being abusive. You don't have to use misogynistic words to flirt with a woman. What would you think if a woman called you "sweetie" in the workplace? Would you suddenly feel obligated to take her to bed because in your damaged mind, that's what she meant?

In my experience, domineering flattery is the most frequent kind of verbal abuse that women suffer from men. If I had to guess, I'd say that almost 90 percent of men have used verbal assault to intimidate women somehow in their lives, especially when they're in front of a beautiful one. Beauty can be a problem and a curse. For me, it's a curse that follows me everywhere I go. There's always someone giving me hard time. Men don't care if you're married or not. I call it "men's chauvinist acts against women."

I was forced to see Toto every time I went on vacation to my grandparents' house. He showed remorse and embarrassment over his abusive behavior in the past, but I didn't care. To me, he was a nonexistent creature. I never went back to Mr. E. S.'s house and had no relationship with any of them. Therefore, I put everything in God's hands—not for revenge necessarily but for whatever he judged necessary to do with this type of bestial man. My mind was too preoccupied with other stuff to remain haunted by these nightmarish times. I completely swept away all traces of these bad experiences from my head. Psychologically, I was free of wrath and liberated from abhorrence. There was no reason to have this sad and distressing part of my past ruin my future. At the same time, however, I vowed to teach my children about rape, specifically about the bad effects that it has on victims.

I told myself I wouldn't make any more allusions to these incidents—not only because I didn't want to revive my painful times of yore, but because it would be embarrassing. Eventually, I buried these memories into a deep hole, covered with tons of concrete. These instances of sexual violence solidified my notion that our conceptions of our lives are not anchored in myth but rather in reality. What we make of life becomes our individual myth. We cannot change the fundamental story as we please. Largely, we don't get to choose, and no matter what may come, we have to follow through to the end. Life is made to fit each of us, like a particular space that belongs only to a specific person. We are given a plan and supplies prior to our arrival on earth, but we build our own lives. Life isn't a place where we can do whatever we want, but rather, it a living space where we stay briefly to do what we were meant to accomplish. I learned a new trick—to ignore. To this day, I try not to pay attention to abusive men because usually, I'm in their presence just for a moment, and then it's over. It's hard to be a female in this world we're living in. It's owned by men, men with force and power who still believe that they live in a world where women are their property—living objects who reside in their proprietary colonies for their enjoyment.

9

Why Now?

BY THE TIME I was in my forties, after decades of successfully sweeping away my memories of sexual violence, they started troubling me again like visionary souvenirs. Suddenly, it seemed like yesterday, and I couldn't let it go away anymore. At night, I was constantly visited by the shadowy images of my past. I couldn't sleep anymore. It became torturous to maintain my ignorance about what happened to me years ago. Going to the police after so long and releasing my aggressive history to the public would be too scandalous, I thought, and besides, I'd left the country for almost eight years. I considered that at forty years old, I was still young enough to be vulnerable to public scrutiny and judgment from my friends. What would be the purpose, I thought, especially given that I hadn't seen my abusers in many years? In my country, I'd never heard of anyone being accused or judged for assaulting a woman. Why did these memories come back to haunt me, I wondered, and why now? Truly, I couldn't find an answer to my unexpected and new trials. I pictured the shocked expressions on my family's visages, how they would play their roles of encouragement and support, victim as I am. Then they would be done with it. I couldn't divulge my hole-and-corner childhood to anyone yet. I didn't want to face the eyes of the people, which would be happy or careless. I didn't know how people would react, so I obligated myself with keeping it a secret.

In my fifties, however, good and bad memories and reminiscences came to my mind more vigorously, one after one, like arrows soaring rapidly upward my direction. I felt more hurt by it than ever before. Suddenly, I was dealing with mementos of everything, even the things that I thought were forever buried in the den of the forgotten. Some souvenirs came back with lot of joy, which made me laugh at myself, and some came back with deep sadness that I had to deal with. Morally, I was suffering, and I had to hide my mental instability. I joked about everything, I laughed, and I got crazy sometimes. When I went to a party, I made people believe that I was a happy cow, but in reality, there was a constant burning sensation inside of me that consumed me to the core. Sometimes, these visions of the past even got between me and my spouse. My mind recreated the scenes of my assaults when I was in bed with him. Thanks goodness that women can fake it easily. The animosity I have for men made me believe in the similarities among them. Their sexual appetites for pistil stigmas is above everything. Females of any ilk, of any age, can make them lose their sense of reason, their capacity of clairvoyance. Sure, they are all different on the outside, but sexually, they're all the same. Our husbands, fiancés, and boyfriends—anyone that you have chosen to share your life with—might one day force himself on you like a rapist does. When it comes to sex, men don't have the world "no" in their vocabulary. No should always mean no, not a caprice or a game. I found out that even the men we love didn't always take no for an answer. They're uncontrollable. Most male minds are focused on one thing, sexual activity, unless if they are impotent, and then of course, they project their incapability onto women because they're unable to face their own reality.

It seems to me that men are from some sort of wild, dangerous planet whose inhabitants won't accept any kind of defeat. All human beings should be able to distinguish what is wrong from what is right. Oh no, I forgot—men don't have custody over their actions and thoughts. They are shameless, and it's normal for them. Men: why are you so obsessed with that particular part of the female body that it makes you forget that you are an engaged or a married man? My thoughts regarding men of all classes is that when they are not raping, they are cheating. Raping somebody isn't only when a stranger escalates into your window and aggressively attacks you. *Rape* is the Latin word meaning "to seize." Every time you use force to have sex, even if it is with your girlfriend, fiancé, or wife, it is an act of rape. Rape is when a woman says no, and a man doesn't listen, forcing himself on her like a beast, leaving her afterward feeling like she is a belonging, and that there is nothing she can do about it.

Raping is forcing or coercing someone to have sex without a mutual consent. Raping is when you go out with a friend, get drunk, and use that opportunity to abuse their moment of weakness. Raping is a criminal act, no matter if it is of a stranger, friend, or loved one, when there is no reciprocal acceptance. Women should be free to change our minds as well. I can say yes now, but later, I can say no without being obligated to do it anyway. My yes isn't a commitment to you. When you engage in the kind of hypermaniac sexual behavior that leads to rape, you are destroying the confidence and reducing the power of your victim. If that person loves you, you are degrading that love and causing her to live in fear. It's frustrating for every woman to deal with somebody who refuses to listen. When she says, "Not now," and he does not get what he wants, he does it anyway because he knows that he can physically overpower her. He has a militant power. Similarly, after he has done a great deal of begging and pleading, a woman might say yes in order to get it over with or because she is scared of the consequences of holding onto her no. This too is coercive and abusive behavior. I've met many married women who think that their husbands are angels who would never cheat on them. Hello, friends, don't fool yourselves; there is no such thing. For a long time, I held out hope that there was one good man out there in my country who was levelheaded on the issue. However, after discovering some national figures about how many men keep mistresses—including powerful men who do it outside of the home—I sadly lost hope. From the top to the bottom, they are all the same. No man is immune to the sex virus. It's contagious. One man trains the next one.

I'm trying to understand this side of the male brain with logic. I understand that men and women are anatomically different; it's a fact. But so long as you're not deaf, can't you hear when a woman says "no" or "not now"? Don't you have the brainpower to consider it? Can't you understand that being nice to you doesn't always mean an invitation for sex or that we are at your disposition? Dudes, it's time for you to consider that we are not living in the barbaric times when you could jump on a female wherever and whenever you felt like it. Before, she couldn't say or do anything to object without fearing for her life, so she just obeyed, but we have evolved beyond this. Stop visualizing women as sex toys to play your dirty games with, or as objects that are available to you at the snap of your fingers. This also pertains to married men; there is no difference. When a woman is tired and stressed, she might prefer not to be bothered with sex. She might only need affection and conversation. Can't you wait for another time? Is it necessary and urgent to have sex, even if it is unwanted by your partner? It is necessary like taking medication?

I don't call a sexual encounter a *tête-à-tête* when consent isn't enthusiastically given and affectionately shared. Personally, many times, I have had to balance my feminist thinking with my husband's masculinity in order for us to achieve a successful married life of mutual understanding and love and to keep my psychic burdens at bay. I'm not going to parade by saying that he had been faithful to me. I'm not an idiot nor a visionary. I'm real, and I don't look for such things. God created Eve to complete Adam, and I have no doubt about it: it is so we can have babies. But men must be reasonable. That doesn't mean that when your brain is empty, sex is the only thing that can fill it up back up. Women make efforts to compromise with your too-frequent demands, and certainly, life requires that we understand each other, so why can men not reciprocate this understanding? If we strongly say no, why do you get extremely upset? Don't you know that we cannot pretend all the time?

Mothers should educate their daughters as well as their sons about the many kinds of sexual abuse. Women are not instruments that you can pick up and play with at your own discretion. It's okay for men to attempt to flirt with you, so long as they don't cross the line, but it's also all right for you be conscientious of possible hostility. Fathers tend to put their boys in the streets as roosters, urging them to pick up all the grain they can find. This is probably what they did in the past, and so they are proud of it. They think it's normal, but it isn't. It ruins human freedom—the rights a woman has to be out at any time and to wear whatever she feels like wearing without fear of getting attacked by a sex devotee. Be civilized!

I realized that sharing stories of my own sexual attacks to the public wouldn't be an easy task, but at least I would feel free of the heavy load that has been on my chest for a long time. What you might not understand is that we, the victims of sexual harassment or abuse, live with that embarrassment forever. The mark doesn't go away—it's always there, reminding you of something. When something like that happens to someone else, you feel it in your nitty-gritty body, in your bones. I wonder about all the children, who, like me, live with their parents but are continuously attacked by insiders. I wonder about the children who stay silent. We all can see in the media how risky the world has become for youths, given the prevalence of sexual addiction among men. Now more than ever, mothers need to understand that she must always be with her child, no matter what life throws her way. Parents leave their children with strangers, friends, or even family members too often. Don't make it a habit; it's too dangerous. I don't make it a general abnegation, but preventing is better than grieving.

My mother has now left this world, and I was never able to tell her about that part of my childhood. I've tried many times, but there was never a way for me to start this difficult conversation. I prefer it that way, though. She left earth without grudges for anybody because of me. I beg you, mothers: your presence can forestall that kind of casualty. It's not a matter of gender; in that circumstance, there is no sexual dimorphism. Girls and boys can be raped in the same context. We can't always shadow our kids, but we can monitor their actions and the behavior of the people who surround them.

10

Deception

OF COURSE, I COULDN'T forget that I was raised like a bastard, born from married parents but with a mother I hardly saw and a father I never met. What's the difference? Tita came to see me once a year, and I saw her when I visited her on vacation. She lived like a single mother and worked far from her parents' home to provide me with the best. She walked away from my real father five months after their wedding. I was very lucky to already be an embryo moving inside her. Their separation didn't affect me at all in the beginning. I was cherished by my maternal grandparents, and they became my "real" parents. Tita was an "other"—someone who brought me fancy clothes, school supplies, stuff of all kinds—everything that a middle-class child could dream for. I never felt like I was missing anything. Even though I was living with my grandparents and my aunts, I truly believed that I was living with my mother, father, and sisters. How dumb a baby boomer could be!

    By the age of fourteen, I became greatly confused and struggled with the fact that my grandfather wasn't my real father. I asked my family, "Who is my real dad? I became obsessed with knowing, and even though it seemed like a normal question, I couldn't get any tangible responses. So my hunt began. I had to meet the man who caused my birth. I was very preoccupied with the idea of finding him. It was a hunt—a hunt to find my biological father. At first, my decision to find him was simply interesting, but it soon transformed into an obsession and a rush. I needed to meet my natural father. I knew that he lived near my city and that he came to town regularly, but I didn't have a clue who he was. When I asked my aunt, she said, "If you ever meet him in the street, you'll know, because you look exactly like him. He has lighter skin tone than you do, though, and his hair is different. He is a mulatto."

She didn't say more—likely because she didn't want to displease the other family members. But she'd given me a clue for my investigation. I took a good look at myself in the mirror to find any characteristic that could make it easy for me to recognize him by. I was more than obsessed—I was so excited by the thought that I might see him soon. Maybe he would apologize for not being a part of my life. Maybe I could forgive him and tell him that my love for him has never faded out, that he is part of the reason I'm here on earth. I learned my speech and practiced it every day in front of a mirror. I didn't want to miss a word. How could I not pardon him? We spent so much time apart. It would be a time for reconciliation, which we couldn't waste on anger. I had so much to tell him. I imagined myself telling my friends that my father, the man who missed my childhood, now regretted his absenteeism. I imagined all kinds of conversations with him. I thought he would try to explain what went wrong between him and Tita, but I would pay that no mind—not because I'd ignore him but because all I'd care about is his presence. The rest wasn't important.

As I walked through the streets in the coming weeks, I looked hard into the faces of all the light-skinned men old enough to be my father—any man who might have a little resemblance to me. However, his face never faced mine. I knew that my heart would race when I saw him, like a lover on her first rendezvous. It was a game that I was determined to win. Sometimes, people in the streets called me insolent for disfiguring them with my eyes. I didn't mind, though, and just kept looking. I began wondering if he'd seen me looking for him and had hidden from me. I thought there might be a chance that he was ashamed and regretful of abandoning me, that he might not want to revisit the difficult situation of knowing me. I couldn't believe that I was the only one who'd never crossed paths with him in the small town where I went for vacation, or in the city, where he went to see his other children. (I learned this about him in my midthirties.) My hope turned into hurt at his deception. I was losing my battle and wasn't proud of it. Pity for him, I thought. He won't ever get to experience the vast affection I'd reserved for him and would be delighted to devote to him.

He died two years later. He remained a stranger without a face who didn't give a damn about me. His only duty in my life was his participation in conceiving a fetus. I tried to forget his cruelty, and yet I thought I could be his friend, even if he didn't want to see me as his child. For all daughters, their first lover should be their dad, but when you've never experienced that, how deeply can you love someone else? Among all my other secrets, I found a place inside of me to hide my anger, my deprivation, and my misery. I filled up my mind with how much my mother's family loved me and cared for me.

One day, I was outside at my grandparents' house, and I saw a beautiful woman with keen, greenish eyes looking at me. She wore a flowering, multicolor dress with a hat made of palm leaves. She was in her forties. I thought that the lady looked so *jolie* (beautiful) that I could kiss her chin and tell her how good-looking she was. She was sitting on the neighbor's patio with her face turned toward our domicile, staring at me. She knew who I was, surely, but I didn't know anything about her. All I knew was that I was enticed by that gorgeous woman, and that she was eating me with her green-gray eyes. These piercing eyes were not only looking at my little body, but they also entered my core, trying to tell me something that I couldn't quite understand. I profoundly felt it inside of me. People always say that you can recognize your own blood easily, and I wondered if that might be happening. I was aware that something hot was going through my veins, but I didn't know what it was. Unconsciously, I felt a parental sensation. Instantly, a delicate bond was created between us. I couldn't stop looking at her. Comfortably in her armchair, she wasn't going to break her gaze at me either. I felt my heart opening widely for that unfamiliar person. I didn't want to gaze at her, lest I be rude, but I couldn't resist my need to look. Indisputably, that woman came to my neighborhood just to see me.

I cannot say how long this romance lasted, but I would have liked it to remain for eternity. Every time I turned my head toward her, her eyes crossed mine with a gentle smile that made me hot in my heart. With my head down, I gave her a glance from time to time. My grandmother soon noticed that there was a relationship between us—that we were feeling connected, bounded to each other, so she grabbed my arm and pushed me inside the house. Later, in 1971, after my grandmother had passed away, I found out more about that woman. She was my father's aunt and his godmother.

After my grandmother pulled me inside and away from her gaze, I completely forget about her. Children have a kind of Alzheimer's! At least she tried to communicate with me. When I became adult, I went to meet her. She was lovely and even more beauteous than I remembered. She passed away at the old age of 102. I bitterly regret that I only saw her face-to-face twice in my life. Her sister, my paternal grandmother—I had no clue what she might look like. Not too long ago, I found some pictures of them in photo albums while visiting his brother's wife. Unfortunately, she didn't have any of my father.

My mother never told me why she and my father separated, and she never taught me to love him no matter what. I don't know why he never tried to meet me. Was there a good reason for that, I wondered, or in addition to his ignominy, was he afraid of my mother's parents? Was he still mad that a woman had dared to leave him— had breached the contract of their marriage? I tried to find evidence to answer my questions. I didn't want to settle for the latter. This could not be it, I thought. He couldn't have cared nothing about me because he had other children. Did he abandon them too? These were all possibilities, each of which was harder for me to believe than the last. I kept thinking about what shouldn't made him so ambivalent toward my existence, and I couldn't find an acceptable reason.

These days, I would like for him to answer to these questions himself, but regrettably, he is no longer alive. I didn't blame my mother's family for trying to protect me, but they were certainly all complicit in shielding me from the truth. They didn't even give me the chance to say hello to the man who'd germinated me inside my mother's womb. I thought that just meeting him once could give me the opportunity to know what kind of man he was and that it could help me entomb forever an unnecessary dream. I was burning up with wrath about the irresponsibility of both sides of my family regarding what was right for a child. In this regard, they seemed to me to be egoistic progenitors. They couldn't see that I needed to put my obsession to rest, that I needed the chance to adjudicate and clear my mind by talking to him.

I have to say, even if my grandparents didn't want him around me, he should've tried to overrule their decision. He must've known that he had a legal right to see me, or was he a coward in that case too? I didn't understand what kept him away; my mother decided to take care of me alone, without ever taking one dime from him. Was it a mixture of pride and madness? Despite all the respect I have for my mother, I can't believe how idiotic and ridiculous that was, especially when there wasn't any legal documentation of separation, just a form from a judge that let her enter the house and got her belongings. The way I see it, Robert, my father, should've paid for child support. That would've been the logical solution. She should've made him pay for what he did to her, especially because he could afford it. It's absurd that women think that it's all right to let men walk away from their responsibilities, even if they are angry. I don't agree with this; the seed would not germinate if you didn't scatter it. She was doing the job of two persons, mother and father together. I was her life, I know it, but I was also a heavy load that she had to bear without the help of a husband. Had she forced him to pay child support, I could've been raised by my mother instead of my grandparents. I could've spent more time with my mother because she wouldn't have had to work in a different town. I had a good childhood with Grandpa as my father and Grandma as my mother, no doubt about it, but I would have loved to have my real mother with me in addition to a grandmother and grandfather. I might have even skirted every bad thing that happened in my life while she was absent. I love you, Tita, and I'm grateful for all you have done for me, but I disagree with how you chose to raise me—how you prioritized your resentment toward my father over my care. I don't know what it feels like to have my own father, no matter who he was. I missed his affection and getting to know him. Who knows—I might have treasured him, or he might have disgusted me—but you didn't give me the opportunity to find out for myself. I might've been able to do so if you had, for one moment, taken into consideration your child's feeling.

My desire to meet him was so strong that I didn't care about what had gone wrong between him and my mother. I've heard that it was verbal and physical abuse, which gave my mother reason to leave him, but she could've at least let me see my father once. Children have nothing to do with their parents' arguments and incompatibilities. I didn't ask for them to get back together—no way, that wasn't my mission, to tell them how to conduct their relationship—but I did want the opportunity to keep in touch with my father. For many years after his death, even though I had no chance of meeting him, I still looked at everybody who had a father and envisioned having my own. I became sensitive and envious of anyone who had a dad. His absence harmed me more than you can imagine and left me with an awful, indelible mark in my heart, which has distracted me too often from my priorities. The feeling of deprivation is with me all the time, and I have to live with it—a weird sensation that intermittently firestorms my heart. I profiled my father as a poltroon, afraid to face his obligations. I felt rejected by the one who had procreated me. To ease my frustrations about this fraction of my life, I gave myself a reasonable understanding of: if my father didn't fight whatsoever to keep me in his arms as his daughter, even under pressure of my mother's parenthood, he doesn't deserve my anger. He didn't deserve to have this power over me, so I should stop making myself sick over him.

But this was just the beginning of my life. Let's move on. This shouldn't stop the process of my story, or even slow down my steps on the road. I couldn't let my emotions be swayed because of this matter. I couldn't let myself be a cripple before my life had even started. However, despite it all, to this day, when I see a father with his little girl, either in a movie or on the street or through friends, I feel so much envy I could cry.

I think about my father time to time. I still don't understand some married couples. Now it's even worse with the millennials.

Young men are scared of having families, and young women are so well-educated that they don't need marriage to get by. The few that consent to get married often don't have the patience to make it works. Many children are indulged by the love of one parent, if they are lucky enough, or they live alone in a foster home. This is sad. I promised myself that if I ever got married, I wouldn't divorce for the peace of mind of my children. However, I don't think the same anymore. At my age, if destiny decides otherwise, my children are adult enough to understand and take care of themselves. If the possibility of marriage arises, I thought, I would carefully look at all the marital side effects before engaging in a holy matrimony. No, I don't think I'll do this sacrament twice.

11

Turbulent Adolescence

Tita always worked far from home. Was she trying to obviate her memories, or was it her destiny's determination? I soon became a teenager and was noticed by men everywhere I went. I dealt with constant remarks from people telling me that I was cute, and I heard it so much that I began to believe it. I became popular at school because of my beauty and because I was a troublemaker. I was troublesome for my teachers and peers, and my mouth was my biggest, worst instrument. I couldn't control it; I said whatever I wanted to and to whomever I wanted to. I seemed to enjoy it. Despite the fact that I made fun of a lot of people, they still thought I was a good person. Hey, I probably am! Truly, my intention wasn't to hurt people with my jokes and funky acts, but to let them know that I was in control. My sense of humor said to others: I know what I'm talking about, and I'm not scared of anything. I would rather make you upset than have you make me mad. That was my dogmatic rule, and I intended to keep it that way.

I liked to play with peoples' emotions, which made me seem like a mean person, but I wasn't really. I just wanted people to accept the things that made sense to me. To achieve my goal of "I'm always right," I snubbed the fact that I could hurt other peoples' feelings and ignored the fact that everyone was free to have their own opinions. I wasn't scared to say to someone's face what I thought of them—good or bad—so that they could change their attitude. Lo and behold, I found out that most people were afraid of the truth, and so was I, but I used that as a strategy to win. I would tell the verity of things, like it or not. Part of my satisfaction was being able to say afterward that I'd made the person lose his or her control. Sometimes, other students didn't talk to me. Should I have considered them my enemies? No, they were free in their actions, and I was free is mine. Having enemies put too much stress on my body, so I managed to avoid it. I thought that it was up to the others to talk to me if they wanted to. I will survive without you, I thought, and you'll need me one day anyway.

I can't explain how I did that, but I was a pro. My grandmother used to say, "If God is with you, you don't need anybody else, just have faith in him." Perhaps I used my grandmother's thoughts in this context? Or maybe I was just messed up and confused. I don't think that God was happy with me doing what I was doing, telling people the cold, hard truth even if it hurt them. The truth is so hard to accept. I used it as a game to play with their minds. I made so many children unhappy, but in reality, I was so afraid that one day the medallion would reverse, that somebody would do the same to me. I feared that someone would tell me things that I didn't want to hear—the truth about my funky character—or would make me lose control of myself. I considered weakness to be a flaw, which is why I started the antagonism in the first place. I also wanted to ensure that other people wouldn't abandon me. I had a big mouth and said crazy things, but I also had a sensitive heart and empathized with other people's troubles, believe it or not.

In high school, I had a teacher and counselor, Mr. L., who had a funny way of speaking. I used to imitate him because of the way he talked—two of his front teeth were missing, which made it difficult for him to pronounce the letter *S*. Teens can be inhumane sometimes, and I was one of them. At sixteen, I liked to hang out with older students in *rhetorique* (twelfth grade). I felt that I was too autumnal to be with students of my own age, which was another way to show my popularity. One day, I didn't notice Mr. L.'s presence behind me as I was imitating him. Nobody had time to tell me to shut up. He got pissed off, and pari passu, requested that I go home and return to school with my parents. My mother worked in the north section of Haiti at that time, so I was still living with my auntie Farvel, who'd grown tired of always coming to school to deal with my poor conduct. It was embarrassing for her—she was a sensible and analytical lady. It was terrible that I always plunked her in a situation where she had to apologize for my silliness. She thought that I was a lost case. I took a real pleasure teasing and bothering people no matter their age. To incrust my knowledge and establish my trust in people's minds, I'd listen to the news on the radio and go to school, where I'd discuss the problems of the day with others and make a big ta-do out of it. I would build drama around it or justify the cause, even for the criminals. I was the lawyer of high school, even though I never intended to be, and I was so good at it. When we weren't in class, I was the teacher of life. I was the dramatic actress that I'd always wanted to become, and I was the class counsel, of sorts. Like Jesus at the temple, everybody paid attention to my eloquent orations.

Seeing things differently than other people did caused me lots of trouble. Many times, I tried to accept the common ways of seeing things so I that could pass for a normal person, but I couldn't manage it. Shutting up and approving their ideas persecuted me too much. I must say that my humdingers and my thoughts were far better than their viewpoints were. I saw things in my own way, and my beliefs were uniquely my own. For example, I held that all people on earth were groovy and great and that we each had a mission to accomplish. I thought that what changes people from good to bad is the society we live in, which wants everybody to be uniform. We're all here on earth with a mission to accomplish, either from God or from a demon. What you call "bad" is not bad in the eyes of everyone. For instance, a military receives an order to go to war, to kill enemies—to kill people that they don't know, people that did nothing to them. Does that make the individual soldier a bad person? This is the mission of a soldier.

I've often heard people say, "We are all God's children," but I wonder, how can the entire hemisphere have come from the same father? I'm not sure of the accuracy of this notion. What happened to

Satan? He didn't procreate at all? Undoubtedly, I think that destiny is inevitable and uncontrollable and that we are all either from God or from demon progenitors. The slaughterer uses the name of God to kill, and so do all of us in different circumstances. People often act in faith, thinking that what they are doing is right, when really, they are acting upon a misinterpretation of what God wants. They might be doing what Satan needs. A killer's mind thinks that he is accomplishing a mission like the soldier is. If you think that we are all God's creatures and that we shall not kill but shall forgive, why do we use capital punishment? If you think that murder is bad, why don't you use another strategy instead? "An eye for an eye" is from the Old Testament. If I remember it correctly, Jesus on the cross said, "Father, forgive them, because they don't know what they are doing." Maybe you as the jury, you as the judge don't know what you're doing either. Killing should only be done in defense, not revenge, hate, or pleasure. Not everything can be credited to God's wishes though—a storm, sickness, loss of family or friends, bad luck, and so on. It is up to us to make meaning out of it. An old saying goes that the master of universe is never mad. Wrong—we saw with Noah and the deluge that God was so mad at us that he decided to inflict massive destruction. Jesus was mad at people for using his temple as a flea market. The list goes on. Why do people always say that "God is never mad at us?" I think that it is all right to be mad sometimes, but we should be able to control our madness, that's all. I will leave the rest for you to think about. These are some of my opinions that differ from others. I see the world differently, and that created problems for me in my teenage-hood. I didn't always enjoy it then, and I don't always enjoy it now. I suffered from injustice and unfairness. I was sensitive to other people's issues, but I used my contrary character to oppose other people who were like me—fragile and weak—and to cover up my own fear about what was happening in the world.

My battle with Mr. L. didn't end there. Every day at school, I stayed under the desk bench as soon as I knew it was time for his inspection, particularly when he wanted to make sure that I wasn't there. The students weren't always mad at me; they even liked me, for the most part, despite my want to make some of them miserable.

THE DAILY BATTLE FOR A NORMAL LIFE

It wasn't a joke to me; in my head, I only spoke up when I wanted a person to change for the best. Maybe my approach was ridiculously inept. I also cared, spoke up for, and embraced their causes, no matter if they were friends or not, even if the principal had to send me home because of it. That is the way I am—I cannot see injustice or unfairness and say nothing. The teachers knew me so well that when something happened, they didn't even bother asking the class about it. They would come directly to me, having already sentenced me with guiltiness.

"Olivia, why did you do this?"

They always assumed that all bad things came from me. Therefore, I thought, I could deceive them with their own ideology. I continued the fun, which I enjoyed so much. I kept up my bad behavior largely so that I would be blamed for something that I really did, for once. I could also be serious about serious matters and didn't let my friends down. I was their lawyer, consultant, social worker, and physiologist. I always listened to what they had to tell me and tried to help them. A friend's problem became my problem, and I could stay awake an entire night thinking about how I might help someone. If I thought someone hadn't been fair to someone else, I'd bravely give them a piece of my mind. I had big mouth, which I had repress as I got older to avoid complications. It wasn't easy to chase away my nature, but I trained myself to be more accepting of people the way they were.

One day, Mr. L. came to school late. We were in mathematics class, and my friends who were sitting next to the door screamed too late to tell me that he was coming. I flattened myself under the desk like I always did.

"Has Olivia came to school today?" he asked in French with the same missing-tooth accent. Man, that made us all laugh. The only *s* in that little sentence in French sounded terrible. Did I create devil teenagers around me? Innocently, everybody answered him.

"No, she isn't here."

Nevertheless, the math teacher, without hesitation, corrected my classmates. "Oh yes, she is here under the desk," he said.

He escorted me to the principal's office, and the principal sent me home again. How cruel! I liked to be at school. I silently cursed my math teacher. As a teenager, you think that you cannot be wrong. Especially in a city where most people know each other, how dare he be so inconsiderable? I hated Mr. L. for a long time.

My aunt didn't return to school with me this time. She was tired of making exculpations and excuses for me, so she sent me back with my cousin Johnny, who wasn't a blood relative to me but was her nephew-in-law. That was humiliating. The principal was so thrilled for the opportunity, however. He asked Johnny to whip me on the hands six times—three on each with a wood ruler, what he gladly did to show his superiority. What a shame! This was one of the most barbarian punishments they inflicted on children for bad behavior, and it was in harmony with their parents' consent. Teachers were seen as third mothers or fathers for a child. Godfathers and godmothers were the second. Wrong philosophy! We were freed from slavery more than a century ago, so how could they still use the same brutal method of discipline? Was this kind of barbarity in our blood from the masters? Had it become hereditary? That didn't shut off my mouth but only aggravated the situation. They were savage beasts. I didn't talk to Johnny for many months, but later, we became best friends until he died at an early age.

When my aunt found out about that day in the principal's office, she laughed and said that she wouldn't have been able to do it and that the principal wouldn't dare ask her to because she was a woman. He wanted to abase me by asking Johnny to do so. I never said anything to Tita about it because it would require too much explanation. I knew she wouldn't like it; in her eyes, her daughter was a saint. Thank God I was a smart student, despite it all. I learned and understood stuff quickly, which gave me the advantage of enough time to bother others and to be confident with myself. I wrote "I have to keep silent in class" on the chalkboard thousands of times between elementary and high school. Some professors put adhesive on my mouth and made me stand on the sidelines while others played on the playground. I had to talk to pass my messages around, so they prevented me from trying. In my mind, if you wanted to be respected by me, you needed to prevail respect to others first. This I truly believe. Back then, I was so out of control. Too many bees on me to deal with.

12

Vacation

One thing that amazed me in my puerility were the strong, powerful horses that people rode from town to town. Three of my cousins, however, came into town riding on a poor donkey, carrying their weight without protestation. They were little, their weight adding together didn't equalize not even an adult weight. My five cousins from my mother's side, her brother, and my godfather who lived in another district come during the summer for a month to stay at my grandparents' house. That's when the fun and the war started. I was the oldest grandchild, so it was expected that the rest of them respect me. With that unreasonable expectation in mind, I built a wall of power around me.

Before going to war, you have to assemble your munitions and get prepared, that was exactly what I did. They were like imposters, five against one. They don't care, and they weren't looking for fairness. If I hadn't built a fence of security around me, I wouldn't have survived the massive invasion of their presences in what I called "my house." They were very bonded in sisterhood and brotherhood, and together as one, they battled against me. I was alone on my side. I had to create that motion to oblige them to back up from me, and thank God, they were afraid of my grandmother too. When she was around, they eased up on me a bit so that they would not get reprimanded all the time. However, when it was my turn to go on vacation to their house—Lord, have mercy—I was in trouble. I didn't want to say anything to my parents that would worsen my case or show them that I was weak. Instead, I wanted to prove that I wasn't a coward and that I didn't need my parents' protection. I wanted to show them that I was self-sufficient.

Well, they nearly killed me once. They forced me to lie down on the floor facedown and put a mattress on my back. Two of them sat on the heavy, handmade cotton pad, one at each extremity, and pressed my head toward the floor with their whole weight. They left just enough space in the middle so that they could beat the mattress with a tree branch, like they were killing a martyr. I couldn't breathe. I kept yelling at them to stop, but they didn't care, and instead they laughed at my helplessness. They didn't understand that this kind of play could cause injury or even death. They kept beating the mattress with that stick until they heard their mother's steps approaching. My guardian angel sent me their mother to save me. I could've died from suffocation! But it wasn't my day yet. I tried to make them understand that it was a dangerous game that we couldn't ever play again, but it was like talking to animals or to strangers who didn't speak the same language. Their ears were closed to my complaints. My teaching didn't change anything. Children can be silly sometimes. Still now, when we all get together and need a good laugh, we just talk about that cockamamie time.

When I was nine, I started traveling by myself to visit my mother wherever she landed to work. I traveled throughout the south of the country and then the north. During the summer, nights and days, I traveled by truck or by horse, accompanied by strangers. It was pretty fun, but in retrospect, I can see how dangerous it was. Unintentionally, my mother put my life at risk. At the time, though, it seemed amusing. It's scary to think about it now. How could she consider doing something like that? Most of the time, I was traveling with strange men and priests. *This is gonna be my life*, I thought. *Like a Bohemian, I'll go from place to place.* I saw what others didn't during my trips. I observed everything.

As I get older, I went to the center of Haiti to Artibonite. The priests there paid my tuition for a month of summer school. It offered advanced courses that were meant to prepare me for the start of the next school year each October. It was a quick review of what I could expect from the coming year. These preschool classes gave me an advantage over the other students who didn't have these classed. Whereas other kids had three months of vacation, I had two, but I thought that was okay because I had fun no matter where I was. At the archbishopric, I had a big bedroom for myself on the third floor. The monsignor and the priests stayed on the second floor. The third floor was also used for visiting priests and visitors when there was a big event and when the monsignor's and priests' families came to stay on vacation. I ate with them every day, including the excellency himself. They didn't wait for me to have breakfast—they ate right after 6:00 a.m. mass. I didn't go to mass every day. I wasn't too religious or holier-than-thou at the time. The cook would wait for me, though. As soon as I showed up downstairs, they fixed my meal. For many years, until after high school, I stopped in Gonaives before I went to spend time with my mother. It was fun on the third floor—especially when all the monsignor's and priests' nieces and nephews, relatives, and friends were there. The monsignor's family usually only stayed for a week, and the young people didn't go to summer school with me because they had tutors in Port-au-Prince. My aunts also went there for vacation. I made friends with the children there. Sadly, I knew some of them for only during summer and only saw others once a year. They were my vacation friends.

While I was there, I traveled with the priests when they went to different provinces for mass, first communions, or baptisms. During these trips, I often said improper things, which caused me trouble. As punishment, I had to recite a rosary prayer, but this kind of punishment wasn't particularly effective because I didn't change. My mouth said everything that passed in a flesh through my mind. I was incorrigible. One time, I lost the monsignor's ring, and he was mad at me to an extent that I never seen in him before. At supper, complete silence floated in the air. The tension in the dining room was intense. The monsignor kept his head down, looking at his plate, and didn't say a word. Maybe he didn't know how to talk to a problematic child. Suddenly, he started talking about the loss of his ring without looking at me. I felt embarrassed and ashamed for the first time in my life. He had another ring on his finger. I was waiting for him to lose control and forego his clergyman's manners so I could add him to my collection of "huffy-tempered people," but shockingly, he didn't. The monsignor was very tall with an imposing stature. He didn't need a microphone to be heard—his voice resounded far from where he stood. But this time, he just mumbled in a breaking voice. He didn't say my name but turned his head toward me.

"A devil child has lost my ring," he said with a genteel, sneaky smile.

I was afraid of his reaction, but he seemed quiet and calm. The next day, I was called into his office, where he reprimanded me for my abominable, imprudent action. From then on, they made me stay in the chapel for an hour at night, repenting for my sins loudly and in my own words. It wasn't easy, but I had learned some prayers by heart in my childhood, such as the "I confess to Almighty God" prayer and the holy rosary prayers. I was petrified to have to sit alone in the obscurity of the room, which contained more religious statues than it did benches. I was scared of seeing the phosphorescent eyes of the saints looking at me, likely asking, "Child, what kind of evildoing have you done?" I was especially afraid of looking at Jesus Christ on the cross, who was right in front of me. He seemed to blame me as if I was one of the reasons he had to die, to clear away my sins. And there I was, violating the God-fearing rules. All of them were there to judge me and find me guilty for my rowdy conduct.

Their judging looks troubled me deeply. I felt the remorse for saying so many hurtful things to people, for losing the monsignor's ring, and for everything I'd done that put me in the presences of these glorious, chastely Bible figures at this unworthy time of the night. Sister Mireille, the nun in charge, would come visit me there illicitly, reassuring me and allowing me to put my head on her cozy, soft chest. She tried to make me understand why what I'd done was improper and then left. I lost myself in the solitude of the statues and forgot to recite my rosary. My mind went to heaven and hell, questioning everything that I could think of. I was talking to myself like someone else was there. This was the best recipe to fight your fright, I discovered.

THE DAILY BATTLE FOR A NORMAL LIFE

I was a spoiled little creature and was probably only well-treated by the nuns because I was related to a Presbyterian priest. But no matter of what, everywhere I went, people always seemed to love me. I don't know why. I don't know what it was about me that gave others this emotional incentive. Perhaps it was because I was adorable, with a look of pure innocence about me. Maybe they were endeared to my long dark-brown braids that hung in cascades surpassing my shoulder and my skinny body, which was like a long nail standing up. I felt comfortable around the nuns. I wasn't afraid to take part in their activities, such as preparing for mass, fixing the flowers, and even helping clean the monsignor's bedroom. I remember being so curious to enter the private room of the respectable bishop. That is how I learned everything I know, from my curiosity. Sometimes, I served as an altar girl, but even in God's house, I often behaved like a desperate child looking for attention. My younger aunt wasn't better than I was, to be honest, and one day, we were nearly pelted after mass, with rocks for bad behavior toward a few children at church. What else could justify my bad actions during teenage-hood? In the grand scheme of things, my behavior wasn't really all that bad—I wasn't hurting anyone—but it was abnormal and astonishing in the eyes of the people there, especially the chaste religious leaders. My mouth was always open, verbalizing what my brain didn't want me to say. I couldn't help myself. I needed to change my pattern, which I did, little by little over the years. I worked very hard on my alter ego. Remember, nothing is impossible in life as long it's fallen on your path.

Once again, my naive mother allowed me to be in the company of a male friend of hers who wasn't related to me in any way. This time, I didn't think that anyone, not even my guardian angel, would be able to save me. Who knows! Daniel in the Bible was "thrown into the den of lions," but the lions couldn't eat him. Similarity, I was thrown once again to the mankind's mouth. From Port-au-Prince to Camp Coq/Limbe, I used to travel on a big transport truck with merchandise and people of all kinds. The buyers all sat on top of big sisal bags, which towered over the height of the truck. The owner was the driver. In one instance, I sat in the front with him for the entire night. We departed at 9:00 or 10:00 p.m. to arrive by 7:00 or 8:00 a.m. There I was once again, alone with a man who wasn't my father, left to my own devices to pass the entire night with him. The first time I traveled with him, I didn't know him at all. My mother explained to me how to get to the truck station, how to look for a truck marked so and so—I don't recall the name now—and ask for Moline, so I did. He was waiting for me. He called me Oli likely because my mother had instructed him to do so. He made me feel comfortable from the instant that I shook his hands. He had a great sense of humor and made me laugh. Over the time, I got familiar with him and kissed him on his forehead in a gesture of fatherly kindness.

He was never in a rush to depart or arrive at destination at a specific time. The truck was so fully loaded that I could hear cracking metal when the truck turned and feel the disequilibrium as it balanced from right to left and vice versa. It felt like it was going to crash each time it jeered to one side or the other. For most of the trip, we were the only ones on the dark road, which was lit only by the truck's beam lights. Light and shade. The road beyond the beam lights was invisible. Once in a while, we faced another truck that was coming in the inverse direction. Both Moline and the driver of the other truck honked their horns at each other in a sign of salutation and solidarity. The streets were very narrow. If we were traveling behind another truck, we were stuck there for a long time because there wasn't enough space for one truck to jut out in front of the other. I wasn't scared, though. Children of that age have no fear of accidents, and so far as I knew, he was a good driver with no record of crashing. Perhaps that was the main reason for my mother's trust in him. She was unperceptive to the rest.

During those trips, we always made two stops to refuel and buy food. I loved these stops because Moline bought me food and lots of candy. I ate all night and slept little. I was thirteen when our trips began, and it went on for many years like that. The buyers, who we called *machan'n sara* in Creole, often went to the bathroom in nature if we didn't have time to stop at a restroom. Women went in the tall grass and weeds. They kept cans to hold the refuse, which dripped onto their bags of rice, sugar, or whatever they were sitting on. The urine didn't penetrate the goods, however, because the bags were covered with plastic to protect them in case of rain.

Moline was in his late forties—a man of respect. He never made any sexual jokes and never touched me in any unpleasant ways. He took care of me like I was his child. I made those trips with him at least twice a year for almost five years, except for when I went directly to Gonaives once a year during summer. I took buses for those trips so that I could arrive by daylight instead of at 1:00 or 2:00 a.m., which was when Moline passed through there. Moline was always an exception to the rule when it came to men's sexual addictions, but I cannot say the same about one priest at the archbishopric.

Like I said, I spent one month each summer on vacation in Gonaives with priests who were always coming and going, to and from the surrounding provinces. There were little towns nearby without a lot of resources, so even though they might have a church, they might not have a designated priest. So once in a while, a priest from our archbishopric traveled there for confession and to conduct mass. The archbishopric was vast, and we received many visitors. Lots priests came for one day or one week. I often observed unusual, clandestine comings and goings during the nighttime. I used to be very curious and overzealous to discover things that most people ignored or believed didn't exist. I liked to inform people about what I found during these exploits. One instance, however, was too unspeakable for this kind of gossip. I couldn't tell anyone, mostly because no one would believe me. I certainly couldn't tell my mother because she might order that I leave. I liked it there because I was treated like a princess. I believe that my aunt saw it too but she never talked about it.

Every year, I witnessed it, and every year, I kept it to myself: one of the priests, cloak-and-dagger and obscured by darkness, snuck into a girl's bedroom every night and then retreated to his nest early the next morning before mass. I couldn't say for sure what they were doing there at night, but one day, I saw them in the same bed, her head resting on his shoulder. I surprised them by opening their unlocked door. This goes to show just how dysfunctional I was. He inveigled me into joining them! I did, my head low with embarrassment. I sat at their bedside, and he invited me to lie down. Without resistance, I obeyed. He stayed in the middle and pushed me closer to him, his right hand embracing my neck. Without a word, my head gently glided onto his other shoulder. He was probably trying to show me that there wasn't anything bad about it. I slept there until morning, and when I woke up, I discovered that he'd left both of us in bed. The priest had left to perform the daily mass. We three never said anything about that night. It was like a dream I invented. I never said anything to my aunt either. The day after, I went to 6:00 a.m. mass. I looked at him with disdain because my imagination jumped to a far conclusion. I couldn't understand why he left his bedroom to go to hers, but still I felt the wrongdoing of his actions.

Since then, I haven't held a great respect for priests and regarded men with even more disdain—even men of the cloth. That priest vowed to be single and stay single. What I knew was that if his actions were appropriate, he wouldn't have to go on tip toe when everybody else was sound asleep, passing through the night and crawling back to his room early in the morning. What could they be doing? While I was there, they slept like angels, but I knew that something was going on. I know that men were men, period. Over the years, all the news about priests being predators hasn't surprised me at all. I've thought about this monstrous act for a long time. I should not have called it a monstrous act because under the priest's cassock, first and foremost, he was a man. The girl was around eighteen, a few years older than I was, and the priest was in his late thirties. They were old enough to choose whatever they wanted. I saw so much sexual abuse in my childhood that I'd lost my faith in men's intentions. I always assumed that men were faking, bluffing, and manipulating, and I still do. Around that time, a new song became popular about a priest and nun who were sexually involved. Even though it was a dirty song, it appeared in my mouth. Without hesitation, I sang this song while they were having quietly their teatime. In my childish mind, I didn't think that it would hurt them. I can't say that I was totally innocent, though. I sang this song to embarrass them, but I never meant to humiliate them to the point where they had to disperse. They stood up and left their teacups cooling on the table, and I regretted my behavior profoundly. I didn't know that in life, we shouldn't always say what we think, lest we regret it later.

Here is my philosophy, how I see things around me—straight and incongruous devotion to reason always put me on the other side of things, and as such, I have always been alone in my camp. I've always felt the need to inflict my ideas onto my friends and peers to make them understand something that makes complete sense to me—something that might make sense to them too if I can get through to them. For example, I'm against the death penalty. We are too smart and too well-educated to justify that kind of premeditated Machiavellian punishment. We blame an individual for willingly taking somebody's life, but then we go and do the same thing in revenge. What if we wrongfully charge a guiltless person? It's nonsense to me that we kill in any circumstance, except in legitimate self-defense. In our century, is justice doing its job? Does it eliminate people who might be innocent? What gives you the right to kill, whoever you are? To take someone else's life, we have to be crazy, real crazy—kind of sick. It's insane to condemn someone to die at a specific date and time and to kill them in an excruciating way. Is that logical to you?

At school, my position of seeing things differently than others did resulted in ceaseless arguments. That's why I was frequently in trouble. I talked too much. My ability and willingness to see the unfairness of things always put me at odds with many of my peers and teachers. But I'm glad that I'm different. I have excuses for all my actions. I forgive easily. These days, it's hard for me to imagine how I behaved like that. I don't like to talk in public anymore, especially not in big crowds. I believe that I was only acting back them. I had such power over people with my dialogue, and that made me feel good. I always had to thrash around and bloviate about one subject or another so that people wouldn't get bored of me. Strangely, in my adulthood, I spare myself from the need to speak in public. I became pacific. What a way life changes! I like this self-more.

13

Ineluctable Deaths

IN 1970, MY GRANDMOTHER, whom I always called Mother, became very sick. She was transported from our little village to the hospital in the city. I was fifteen at the time. The doctors couldn't determine what was wrong with her. They eventually diagnosed her with fibrosis and said that she would need to have surgery. She was always anemic, so they had to give her blood many times before each scheduled surgery. Even so, every time she went in for a procedure, it was as if she'd never received extra blood at all. Nobody knew where the blood went, and it remains an enigma to this day. Perhaps we couldn't understand the medical slang that they used to explain the problem, so that was all we retained.

Finally, the doctor released her to go home, but her illness worsened. In a way, I would say this: she had cancer, and there was nothing they could do for her. Looking back, I think that the doctors knew but didn't want to take any chances. That's comprehensible; medicine wasn't so advanced back then. She was only sixty-four years old, though, a woman with a lot of energy and hope, and they sent her home to die. Life is full of surprises. All she could do was lie on her deathbed waiting for her expiration date on earth. Six months later, she died. All her family members were present except one of her daughters who was expecting a child herself. In our culture, when you're pregnant, you can't go near a sick person, wear black clothes, or go to a funeral. Giving life shouldn't interfere with losing life. My mother came to take care of my grandmother as soon as she heard that she'd been released from the hospital, and she did a good job. I promised myself that when it was Tita's turn to go, I would do the same.

In the morning of her last day, in April 1971, we all sat on her front porch, facing the ocean, having a simple breakfast of coffee and bread. Something irrational happened. The weather was nice and calm, and we were resting and relaxing, a privilege we hadn't had since arriving there. At that time of the year, it was usually around 72 to 75 degrees at sunrise, whereas where we lived, up in the mountains, it was cooler. The atmosphere and the scenery evoked faraway souvenirs—the times we used to sit down there and sing. Drizzling drops of condensation fell from the wet, zinc roofs, making little, wet spots on the concrete terrace. Crystalline dew on the plant leaves shone in the blossoming day light. The odor of the ylang-ylang tree with its yellow flower filled the air, and under the gray-bluish sky, the sun timidly emerged like an apparition. There was no wind, only a cool breeze intermittently refreshing the atmosphere. The fresh air made us lazy, and we almost forgot that inside, at that early hour in the morning, our loved one was agonizing, waiting for the angel of death. As we sat there, we heard a strange noise, like something that had fallen down. My grandfather stood up to find out where the sound had come from, but he didn't have time to search. Right in front of us, a sugarcane tree collapsed. It happened so fast that we didn't see it at first. We were very surprised; there was no strong wind or any other force that could've broken it into two pieces like that. My grandfather looked out at the jagged remains of the tree. Calmly, without too much emotion, as if all his energy had been drained away, he spoke.

"This is it. It's a sign," he said and then paused. "Get prepared." He spoke like he was out of breath. "Today is her last day with us."

How does he know that? I thought. But we believed him. My grandfather was a very wise man—reserved and predictable, contrary to my grandmother, who was tough, outgoing, outspoken, and mean businesswoman. Was his prediction truly supernatural, or had he given her the liberator tea of death to cease her pain as a gift of love? I assumed the latter, given that he was so sure about when she'd die, but perhaps the sugarcane tree truly suggested otherwise. She was two years older than her spouse was and more mature than he's too. That day, he looked very old to me with his gray hair and pale, mulatto face, which was contorted in anguish.

After my grandfather's predilection, we couldn't eat anymore. He forced us to finish our food and be strong for the sad event that was upon us, but fear monopolized us. Our dogs knew that it would happen soon, too; a week earlier, they'd had a farewell concert for her. We couldn't sleep at night because of the lamentable tone of their voices, weeping and wailing. They were already crying for their loss. My grandmother was an animal lover. We had many dogs, cows, and horses who were often restrained together when the farmers had to change the pastures. When my grandmother was dying, she was in unmanageable pain, and she constantly asked my grandfather to end her misery. I thought that her pain was like that of patients who fell into comas because their hearts couldn't take it anymore. She was in that kind of pain, but she was a fighter—too strong to let something like that happen to her. She still had her lucidity. I saw people dying from cancer, under strong medication, screaming like hell. Imagine how would it be for someone without painkillers like morphine to endure such torture? Even so, I couldn't understand her request to die instead of live. For years after, I imagined how terrible her suffering must've been to make her wish for the relief of death. She couldn't wait for the black cloak with its hood to come when the time was right. She preferred that her husband commit homicide.

All I knew was that she was screaming like an animal. That is the way it goes when there are no medical supplies available to comfort sick people. One of her cousins brought her a sort of potion that she claimed could ease her pain, but for some reason, my grandmother refused to drink the black oily medication. We didn't know what it was made out of, and neither did she. It was a gummy, dark mixture with a terrible smell. She had one mouthful of it, trying very hard to swallow, but she couldn't get it down and spat it out. She held my grandfather's hand as if to give him courage and derive the strength she needed to finish her path on earth with dignity. I was heartbroken; she wasn't only my grandmother but was the woman I called Mother all my life. I was sad, dejected, and crushed by my grandfather's prevision and the way it was coming to fruition.

We waited like Jesus's apostles at Oliver Mountain. By 11:30 a.m., my grandfather called all of us in, one after another, and we went to her bedroom to say goodbye. We performed what we had been told to, kissing her *adieu*. For me, it wasn't natural to do something like that. It felt like we were rushing her toward death, but the logic was if we didn't do it then, we might never have the chance to. This was our chance to see her alive for the last time. That was the first death in the family that I experienced. It was shocking. Later on, when I heard something like that was happening in one of my friend's lives, I realized just how hard and awful it is to be left behind by a loved one. I only said goodbye to my grandmother as a simple formality. At the time, it carried no meaning to me. I didn't understand much about death at all, just that I wouldn't get to see her anymore and that I couldn't apprehend the Lord's decision.

At about 12:30 p.m., she was gone. Yes, you heard me. She left us. Her pain was gone, silent. She was free from of all her hurts. Tita cried out for many minutes, and the others, including my grandfather, seemed to be holding everything inside. I was hurt, heartbroken, and terrorized by what diseases could do to the body. And at the same time, I didn't realize that her death was bloody real—I was too young. I couldn't believe that I would never talk to her again and that she was truly dead. I don't know how my grandfather pronounced her dead because there was no doctor or nurse to confirm this. I guess they just knew. Later that afternoon, an old woman came to bathe her, dress her, and install her in into her coffin for the wake. There was no time to waste—there was no funeral home, mortuary, or morgue, so everything had to be done the same night. The body had to be buried within twenty-four hours. There was too much to do, all things considered. After their fiftieth birthdays, my grandparents had bought a coffin and kept it in the *galeta*—a sort of open attic—so that it would be ready for whoever went first. It must be funny to live with your own casket every day to remind you that your days are counted! Life on earth is about moving rapidly toward the end. Nobody gets younger, but everybody gets older, which is the biggest rule of our destiny.

Like me, my grandmother was a woman who loved music and dancing, was full of life, and was tough on principal. She was the force of the family. I can't forget that my grandmother built an atmosphere of security for all of us and brought our family a good deal of respect in the village. She wasn't loved by the majority of the people, but this didn't stop her from doing what she strongly believed was good and appropriate for the welfare of her family. At the beginning of her legacy, the specter of the death took her away from all things she felt affectionate toward. No one thought that she would be gone so soon, but there is no escaping to your destiny. Before she died, she told us that she wanted a band to play as she was lowered into the ground at the cemetery. That wasn't a problem for us at all. It was an honor for that band to perform at her funeral, but they turned out to be a torment for us to listen to. We didn't pay for it ourselves. Rather it came out of her own pocket, which was the last gift she ever gave us. Every clash of the trumpet, cymbal, and drum filled the air with sadness that went directly to our cores. It was as if somebody was stabbing us with a knife. It was torture, and teardrops ceaselessly ran down our faces. Some family members had crisis reactions, contorting with epileptic movements. They threw themselves onto the floor and rolled up like serpents. I couldn't know whether it was supernatural or not, but it seemed to me like they were overtaken by maniac spirits. No one could stop crying—the band didn't permit it with their mournful musical rhythms. The musicians were on a mission, and they were willing to accomplish it no matter what.

After the service, our family members and friends from all over the region went to my grandparents' home to eat and grieve. Goats, pigs, and chickens lost their lives for the occasion. We had a legion to feed. It was a big celebration. Everybody was dressed in black and white, which made it all even more solemn, except for a few people who wore light colors like blue and gray. Maybe those were the only presentable things in their closets. Before they left, they made sure to see each of us—my grandfather, my mother, my uncles, and my aunts—to compliment us for having such a great ceremony. Some of them seemed to forget that we'd just buried someone close to our heart. All they talked to us about was the food and the beautiful, touching music. This culture of death and mourning is so erroneous. Even at the time, I thought that we needed to change this way of recognition, this manner of being ungrateful to and disrespectful of the dead.

Days after the funeral, I told my grandfather my point of my view. I told him that I thought the extravaganza funeral was a waste. "Why did we have to spend all that money to feed a horde of people, like we were having a party?" I said in an adult tone of voice.

He gently answered me with a hypnotic smile. "Oli," he said, pausing and catching his breath. Certainly, he didn't expect this kind of remark from me. "Your grandmother was a public figure in the region. Over the course of her life, she fed lots of people and enjoyed doing it, and so the day of her funeral was the last time she could do it. I'm sure she would've wanted to keep doing it if she could." He paused once more and then continued calmly, this time with a mournful tone in his voice. "Don't you see? Those people traveled far to express their feelings, show their respect, and share in our sorrow. How could we let them go back home with empty stomachs?"

Man, he was right! He always found the right answer to any question of mine. It really made sense to me after he explained it, but I still thought that the guests had eaten and enjoyed so much that they'd too easily forgotten my grandmother's memory. I was too hurt to see clearly. She was the one I called mother for sixteen years, and she was gone. I fought for a long time with the sight of her dead body, inert in that rectangle box. After her funeral, I tried to understand our purpose on earth and what happens after death. By the way, I have to joke about something. During the procession to the cemetery, they didn't let my grandfather walk behind the coffin in case he wanted to wed again. According to our traditions, that would be bad luck for him. He was furious at the people who told him what to do at such a difficult moment, furious that they were already considering the future to such an extent. "I'm not thinking of getting remarried! That is disrespecting me," he responded.

Oh, sure, he wasn't looking to remarry that day, but a few years later, he hooked up with a woman who was as young as I was. She shouldn't been his granddaughter. Men, men, men—all the same.

It may seem unbelievable, and I've always tried not to talk about it, but I find our death rituals to be so distinctive, so I want to describe them. Here is what happened to the corpse of my grandmother after her death. She wasn't loved by lots of people because of her character. As I said before, she was a woman with strong stamina and was tough on principle. My grandfather believed that his wife's death wasn't natural. He thought that the *malefici* spell from them killed her and that they might torture her for eternity if they could get to her entire body after death. They could change her into zombie for their own purposes—a sort of animal that could work for them. Who are "they"? They are the night members of voodoo, the Zobop's Clan, or the *lougarou*. We believe that malefic things can still happen after death, especially when we think that the death was supernatural. Had her time scrupulously expired? Perhaps not. The devil is always part of the crime, and he's always waiting to transform victims into zombies for the imminent zombie revolution. After we took her coffin to the cemetery, the undertaker was advised to separate the head from the body and place it in the backyard of our house, which was quite far from the graveyard. Like that, even though they tried, they weren't able to assemble both the head and the body. We're not the only culture that engages in these kinds of traditions. I've heard that there are others like ours. By separating her head from her body, we prevented the devil from changing her into zombie because he couldn't access all of her at once. That said, my grandmother's head was buried in our backyard, and the rest of her corpse was buried at the cemetery. I found this to be very interesting, but I wasn't disturbed by it. Who cares? After we die, we are nothing.

That year was an exceptionally sad one. A few months after my grandmother passed, on October 17, 1971, my biological father died. I was sixteen. I wasn't at his funeral, and all in all, the news didn't mean much to me. The enthusiasm I had for searching for him faltered when I had failed to locate him, and I didn't care about his death. I had more hate for him than I had love for him. I didn't take that defeat very well. My mother didn't go to the funeral, and no one from her family did either. I could've gone because I wasn't a child anymore, but I thought that it would've been better to meet him while he was alive than to meet him as he lay in a casket, probably disfigured from what had killed him so early in life.

Tita never divorced him, so she sent a notarized release form to authorize the burial in her absence. With my mother's authorization, his parents were able to bury him. Later on, the funeral bills were sent in totality to Tita for reimbursement, which probably she paid, though I don't know. From what I heard about him, he wasn't different from other men. He was a Casanova who never worked in his lifetime and lived on his parents' wealth. He had mistresses everywhere, and I thought that they should chip in to pay his funeral bills, considering they'd spent more time with him than my mother ever had. These rumors made me furious to the point that I said to myself: I survived the death of my grandmother, so his won't change me. I never met the man, not even once. His passing was nothing for me. He was an uncharted personage who never existed in my life. Less than a year later, his only brother, my biological uncle, passed away too. I'd seen him only once in my life, and he didn't talk to me. I was with my aunt at the time. He and my father were the only two children in their family, and they both died young. Another year passed, and I heard that their mother, my biological grandmother, also left this world to join them. I found out about her death months after it happen, but I wouldn't have gone to her funeral even if I'd known about it. In my record, she was classified as a bad mother-in-law and an apathetic grandmother with whom I had no relationship. I don't want to judge her, but I have a motive; she never looked for me either. Three people who should've been close to my heart chose to pass through my life as mirages. They've all since left the world, leaving me with no hope of knowing the truth behind their silence. Only my father's aunt was still alive at that point, and she never had children. The similarity between the two generations in his family was so coincidental; they were two sisters, and one gave birth to two sons. Many years after the death of my grandmother, the wife of his brother, my biological uncle, called my mother to arrange for a separation of the inheritance. By then, I knew that I had four half-brothers and half-sisters. I was twenty-five years old at the time. I tried not to blame him, to detest him, but all of a sudden, it became very difficult to do so. He preferred not to be the first man in my life, so be it. May he rest in peace!

Did I make everything difficult with my queer personality? I don't think so. I was just a realist. I didn't want to waste my time thinking about the past, even though the past was always present for me. I paid less attention to the past, so it became largely meaningless in my life. I had no trust in most of what they told me at school and in catechism study. I became mentally disorganized. I had faith in God, but not everything in the Bible stimulated my brain. My mind went into another type of mental manic disorder. I went back to my early childhood, where I was alone in my camp. I criticized everything, even the Bible that I couldn't and still don't understand. I didn't go to church that often either. I was especially mad at people who compared the old world to the new. The various authors who have rewritten the Bible book according to Christianity are just telling stories. I don't think that the Bible has anything to do with the actual world. Our times have changed; before, they didn't have cars, big homes, electricity, water that arrived through hosepipes, airplanes that flew like birds, and so on. How could ancient values apply to our existence after so many centuries? Are men still wearing those long robes? No! They wear pants now. Even our priests don't wear the robes in the street anymore, except of course some of our pals in the Middle East. Civilization has changed.

I have my opinion regarding the Bible, and of course, everyone is free to have their own. At many points in my life, I have been close to becoming an atheist. The way I see things, we cannot follow everything we read in the Bible. With so many things still changing in the world, and considering how many times the Bible has been translated, how could we claim to follow the history in the Bible word-for-word? There's a big difference between what happened in the past and what is happening now. To this day, however, I fundamentally base my life on the Ten Commandments, which make logical sense to me. They were written under God's dictation, and they will never become outdated because every line still applies to our daily existence. If we merely follow the Ten Commandments, we go in the right direction. We do exactly what God told us to do. So I went through the world rejecting almost everything that seemed to make sense to other people. I suffered in silence despite the deprivation that persecuted me. Why did my own family abandon me? I didn't always appreciate the side of my family that adored me and instead focused on the side of my family that I called the villain.

14

Meeting Sam

A FEW YEARS LATER, I met Sam, my now-husband, while I was on vacation. I was on my way to stay with my mother for the summer, and I stopped in Port-au-Prince to see my aunt Coye, who lived there. Sam was a friend of my aunt's boyfriend. We dated for five years, mostly by correspondence. We were in the same grade at school, but we didn't live in the same city. He was from Port-au-Prince, the capital in the west side of Haiti. At the beginning, when he commenced flirting with me, I thought that he was too immature for me. I thought that I needed somebody who'd already finished school, someone far older who had an adult, levelheaded mind. During my teenage years, I considered myself to be very mature and thought that I had power over other people's lives. As such, Sam was definitely too puerile for me.

At that point, I was already dating an internist. My best friends Katie and Lucy asked me to say yes to Dr. D. so that we could have free consultations and medications. One of them said yes to a musician for free festival concert tickets, and the other one said yes to an engineering student. It was kind of silly, but things got serious. My parents were in love with the doctor, though. He was a very nice guy, but I was too batty for him. I had to find someone who matched my strange, wild character. The doctor maintained a good relationship with my family, even after we parted ways. I couldn't say if I was in love with him because he reminded me of my teachers. He had that kind of formal protocol and etiquette that I didn't want from a boyfriend at that time. I was far too liberal. I didn't know if he was truthfully in love with me either. Katie, Lucy, and I all agreed that we wanted to have fun and not get stuck to a man too soon. For fun, we got dressed up for walks in the streets, and they called us the trinity. Almost every day, I shared my food with them in three equal portions, and they did the same for me. We usually went from my house to Katie's house to Lucy's house, nothing else. We were crazy, for sure. Hey, we didn't have a television, cell phones, computers but we had comic and romantic books to entertain us. What else was there to do than get dressed up for a tour of the city? The movie theater was only open from 6:00 to 8:00 p.m., which was too late for us to be out in the streets. Our families wouldn't ever permit that. When we got tired, we came back home, slept, and repeated the same routine the next day if there was no school. It was a simple and easy way to get through life. There was no need to have cars because we all had bicycles, and our families didn't have cars either. We could walk across the entire city in one day. It just wasn't necessary to have a car payment. Looking back, I can see that it was genuinely a simple and affordable way of life.

At the end of the eleventh grade, my mother decided that she would move me again, this time to Cap-Haitian, where I would finish my last year of high school. I was excited, but unfortunately, I couldn't stay with Tita because my high school was miles from her workplace. She placed me with a good friend of hers. This time, the friend was a woman who I already knew, and one of her daughters, Irma, was a good friend of mine. I'd known her since I was nine, and she was a troublemaker like I was. I saw her once every two years, but we stayed friends. It's dreadfully true: Irma was also one of a kind, and we had nearly the same characters. I traveled from the south to the northern end of Haiti. I'd traveled almost everywhere in Haiti since I was eight years old. How exciting! I felt like a free spirit searching for a body to make my home. I was constantly moving from place to place. My mother didn't see the impact that these constant changes caused me morally and psychologically. I knew that she was looking out for what was best for me. This time, she thought that I would like to be closer to her so that she could visit me more often, but I felt otherwise. I was happy to be nearer to her, but I felt like she was perpetually dumping me wherever she pleased. I was always on the go, living with strangers who she trusted. I traveled from south to west, from central to north, and into the northwest of Haiti during school breaks, either with the clergymen or to see my missionary mother. I met people of all kinds.

This time, I had to leave my two best friends behind in Cayes to build new friendships in the north. Irma wasn't a new friend, but we weren't that close before. I went to live with her. Over time, though, our friendship bloomed, and I couldn't have had a better friend than she was. We argued sometimes and went without speaking to each other, but we always laughed about it one or two weeks later. I couldn't have been in a better place than Irma's house. It was even better than my aunt's house. Irma's mother was one of Tita's best friends. She was a very good person. I had a little, separated bedroom of my own, and I became a good role model for her own children, who didn't like to clean their bedrooms. I learned the principal rules of life from my grandmother: "We never leave the house without making our beds and eating something, and we never wear dirty underwear." I still follow these regulations. In Irma's house, there were four children, two boys and two girls who shared two bedrooms, separated by gender, but I had my own room, which made them all a little jealous. It was a privilege that their mother offered to me only. I became the big sister of the house even though I was only a few months older than the eldest, Irma, was. Irma's mother had a fabrics boutique, and she didn't hesitate to give me pieces to model or make dresses for me. She treated me like her own daughter. We had an amazing time together that year. We are all still good friends and keep in contact. I'm even the godmother of her second child.

My hometown and this new town were very different, each representing two geographical extremes of Haiti. We even spoke Creole differently. When I first arrived, it wasn't easy for me to correspond with the other students at school. Our accents and word usages were so obviously different that they'd say things that I don't understand and vice-versa. But I acclimated. The kids at this school were very intent on passing their baccalaureate tests with success. It was like a competition between schools, a fight for the laureate award on the high school's final exam. Let me tell you about that test. We spent an entire year memorizing facts, working hard, going without sleep, and studying subjects such as math, essay writing, French and Haitian literature, geometry, algebra, Latin, Spanish—you name it. Every year, all the twelfth graders in the country had to go to Port-au-Prince, the capital of Haiti, to take an ultimate test for five days under very strict regulations and surveillance. The educational department assigned each student with a school location and a seat number to sit these exams. Even those of us from the same school might have had very different exam assignments. That week, they used a few local schools for that purpose only. It was very difficult and complicated to pass the exam, which is why we had to work very hard for nine months prior.

The results of each year's test were announced publicly on the radio. The broadcaster would reveal, alphabetically, the name of each student who had successfully passed the test, regardless of which city they came from. If your name wasn't listed, it meant that you didn't make it through. That day, parents and friends listened to the radio, expecting to hear your name. Luckily, if we failed, we could always take another exam in September or redo the class the next year. That said, not getting acknowledged on the radio meant public embarrassment. Neither my name nor Sam's was announced on the radio when we were in twelfth grade. We knew that it wouldn't happen, though, because we hadn't sat the last portion of the test. Instead, we went to the beach that afternoon. How crazy does that sound? No one knows about that until now. My mother's expectations for me to become a doctor or a lawyer are absolutely taboo now. We had fun, though. I wanted to become an actress, that's all. Don't ever push a child to do something that he or she doesn't like. You might find yourself the laughingstock of the people.

15

Engagement

AFTER A YEAR IN Cap-Haitian, I was installed in Port-au-Prince with another family to go to secretary school. I'm still in contact with them today. I loved them very much. They were very graceful people who were recommended to me by Sam's godmother. The lady of the house was friends with his godmother. What amazed me the most in that place was to see the solidarity among the family members. Mercia, the owner, had three children with a married man, but her sister had two daughters with the same man. One of his other mistresses died from a car accident, leaving two sons behind. During the school year, the children stayed at Mercia's house, including the ones from her sister. The man came almost every day. When we had a party at his house because his wife had died, all of them reunited like they were from the same mother. She fed all of them after school before they went back home. Food was limited with that kind of crowd to feed! They were all synchronized with each other, even though they knew that some of them were siblings and cousins at the same time. Mercia seemed to love all these children equally, as if they were all her own. In addition, I wasn't the only pensioner who lived there. We were two, and the house was small. Furthermore, after a few months, I became her protégée like the others were. She was a woman with a big heart. I liked her more because she showed that children have nothing to do with their parents' behavior and shouldn't pay the price of it. You need to have a very high level of skill and love for others to act like that. I salute you, my dear Mermer.

Sam and I became very close at that time. I was having fun with him and found him very comfortable to be with. We always found common conversations to have. I never get bored by his presence. His concept of life made sense to me, and we were quite similar and agreeable about most things. I was more a spendthrift than he was, and although Sam said "no" to many of my hasty, thoughtless expenses, he never made an argument out of it. Did I love him? My character didn't allow me to show him my love. Did I have to love him in order to feel so at ease in his company? I don't know. Amazingly, I had the freedom of language and the freedom to do whatever I wanted to. I think he was crazy about me. My intuition never lies to me. The man was in love. At that age, I thought that showing too much love to a man was a sign of weakness and desperation and that men didn't deserve passion. *Let him be crazy*, I thought. As a girl, I wanted to be real and stand on my feet. I didn't want to allow myself to dream, and so I didn't communicate my feelings to him. In retrospect, I see that this was terribly, terribly wrong. Was it because of the separation between my mother and my father that made me think like that? My conviction was to let the man love me more than I loved him. I thought that if I showed too much emotion, he wouldn't appreciate it and would abuse my feelings. My inability to show love notwithstanding, we ended up engaged before he left to study ceramics, in Mexico. I didn't have a ring, but before his departure, my mother met his parents and we all had dinner together like they did in the old times. On the side, I continued to study administration. I was learning how to be a secretary even though I profoundly disliked it. It wasn't the right profession for me. I wasn't even good at serving coffee to my boss, customers, and friends. I have to confess that I could be discourteous sometimes, like to the people who shook my hand and held it for minutes, like they were telling me something that I was trying to ignore. It wasn't my dream job, and I planned to study something else. I also had a temporary job to keep me busy while Sam was overseas.

Surprise, surprise—he was in Mexico City, and it seemed like he wanted to do business like a gentleman. I received a white gold diamond engagement ring and flowers, which were brought to me at work by two of his friends who were studying in Mexico too. They were coming home for a few days, and he'd asked them to deliver the ring to me. God in heaven, that was the sweetest thing that ever happened to me. I was excited, joyous, and ecstatic about that ring. By the way, it was like the ancient era when the warriors put chastity belts on their wives before they went to war. Sam left me with his family. Was it to guard me? I stayed in his bedroom, which was well-decorated, just for me. My bedroom was the most beautiful room in the entire house.

You might call me a wandering child who never had a permanent place to stay. To that, I would answer, "Yes, I am," because I have lived in so many abodes in my life. I wondered if my destiny was playing games with me. Did I want to be like that, or did I let it happen because I didn't have a choice? *What is the alternative?* I often wondered. I saw none. I accepted the verdict of my tormented life because I was a true believer in destiny: "It is meant to be as it is." I was too young to decide for myself where to go and who crossed my path. This was the pathway that I was meant to follow from my birth. We don't select our destiny, I thought. Rather it's dictated by the nature of things that we cannot change. It has already been closely determined by the Creator before our existence even began. I realized that on many occasions, my mother could've decided to be there for me, could've decided to live with me. Nevertheless, she couldn't, because her destiny was to be separated from me during my childhood, my teenage-hood, and my young adult years. Unlike my father, however, she maintained the exception that she would continuously provide for me. The only time we lived together was when I was young in Canada for those two years. She did her duties to supply for me and love me as a mother should, but she forgot about being there for me. I'm not blaming Tita; she didn't see it the same way I did. You need to live through these moments of parental deprivation in order to understand what I'm saying. She bought me many nice things, but I would've preferred to be with her more often than have fancy things. As usual, we the people are perpetually unsatisfied. Perhaps even if everything was normal, and I lived with a mother and a father, I'd still find something to complain about. Who knows? Her destiny blindfolded her from doing what was truly best for me, from being with her only daughter. She operated in a mannerly mode toward me to make sure that I didn't miss anything, but she wasn't with me often. Unfortunately, nothing is worse for a child than to grow up without a father and with a long-distance mother. Disillusion from one's principles and running from place to place can damage a child for life.

We shouldn't presume that our circumstances are unique in the world. We have to remember that there are always one or two other people around the globe who are facing a similar or worse situation at the same time we are. This is the beauty of it—the beauty that tells us, "We are never alone, we are just going through a bad storm." Often, we may think that there isn't anyone else in our situation. I said the same thing when my faith was wrecked, but we all live in the same world. Whatever our trials and needs are, our loads are somewhat analogue and connected. When I talked to my sister-in-law in California, she told me about the trials of her childhood. She met her mother for the first time at the age of seventeen. Besides infrequent stays with her father, she was constrained to living with other families, nuns, and strangers. She told me that living with her stepmother wasn't pleasant. Her circumstance was little different than mine was, no doubt, but what a coincidence! Of course, I never had the leisure of meeting my real father, but I'm not comparing her life to mine. I just mean to show that we had something massive in common—a flagrant similarity in our life. I never told her how many places I'd lived before I got married. I didn't like making that comparison. However, I had a mother and a family who loved me. I never felt deprived of anything until I reached the age of understanding.

It's so unfortunate that a lot of children in the world have to pay the price of parental neglect and selfishness. As such, these are the lessons I've learned through it all; when life seems hard-bitten and it's difficult to step forward, it's because God knows that we can be tougher and stronger than our adversities are. He supplies us with the ability to handle anything. I never met my father and passed through different boarding houses, living with people that I called strangers.

If he'd wanted me to have an easygoing life, he would've provided that for me. Of course, I would've preferred to be with my father from birth and have my mother there when I came back from school to help me with my homework, but that wasn't his will. Instead this job of raising me was left to my grandparents and aunts. That was the little cross that God gave me to carry, and he knew in advance that it would fit me perfectly. The crosses we carry take on different shapes and weights to perfectly suit our bodies. What we should understand, however, is that whatever crosses we might bear, we shouldn't compare ourselves to others. I chose not to be judgmental toward my parents. I knew that if I did, I'd to start with my mother's family for their reckless behavior and finish with my father's family for their abandonment. Instead, I've always preferred to see the good side of it, so I focused only on the love my mother's family extended toward me. I also know now that the emotional hardships I encountered made me a strong person. They turned me into a woman I didn't know I could be. Look at it this way: hindrances in our lives move us toward different dimensions and advantages. Each stormy day is just another footstep in life, not the end of our existence. The sun goes away but always comes back to radiance again, as do our lives. This is the law of nature and of our metabolisms.

16

The Return

On June 4, 1977, after Sam had been overseas for one year, he returned home and became my husband twenty days later. Only three witnesses, three of our good friends, were present at the ceremony. We got married at civil court without telling our parents. I was weird, and Sam was peculiar in the same way. It's not that we didn't want to tell anyone, we were just too excited. We didn't want to wait, and I knew that my mother wouldn't understand. He called me on Monday at work and said, "Let's get married on Friday" and I, the silly one, said, "Okay, no problem." No questions asked. It was an order, and blindly, I accepted his direct proposition. I could've said no, but I didn't. No time to buy a new dress. I considered it a normal day. I wore the dress in my closet that seemed most appropriate for the occasion. We popped one bottle of champagne, which was all we had. We were happy, and that was all that mattered to us.

Nervously, I mailed a letter to my mother announcing our court wedding, but she wasn't happy with our decision. In a word, she was furious. She declared that it wasn't a wedding but a law-abiding concubinage. She said that I needed to go to church to be properly married, which we did in December of the same year, just to please our parents. I was so used to Catholicism's rules that I expected that kind of reaction from her and the family. I didn't think it was important to go through all those hoops just for people's acceptance, but I did it anyway. Around the same time, I received a letter from my family's priest requesting the same as my mother, that I forthwith get religiously married. My big mouth…I wrote back, asking him to show me where in the Bible it said that Mary and Joseph were married. I think I made my family madder with that blasphemous insinuation, but truthfully, that question needs a response.

The worst part, perhaps, was at the time we were planning our wedding, they were playing the movie *Le Ciel et Toi* (French), *El Cielo y Tu* (Spanish) on every TV channel. In it, a priest marries a woman in front of the ocean. The two of them were alone in front of this vast nature's splendor as the only witness. I liked it very much. We were so thoughtless about what our families would think that we assumed we could do the same if there wasn't a law to follow for our wed to be legal. Would God attribute it as a foolish act or as a lovely human action? I had no idea, but we didn't care. We only went to the court to be legally married. Six months later, to avoid a family's crisis and to please my mother, we were religiously wed in a very nice chapel, St. Louis Roi de France. We had our own attending priests and Sister Mireille was also present. Yes, I married a lovely, charming man, and I became mother of a marvelous child eleven months later.

In November 1978, I gave birth to my first lovely, beautiful baby boy. Sam and I were overwhelmed with joy and excitement. Sam was a very proud father, and I was a proud mother. Friends said that he was too cute to be our child, and really, he was and still is. I went back to studying to be a ticket agent and later worked as a stewardess. Two years later, I got my diploma. I decided to leave for Kingston, Jamaica, to learn English. I needed English to speak to the travelers.

Nothing seems to be easy for me in life. The agency that arranged the details for this student's program didn't knowledge us about the chaos over there. Surprise! Here we're in the middle of a bloodstained political campaign between the popular Prime Minister Michael Manley and the leader of the opposition Edouard Seaga. The country clambered, day after day into a violent transmutation of the parties, where shooting and killing people were normal. It was frightening, almost impossible to live. Food was limited and buying

THE DAILY BATTLE FOR A NORMAL LIFE

luxurious imported items such as perfumes, liquors, etc.…weren't permissible to the residents unless you were foreigners. It was like watching a gangster action movie. Days and nights, armed gangs from both parties are in the street to control the constituent's tendency. They're targeting, gun firing at oppositions, and innocents. Even the color of what we wear, as clothes, was controlled and needs to not offend either parties, otherwise, you'll be killed.

On our way going to school, it's always a running away from the shooters because the life of any individuals was in danger. There I learned the difference between a Democrat and a Socialist. If you're inclined to be too much on the poor people's side, they attribute you as a socialist, which is still, nowadays, what some people believe in our society. It was new to me because in my country, at that time, they called it "Communism." That was for me like an initiation to politic, how dirty and bloodily can it be. Despite all this, while in Kingston, hurricane Allen made its apparition. Food was rarer, even with money we couldn't find groceries. My roommate's sister flew from Port-au-Prince to bring us food. Some of the students scattered to other locations or returned to Haiti because of the aggravation of the situation. We were the only two left in the house. We thought that moving out or staying at the same place won't change anything, because the blitz was everywhere. She was like me, very determinate to finish what we were there to fulfill.

I stayed there for four months. I came back home, and we had our second sweet baby boy in December 1981. I wasn't ready to have a second child right away, but it was God's will, so I just accepted it. I was miserable and angry because I was pregnant again so soon. I had other plans. The baby resisted my anger, though, and didn't give me any pregnancy problems. Silently, he waited to come out of my unappreciative stomach. Maybe this is why the baby was so serious after he was born; he didn't like to smile then, and he still doesn't as an adult. I love him deeply. He is one of the most compassionate and caring people I know, and he's like that toward everyone. I call him my sunshine, and this epithet name fits his character. He is a joy. He likes to help everybody and loves every living, crawling creature on earth. He soon became a consultant of mine; whatever advice I needed, I could just call him up and ask. These days, he comes home every two weeks. Now, we can just lie in bed and talk like two adults.

Soon after giving birth, my husband left again to study in Panama. He came back, and we had our third baby boy. He soon traveled to Italy to study further, but this time, things went wrong. His government grant wasn't approved, so he decided to go to New York for a while instead. As soon as he came back, he went to Atlanta for an exhibit. It went on and on like this. In retrospect, I think that my husband was scared to stay with me for too long. Like my mother, my husband was always traveling, if not overseas than around the country. That's my destiny: someone would always be absent from my life.

17

The Third Pregnancy

My health changed completely during my third and final pregnancy. I was sick from the beginning, which is why we all thought that it would be a girl. This pregnancy was so antithetical to the two others. I bled periodically, as if I was menstruating. One of my best friends, Mary, always volunteered to take me to the doctor. I spent so much time going to the gynecologist or to my family doctor. It was always something: an infection, shingles all over my right side and back, etc. That baby wasn't moving but running inside my belly. I had very good appetite. I could eat half a loaf of bread with oatmeal at night. When Tita brought me my meals while I was on bed rest, I asked her if she was feeding a cow. Somehow, I ate it all, but when she returned, I covered the tray and told her that I wasn't finished yet, that I was full, and that I would eat the rest later. I was ashamed of how voracious I'd become.

Tita left her job after I got married to stay with me. We tried to make up for all the time we'd lost. It was very nice to have her wholehearted efforts directed toward me for once, which helped compensate for the time we were separated during my childhood. The baby was born weighing eight pounds, five ounces at 10:15 a.m., whereas my other children respectively, had come into the world at 4:15 and 4:30 a.m. He had to make his arrival in the daylight, a controversial baby boy. We'd only picked out girls' names because we were certain it would be a girl, so we didn't have a name picked out for another boy. They needed something to put on his hospital wristband, so we temporarily gave him his father's name, Sam Jr. We assumed that later on, when we registered him for his birth certificate, we would give him a real name. Unexpectedly, they used this name to issue his birth certificate without advising us. Three years later, the hospital's policy changed, but it was too late for us. The temporary name became permanent and has stayed with him since. Sam's mission was for all his children to have the same initials as he did, S. G. It was fine with me. I accomplished two things that he would never be able to do in his lifetime: giving birth to and nourishing our babies. I was already happy with and proud of my creations. I had three boys and a husband to protect me. What a blessing.

After giving birth, everything went pretty well, thank goodness. I had a few visitors, and Mary, who was excited to be a first-time godmother, never left my side. I received flowers from my husband, from friends, and from work. They flourished in my bedroom. I could smell the mixture of freshly cut roses and orchids everywhere in the room, but the disappointment of not having a girl was floating in the air too. I didn't believe the doctor when he told me that I'd given birth to another boy. I had to check his genitals myself when they put him in my arms to believe that the force of my subconscious didn't obey my irrational desire to have a daughter. I was shocked. I had a somber pride.

The doctor saw my dissatisfaction, and he whispered to my ear, "If it'd been a girl, you would have to have a fourth baby to make it even."

I didn't say anything. What else could I do? I felt kind of embarrassed because everybody was expecting a female to come out of my body like I was God. But the baby was so cute with his stick-straight black hair from his Indian heritage. Promptly, I found myself maliciously grinning, reasoning that I would have more loving men to myself—a psychological moral victory to cover my despair. Without glamor and without glory, Sam entered the room, kissed me, and didn't say a word for a while. I didn't say a word either, just looked at him. For a moment, I felt guilty for not giving him the baby girl he was anticipating. He had an unexpressed smile on his face that seemed to ask, "What did you do?"

"You're okay, and that's all I need," he finally said, but for me, that one sentence had a lot of meanings, namely, "I will survive despite your plot to have only boys." It was normal and logical for a man who was expecting to have a daughter to feel defeated when he got a son instead, but he was too strong to show me his clear disappointment. I'd asked St. Joseph to give me a girl, but he gave me a boy again. I blamed him for his mistake like he was my husband. From then on, I stopped going to St. Joseph's church. I stopped celebrating St. Joseph's anniversary on the ninetieth of March, and I stopped believing in saints all together. I had been so sure that I'd get this favor during my pregnancy that I refused to have the baby's gender tested in the womb, which was a new technology in my country. I had deep faith and look what happened! As a Catholic, I had a religious belief in saints; they are our intermediary messengers, our ambassadors who carry our requests to the Lord. What went wrong? Didn't he listen to my prayers? I didn't ask for much. I thought it was necessary to have a little girl who looked just like me. All my other children were portraits of their father. What would happen to my face and my femininity? Would it disappear at the hands of St. Joseph, giving everything to Sam? After that, I thought that God must be a man who couldn't care less about women's rights. He gave us so many scrapes, such as our monthly discomforts with menstruation, giving birth, and so on—all the crap we have to put up with in life that men don't. Although I called it a victory to have four men in my life, it was just a semblance. I was pretending that I was one of the most powerful mothers in the world. In reality, I was mad at the entire universe. I carried this madness with me for a long time.

At 6:30 p.m. on March 7, 1984, I should've been relaxing, feeling free of the complicated pregnancy that I'd suffered through for nine months. However, another daze was awaiting me. Suddenly, I felt that something wasn't right. I started having a mild stomach ache. The later it got, the stronger the pain became. I was still in the hospital, so I called the nurse to tell her that I had a low abdominal ache and was bleeding more than usual. She gave me painkiller pills and changed my pad, which was very damp with blood. By 9:00 p.m., all my visitors had left, leaving me with Sam. That was the first time he stayed with me at the hospital. I told my husband that I was overwhelmed with pain and was bleeding too much. He called the nurse again, and she came with a painkiller shot, which was administered into my rear. Nothing could stop the hemorrhage. I was bleeding so much that my pad was like a baby's Pampers. Sam didn't seem to understand that I was exiting into hell. I was getting pale, my blood was draining out of my body like a river, and my respiration was slowing down. I couldn't talk much anymore. I was already buried in my own blood. I used the clean folded bedsheet left by my side and use it as a sponge to better soak up the blood that was pouring from my uterus. I really thought that I was going to die. I lay in the bed, still and silent like a wounded, sacrificial wounded lamb, waiting for a miracle.

Ha—what miracle? Sam was snoring. The mask of the death already encased my carcass. I wouldn't be able to raise my three sons, I thought. How many women die right after giving birth? As usual, men can sleep regardless of women's suffering. I was in that obscure room of the hospital with only my thoughts, pain, and agony to keep me company. Could I blame anybody for that? No. That's just how it is; women are mostly alone in this type of situation. I couldn't sleep because of my worries and the severe pain I was in. I begged to have the doctor called that night, but my demands didn't reach the people around me. They were confident that the hemorrhage would stop by itself, which I wasn't sure would happen. Angriness covered my soul, which left me with no hope. I had faith that a miracle would come, but God says, "Help yourself, and heaven will help you." I couldn't help myself, though. I was too frail, so someone else had to do it for me.

Humor is my normal way of dealing with things. I always make jokes in a sarcastic way to deal with difficult situations. I got the stupid, antagonistic idea that if I died, my husband would be penitent all his life, cursed with the regret that he didn't listen to me. That thought made me smile with bitter, ill will. After many years, I realized that this was the most imbecile, dumb viewpoint. If I had died that night, I know that I would've been forgotten and that my children would live with a stranger called stepmother. The next day at 7:00 a.m., which is when the doctors made their rounds, Dr. F. visited me. My exceptional gynecologist was just on time. By the way he was also the gynecologist of the First Lady of Haiti, he's indeed one of the best. He opened my eyes, took my pulse, and realized that something had gone very wrong. I could barely open my mouth to tell him how I felt, but he already knew. I heard him telling the nurse to call Dr. L., a well-known surgeon, right away and to have the anesthesiologist come ASAP.

"It sounds serious," I murmured to myself, but because of the severity of my illness, no sound came from my mouth. I was too weak to talk. Abruptly, I was surrounded with nurses beginning my preparations for the surgery. He turned back, face-to-face with my husband, who was standing behind him.

"Mr. G.," he said, "she will need a blood transfusion, so you need to go gather some friends or family members who can give blood to replace the liters we will give her during the surgery."

I was listening, but I didn't have the energy to ask the questions that were buzzing in my head: *What kind of surgery do I need? What illness do I have?* Sam didn't ask any questions to find out of why I was going to the operating room, he just obeyed and left the room to complete his mission. I speculated that he was shocked and that he already regretted the fact that he hadn't paid more attention to my supplications. My life was in jeopardy—not his. Typical man: they don't listen to their wives. *Good for him, I don't care*, I thought. I was numb, like there was no life inside of me anymore. I had already given up my fight and was ready for whatever came next. I was sure of one thing, though, that if Sam and I had switched positions, if he had been in that kind of pain all night, I would've made the nurse call the doctor before it got too bad. I would've found out why my husband had to have emergency surgery. This is the archetypal man, though. They don't listen to their women, and they don't ask questions when they're supposed to. In this situation, if there had been another person present, something might have been done before it got to that point. When all was said and done, the surgery was a success. They were able to stop the bleeding. It turned out that when

I was cut open for the passage of the baby, my uterus ripped and caused the bleeding. I was so happy that I was a Catholic, so I didn't have any problem receiving a blood transfusion.

I stayed in the hospital for a week. I wanted to breastfeed my baby, but I couldn't. Less than a month later, my breasts were still producing bodily fluid instead of milk. I didn't have cancer, but blood was coming out of my nipples. I didn't think that I was a vampire who needed to feed my baby with blood, so I stopped breastfeeding right away. I was deeply concerned about that because I'd never heard of this happening before. My gynecologist told me to stop giving him my milk and to come to the doctor's office. Of course, I'd already stopped. Who would give blood to a baby? I gave him bottle instead. My baby grew up healthy except that he had problem with his legs, which were not straight. He had to wear a cast on both legs and especial shoes without a left-right orientation, which I had to order overseas from Miami. They came marked so that I could recognize which was which.

18

The Aftermath

My conspicuous misery started right then and there. The strange blood they gave me at the hospital wasn't too friendly to my body. I had malaria, nausea, chills, and fevers. I visited doctor after doctor to find a cure for my new illness. To tell the truth, at the beginning, the doctors couldn't diagnose me with any sort of disease. In fact, everything seemed to be all right with me. I had fevers, especially at night, and chills during the day. I was anemic, and I vomited sometimes. I was very sick and wasn't getting better. I took all kinds of bitter pills. I became a lab rat, considering all the medications I took. Sometimes I could see the ruefulness in my doctors' expressions. They didn't know what to try on me anymore. No matter what they gave me to swallow, I did it with closed eyes. I wanted to feel good, to feel better. I was too young to give up on searching for a cure and die. It was a challenge, and I thought that I ought to win it. I wasn't going to let an unfair disease take over my body and make it a sanctuary. The disease should know that I was against this unfairness, I thought. I would fight, and I would win. My goal was to fight for my life. I went to a friend's doctor as well as many others. At that point, if someone had told me that I would feel better if I ate a lizard, I wouldn't hesitate if I could just go back to feeling normal. I could tell that an unwanted outsider had invaded my body, but what was it? I kept laughing to hide my sadness. I thought that nobody should know that I was close to exploding.

As the days passed, I became sicker and sicker. Sam took me to Petion-Ville to see a friend's doctor at the same time he was taking a sick employee to Fermathe's Clinic Center, which was managed by an American doctor for the low-income populace. He dropped me at my doctor's office and continued on his trajectory. I was left at the mercy of the new doctor. He made many hypotheses, and some of them sounded true but not all of them. When I was done, there was no sign of my husband. In vain, I waited almost two hours for my dear hubby to come to pick me up, but he didn't, so I decided to take the *camionette* (little van) to go home. I was desperate, angry, miserable, and in disarray. I felt like the sky was falling on me. At that instant, I really thought that I was the only person on earth with so many tribulations, despairs, and anguishes. I became very egocentric. I had a black veil covering my face so that I could concentrate on my crisis. I couldn't see anything else and thought that everybody should have their eyes only on me. But at the same time, I didn't want to show that I was looking for attention. I had a hypocritical character. Although I was searching clandestinely for attention, I didn't want people to discover my surreptitious side. While I was waiting at the public transportation station, I couldn't stop crying. A lady in her late forties asked me why I was crying, and I explained everything to her like a child. I lost my stealth.

"My dear child," she said, "you are so lucky that you can pay for so many doctors. There are many people who cannot and never will be able to afford the price of even one consultation or medicine. At this moment, they are dying somewhere without the help of anyone. You think that you are miserable, but these dying people accept their destinies, waiting happily for death to set them free from their misery. Despite their bad fortune, they thank God every day for what he has given them, which is nothing."

"Is it the time for French literature?" I muttered, wanting to move away from her. That wasn't what I was expecting her to say to me at that moment. I was asking myself, "How dare she tell me that what I have is nil?" She wasn't the first one to say this to me, though.

THE DAILY BATTLE FOR A NORMAL LIFE

I don't like it when you tell other people of your wretchedness, and they answer that your problem is nothing compared to that of others. Real people should recognize when their friends are antagonizing, and they should just listen. Don't put me down with that incomprehensible nonsense. If there is nothing else you can say—if you're not human enough to understand that everybody is different, or if you're not smart enough to see that I have something ruining my life—shut your mouth. By saying this to me, you're not consoling me; you're making me believe that you don't understand what I've just told you. You asked, and so I answered. I don't want comparison; I want comprehension. That stranger, to whom I revealed my life's greatest sorrows, made me feel like I was talking to nature, my words flying away like butterflies, leaving no trace after I was gone. If I'd known her, I wouldn't have shown that much emotion to begin with. I was decongesting my inner feelings by talking to her. I don't deny that what she said was true, but most people can keep on going with a swathe of bandages around their heads after they get deeply hurt. You might think it is normal, courageous, and brave, but not everybody can undergo the same pains with the same spirit. "Lucky" isn't an encouraging word. We are not lucky in life; we just get that which was predestined for us. Please change this mentality if you hold it and see things as being up to chance. Think twice before saying words to sick people, no matter how sick they might be. You hurt us with what you think are words of support. That woman was truly right, sure, but at that present moment, I needed comfortable words. Can you only try to understand? My grandmother used to say that everybody is carrying a cross. It doesn't matter how heavy it is, a cross is a cross, and it's your cross. Made of paper, wood, or steel, every cross is heavy for its carrier.

At the bus station after that doctor's appointment, I was so crumbled that the wind could've blown me away. The heat and the standing were killing me. From nowhere, a tap-tap (Haitian transportation van) stopped right in front of me. I couldn't see it coming before because I'd turned my head in the opposite direction. It was a liberation to finally be able to sit down. I was shaking with anger and confusion, and I was burning with a fever. My feet couldn't carry my body, and my body was incapable of standing on my feet. The bitter taste that was left in my mouth from all the pills made me thirsty, and I was also hungry. I didn't have breakfast due to my loss of appetite. It was almost one in the afternoon, and I needed something to eat soon. It seemed that all the discomforts tangled over me. I just sat in the *camionette*. Then I saw Sam speedily approaching in his car. He saw me in the van and sped up so that he was next to the driver's side. He asked the driver to stop, explaining that his wife is in the van. For some reason, the chauffeur turned to me and asked if he should stop. I answered that I didn't know the man and to please keep going. That was the angry woman in me talking. Even though I knew I would be more comfortable in Sam's car, I was blind by rage, and so I chose to suffer instead. Men think that they can do anything to women without consequences. He could go and drop off his employee first and then come back to stay with me. He must have assumed that I was a piece of heavy rock, that I could survive any flood. If it'd been female employee he'd was with, I would have been sick enough to think that I was in the same car with my concubine. He was the same as all men are, who act without thinking. I never understood what shouldn't possibly made him act so unfairly toward me that day. He should've been at my side at that critical moment. Why do some men lack common sense? Without a doubt, I take is as truth that they come from an undiscovered planet of their own.

To compensate for what he did to me that day, he tried his best to be nice to me. He lay down next to me on the bed and watched me for a moment. After a few minutes, he asked if I wanted him to stay. I was cold to him. He kept looking at me, waiting for a response, but I avoided looking back, ignoring the question he'd just solicited. *What do you expect from me*, I thought, *to forgive you right away? To forget what'd happened just today? I'm sick, dummy, stay with me*, I thought, but I didn't say a word.

"Am I bothering you by moving too much in the bed? Do you want me to leave you to rest?" he asked.

That was a stupid question. If I answered it, I thought, I would only make it worse, so I stayed silent. Later, I woke up to have my bath, and he continued: "Do you want me to do the bed for you while you're having your shower?"

"Okay," I said in a slow-motion voice.

"What bedsheets do you want me to use?" I stayed mute. He opened the closet and withdrew something. "Can you please tell me where I can find the pillowcases?" he said. "I don't see them."

What a torture! Men can't do anything for women, no less for themselves (make the bed for you, wash the dishes for you, watch on the children for you, and so on). If you really want to help, you should try to avoid these ridiculous questions. Are you helping me physically but at the same time, destroying my morale?

"Leave, I will do it," I said in an attempt to release my anger and stop this interrogation. The marathon questionnaire wasn't over, though.

"Do you want to go outside to have fresh air? What do you want for breakfast tomorrow?"

"Whatever you want," I said, tired of him trying to show-off how much he cared for me.

"You want the eggs soft or hard? Toast or bread? Black coffee or with milk?"

What the heck is wrong with you, man? I thought. *Can you stop posing these ridiculous questions? Are you searching for trouble?* And what would happen if I answered him honestly: "Yes, you're moving too much on the bed, and don't bother making breakfast for me because you will ask me too many questions before you get it done." That would've started a new problem between us. *For God's sake, I'm sick*, I thought. *Do whatever you want without questioning me. Why after so many years do you still not know how I like my eggs and coffee? I know what you like! Have you never paid attention to your wife's lifestyle? Do you really care about what I like or want? If so, you would've listened to me at the hospital, and you wouldn't have left me by myself at the doctor's office. You are not helping, you are just harassing me with all these questions about everything you think I want you to do for me. However, you didn't need my permission for most things. You just do whatever pleases you to piss me off.*

I was debating whether I should answer his verbal questionnaire or completely pay no heed to him. In my condition, there was nothing that I could do than assent to his requests. I needed his assistance. I should've been grateful, I suppose, that he was asking to do something for me. He wanted to philanthropically satisfy my desires with what I wanted, respectfully, without diminishing the rights of a woman to choose. Sometimes it's ridiculously annoying, though. Just surprise me, *amigo*.

19

Emotional Distress

LIKE A MIRACLE, AFTER a few months, I was back to normal. I have no idea what really cured me. I went to so many doctors searching for good health, but finally, it was like nothing had happened, like the sun had risen again. I was myself again. I went back to work like a new person. One year later, however, my well-deserved happiness and good health were threatened by with a crazy stomach ache that woke me up a Friday morning. The excruciating pain increased very quickly, to the point at which I couldn't get dressed for work. It turned into a hellish morning. My lower stomach really hurt. I decided to go to my gynecologist's office because the pain was situated below my abdominal. On the way to the doctor's office, Sam said that he wasn't convinced that my pain was serious. He told me that it might just be stomach gas because I hadn't eaten that much. I got a little upset and told him that we could make a U-turn and go back home, but that I was in too much pain to go to work.

"We already left, so let's go see the doctor anyway," he said.

I pledged to him that if it was him in the same situation, he would be screaming like a baby. Why do men always choose the wrong time to make you upset? I didn't need that remark from someone dear to me who was supposedly there to protect me. I knew that my husband loved me very much, but he made so many idiotic remarks. He could've simply agreed with his wife without the commentary. Silently, he drove me to the doctor's office. It didn't take long to see Dr. F., the same doctor who delivered all three of my children. He examined me and requested that I have an ultrasound right away. He told me that I could come back in the afternoon for the results. In my country, money talks, and I had insurance. After the test was done, we went back home. Amazingly, I was free of the pain.

"I was right," Sam said. "Anyway, I'm going to make you a garlic tea to relieve you of this gastric matter."

Traditionally, we used garlic skin to make that kind of tea, which was served with a pinch of salt. We don't add sugar. He wanted to take care of me in his way. I drank the tea to please him, but my pain had already disappeared completely. I couldn't tell if my hubby's medicine made any difference. At two o'clock, it was time to revisit the doctor for the test results. My right ovary was covered with cysts. He told me to stay in bed for the weekend and rest until Monday to avoid any further complications and to avoid bending or carrying heavy stuff. I figured that cysts were little bumps that cleared up by themselves after a few days. I didn't know that they were something I should be concerned about. He didn't want me to leave my bed, not even to have a shower. He strongly recommended that I come to see him on Monday morning with an empty stomach.

"Didn't eat or drink anything," he said, repeating his own words.

I didn't have a lot of information, but I decided to follow his recommendations, just in case. I went straight to bed. On Saturday, I was all right, but on Sunday night, I had a high fever. What is going on now? I pleaded. This wasn't in my plan. I spent the entire night with a fever. It never went down despite the cold compress that Sam held on my forehead. He gave me a shower of *tafia*, which is white rum mixed with water and was meant to lower the fever, but nothing helped. On Monday, I was the first patient in to see Dr. F. Very soon, he instructed Sam to drive me straight to Canape Vert Hospital because I needed urgent surgery. He didn't know exactly what they were going to find, he explained, but they might have to remove the right ovary completely.

"A full explanation will be given to you after the surgery," he continued. "I will be right behind you, I just need a little time to talk to my assistant."

That sounded serious to me. In my country, doctors are gods on earth, and we truly trust them. Anyway, there was no time to get a second opinion. I had a horrible fever, I had known Dr. F. for a long time and trusted him, and I was in too bad shape to think otherwise. When we arrived at the hospital, I could tell that I was expected. Nurses were waiting to take me directly to the operating room. Right away, they began the preparations—shaving and cleaning me with a lot of iodine. The funky, strong smell of the chemical antiseptic was the same as when they dressed a wound. I felt nauseated. The time it took the anesthesiologist to prepare me seemed very long, but when I regained conscious, it felt like they'd done nothing. The surgery went well, a doctor explained to my husband.

"As predicted, Mr. G.," he said, addressing Sam, "we had to remove the right ovary, which was covered with many cysts, and the reason she had the fever was because some of them had already burst. I drained a lot of blood and fluid that had spread inside her."

I spent a full week at the hospital and three months on disability. Then I went back to work. While I healed, Sam interpreted all my desires as his own personal orders and missions, and he doted on me accordingly. Did he feel guilty for underestimating me? Maybe. All I know is that I was very well-treated at home. This health problem was over, thank goodness, but another had arisen in the process. After the surgery, I woke up with a swollen red eye. It was a mystery. My right eye was coming out of its orbit. The doctors couldn't figure out what'd happened to me during the surgical procedure to cause such a thing. I wondered if I was turning into a devilish person. I'd never had this before. They called an ophthalmologist. After many tests, he finally determined that this kind of problem happens with pressure and that it would disappear on its own with cold compress.

"There is no name yet for that type of disease," he explained. "You'll have to check back with us later."

"Will this be a constant, lifetime issue, or is it just temporary?" I asked him.

"I'm not familiar with it," he answered with great embarrassment.

"Doctor," I said, "during the procedure, I didn't have to use any pressure. I was unconscious and under anesthesia. How can you be talking about pressure?"

"In general, it happens with physical exertion…" He trailed off. To change the subject, he said, "Let's schedule another appointment. In the meantime, I will come up with more answers for you."

As was recommended to me, I followed up with Dr. Al, who was Sam's friend. "There is nothing that can be done for this bizarre disease. There is no treatment," he concluded.

I was so disappointed. I was his only patient who'd ever had that weird condition. Well, I decided, if there was nothing that could be done, there was no reason to continue seeing him. I forgot completely about this eye problem until late 1994. By the way, one of the doctors put me on a food restriction for internal bleeding. There were lots of things that I couldn't eat, especially cabbage. Also, my doctors were scared to give me medicine that had blood thinner in it.

20

An Unceremonious Goodbye

I BEGAN TO FEEL like my life was back to normal. One year passed without any health incidents, and life was good. We decided to start building our house and made other plans for our future. Sam continued to work for Mupanah and Enarts, which were under the First Lady's control. Sometimes, we got invited to the Presidential Palace, or *le Palais Presidentiel*, shaking hands with the president and his wife and going to parties. I couldn't have asked for a better life. Our house was under construction, and I really liked the architecture. We designed the house's plan exactly like we wanted to. Every detail was meticulously planned and agreed upon by both of us. We paid attention to every detail in order to make it our dream house. We made enough concessions to each other to finish it in a way that made us both happy. The sun was so bright and shiny, but the good life suddenly disappeared, replaced by a turbulent storm. The revolution began. People were not happy with the presidential lifetime proclamation that had been issued. There was fire, smoke, strikes, and riots everywhere in the streets. Many Haitians were extremely discontented and wanted a new regime. After a long period of everyday battles, one morning, we woke up and heard that the government had finally given up and gone into exile. You would think that the people would be delighted with their successful battle—after all, they'd gotten what they wanted—but they were still not satisfied. It was time for revenge, and they came after everybody who worked for the formal government, especially those called *Tonton Macoute*, who had committed crimes and injustices toward the poor and middle classes.

My family was suddenly at the mercy of these enraged people, who were looking for a reason to kill without lawful justice. In the streets, we could smell burning tires mixed with dead human bodies everywhere. It was a chaotic revolution, and people were petrified. There was no school. My older son was so scared of the sound of bullets that he always hid under the bed. One time, he asked his grandmother if we were all going to die. We decided to send him to New York on vacation until the storm calmed down. The partisans of the radical war wanted more change—a territory free from corruption and injustice. Instead, it worsened every day. They were killing as many people, burning as many houses, and stealing as many things as they could. Hell was all over Haiti. Before I went to work each day, I had to listen to the radio to find out which streets were safe to drive on. Sometimes, there wasn't a safe route at all. For a long time, I had to stay home, and the businesses remained closed. Downtown Port-au-Prince became an infernal, undrivable, and unlivable place to be. It was a disaster.

Sam used to work for the First Lady as a teacher at Enarts and as an art renovator at Mupanah. During the revolution, he decided to leave Haiti, promising that as soon the calm was reestablished, he would be back home. All his brothers had already left Port-au-Prince for New York. I was left by myself with my second and third sons, Scott and Sam Jr. Steven was living with a relative in Brooklyn at that point. This situation in Haiti frightened me, but at the same time, I missed my son and my husband deeply. I was the mother and the father. I had to run to school, to work, to do the grocery shopping, and sometimes to the gas station whenever I heard that the precious liquid was available somewhere within the bloody scare. I thought that I might get hurt in the streets or not come back home at all. The worst of it was that sometimes, we used the little gas we had left to go to the gas station, and when we got there, we found that there was no gas left. Perhaps we had gotten false information, or the gas station had already closed. Perhaps the owners of the gas station were scared to open their stations or were receiving threats that if they opened, their businesses would be firebombed.

I was stuck forever inside the house. I wished that a Good Samaritan would bring me a gallon of the treasured fluid, but it wasn't that easy. Everyone was cloistered in their homes. Nobody left the house unless it was a life-threatening situation. It wasn't safe to be without gas, candles, or food. It was catastrophic. The crusaders had the power to tell us when we could go out and when we couldn't. We couldn't always trust what was said on the radio or on television because we knew that the producers were as afraid as we were. The activists could say one thing one moment and then change their minds the next moment. The broadcasters just relayed what the activists told them to say. As a parent, I had to provide food to my children even though the protestors were deploying asphyxiating teargas and smoke-fire in the streets, which made it difficult to drive and hard to see when I did. But I had to brave these dangers for the good of my children. Cadavers lay in the street, killed by the tires that lay around them. They had been dampened with gasoline and set on fire, like humans being barbequed. The scent infested our clothes and spread pestilence into the smoky air. I had to protect and feed my family, that is all I knew. Life was impossible, and the country was very unstable. So to secure my family, after nine months, I decided to immigrate to New York City, joining Sam and my son so that we could all be together again. It was another storm, another step forward, another step in the direction of our destiny. I followed the path even as it drove me toward uncertainty. I never thought that I would leave my country. It was hard to say goodbye, especially when my birthplace was in such bad condition.

We embarked on an adventure with no return in sight. It was such a heartbreaking feeling to sell my house, my car, and all my belongings for a pittance. I packed a few things and said bye-bye to my country. It was like I'd entered the gate to the end of the world. It felt like life stopped right there. I didn't know exactly what I was going to find. I was torn apart by the uncertainty. I was miserable. I couldn't dry my tears, but I had no other choice than to leave my country for the future of my children. They needed to go to school with confidence that nothing would happen to them. Sam and my eldest son were already waiting for us in New York. I arrived at JFK airport in July 1987. After what I'd just experienced in my country, nothing could scare me more. Still, I was scared of my new life and the process I'd have to undertake to make it work for us.

That was a new beginning. *Forget about Haiti*, I thought again and again. To start a new life, I had to desensitize myself to everything around me, to be unemotional toward any possibility our lives might take. I was ready to face the impossible, but this was easier said than done. Nostalgia for my country became a disease. There is no pleasure in being an immigrant or refugee. I can't speak for everyone, but for me, it was hard to adjust. Heartbroken, I listened to only French songs, the ones that were written to plunge my soul into deep sadness. I wanted to be sad. I wanted to cry. I thought that it was the only way to stay loyal to my country. I thought that I would never like American songs except the ones that I already knew. The more I cried, the more I felt the need to cry. I wanted to punish myself with crying. I didn't blame the people of my country for what they did to force me to leave, but the United States of America, for not providing me with the comforts I had in my country, especially my maids and my gardener. Everything seemed so hard to accomplish. The route to go to a friend's house seemed longer. Everyone was busy on weekdays. This nothingness was the same everywhere.

21

Unaccustomed Life

My husband became a cab driver, and I stayed home with the children in a one-bedroom apartment. Our attic became a bedroom for all three kids. We had a kitchen but no living or family room. The other room, which could've been another bedroom, was rented to an old man we knew from Haiti. He was in great need of housing, and we needed the extra income. The apartment wasn't too bad. I considered ourselves fortunate to be able to afford a place like that in Queens. I was all right with that. I cleaned, cooked, did all the housekeeping duties, and took care of the children. In my country, I had helpers, so now that I was doing it all myself, so I wasn't too happy. I was willing to serve my family and to learn how to be a wife, mother, and housekeeper at the same time. Fortunately, at the beginning, I wasn't working. Sam overworked to bring the daily bread to the house. I was depressed; the nostalgia of leaving my country was gnawing my insides, bite after bite, but I had to show my happy face to my children. I knew that they were struggling too and that my happiness would support them. I had to take responsibility and be helpful to Sam too, who never complained a bit about his new job. We didn't have a car. Instead, I had a cart that I took to the grocery and the laundry, which were the most difficult tasks for me. In my country, when we needed to shop, I just drove the maid to the flea market and told her that I'd pick her up in an hour. I didn't have to think about what I was going to buy unless I had a desire for something special. She knew exactly what to buy and what I liked to eat.

I had so much anxiety about the multiple tasks that were waiting for me to accomplish every day. I often thought that it doesn't matter how bad your country is, it is your country. This is a fact, and no one can't change that. I missed my country and all the helpers I had, who I didn't appreciate enough when I had them. I was experiencing so many things that I never thought would happen to me. I needed to get adapted to my new life. I constantly cried when I was alone. It became something of a recreational habit, a type of relaxation. I wanted to get adapted as soon as possible. It hurt very much, and I thought that the faster I got used to my new life, the sooner I would be able to relieve my emotional pangs to go back to Haiti. I wasn't willing to be discouraged over it, which I thought was part of my duty as a wife and mother. In a sense, my emotional stability was a contribution I could make to the house. Day after day, I worked on accepting my new life with pride. I wanted to become a new kind of Scarlett O'Hara from *Gone with the Wind*. I told myself that I had to survive and be strong. Being able to take care of my children was a blessing. Afterward, I felt closer to them than ever, and I enjoyed it. The only major problem was that I was afraid at night because I was seeing ghosts. I was the only one in the family who heard noises and saw rats in that nasty apartment. Everybody else in the house managed to sleep, but I couldn't, thinking of the rats like those in my grandparents' house. I couldn't sleep. I detested those rats. I could smell the unpleasant odor of the overrunning animals everywhere, no matter how often I cleaned and swept the place. It was always a strange, abominable odor that came from I-don't-know-where.

One night, I dreamed that a rat bit me. Suddenly, I woke up like I'd had a nightmare. Sam asked me what was wrong, and I explained my dream to him. He hugged me and tried to unruffle me. I was trembling. For the rest of the night, we left the lights on to help me get over my fear. It didn't take long for Sam to fall asleep again, but I couldn't. I needed to go to the bathroom. I was scared to put my feet on the stinking carpet, thinking that a rat might be waiting for me. Suddenly, I felt a sharp, burning sensation on my arm, as if I was cut by a piece of cardboard. I looked down, and what I discovered petrified me so badly that for a moment, I couldn't speak. It hadn't been a dream at all. The bastard had really bitten my arm and left teeth marks! I was bleeding. Afraid that the nasty animal was still around me, I pushed my husband's arm to wake him up and show him my scratch. He finally believed me.

The next morning, I told my story to my children and showed them the lesion. They were all very sorry. All of them needed proof to believe me, and there it was: my arm serving as a piece of meat for a rat. We didn't have insurance, so I couldn't go to the hospital to have a tetanus shot, but I washed it with peroxide and took some antibiotic pills I had from Haiti. I wasn't scared for my children; they had all the proper vaccines before our departure for New York, as was normal for children of their age. Sam put many traps in the apartment, but we would've needed the Home Depot's entire stock to fight these ugly, infected invaders. They were coming from the neighbors' apartments, from the people downstairs, from everywhere. The more we killed, the more they kept coming. Dead or alive, I didn't like them. Before my husband left each morning, he had to make sure that no monster was left in the lures. God bless America, the country of hope and possibly, where the ubiquitous rats were immigrants like we were. Unfortunately, they'd come to the wrong house. We set up traps everywhere, trying to catch them all.

Often, two of my sons went to the local public school. I stayed home during the day with my youngest son, Junior. He was with me all the time, going to the laundry, supermarket, and shopping in Queens Jamaica in New York. We often went to Manhattan for the pleasure of looking at the coming and going of people in the street, like ants searching for food to store before winter. We had fun going everywhere together in cold and warm weather. There was always a funny, funky scene to watch in Manhattan. Sometimes, we had to enter a shop to warm our freezing, trembling bodies. We were not used to that kind of cold, and we weren't properly dressed for winter weather. Did I like my new life as housekeeper? I don't think so. I was pessimistic as I accomplished these hard, new activities. Here are the questions I had to answer:

"Olivia where did you put my socks?" my husband asked.

"Mommy, I don't have a clean underwear," my sons said.

"*Cherie*, darling, did you remember to wash my uniform pants?" my husband asked.

"What are you going to do today? Are you cooking?" my husband asked again.

If it'd only been Sam and me, I'd likely only cook twice a week, but I didn't want to always give junk food to my children, and he always got home late at night. So I did a good deal of cooking. I strongly believe that parents should minimize their children's intake of fast food. Don't you need them to be healthy? They came back from school around three p.m., and I had to give them real food. Sam didn't keep specific work hours, so his arrival time fluctuated. He'd often take a few extra people home at night to make a little extra money. Normally, around 9:00 p.m., we'd hear the click of the door's lock, meaning that Sam was home. After he finished driving, he had to surrender the cab and take the train to get home, which was a long process. If we'd waited for him to eat dinner, we would've always eaten too late, so we always saved some food for him.

There was little time for my husband to sleep because he woke up at 4:00 a.m. to start driving at five. That was when traffic began in New York. He worked seven days a week. Can you ask someone so tired to keep you company? My loneliness was getting to my head. My brain was being attacked by darkness because of my recent life changes. Often, at night, I let him sleep for a while and then woke him up to have a moment with me. You can call this whatever you want—selfishness or narcissism—but that moment was beneficial to me. I needed it to keep me functioning. As a good hubby, he never got upset with me. I would've if I was him! He always found time to talk to me for a little bit with smile, half-sleeping and half-awake. I won't ever forget the kindness of my husband during that time. He was amazing and never complained about doing something that he didn't like, driving strangers from place to place. His purpose was to provide for his family, and I respected him for that. He set a good example for many couples. He took his charge and responsibility seriously despite the hardships, and I vowed to be more like him and to stop complaining.

When I got to the United States, I didn't know how to cook well. I called my friends for help and watched the food network every time I had the opportunity to stay home. The food might've been too salty, the rice might not have been properly cooked, but they supported me by eating my meals anyway. I'm glad to say that now I'm a quasi *Cordon Bleu*. These days, they enjoy my food, and I think it's really good. I learned that we should erase the word "impossible" from the dictionary because there is nothing you cannot make possible. If you use your heart deeply and widely, you will honor your plan. I'm not saying that you can be an athlete when in your blood you're an artist, but if your desire is to be what you want to be, you can be it. Every happiness, sorrow, and frustration in our lives are meant to happen to us. So let it be and don't ever give up. As President Obama said at the Al Smith dinner, "Tribulations produce perseverance, and perseverance produces hope." With perseverance, I became the centerpiece of my family, which I was so proud to be. Soon, Haiti became something in my past—a past that I could never forget, but an antecedent that I could live without.

22

Another Beginning

THE SCHOOL YEAR ENDED, and the owner of our apartment wanted to sell the building. We didn't like the area for raising our sons anyway, and we were looking for a better place. We always said to friends that we might have to move to Miami one day. Soon, a friend said to us, "Why don't you take this opportunity to move to Florida?" Her advice was just right and at the right time, so she didn't have to say it twice. That was a perfect moment to make our transition to another place, which seemed to be closer to Haiti with its hot weather. Two months later, we were ready to make our second move. We called the moving company, packed everything, and drove to Miami. Another adventure and another new beginning was waiting for us there. That is what life is for—taking challenging opportunities and collecting them as memorable moments.

My cousin Ann lived in Perrine, Miami, at the time. She gave us her address and said that we could stay for a few days while we waited for the moving truck and looked for an apartment. At that time, it was easy to find a place to live because nobody cared about checking your credit. All they needed was the deposit and a month's rent in advance. It'd only been ten months since we moved to America, so we didn't have any sort of credit. Within half a day, we were able to find a place to accommodate our family. The gated household was nice, in a very clean and beautiful area, but it was small. My husband had to go back to New York because we couldn't both stay without a fixed income. We were mostly living on the money we made from selling our furniture, car, and house before we left Haiti. The money was spent fast, too fast with three boys to feed and dress. My youngest soon began school. Life wasn't going as expected, but it was getting a little better in certain ways. In the building, we had a public pool, so the children could have a good time for free. Periodically, we walked to the mall as entertainment. I didn't have a car, and in Miami, unlike in New York, this was an absolute handicap. There was nothing else I could do.

Sam soon returned to Miami permanently. After less than three months, he was with us again. He'd missed his family, and we were very glad to have his presence around us. In the meantime, I found a job at Bayside selling shoes. The owner was a friend of my husband; they'd gone to school together, and the job was a great opportunity for me to practice English. Unfortunately, I couldn't stay too long for personal reasons. It was very hard to get from Cutler Ridge, where we lived (now called Cutler Bay) to Bayside. It took me more than two hours to get there by bus. To go to the supermarket, I had to go by foot, until one day, a friend loaned me a car that I could keep for a while. It was very nice of them to trust me with their car. I kept it until we bought an old BMW from Sam's cousin in New York. Rapidly, our income was all but zero, except the monthly payments we received from our house in Haiti, which wasn't honored as it should be. We sold the house to a very good friend who lived in Montreal, Canada, and he sent us part of the balance every two or three months. Life was tough for everybody, and we understood that. We knew that it had to be hard for him to get the money all the time. If it weren't for him, the house would've taken longer to sell, so we took our chances. Nonetheless, a lot of Haitians were leaving the country like birds flying away before a violent tempest.

I'm Catholic, and I believe strongly in miracles. People don't accept that they happen every day in our lives. One day, a miracle gloriously entered into my house. God sent a friend to save my family from starving. I paid all the bills with the money my husband sent and bought clothes for my children to start school. I didn't leave any for the market because there were still some groceries left in the house. I thought that in the meantime, Sam would be able to send more money from New York, but he utilized the money as a deposit on that BMW. There was no way he could send us money that week. Like all children, my children didn't know our finances and business. They didn't know that we were broke, and I didn't know how to tell them, "Don't rapaciously eat everything in the refrigerator—we need to save food for tomorrow and for the upcoming days." They wouldn't be able to understand that. I was desperate, anxious, and worried. But when you have faith and you are good to people, you will never be completely deprived. One day, I heard the bell ring. I didn't have any idea who it could be. I opened the door. It was a friend who I'd helped one time, only one time, and he'd come to see me. I don't know how he got through the gate without a call from security, but he bragged that he had a powerful influence on people. I was very happy to see him because I'd heard that he had a big accident and had to be transported by helicopter to Jackson Hospital. One of his legs was mutilated, and he had stitches from the bottom of his leg to his abdomen. He was pushing a walker to help him totter through our apartment. Despite his bad fortune, he was here to ask how I was doing with the boys. He told me that because of his injury, he would need some help unloading the groceries that he brought me. His car was fully loaded with every kind of food you can imagine. It looked like he'd passed through each aisle of the supermarket and picked out one or two of everything. I told him that he didn't have to be so generous, that his presence was enough for me, but as he turned his back to talk to my eldest son, I made the sign of the cross from my forehead to my chest, from left to right, to praise the Lord for his goodness.

 Would you call this a coincidence or a miracle? I called it a miracle. God sees our needs and he provides, like my grandfather used to say. You might not always pay attention to details like this, and you might take it for granted. I believe that if you're truly connected to the divine Lord, you can communicate with him without having to do anything. Trust him, for he is the master of the universe. He knows our needs and won't ever let us perish. I couldn't thank my

THE DAILY BATTLE FOR A NORMAL LIFE

savior enough for that enormous gesture of love that had come at just the right time. I'm pleased to say that miracles happen in my life every day, and this was one of them.

I left the shoe store in January 1990. Someone gave me an agency's name and address and told me to fill out an application for job searching. After a week, the agency called me for a two-week part-time job. They told me that I'd need to get to the business by 10:00 a.m., meaning that I'd only have two hours to get ready and get to a place where I'd never been before. It wasn't possible for me to accept it. First, the children were in school, and I couldn't make arrangements for a sitter with such short notice, and second, it was my son's birthday, so I was baking a cake for him. I really needed the supplementary income, but I had to decline the offer. A week later, they called me for another part-time job, this time for four weeks. Even better. I'd start on Monday at 8:00 a.m. I'd have plenty of time to arrange for my children to stay after school. I didn't have a clue where the place was, but I had plenty time to find out. On Monday, I left home at 6:00 a.m. Some friends of mine tried to explain where it was located. I got lost constantly. I looked everywhere, but I couldn't find it. I asked a few people, and some of them sent me to hellholes, but God sent an angel to guide me. It was almost 8:00 a.m. I was nervous, despairing, and didn't know what else to do. In the middle of the street, I stopped a person. I don't remember if it was a man or a woman, but he or she offered to take me directly to the address. All I had to do was to follow their car. It had to be an angel; they stopped their own journey at a busy time of day to help me out. I called that another miracle. I wish that I'd had more time to talk to that person, but as soon they showed me with a hand gesture the address, their car disappeared. All I said was "Thanks a lot!" It was almost time to show up for my new part-time job. My eyes were too busy finding a parking space that they forgot to check if my angel was a man or a woman. Perhaps they needed to get on time to their destination too. Thanking that person wasn't enough, but at the moment, it was the only way to express my gratitude.

The part-time job consisted mainly of filing. I had a pile of papers to file. Everybody seemed so charming. I soon filled out an application for a permanent job there. Human resources promised that as soon they had an opening, they'd call me. After four weeks, I had to leave and return to my previous activities, but I had a little more money for groceries. I got a paycheck every week and saved. Immediately after leaving, maybe four days later, I was already waiting for that call. Luckily, I didn't wait too long. After two weeks, I was called in for an interview and was hired immediately. I stayed with the agency for another two weeks before I got on their payroll. That was the agency's policy.

On May 1, 1990, I was officially employed by an import/export company, Greyhound. Three months later, I was promoted to processing customs entries, a procedure that I learned by routine. They laid off a lot of employees, and the name of the company changed three times. I stayed there for almost twenty-three years. I had a job with benefits for my family and myself, and I was fortunate. So many people in the country weren't able to access doctors' offices and hospitals when they were sick. I always believe in getting insurance, probably because I worked for an insurance company for ten years before. For those who don't know, insurance is a necessity that should be available and affordable to all of us. I remembered when I started to work at Greyhound, I had to go to the emergency room. I had insurance, so I got good health care there, but that wasn't the case for everybody. At the same time, a man came with a broken leg, he fell down from a tree, and it took him forever to get registered.

"Do you have insurance?" the nurse asked him.

"No," he answered.

"How will you pay the bills?" asked the nurse.

"F—— you," he said. "Don't you see that I have a broken leg and need a doctor?"

I sadly understood why he cursed at the nurse. When you're in pain and somebody asks you those dumb questions, it's no fun at all. He resembled one of the rednecks who do believe that the government bureaucracy should pay for insurance. Having insurance in America is a real luxury. As we all know, if you don't have a job, health insurance is a privilege reserved for certain people. The out-of-pocket costs are so high that only rich people can afford coverage. God knows how many employers can't afford to pay for their employees' insurance. I didn't see the rest of the nonsense of the man with the broken leg, because another nurse called me to go inside. I think that everyone should have life insurance—no discussion. In the world we are living in, having insurance is a protection for your family and assurance for your health and financial peace of mind. We did believe in angels' protection, but faith or not, we knew that angels never come with a check from God to pay the medical bills. Help yourself by having medical insurance, and the sky will help you by giving you good physicians. That is one of the reasons I stood for Obamacare, which was the best health care reform in the country. Those who don't need insurance might say that it's bad, but I'll be always grateful to President Obama for implementing insurance for all in America. Without it, I don't know what I would've done when I had to stop working due to medical reasons. It didn't provide like my employer's insurance did, but I could fill my monthly prescription, thanks to you, Mr. President!

23

The Grotesque Irony of Fate

Soon, I was able to afford the down payment to build a family house in a quiet neighborhood, bordered by farms. I chose the place myself. As usual, Sam didn't care about the house's details, and he approved whatever I wanted. Six months later, we moved into a very comfortable four-bedroom home. I loved it. However, we had a hard time affording to furnish that house. Sam and I were not making much money, and we could only manage to buy furniture little by little, and even at that, we bought a lot of secondhand pieces. On Sunday, August 23, 1992, we finally repainted and installed all the furniture we'd bought, one piece after another, which had accumulated in the garage. Friends came over and told us that there was a hurricane coming. It wasn't a big deal for us. We never thought that Mother Nature would be so inconsiderate. After we finished decorating the house, we perched on the inside balustrade to look at our nice work. We felt very happy to be able to put our new things in the living room and the dining room.

We forgot about the coming hurricane. Fatigued by a such challenging day, we showered and went to bed. As soon as we turned on the TV, we realized that the news wasn't good, that the hurricane was coming fast and furiously toward Miami. I should've known what was coming. This was the pattern of my life. A time of full happiness was always a signal to let me know that something else was coming, something that I didn't always like. That night, Sam and I were joyfully fulfilled, but we were exhausted. It wasn't a big deal, we thought. We had never seen a hurricane before. We put some tape on the glass windows and sliding doors, and that was all about it. My son was watching TV, and on the news, they were warning people. It just didn't occur to us that something from nature, which I'd made my friends in my childhood, could so viciously disservice me.

Scott was still awake, watching TV. Silently, he came into our bedroom, and with his serious face, informed us about the powerful storm. Its original plan had gone askew and it was predicted to make landfall in Miami-Dade. Per the news, the hurricane was careening toward Broward. I always believed Scott, even though he was only eleven years old. He knew about everything—like father, like son. He liked to watch the planet and animal channels on TV. We immediately turned on the television, and what we saw on the weather broadcast made us really rethink our ambivalence. The hurricane had changed its course and was on its way toward Homestead and the surrounding area. A few seconds later, he was back, telling us that the eye was coming straight toward us. We didn't know what a hurricane's eye was, but by instinct, Sam said to me that it would be wise to fix a bag with some emergency clothes and important papers, so I did. I went to the kids' bedrooms, asking them to do the same, to have their backpacks prepared for evacuation, just in case.

Dead tired, we went downstairs to look for a place to sit away from the windows. Around 3:55 a.m., we heard the most awful noise outside—the most awful noise I've ever heard in my life, to this day. At 4:00 a.m., there was silence. We thought it was over, but my son alerted us that the eye hadn't passed through yet. My husband took us to the garage, which he thought would be the safest place because it had no windows. I thought we might stay in the half-bathroom downstairs, but his instinct told him otherwise. We stayed inside the car, which we covered with a mattress, and we pressed the front bumper into the garage door so it wouldn't open. By 4:15 a.m., we heard a cacophony of sounds, different from the first one, which lasted no more than a few minutes. The noise was a mixture of everything in our house clattering around and crying for help: cracking wood, walls, stairs, and furniture, shattering glass windows, the two front trees being unearthed from their homes, all singing with disturbing dissonance. Our sofa flew into the stomach of the hurricane, breaking the sliding glass door on its passage. Suddenly, there was the deep silence, a silence like a menace.

We debated whether we should go out and see the damage or remain in the stuffy, hot car. Lamentably, no real answer came to us. Scott's duty was over. He saved us with his warnings, but now it was up to us, the adults, to decide what to do next. Our curiosity was too strong to ignore any longer. Sam went outside first, and when he called us, we all rushed out of the car. What we saw was beyond what we anticipated. The wall of Steven's bedroom had collapsed over the other children's bedroom, and another wall had crumbled toward the stairs, forming a barricade and preventing us from getting any closer. All our things and furniture were either broken or misplaced. My couch was reposing in the backyard, waiting for something to tell it why is was there. Hurricane Andrew had passed, but it had destroyed almost everything we had. We'd only enjoyed our remodeled home for a few hours. The fresh paint peeled from the wall like wallpaper, and some of our family pictures and diplomas vanished forever into the air. The only thing it'd left behind was five broken hearts.

In my desolation, I was only able to think, *Vanity…everything was in vain.* What took us a year to build and accumulate was shattered in a manner of minutes, like in the story of Sodom and Gomorrah. The trees in front of every house on the block had disappeared, even the roots. The grass was a golden, yellowish color, as if an atomic bomb had bombarded the place. We were roofless and emotionally confused, wondering *What will we do?* and *Where will be go?* I couldn't help but wonder, was the curse of my life still after me? Why was I part of this? I could've built my house somewhere else. The hurricane could've missed us. However, there wasn't time for those kinds of questions, nor was there time to lament. We needed to find a place to stay. We had to focus on what was next.

In retrospect, I shouldn't have called it a curse. We weren't alone in this situation. It was just another low section of my life. Quickly, I changed my perspective and tried to see it not as a setback but as a change—maybe even for the better. I had to stay focused and keep a positive mind-set so that I wouldn't start screaming! I knew that if we couldn't stay focused on the positives, we would surely be blind to the miracles that happened around us. We were alive, and that's all that mattered. I always tried to stay positive, no matter what happened in my life. It was all part of my destiny, I thought. Also, I had insurance, which helped me keep looking forward. I called my homeowner's insurance company right away, even before I hit the road to find a place for my family to stay. My telephone was still working. The company reassured me that they'd take care of everything and that they'd be there to help in three days. Heartbroken, we left the house with our small bags and ended up at a friend's house in Kendall. On our way there, we couldn't stop gaping at the devastation that'd occurred in a blink of an eye only a few hours ago. We went back to the house to assess the damage and to wait over there for the insurance agent. Gas was difficult to be found, we couldn't make two trips. My fears and emotions were no longer controlling me. "We will start over again," I said. "We will rebuild our home." This doggedness became our declaration in life. There was always something to spice up our existence I called it the salt of life, because salt is in every food, no matter what diet you're on.

    I never got bored because there was continuously something to think or worry about. I always wanted to define life. What's it in reality? Lately, this has become an obsessive question of mine, and it doesn't have a real answer. Everyone describes it according to their *train de vie,* their way of living. For me, it means our passage from birth to death with uncouth, unexpected complications. It's an adventure. We tried so hard to accomplish the makeover of our house and suffered a year of saving and deprivation, and it was all gone in a moment. We wanted to cry, screech out from our frustration, but when we looked around us and saw all the devastation, we backed down and said, "We are not alone." I realized that all we should say is, "Thanks to God for his protection and to my son for his knowledge and warnings. We are all alive and safe, and my neighbors and friends are as well." As I said before, I believe in insurance. Along with my marriage certificate, the children's birth registrations and their green cards, I'd packed my homeowner's insurance policy, which at the time, included flood and windstorm protection for an insignificant cost. The insurance company, Aetna, was very reliable, and just like they'd promised, arrived three days after the hurricane and paid for everything including a hotel room for a month, but there were no vacant hotel rooms or apartments. After a few days of living at our best friend's house in Kendall, we finally found a place to stay. We were very happy that we would soon be sleeping in warm, cozy beds in a place we could call home again. We stayed there for three months, but it didn't take too long for my children to show their discontent. They went to a new school there and weren't happy campers, especially after their bicycles were stolen from the backyard. They missed their friends at their old school and in our community. That was the last drop in our overflowing vase. Likewise, Sam wanted to go back to reconstruct our property. We all decided to go back despite the damage. That was the first time we truly listened to the children. Most of the time, parents decided everything, but this time, we let the children guide us. We decided to return home no matter what, and we all agreed on that. We returned to rebuild our home. We all slept in the family room at the beginning, while the reconstruction was in progress, which was really the only room in the house that was safe. The dust and noise didn't bother us. We were finally home.

During the rebuilding process, we actually had so much fun. We reached out to our neighbors. They had barbeques in the street for the entire neighborhood. Most of the people in our community were military personnel. They'd moved from many different states to work at the Air Force base nearby. There were no break-ins, and we were well-protected. For three months, we left everything inside even though the doors were broken. When we came back, everything was intact. We slept with both eyes closed. The military people living in the community made it safe for the civilians. Food was shared among us as well as information, such as where to find free bottles of water. We helped each other and tried to get to know our neighbors better. There were no fences to separate us anymore. The hurricane left us with none, as if to instruct us to step out of our comfort zones, as if saying, "Get to know your neighbors and be friendly with each other!" Before the storm, we didn't even know the names of our nearest neighbors because we were always too busy or tired to say hi or inquire for their names. Now, however, we were all together like a real community. The neighborhood was as an open book without restrictions. Some of the houses didn't even have front doors. If one of us heard something, for example, where they were giving out goods to victims of the storm, we would go door-to-door to spread the word.

My husband did a big part of the reconstruction work himself, including building a longer inside balcony, which I'd always dreamed of having. Contractors redid the roof and the big stuff. Sam even employed someone to help him. Soon, our home looked better than it had before, with new and more expensive furniture. I don't know the reason why the storm happened, but we were all better off than we'd been before. I truly believe that we must perpetually start over and over again as we move through the stages of life. There is no peace on earth. We always have to keep on going. Keep hoping and have faith. Life is all about good days and bad days, a mixture of joy and tribulation. The end is death, which I believe isn't really an end either, but a chance to restart another life someplace else as a new human specimen.

After the storm, my workplace's administration was good enough to let me have a week off with pay to find a place to live. They also gave me an allowance for the kids' clothes and a loan for the rest of our needs. I continued to go to work while my house was under reconstruction, and everybody was very good to me there. Life continued. Little by little, I reclaimed my existence as it was before. That same year, I lost my best friend, godmother of my son, Mary, in Haiti from a car accident. She'd come to see me in Miami just a year ago. She was very proud of her godchild, Junior. It was a Sunday morning. The telephone rang, and Sam picked it up. As he was talking, I could see his expression change, but when I asked him why, he couldn't tell me and said that was nothing. I believed him. Men control their emotions very strangely, by using their masculinity to solve problems. Later on, he found the bravery to let me know that Mary had died, which is what the call had been about. I was sad and upset. How could he have kept quiet about it—having sex and making breakfast when he knew that she was dead? Is that right? I wouldn't have eaten if I'd known beforehand. He lied to me. I respected what he did in order to protect me, but at the same time, I couldn't forgive his selfishness and coldness during a moment like this. I'd lost one of my best friends at an early age, thirty-five, and I was helpless and going about my life in ignorance.

A saying goes, "We are helpless twice in life: the day we were born, and the day we find out that we have an incurable sickness." I believe, however, that this kind of circumstances makes it three. I lost my friend and could never bring her back to life to see her. I missed her so much. I couldn't stop visualizing her dead. I had nightmares about her almost every night. Not too long ago, we'd gone to Falls Mall during Christmastime. We laughed, shared secrets, and had a gorgeous time, and now she was gone like when a feather flies away. Without justification, the wind blows it away, farther and farther. You can run after it, but you won't be able to catch it, it just disappears forever. Life is like this. We arrive with lot of expectations and we leave without admonitory. Mary was too young to join the dead people in the beyond. A year later, her husband passed away from sickness, leaving their three underage children orphans. Talk about bad luck. Those poor children. I cannot picture their souls when they had to say goodbye to their mother and father and make their aunt's house their home. We don't know our futures, and we can't erase or add anything to our destinies. Mary had planned to accomplish lots for her three youngsters, but she didn't plan to die so early and to leave them behind. How could she change her destiny? There isn't such a thing. We're all born with our own fate. Everyone has their own path, and it's not changeable or correctable.

24

Full House

IN NOVEMBER 1995, MY godchild Clara came to see me in Miami. Her mother, my aunt on whom I'd afflicted so many problems when I was in high school, was very ill. She had ovarian cancer. First, she'd had breast cancer that was completely removed, but two years later, a malignant tumor came back in the other breast, and by the time they could do something about it, it'd already spread to her ovary. She was dying. Clara was the oldest of her five siblings, and her mom wanted her to have a break from being emotionally and financially involved in her illness. She sent her on vacation to stay with us in Miami. Two days after her arrival, I received a collect call from her mom in Haiti, demanding that I take care of Clara after she was gone. Sam and I didn't know how to answer, given the circumstances, but we accepted anyway. Clara's mother wanted her to stay with us and supplicated us not to send her back. That was a very difficult task because she was an adult, not a child. In the United States, of course, we couldn't decide something like that for a grown-up. For her peace of mind, we said yes, but that we'd need to consult her daughter on the matter. The fatality happened sooner than we could've imagined. Four days after, on Clara's birthday, they called to let us know that she'd departed. What a fateful gift to have your mother pass away on your birthday. It was unbearable for her. Sam went with her to the funeral in Haiti, but because I'd promised her mother that she could stay with us, I instructed Sam not to come back without her.

I deeply regretted that I couldn't go to the funeral to see her one last time and say goodbye. I had to stay in America with the children. She wasn't only my aunt but my big sister. I was raised by her, sang with her, and resided for more than four years at her house during my teen years. It took me a long time to get used to her departure. When I was alone, when Clara couldn't see or hear me, I sang and cried in grief. But I had to be stalwart. She was already a very steeled person. She wouldn't show me when she cried either, but I knew that inside she was screaming at the loss her mom at such a young age. She was horrified to see things around her take such a drastic turn so quickly. She had to pack and leave her family and her country behind right after the funeral. She often told us that she felt guilty for letting her mom have a second surgery. What she didn't know was that destiny never lies. It was written as it was written, and she couldn't have changed a step of her mother's footpath. We all feel some guilt when we lose a loved one because we need a reason or something to hold onto and to blame. I was pleased to have her with me, and she seemed to be happy in our home. In a way, that part was good. I was willing to do my best not to betray the dead. I vowed to keep my promise to her mother, and Clara became like a daughter to me.

For a long time, my mother came to visit twice a year for summer vacation and in December, but soon, she moved in with us permanently. After her sister's death, the people were stampeded out of Haiti. Back home, they were killing people in the streets for no apparent reason. My cousin, the priest, got shot in the leg and had his car stolen. The security there was very bad. Like birds do before the cold season, Haitians were flying to America and anywhere else where they could feel safe.

So our family grew from five people to seven people, all of whom shared four bedrooms. Both my mother and Clara filled in for US residency with the department of immigration. It was so wonderful to have a full table on Sundays for dinner. We discussed current events and difficulties and what had happened to each of us during the week, and we sat around a table of Haitian soul food:

macaroni gratin, rice, bean soup, meat or poultry, salad, and cake, all prepared by me. After lot of practicing and experimenting with crazy ingredients in my food, I cannot say that I became a *Cordon Bleu,* but I became a good cook. We were all grieving and coping. I'd lost my favorite aunt, my mother had lost her little sister, and Clara had lost her mother. We were all grieving behind our inexpressive appearances.

(By the way, I still experiment with my food. I've never been able to follow a recipe word-for-word. I'm never able to say exactly what ingredients I've used to make something because I always improvise. But isn't life itself a daily experiment? We must always seek to enliven things so we don't get fed up with the same stuff.)

25

An Alley through Sicknesses

ONE NIGHT, I GOT a headache, and not the kind of headache I was used to having. It was a sensation inside one eye that made me touch my eyelid while I lay in bed. It was very swollen. I realized that the orbital globe overpowered my eyebrow in size. I went to look at my face in the mirror, and to my stupefaction, my right eye was so big that it seemed to be closer to my nose than the other one was. I was a becoming a monster, sleeping next to Sam, and he didn't know it yet. I went back to bed but couldn't find a good position to rest my head. It was very uncomfortable. In the obscureness of the bedroom, I was thinking that maybe I'd inherited some kind of spiritual power, maybe the power to move or elevate items without touching them. I'd watched too many *Bewitched* episodes, that's for sure. I concentrated so intensely on that thought that I was lost in time, misplaced and confused out of my human mind. I was waiting to transform into a legendary animal. I couldn't even sleep like a normal person. I had to be half sitting; otherwise, my eye would get bigger and more painful. It felt like my eye was coming out of its socket.

After a moment of hesitation, I shook Sam to show him this paranormal transformation of my body. I thought that I was changing into a surrealistic creature and that he had to be awakened to witness it for his testimony. I concentrated so hard on the possibility that I was able to move things with my thoughts, so much that I felt the need to go to the bathroom. Sam nearly choked when he saw me. He silently looked at me, turning my face right to left and left to right with his hand. Then he remembered the last time I had an eye problem, and as if weren't a big deal at all, he calmly murmured, "Here it is again."

The first time it happened, I never had the chance to see it for myself. I was at the hospital regaining consciousness from the anesthesia and recovering from the half circle that they'd cut under my belly. I never pictured my face with a horrible eyeball like this. The next day, I urgently requested an appointment to see my PCP, Dr. Joe. He referred me to an ophthalmologist, Dr. H. After many tests, he told me that there was nothing he could do about it. It was called an orbital varix tumor, he explained, and there was no cure for it.

"Do I have to live for the rest of my life with this unpleasant pain and sporadic disfigurement?" I asked.

"I'm sorry about that, Mrs. G. Let's hope that they come with a something for it in the future." He continued. "I'll see you every year for follow-up."

After that episode, it didn't bother me again for a long time. Every so often, I would feel a little discomfort, nausea, tiredness, chills, or fever at night, or mild pain in different parts of my body, which made it so that I went to the doctor very often. My primary care physician was Dr. Joe, who was tall but not handsome but not ugly either. Very mannish. The sound of his voice made me feel like I was in the same room with Eric Roberts, the celebrity actor who I had an eye for. Everybody has actors that they like more than others, and mine were him and Alain Delon, the French guy. I liked Dr. Joe; he made sure that he knew my family's story well so that he could find out why I had so many complications. Now, I laugh at myself; if only I'd known that, those small pains were nothing at all in comparison to what I would go through later! When I went to see Dr. Joe, I paid more attention to what I wore and tried to look chic. I fix my lipstick, seeking his compliments. It's so stupid, but women like to be awarded for their troubles, especially when we have been married for ages and don't get attention from our husbands. We're happy when we find it somewhere else.

I was taking vitamins, but nothing seemed to make my new troubles go away. Despite all this, I was doing well. I was going to work regularly and partying with my friends. Life was good. These symptoms were mild. My PCP was tenacious and eager to discover the problem. I was too young to be like that, he said. It had to be something. He made me laugh by telling me that my file was so big that they had to split it in two, like an old lady who'd been with the office for many decades.

"Are you sure you're not an alien from outer space?" he jokingly asked.

"Oh yes, I am," I said, laughing. "I even have an alien number."

One day, a blood donor truck came to my workplace, and human resources was looking for blood donor volunteers. I volunteered. I was very proud to have the sticker on my blouse that stated, "I donated blood." A few days after giving blood, I received a letter from the Red Cross stating that my blood was abnormal and to follow up with my family doctor. They didn't have to say it twice. I was curious to find out what the company meant by "abnormal." How come so many things in my body were so abnormal? I scheduled an appointment to see Dr. Joe. I showed him the letter, and he immediately called a nurse and ordered a blood test, which was done in his office. At least six tubes of blood were withdrawn. I was very excited to find out what was going on.

I won't ever forget Dr. Joe's persistence. But also because of my good spirits and my desire to help save someone else's life, I ended up saving myself. I was able to find out about my disease in the early stages. I was also able to bargain with it by changing the way I ate and stopping over-the-counter medicines that could do further damage. I really didn't think that I had something major, but I wanted to know what troubled me. Dr. Joe called me himself early in the morning. I was at work. He asked if I could come to see him at my convenience, that the results had come back abnormal. I was very happy to know that pretty soon, I would found out what kind of devil was sucking on me inside. I decided to go to see him the same day, in the afternoon. This is my nature. I'm impatient.

When he entered the exam room, his gray-greenish eyes were avoiding my presence. He sat down with his face affixed to the file as if he hadn't seen it yet. He went straight to the point, which wasn't his usual habit. After a moment, which seemed to me like an eternity, he spoke to me in a groping, ceremonial, aristocratic way.

"How do you feel, Mrs. G.?" Without letting me answer, he continued, his head still lowered. "Looking good as usual?"

Was that a compliment or a question? I paid it no mind.

"I'm okay," I answered, disinterested in his flattery for once. I just wanted to hear the diagnosis. I could see that he was searching for the right way to give me the news.

He finally looked at me. "I have bad and good news for you. Which one would you prefer to hear first?"

"I hand off that choice to you, the doctor, who will know which order is more appropriate," I responded.

"You…you have…the hepatitis C virus. The good news is there is a treatment for it."

"What is it?" I naively asked.

My question was answered by other questions, as if he was interrogating me like a criminal.

"Have you been taking drugs?"

"What kind of drugs?" I asked. I was lost. I didn't know what he was talking about.

"Recreational drugs…smoking marijuana…sharing needles with others?"

My eyes opened widely. I was starting to get frustrated and upset. "I don't get it," I said innocently.

"I mean—have you shared needles with other people? That's probably how you got it—by sharing a needle with someone who had that virus in their blood."

"Why would I share needle with other people? Please explain!" I became edgy because I had no clue about what he was saying. He could see that I was getting nervous, and he promptly responded in slow motion, accentuating the way he spoke as if he was educating a child. Then again, I needed to be educated.

"This disease you have is caused from blood-to-blood interactions. When a person comes in contact with a person who already has the virus, they often get it. For example, a group of people might share one needle to insert drug into their vein. Cocaine or other drugs. They might use the same syringe over and over, transmitting the virus to others." He paused. "Sometimes, people reuse the same needle with multiple partners, which is the most common means of transmission for hepatitis C. That's what I meant. You can be infected sexually too or through IV drug use. Patients who use drugs are at high risk for this malady, so that is why I asked you the first question."

I was pensive. I didn't know what to say. I wasn't shocked by the diagnosis itself because I didn't yet know what is was, but I was blown away by the questions that I had to answer.

"Did you have a blood transfusion in the past? he asked.

"Yes, when I gave birth to my youngest son, in 1984."

"You already answered my next question! In 1984, huh? That is how you got the virus. Back then, we didn't have the technology to screen blood before transfusions. I will send you to a specialist, a gastroenteritis, for treatment, and I will request a blood test for your husband also."

"What the heck is it? And how does it possibly involve my husband?" I muttered to myself. *Heck* was English slang I had just learned. I used it as a curse in many of my sentences to stay cool. I left the office, smiling and talking to the nurse like normal, without realizing that she was probably disgracing me as a drug user. Maybe she didn't read what was on the chart: "hep C from blood transfusion." Honesty, I thought it was like a flu virus, that I could just take an antibiotic and be done with it. On my way home, I kicked myself for not asking him why he didn't just give me the antibiotic himself instead of sending me to see a specialist. I didn't know a thing about that disease.

The next day, I went to work, and everybody asked me what the doctor told me. I told them the truth. Some of them knew about the ailment, and looking back, they probably thought that I was contagious and looked at me with apprehension. Anyway, I didn't pay attention to that. I was a nescience about my blood-sucking killer. I wasn't aware either of the gravity of my illness. I shouldn't told the whole world that I had HCV, and I would never have known that some people would see me as a contaminated person. When I told my husband, he went cold, like he had seen a ghost. He told me that he didn't know anything about that disease. I was very surprised that he didn't give me a lecture because I knew that he knew everything. I called him a *conosco* (Spanish word for a person who knows everything). He could keep up a conversation about any subject, from medicine, to law, to world history, but this time, he knew *nada*. As I thought about it later, I supposed that he didn't want to bog me down or scare me. The next day, I called to schedule an appointment with Dr. R. S.

Within two days, I was seen by Dr. R. S. He was petite, with a brain larger than his body. He had many awards hanging on his wall. My PCP had referred me to him because of his reputation as one of the best specialists in the area. However, that made him very arrogant and rude. I noticed it the moment I entered the room. I didn't go to the consultation room first but directly to his office. With a smile, I said "Good afternoon" as politely as possible, but he replied with a dry "Hi" without lifting up his head. Startling me, he began abruptly reading my record that my PCP had sent to him in advance. He sat behind a big desk piled with all kinds of medical papers and files that crested so high that I barely could see him. He explained to me that he was going to send me out for more tests and that he would schedule a biopsy of my liver to find out how bad it was already damaged.

"From there, we can start the interferon treatment, which means three injections per week and five pills every day," he said. "The treatment will last twelve months. It has some side effects."

He questioned me about my lifestyle. Right off the bat, he didn't hesitate to ask me if I was using drugs. I was sure that Dr. Joe had noted the cause of my disease in his memo, but Dr. R. S. had to hear it from my mouth, I guess.

I answered him with tears filling my eyes. "No, I'm not and wasn't. I had a blood transfusion in 1984." I told him everything so there wouldn't be more embarrassing questions. Then there was the silence, silence like he'd not expected to see me so vulnerable.

Finally, he repeated what I'd just told him. "You had a blood transfusion? When?"

"Yes, I had it in 1984 after a hemorrhage from a rupture of the uterus."

I had to repeat the story to him. Maybe he couldn't remember all of it at once. He was writing notes like a collegian but then stopped to explain to me what my disease was all about—without reticence, just the rough truth. Then he called the nurse in to take me to the exam room. After a long time, he finally came in and asked me to lie down on the examination bed. As if he suddenly realized that he had given me too much of his time, he rapidly put both of his hands on the right side of my abdomen, pressing my stomach down as if he was giving me CPR, which at the time didn't hurt me at all. After that, he stretched and lifted my eyelids, and made me open my mouth to look into my throat. Afterward, he left me without saying a word. The nurse stayed with me and withdraw more blood for more blood tests. His character didn't bother me, I was more concerned about my health than his ill-mannered behavior.

The nurse gave me some pamphlets about the disease. I knew then exactly what HCV was: the quiet oppressor that wouldn't spare my life, the pitiless killer that had no compassion toward anyone. I drove home with my face wet with tears. I screamed and didn't care what people in the street thought of me. I needed to empty my chest from the humiliation and worriment that this illness had caused me. I went home and was inconsolable. I tried to explain to Sam what I'd gone through at the doctor's office, what exactly my disease was, and what needed to be done as care. He was powerless. All he could do was to listen. After a moment, he murmured, "Let's go out to relax a little." He spoke like his voice had run out.

26

The First Treatment

A FEW DAYS LATER, as scheduled, I went to Baptist Hospital to have a biopsy. As advised, I hadn't eaten anything since midnight the night before. I soon learned that my procedure was delayed from 10:00 a.m. to 1:00 p.m. I was very hungry. I didn't know why it was rescheduled, and when I asked, they told me something banal. The doctor had to deal with an emergency before he treated me, they said. I was novice in that kind of medical environment, but I asked the nurses again and again when he would come. I wanted to at least drink a glass of juice, but the nurses refused to give me anything at all. I was already there, so what could I possibly do but wait? As usual, without saying a word to me, not even an excuse for being three hours late, the doctor finally arrived and started the short procedure.

He made a tiny little hole under my ribs as if it wasn't a big deal. He was used to it, sure, but for me, it was the first time. I had local anesthesia, but that didn't go very deeply under my skin. I wasn't asleep because I needed to hold my breath at certain points during the procedure. Before he started, he'd only told me how it would feel when he pulled out the piece of the tissue from my liver. I could never have imagined that the pain would be so uncongenial and uncomfortable. I felt everything. When he pulled out that little bit of my organ, my heart had stopped. For me, it felt like the end. That was an awful sensation and a bloody terrible experience. I was dead for a moment, no doubt. The pain was indescribable, and afterward, I had to lie on my right side for an hour. After less than an hour, the pain was gone. I stayed the night so that they could check on me for side effects, and then they released me the next day. As usual, wherever I went, something strange happened. Once, in the night, I woke up to go to the bathroom to find that room floor was wet with water, which was coming from I-don't-know-where.

Five days after, the nurse called me to come back and review the results with Dr. S. I went, and he told me that my liver was already damaged and that my alfa-fetoprotein level was already high, meaning that I was at great risk of liver cancer. I would have to consider having the treatment as soon as possible, as well as alpha-interferon therapy.

"Is interferon a kind of antibiotic?" I asked him.

He looked at me as if I was totally ignorant. "No, you will be on treatment for one year, as I already told you. You will take three shots per week and five pills every day. The treatment has some mild side effects, which are tolerable for some patients, but others complain that it makes them ill."

Yeah! He didn't want to tell me the truth, that the treatment would kill me before the illness did. I stupidly kept on asking him about my liver.

"What makes you think that I should consider myself at risk for liver cancer in the forthcoming years?" I said softly.

"Don't you know that when your liver is damaged and your fetoprotein level is as elevated as yours is, your chance of having cancer is higher than that of a normal person?"

I persisted, posing more questions. I needed to know. "Do I have to use condoms for intercourse?"

"You should. Did your husband have a blood test yet?"

"Not yet, but Dr. Joe suggested it."

"Well, he should do so as soon as possible to find out if he caught it too."

Wow, I thought. It was officially serious. I didn't stop asking questions. I had so much going on in my mind that that I couldn't stay silent. I kept going, politely searching for the proper words even though my mind was racing.

THE DAILY BATTLE FOR A NORMAL LIFE

"Dr. S., I heard that the liver can regenerate itself. Is it true?"

"Yes, but not in your case," he answered. "When the liver is damaged due to a virus, it's permanently damaged, period. You have chronic hepatitis C. We can't fix your liver unless we cure the disease."

That wasn't the answer I was expecting. I wanted him to say, "Yes, it can!"

"Why not, Doctor?" I said.

He pretended not to hear me. Man, that doctor was ill-mannered. Only his mother could love him, not even his father. I guess that his knowledge in the field went to his head to compensate for his small size. He was probably less than five feet tall, which probably gave him some kind of Napoleon complex. He gave me some papers to read, and as usual, he left me with the nurse for more details. So often, doctors think that their patients are supermen and that everything they prescribe will be both bearable and acceptable. How can you know so much about my body after only two visits? What do you know that I don't know? What gives you the right to imply that the treatment wouldn't hurt me?

My husband didn't want to have a blood test, but I insisted. I told him that from now, we'd have to use condoms.

"During all the time that we didn't know about it, we never used protection, so why should I start now?"

"Because now, unlike then, in the eyes of God, we aren't innocent anymore. We know. He spares people from harm when they don't know what they're doing. On the cross, Jesus said, 'Father, forgive them, for they do not know what they're doing.'"

That was a very risky way to show me support, but I liked it anyway. To tell the truth, at that time, I wanted to hear this answer from him. He was sincere, and life granted him the gift of not having to deal with this disease. Still, to this day, he's safe, which made me really believe that the risk is very low if you are in a long-term monogamous relationship. Sam's blood test came back negative.

Back to Dr. S.'s response: Was he telling me that I wasn't normal anymore? Was he saying that I might have to live with that stress for the rest of my life? Conversely, I felt all right. At forty-two years old, I couldn't die! Was he trying to warn me about how harsh it can be to live with HCV? Perhaps the rudeness in his language helped, in a sense—not for my self-esteem, of course, but for my health—because I took his diagnosis very seriously. Right away, I decided to start the treatment in the hopes that I could live a normal life as a normal person. That was my goal.

With a tap on my shoulder, Dr. S. was gone, leaving me with the nurse, who had seen so many patients like me with different stories. Her eyes were telling me that she didn't believe my version of the story one bit, because of my ethnicity, no doubt. She thought I must've been on drugs or that I was so mentally instable that I couldn't know if I was or not. She said to me that she would request authorization from my insurance company and order the medication. As soon she received the treatments, she said, she would call me to return to the office to pick it up and to teach me how I could administer my shots myself.

"Can I get the interferon from the pharmacy?" My voice sounded crazy, even to my own ears. I wasn't myself anymore.

"No, Mrs. G. You either get it from our office, or we send it directly to your home, but in that case, somebody has to be at your house at the time of the delivery. Also, the shots have to be kept refrigerated," she firmly explained.

In my head, I felt incredulous. *I don't have any pain or discomfort now*, I thought. *Why should I go through all this misery? However, do I have a choice?* I asked myself that question again and again. Rather than live with an uncertain future, I figured it was better to deal with the side effects and get cured. In life, you always have a choice, but your destiny makes you pick the one that suits your mission on earth. I wouldn't pick "later." "Later" isn't who I am. My decision was made. The doctor sent a letter to the human resources department at my job so that my boss would be aware that I'd only be working three days a week. To think, I was excited about it! As planned, on the following Friday afternoon, I left work early and went to the doctor's office, frightening inside but audacious outside. The nurse injected me with the first shot and gave me boxes of shots, pills, and syringes, enough to last a month. She told me to buy alcohol pads at any pharmacy to clean my skin before I injected myself. So that's what I did.

THE DAILY BATTLE FOR A NORMAL LIFE

At bedtime, I took two ribavirin pills plus a Tylenol tablet to prevent me from getting a fever. The first night wasn't too bad. By 3:00 a.m., I had a mild fever, so I took another Tylenol and had warm tea that I had in a thermos on my side table. I couldn't sleep after that, anxious about my fever and what would come next. I spent the entire following Saturday in bed resting, and the next day, the fever was completely gone. I was fine. On Monday morning, I went to work. When I came back, I prepared everything for the second shot, but this time, the fever lasted longer, and I was nauseated. In meantime, I was also taking five pills a day, three in the morning and two at night.

After a month, I went to Quest for a blood test. The viral load in my blood was the same, and nothing had really changed. I continued the treatment, the same process at the same time on Monday, Wednesday, and Friday nights, plus five pills every day. Human resources, at the recommendation of my doctor, gave me permission to use my sick time to stay home and rest in the days after I had interferon, so I got paid time off. I wasn't going to give up, but I started feeling depressed and irritable. Suddenly, people needed to tread carefully around me and pick the right day and time to talk to me. I was going through a very traumatic time. I was poisoning my body without even the certitude that it might work. The HCV wasn't an easy target. My chance of remission was only 40 percent. Was I lucky enough to fall within that range? One day, almost three months later, I was home alone. Sam went to work, my mother went to her medical care program, the children were at school. I was walking around the house, talking to myself. I felt that I should let myself fall down the stairs. I cannot explain that strange urge. I call it strange because at that time, it was a normal thing for me to let myself whirl down. I didn't feel like I wanted to commit suicide, but I thought that if I died, it would be a deliverance rather than a tragedy. I was getting confused. A real darkness veiled my mind. My brain was focused on my well-being, and it told me that this action would be good for me, the only thing that could make me feel right again. I remembered that I stood on the balcony inside our house looking down at the living room, thinking I might let myself fall down. I had a baby's mind, completely void of realism. For me, it wouldn't be a suicide at all, just something that popped up in my brain. I thought that it would be beneficial for me, for some reason, that it would ease my wild sensations. I didn't have pain or a fever, but I was occupied by the darkness. I felt lost and worthless. Precisely that moment, the telephone rang and woke me up from the darkness.

"Hello?" I said

"Is this Mrs. G.?" It was Dr. S. himself.

"Yes, it is," I said.

"The treatment isn't working. Stop everything. My assistant will call you soon." He spoke like a robot repeating something it was programmed to say. He went straight to the point as if his time was limited. I didn't have time to ask him any questions. He hung up. Less than five minutes later, a nurse called to schedule an appointment for me to see him. I regained my consciousness. I already forgot about the action I was about to commit. My mind had another preoccupation: defeat. *This is it*, I thought. My hope to be free of this virus was gone. The news was like a wake-up call from my guardian angel. I suddenly recognized the weakness that had almost killed me a few minutes ago. I trembled at the idea that my mind could play such a dangerous trick on me.

I went back to bed to cry, as if mourning my own life. I cried and yelled as much as I could. My brain told me to keep going—cry more to relieve the pessimist ghost inside me. There was no alternative, no other cure. "What am I going to do now?" I wailed. I merely wanted to be released from the disease because of the shame it caused me when I went to any doctor or lab. The disease was ruining my poise and my dignity. I knew that I'd have to wait for another treatment to become available, perhaps in two or three years. As a matter of fact, I knew I'd have to make a terrible choice: live my life as it was before or be miserable and die. Nothing was going to change the reality. I chose not to let the disappointment attack my brain or bother me too much. I figured that even if I stopped treatments completely, I'd still have plenty of time ahead of me. I decided I would wait for the next option to emerge from scientists and jump on the chance to try something different. If I had to start all over, again and again, I would. I wasn't afraid.

THE DAILY BATTLE FOR A NORMAL LIFE

I remembered the story of Robert the Bruce, who lived in 1306, and the spider that he watched: "The spider swung from one rafter to another, time after time, in an attempt to anchor his web. It failed six times, but on the seventh attempt, it succeeded." You can defeat me once, even twice, but I will continue the fight. I won't give up my battle. As many times as it took, I'd keep fighting until I was well again. By and large, I was in charge of my life. I kept on doing the things that I enjoyed, but the one thing I couldn't control was the burning sensation in my chest and my upper breasts at all times. I had intermittent pain. I took Maalox and Tagamet, but nothing seemed to bring comfort to my dysfunctional gastric system. I was stressed about the HCV. Although it didn't trouble me with symptoms, I knew for fact that it was always there, waiting to ruin my future. I was still upset that the treatment had failed. Even though I was laughing, the laughter only masked my tears.

I had the déjà vu hurt in my stomach and I needed to relieve it. My PCP referred me to a gastroenterologist. Dr. Fred didn't say too much, just told me that he wanted me to have an upper endoscopy test. I tried to make him understand that I'd had one just the year before, but he was sure that it was the only way he could see what was invading my innards. To tell the truth, I started to really like the sensation of anesthesia. That absence of sensation and lack of bodily awareness was genius. I knew for sure that one day, I'd be free from pain and feelings. It was a fast procedure. When I woke up, I thought that they hadn't done anything yet. When they showed me picture of my insides, I wasn't too interested. All I wanted was for the doctor to leave me alone so I could sleep. The anesthetized Olivia had traveled to a magical country, and I wanted to go back. The doctor told my husband that there was some narrowing at the CE junction of my lower esophagus that they'd able to dilate and that there was a polypoid tumor in the greater curve of the stomach that they'd have to remove as well. The duodenal cap and the duodenum were normal. Because of the lower esophagus spasms, food was getting stuck there and didn't travel easily into stomach. That might be the cause of the burning sensation, he explained. He prescribed Levbid and Zantac and said he hoped I felt better soon.

Living with chronic diseases is similar to living normal life, except that you're sick with no chance to get better. Despite all my entreaties to God, nothing changed even a little bit in my life. It became something I just had to live with. I tried living without thinking about death, but I wondered, would that always be possible? How long would I survive? I was alive, and the doctors never gave me an expiration date, so I was happy about that. I can call this being fortunate, sure, but in the Lord's book, this is the way it had to be, so I don't call it being "lucky." I knew that I was just following my own destiny.

I don't like being compared to other people. We each have our own encumbrances, occurrences, and purposes on earth. We cannot know what life has reserved for us, and we don't choose our paths. I believe that I'm still alive on this terrestrial planet because God has willed it so. I'm still on his schedule and approaching his deadline, but I'm living in a wail of mournful apprehension about my future. It's like a suspense series on TV. We like to watch them because we want to know "what's next." This question got stuck in my mind, no matter how hard I tried to fend it off. I asked myself that almost every day, especially when I was in pain. What's next?

I didn't choose to go out into a storm, but throughout my existence, inevitably, the storm has always caught up with me. Sometimes, I feel defenseless and like I have no stamina to help me reach the next stop in life. I consider my ailments to be like tornadoes that have caught me by surprise. I have no resistance to fight off their devastating rage, which hits me with one blow after another. Throughout my life, even when there was no reason to panic, there were many reasons to be afraid of the future. That was the pattern. You won't always get a category-four hurricane, of course, but you need to be prepared for and understand that over time, a category 1 hurricane can turn into a category 4 when you least expect it. The question is how to be prepared for this catastrophe when there are not enough supplies available to you, so do health in that case, and there isn't no other treatment for now.

These days, when it comes to my illness, I'm at the border of category 3, with only one stage separating me from the catastrophic category 4. Medically speaking, this should spell the expiration of my life. I have liver damage. This is a fact, my friends—an eventuality. It isn't a dream. Some people have said to me that healthy people die all the time from car accidents and such. Yes, that's damn true, but it's so easy to say that when you are not in the situation and don't feel what I'm feeling. Let me speak from experience about HCV. It's not a terrible disease when you're in the early stages. Hepatitis means inflammation of the liver, and C is the type (A, B, C). I hope that the scientists don't discover a D, because then hepatitis would become a sort of vitamin! The V stands for *virus*.

At the beginning, when I learned that I'd contracted the virus, I wasn't scared. I didn't throw myself into a panic. I only had a few mild symptoms that occasionally reminded me that I wasn't normal. I thought I could cure it by taking it easy on what I ate and drink. However, I soon learned that the virus had been inside of me for over a decade and that it had gone untreated for so long that it manifested at a dangerous level. I didn't have any symptomatic awareness because HCV operates in a vicious cycle. Obviously, after I knew about it, I had to constantly reckon with the fact that I had something inside of me that could get worse and worse if I didn't take precautions. Safety measures were essential, such as changing my eating habits, drinking little to no alcohol, and not smoking, which I didn't do anyway. The liver is very powerful. It is the largest organ in the human morphology, located on the right side below the diaphragm and slightly above the stomach. Our livers, ostentatiously, fill many major roles in the metabolism—so many you wouldn't imagine. The liver regulates a wide variety of biochemical reactions and acts as a kind of storage place and filter for our systems, removing poisons from air pollution, debris from our food and drink intake, and medications that go to our immune system.

In one word, the liver serves as the detoxifier for the body. We cannot change the filter like we can in a car or air conditioner, but we can keep it clean by intaking less impurities. From the time I was diagnosed with HCV, my doctors told me that my liver wasn't going to be like it was before, clean and smooth, but that I could still be functional if I lived by certain instructions and restrictions. This organ is as important in our metabolism as our heart is and plausibly more important. We always think that the heart is the more vital organ, but what would happen if the liver lost the capacity to filter? All the toxins we intake would clot inside the arteries, leading to atherosclerotic damage and blood clots. At that point, the heart would certainly stop functioning, likely succumbing to stroke or heart attack. This is how powerful the liver is. For some reason, telling people that I have liver damage often seems like nothing to them, but if I said that I had "heart problems," they would be astonished and concerned, wouldn't they? Both organs do amazing jobs in our biological human processes. According to research, HCV has affected more than 3.2 million humans and kills more people than HIV/AIDS does. Since 1989 when it was discovered, scientists have been working relentlessly to come up with a real and efficacious treatment for the non-A and non-B viruses. It has been a big challenge for long time.

    We all need to go to the dentist often to take care of our teeth and gums. A HCV-positive person, however, goes for two reasons; we cannot have bleeding gums. Certainly, it's not always a threat, but if we bleed on our mouths, we might infect our loved ones through kissing. Keep in mind, it's a matter of blood-to-blood contact. My blood cannot touch your blood on the inside. Hepatitis C is all about that. We are not contagious by saliva, air, or physical touch. They say that a good remedy to this ailment is to abstain from stress. Who can do this? Stress is in the air, and we're always breathing it no matter what. Stress becomes more difficult for people with HCV. The best we can do is develop a positive attitude, which is one of the keys to dealing with it. That said, I decided that I wasn't going to be ashamed anymore. I decided that I had to change my unreasonable ways of thinking and that I would tell whoever I wanted to that I had hepatitis C.

    It is a malady like all others. Why should I be embarrassed when I didn't do anything wrong? Friends of mine who were Jehovah Witnesses accused me of being a sinner for taking blood. So be it, I thought. I'm a sinner in your religion, not mine. Instead, religiously speaking, when I went to church, my priest gave wine to the parishioners as a sign of Jesus Christ's blood. "This is my blood," he says. "I give it to you to wash away your sins." Well, if I had to take blood again, I would. Witnesses of Jehovah need to have some blood to wash their poor minds. Without that blood transfusion, I would be fifteen feet under, as they said. I would have been dead twenty-nine years ago. But by receiving blood into my body, I stayed alive and could enjoy my baby son as he grew, as he learned to walk, as he walked the red carpet in LA, and as he became a well-known artist in San Francisco. I'm very grateful to the person who donated my blood. After I germinated that positive mental attitude, I became very confident with myself and happy with my new resolution. "I'll fight that sucker," I said, and I meant it. I would try everything to make my life as normal as I could. I started taking a yoga/meditation class where I learned from a good instructor.

 I don't resent any pain except that of my mind, which from time to time bothers me around the clock. I needed the "shadow of life" to be on my side, not against me. HCV is a dormant killer. It can dramatically change at any time, so I couldn't take the chance of forgetting about it. Whenever there was a trial or something new, I tried it. For five years, I was drowning in the darkness of fear. My disease was like a stranger who followed me around. Years after, it become a critical issue for my health. Even though I tried to live my life and laugh, I was concerned. There was no immunization for HCV and no cure. In 2000, more people than the years before were affected by the disease, and thousands die from it every year all over the world. I know that numerous efforts had been made to find a cure for this virus, like for HIV, but was that going to be enough? The number of people with this disease is surely decreasing with the blood screening test we used now in health care, but we still need to campaign against this virus to prevent it from spreading. People with financial power who could do something about it are ashamed to let society know that they are victims. We discriminate about everything. It should be procedural that everyone who goes to the doctor gets tested for it. If it were more normalized, and people were more informed, we would know what kind of precautions to take. It's so easy to catch that disease and so difficult to get rid of it. We don't all die from liver cancer, jaundice, cirrhosis, and liver failure, we can also die from a heart attack attributed to the malfunctioning of the liver. I don't like using the term "silent killer," because for me, HCV has never been silent in my body. I could always feel the nuisance of something menacing my health with tiredness, body aches, chills, nausea, and fevers at night. We all get these symptoms at one point or another, so I didn't pay great attention to it. I don't deny that for some, it can be completely symptom-less. That's the ruse of it. It's a silent killer for someone who hasn't acknowledged that they have a problem. If you really know your body, however, you can know when something isn't right. I spent a lot of time going to the doctors, trying to find out what could be making me unhealthy. I really thought that I was an alien from another planet. I pledged that I was on earth by mistake and that the inhalation of the air wasn't good for me. I had so many futile problems that made me constantly want to go to the doctor's office. Luckily, I managed to have more good days than despairing ones.

Unfortunately, not all of us have this chance. Other victims might find out late, when cirrhosis, liver failure, or cancer are already present. In the late 1990s and at the beginning of the 2000s, when the disease was first discovered, people talked about this monstrous illness, but as time passed, people became too afraid of criticism and largely chose not to disclose. I understand how hard it is to disclose about HCV to the public or in the media in general. I'm one of those chickens too! Now, we need to talk more about it, to make society aware of our situation. Airing an ad for medication is different than talking about it. The manufacturers only did it to make more money. Even when they found a treatment that could give us a 90 percent chance of remission, it was still not enough because the price was out of reach for most of us, and most insurance policies didn't cover it. Doctors need to catch it earlier to prevent progression. All it takes is a simple blood test. Young people need to be aware that like HIV, HCV is transmissible through blood-to-blood contact and sexual activity. Even if you've never had a blood transfusion in your life or haven't done any recreational drugs, there's a possibility that you've had it in your blood since birth. The abbreviation of HIV and HCV are so similar too, and they're treated in largely the same way. Don't hush our voices like the disease itself. Let's talk about it.

Some studies have shown that the rate of HCV transmission is mild in comparison to that of HAV and HBV, but you must be aware of what can happen and be prudent. How many of us go to the dentist for bleeding gums? It's a blood-to-blood affair, so wake up and get attentive. Living with this illness is stressful because in addition to the symptoms, we also have to control our lifestyles. We must also be attentive that we don't give the disease to someone else, especially family members who we are with most of the time. That said, it isn't as highly contagious as some may think. Let me remind you that I got a blood transfusion in 1984, and it was only in 2000 that my life became tormented by the virus.

27

What's Next?

AFTER THE FIRST FAILED treatment, I tried to live my life as if nothing was wrong with me. It's not that I forgot about it, but I had to make a choice: continue to live my life with a positive attitude or stay constantly worried about my insidious disease. I chose to go to the doctor regularly so that they could monitor my health. I went in for checkup every three months, had a liver ultrasound every six months, had a blood test every month, had a biopsy every three years, and closely watched my diet, as was advised by my doctor. Religiously, I followed all the steps to stay on the top of that disease. I seemed normal to the people around me, but I couldn't negate the fact that inside of me, I had rodent parasites, which scared me sometimes. Any time I heard on the radio or television that someone died while waiting for a liver transplant from liver cancer or failure, I freaked out. This is how frightened I was! I'm human, and my soul weakened sometimes. I felt like I was a condemned person waiting for my execution day. What else could I do but wait and hope that maybe one day, a miracle would find me? Like when the governor calls at the last moment to stop a prisoner's execution! "Stop, he's innocent!" Maybe the disease will become the governor to find me not guilty and to discharge me of any hurt.

Every time I went in for a test or an office visit, I had to explain to the new doctors, nurses, and medical technicians how I'd contracted the disease. Sometimes, even just out of curiosity, even an ultrasound technician would ask, "Why are you here to have a sonogram of the liver?" A nice way to satisfy their curiosity, isn't it? Did all of them believe the response that I gave them? I doubt it, but I didn't care. This chronic illness is a load of burdens that has no end. When I changed doctors, depending on the insurance, I had to be prepared that explanation would be required. Was that normal? Why did the doctors care more about how I got it than how they were going to fight it? How I got it wasn't the problem. I just wanted to get treated for what I had. You already know all the possibilities, and the treatment is the same, no matter how I got it. This is the kind of nonsense that makes people avoid going to the doctor's office.

As soon I was diagnosed with that ailment, I was wantonly rejected by part of society. I was deemed high-risk for all insurance companies. I have been denied life insurance by all companies, and lately, even by my employer. They didn't even have the decency to offer me a higher premium. They just denied me that right. I felt lucky to have medical insurance through my employer; otherwise, I would've had a big problem. There is no way I would've been able to afford the cost of it otherwise. Without medical insurance, I wouldn't even be able to follow up with my doctors. Insurance is right, not a privilege. To repeat President Obama's slogan: "No one should be left without insurance regardless of their preexisting diseases." He was so right about that, and thanks to him, I was able to stay on top of my disease. To this day, I can get medication through Marketplace even though I'm not working anymore. Even though some insurance providers refuse to pay for my HCV treatments, I can still have sonograms to monitor the progress.

Despite all our medical knowledge, only a small percentage of people are organ donors. Why aren't we all? We should consent to giving our organs if we are fortunate enough to have healthy ones at the time of our deaths. I'm not trying to constrain anyone but rather to bring their minds to reason. A cadaver doesn't need a good organ that could be donated to sick, living people who has waited ages for an organ transplant. Doesn't that make sense? I'm sorry to say this in so many words, but please don't be selfish. Sign up to be an organ donor at the time of your death. It's a way to make one last contribution to earth, and your soul will find peace and salvation beyond the threshold of eternity. I won't ever be able to give my organs because of my disease, and there are millions of people like me with the same issue. If your blood is clear of diseases, please sign up to be an organ donor.

Later in life, I decided to get involved in this cause. I started going to group meetings. I became friends with a woman who had already developed cirrhosis. We went to the group meetings together, and holy moly, she ate like a cow while she was on interferon. All her hair was gone, and she wore a wig. Contrarily, I couldn't eat anything, and I was on the same treatment. We're all different, that's for sure. I'm certain that the treatment worked for her because during our friendship, she told me that day after day, her health was improving considerably. She moved away after a while, and I never heard from her again. I went to four of those meetings, but after that, I was too sad and horrified to continue. I wasn't strong enough to see people who were so sick, far worse than I was, fighting for their lives. I couldn't bear to hear it when despite all their battle, someone didn't make it. During my third meeting, I remarked that a man who was always there asking all kinds of question with a feeble voice, wasn't there anymore. I learned that he'd departed suddenly when he didn't respond well to a liver implant.

Life can be so discriminatory. Some of them managed to get rid of HCV for a while via liver transplants, but this is only ever a temporary fix because the virus is ever-present, waiting to destroy the new liver too. Some people lost hope and were crestfallen to a grave level that wasn't movable. I didn't want to see all these calamities that would very likely occur in my own life. I was already afraid of what I had, and I didn't want to hear more sad scenarios or see images of people struggling with cirrhosis, jaundice, cancer, and liver failure, people who were waiting desperately for a liver, a miracle. I was still young, and I didn't want to live with the certitude that I would turn into them. My disease was still at an early stage, and I intended to live my life without additional complications. I didn't have the heart to face the ill-fated people who were on a path that they didn't select.

For me, it was always a "what next?" Soon, another complication arose. I had moderate pain in my lower abdomen. As usual, I went to my PCP for my three-month checkup, and while I was there, I explained to him that I was having intermittent pain in my lower stomach next to my groin, which could be moderate or severe. He sent me for a sonogram. When the test results came back, he mailed them to me as well as a referral to see a specific gynecologist. I tried without success to understand what the test results revealed about my ovaries. I gave the info to the referred specialist, Dr. E., who I went to see shortly after.

"What happened to your right ovary? It doesn't appear anywhere in these results."

I explained that it had been removed and the reason why.

"The same problem is happening with your left one. Do you have relatives who had ovarian cancer?"

"Yes," I said, "my grandmother and my aunt both died from that."

"Are they related on your mother's side or your father's?"

I answered him without alacrity. "From my mother's." I began to understand what these results meant.

"It's indicated that the left ovary is enlarged and contains a central cyst region, and a small amount of fluid is already there in the cul-de-sac." He told me that I had a choice to make: keep monitoring the cysts on my ovary and hope for the best, or have a complete hysterectomy, including the removal of the uterus (and lots of medical words that I didn't pay attention to because it would've be too much to ask for the definition of each one). I already felt pain, and I figured that monitoring my ovary would cause me more of it, plus more doctor's visits. In a split second, my mind turned back to what he had said. *What kind of question is that?* I thought.

"What would you suggest?" I asked. He didn't answer right away, so I asked him again. "If you were in my place, what would you do?"

"Because you've had this problem before and because it seems to be genetic, I think that you should opt for the removal, unless you wish to have more children."

I was silent for a moment. He was waiting for my answer

"If you think that's the better choice, let's go for it," I replied with hesitation. I was glad that he'd been respectful enough to give me the option. It was my body, and I got to choose. My memory went back to when I had to have the first ovary removed. I wasn't in a hurry to go through the same pain again.

"You will also be free of worries," he said. "You won't menstruate anymore and will be on hormones for a long because you're still young."

"Doctor, what will the hormone do for me?" I gently said.

"You might suffer later from chronic pain from the procedure, and in conjunction with the diseases you already have, some days might be difficult, too difficult, even, for you to leave your bed."

My mind, however, was stuck on the fact that I wouldn't menstruate anymore. Ironically, I was happy to have that extraordinary surgery, not because of the intermittent pain, or because I feared my genes, or because I wanted to prevent cancer, but because my annoying monthly period would be over! The idea of being free from that vengeful gift from God was a triumph for me. I wouldn't have my monthly menses, and that was fabulous!

Dr. E. was tall, in his early forties, obese, and extremely kind. Yes, he was a pussycat doctor. He was so sweet that I felt comfortable from the beginning, not only at ease but also confident in him. He was a gynecologic surgeon who had changed careers from surgeon to professor and researcher. He was a very intelligent doctor, according to what I read about him on the internet. I had to—it was a very serious procedure. I didn't want any charlatan cutting my stomach open. One question remained hanging in my head, though. Why would a well-known doctor, with all the knowledge he has, let himself succumb to extreme fatness? Should I really trust him? I wasn't judging him for letting himself go, but it confused me that a doctor wouldn't take better care of himself. That was another reason I had to research him and read all the comments from his former patients on the internet. I had to investigate his practice, and thanks to modernization and free information, I was able to. When he hugged me after I gave him my consent for the surgery, his plump chest and belly were so soft that I could've rested there forever. He was too gentle for me to pass judgment on him. I liked his character and his devotion to what he was doing, and that was all that really counted.

Before the surgery, I had to go through many preparations. I had to be seen by a counselor at Jackson Hospital, have a few psychology sessions, and have stress and blood tests done. I was so nervous and anxious that I almost didn't pass. Dr. Joe was absent at the clinic, and the substitute doctor didn't release my papers to Dr. E. My stress test was abnormal. The day before the procedure, I had to redo the exam. I tried to calm down. Fewer than twenty-four hours before the surgery was scheduled, I was in the hospital waiting room, bracing myself for another test. I told the technician to send the new results as soon as possible to my surrogate doctor so he could release me for surgery. He had to give his okay, confirming that everything was all right and that he approved the surgery. But the technician didn't want to rush. I wanted to have my operation as scheduled. Despite my plea to the technician, he wasn't in the mood to be liable.

"Everything must be done by the book," he said, "we need at least twenty-four hours."

There was no doctor available to approve my case, and there was no possible way I could've compromised with that hardheaded technician. But as I've said, the word *impossible* wasn't in my vocabulary. I figured that even if I had to stay until I saw a manager, I would. My mind was already focused on the procedure, and I'd already requested a leave of absence from my employer, as did Sam so that he could stay with me at the hospital. All that said, the technician explained to me that I'd have to reschedule the procedure and that because of all the waiting and anxiety, some of my tests wouldn't be good anymore. What a mess I was in! The lab tech wasn't at all interested in my *palabras* and certainly not in listening to my angry voice that revealed my French Creole accent. He wasn't going to give me a chance at all.

I had to go for plan B, so I went to the information desk and requested to talk to the manager. The manager emerged, and I explained the reason for my request. Within thirty minutes and with exemplary kindness, he came back and handed me a copy of my signed test results. He told me that his assistant would promptly fax them over to my doctor. It would've been so simple if that technician had made a small exception to his rules! Sometimes, people make life complicated by not trying hard enough. Thank goodness, I didn't have to have the stress test redone; I could feel my blood pressure going through the ceiling. If I'd had to redo the test at that moment, it would've been abnormal again. This is my nature. Most of the time, when I'm facing a hardship and have to accomplish something difficult, I find that perseverance and patience always pay off. In life, we must always make compromises. For example, this lab tech was too lazy to help or didn't have the real qualifications of a caregiver, because if he had, he would've at least made an effort to comply. When I got to my car, I called my PCP's office and learned that the test results had been received and sent on to the surgeon already. Hallelujah!

I had the surgery. My left ovary and my uterus were removed. Contrary to my first surgery, where I had a half-circle shape incision in my lower abdomen, this one was done with a laser that made two little holes in my tummy. I thought that the lasers would minimize my pain after the anesthesia was gone, but I had severe pain that night. After my surgery, only a few hours after they'd taken out my body parts, two nurses, one man and one woman, came to my room to make me walk. *Isn't it too early for this sort of therapy?* I thought. I thought it was very cruel to make me move from my bed while I was still sleepy and in pain. They said that it was for my well-being. Their insistence pulled me out of bed, and I tried to walk, but as soon as I stepped onto the floor, the pain was so severe that I couldn't do it. They left me and came back the next morning.

During the surgery, my right eye scared the hell out of the doctors, anesthetists, and nurses. They questioned my husband about the puffiness of my eyeball, and Sam answered that this problem had occurred when I'd had my first operation. My eye didn't tolerate anesthesia for some reason. I was released after three days, but the pain was far from gone. Dr. E. prescribed pain killer and hormonal medication and recommended that I stay in bed for two weeks. I shouldn't carry anything heavier than five pounds, he said, and I shouldn't drive for a month.

"After enough time has passed," he instructed, "you should see an ophthalmologist about the unusual eye reaction."

I couldn't take pills because of my liver, so I was prescribed with a vaginal cream that helped me generate hormones. When I told my friends about this, they were incredulous.

"Why do you have to take this?" one asked, citing somebody she knew that had the same surgery but didn't have to use the cream.

"Why do you have to take this medication?" another asked. "Don't you know it will make you fat?"

"Per my doctor," I said, "I will be in pain if don't take it."

She continued as if I'd prescribed myself to the medicine. "It's not true. I have a friend that had the same surgery, and she doesn't take anything"

"Well, I don't know," I said. "I'm just following my doctor's orders."

"Anyway, I only wanted to warn you about it. What the doctor told you doesn't make sense to me." She went on and on like she was my mother. "It's up to you if you want to continue this nonsense medication. Does your doctor know that every prescription costs money?"

Hello, my friends, don't you think that if I wanted you to be my health care adviser, I would've contacted you before I went to the doctor? We're making a conversation, and all you have to do was to listen. You questioned me, and I answered your question—twice, actually—because you didn't accept my response. When you talk to your other friend, do you say, "Why doesn't your doctor prescribe you hormones? My friend had the same surgery, and she got them!"

My friend also told me that the medication came with a load of side effects, and I understood her point, but telling me what do was unacceptable. Why are you putting me on the defense with your commentary? People have no right to judge or make comparisons, regardless of the circumstances. We all have a different genetic make-ups and metabolisms. Therefore, we have doctors to identify what works best for each patient. Treatments might vary from patient to patient, even though they have the same disease. I've found that it's best not to tell your business to other people because they make it theirs. I've always condemned the comparisons that most people make between two people with the same illness. Our immune systems are not all built to react the same way. You don't know my body, so you shouldn't tell me what to do. I'm a fan of the Dalai Lama, who said, "Do not let the behavior of others destroy your inner peace." I'm not as peaceful of a person as he is, but I declare that I won't let these sagacious attitudes bother me. I will do what I must do for my own benefit, and I will ignore the mudslinging.

As was suggested, when I began to feel better, I went to see an eye doctor. He couldn't tell me in simple English what was going on, so I decided to see another one. That doctor was certain that he could correct this abnormality through surgery. He made me do all kinds of tests, and I was going *cou-cou* at the Miami Vascular Hospital. The eye became vindictive because the tests put it through so much pressure. I couldn't even sleep in a normal way anymore.

When I returned to the eye specialist, he was more scared than I was. He probably realized how wrong he was to give me hope when there was none. I understood his enthusiasm and appreciated that he wanted to help me, but he should've waited until after the results came back before telling me there was light at the end of the tunnel. Without an apology, he told me that there was no surgical procedure that could correct my eye. I was already scheduled for the excision of a lower lid lesion. He told me that only 1 percent of the world population suffered from that disease and that scientists didn't know anything about it yet. This meant that for me, there was no cure. The kind of orbital varix that I had was so different from the other cases he'd encountered, he explained. The whole time I was there, I bent myself into all these uncomfortable positions, expecting that he could do something to make my eye normal. He made me bend my head down and up to take x-rays of my skull, even CT scans, and in the end, it was all for nothing.

I could tell that he was sorry by the tone of his voice. "This disease is very new. I cannot take any chances trying to fix it surgically, especially because your tumor is placed behind the orbital venous varices."

Although he was talking, I didn't hear a word. I was thinking that all of this had just been to satisfy their curiosity and fuel future research. It was never about me or my well-being at all. I went from having hope to having no hope at all. I felt like I was in a dark tunnel that I had to keep moving through, never knowing what was in front of me. His words felt like a very cold shower; like freezing water, they hurt me and gave me chills. There was no solution that could to control this disease, not even a pill to ease my discomfort. I didn't say a word, and no questions came to my mouth to ask. I was just seized by the reality. For the first time, I had tears rolling in my eyes and my eyelashes were wet, but there was no sign of salty tears on my face. Maybe unconsciously, I was retaining my tears so they wouldn't mess up my makeup. I was like a robot, exiting the premises without a word. I couldn't even ask questions. All I could do was shake my head from right to left to say no and up to down to say yes. *I have a weird disease*, I thought. *Everything is so weird. Maybe I'm weird too.* This was another defeat, but as always, I tried to look at it as a challenge I could overcome. I tried to be realistic about it, so I kept repeating "There is no cure…there is no cure…" to inculcate this notion into my cranium. I went straight home in awful desolation, surprised that what he'd told me was the opposite of what I'd heard during my first visit. I expected the other side of the medallion, the side that says, "We can do it."

At home, I exploded into tears, the tears that I'd held back in the presence of the doctor and assistant. They were finally permitted to freely run down my face. The more I cried, the longer the eye stayed swollen and painful. I didn't see that I was creating more pain for myself by expressing my emotions, I just saw that the swelling wasn't ever going to go away. I wanted to look normal, to be normal like everybody else. My case was so different from the others that the doctor wasn't even sure if there was even a case exactly like mine in the whole world. For some people, the swollen is permanent, but mine comes and goes as it pleases. It swells only when the pressure is too intense for the eye to manage it. Since it first happened, as advised by doctors, I slept on three pillows and requested additional pillows wherever I went. My head had to stay high when I slept if I didn't want the painful puffiness to materialize overnight. By looking at me, nobody would imagine that I had a wondering, abject, threatening thing hiding in my face. I masqueraded it with makeup and smiled all the time, in case my frightful phantom appeared while I was talking to somebody. The only good news was that the ophthalmologist came up with a name for that illness: an orbital varix tumor. Was that the real name for what I had? Who knows, but that's what he told me to call it.

Then one day, I received a phone call from a doctor at Baptist Hospital asking me if there was a possibility that he could see me the next day in the afternoon. He asked for permission to take pictures and have a few students present. I said yes because I thought that he'll be able to do something for me. My eye got very fragile. I couldn't bend, put pressure on it, or cry or laugh too forcefully. Everything made my eyeball swell and feel heavy. My coworkers even questioned me about it. It's wasn't just a nighttime problem anymore but happened during the day too. One moment, I would be all right, but then somebody would make me laugh, and my eye would swell up. It was so embarrassing. I didn't even have a name for this weird illness.

The next day was December 24. It seemed bizarre for a doctor to be receiving a patient in the afternoon of the day before Christmas. When I got there, they're waiting in the lobby with coffee, cookies, and sandwiches, all for me! Probably some leftovers from their Christmas party. I had become a celebrity, or at least my eye had! I was so naively happy. Soon I realized that he was only interested in seeing the proptosis of my eyeball himself. He also requested my authorization to release the pictures he was about to take to a medical book. He didn't touch me or check my eye. He just took pictures because in reality he wasn't concerned about my health at all. I was wrong about that. He just wanted to use my incurable ailment as a subject of discussion with his colleagues. They all thanked me for my patience and my contribution to science. I was blissful to do it for science too but mostly because I wanted to rid myself of the embarrassment of the ridiculous, monstrous ailment that affected my sight.

Orbital varix is a vascular malformation of the eye's orbit. The vein is enlarged due to pressure or position. When the vein is dilated, the eyeball swells. It bothers me most when I'm sleeping. I don't know why, because I'm not doing anything while I sleep that would exert strain on my eye. I don't sleep differently than other people do, but what I know for sure is that my eye doesn't like sleeping or anesthesia. Fortunately, the vision and movement in my right eye are equal to that of my left eye, but maneuvers like straining or bending down can make my eyeball pop out. According to some studies "Any stooping position increases the blood flow as a result of intracranial arteriovenous malfunctions and carotid cavernous fistula, which drain via the orbit and make the eye swell." However, in the early stages, I only felt slight discomfort, but as I aged, I started having mild headaches in the morning and mild pain at night around the eye. There was no good position for me to sleep in some nights. Even though this was a rare, untreatable, and difficult condition, I thought that I needed to find an adequate position in which to sleep. Sometimes, as if protecting it from falling out, I pressed the palm of my hand into my oculus, which was so uncomfortable.

By having surgery, the doctors said, I would be at risk of internal hemorrhages or blindness. They said that they'd only do the surgery if I began going blind. Thank God, I can see fine. I check every year with my eye doctor to find out if there have been any changes in my vision, and every year so far, everything has been all right. Sometimes, this eyeball can become a real incubus. Sometimes, for a full week each month, I can't sleep well because of the swelling, heaviness, and pain. When I drive, I must stay in one lane because I can't spontaneously direct my eye to move right or left—it's slightly painful when I do so. Laughing and crying cause much pressure and cause me soreness, so I try sometimes to avoid both for my welfare, which isn't easy for me to do.

28

Life Goes On

I HAD TO LIVE. I decided that these diseases wouldn't stop me from doing what I used to do. I wouldn't let these ailments take over my life. I felt like I was strong enough to deal with them. I was determined to savor everything and enjoy every moment. When there was a party, I was always the first guest to arrive and the last guest to leave. Every paycheck, I went shopping, which was a sort of therapy for me. I would buy something and return it the next week if I had no use for it. I didn't necessarily buy things because I needed them, but to feel good about myself, to help me forget about my unwanted, shadowy diseases. Even if I bought something tiny, it helped make me feel better. Because I had liver damage, I had no way of knowing how bad it would be tomorrow, so I didn't want to live with any regrets. I didn't want to find myself saying, "I should have enjoyed more pleasure when I could!" When my force abandoned me, I didn't want to express any remorse: "If only I had known, I would have done such and such…"

I did only what I wanted to do as a means of challenging these monsters. My time was limited, and life was treating me badly, so I needed something to hang onto, to maintain my spirit, to prove to myself and my loved ones that this quickening darkness couldn't break me down. I call this the essence of being alive. I endeavored to be joyful most of the time, even when I felt extremely haggard. I tried to practice these words: "I have what I should have, not more, not less." Of course, sometimes the negative side of my brain overmastered the positive, and that's why I had to repeat those words often. Opening my door to the public to tell my uncanny story is also helping me rid myself of shame. I always sought to walk carefully and joyfully on the path of life.

Boom! I was faced with a new health challenge. One day, I heard a *tam-tam* sound in my head, like there was a division between my brain and my mind, a rupture, like the bones of my skull were cracking. For some reason, my mind was sending me all kinds of sounds, and my brain couldn't stop them, which give me the dominant sensation that I was possessed or demented. I had no headache, but the noises and the ticking were like sudden electrical shocks that were demoralizing me. This part of my body was suddenly ungovernable. Dr. Joe sent me to see a neurologist. As usual, I scheduled a visit to see him as soon as possible.

Dr. A. was practical, jovial, and professional. As he entered the room, my first thought was that he could make those audible disturbances go away. I positively wanted this to happen. I was stunned by his imposing appearance, so I was sure that he would implore my new ailment to leave my body. Along with my file, he held a tape recorder in his palm, and he started recording right after he introduced himself to me.

"Today, I'm seeing Mrs. G., who was referred to me by Dr. Joe. Visually, she looks all right…" He looked at the nurse's note. "She is forty-five years old, and she has hep C."

He examined me, gave me a prescription for Neurontin and a relaxant drug, and told me that his assistant would mail me another prescription to have a scan done of my brain. I believe that he thought I had an unusual constellation of symptoms—migratory electrical symptoms and presyncope. Thus, he ordered an MRI of my brain. As I was exiting the building, his assistant called me to schedule a follow-up visit in two weeks. The drugs worked perfectly for the first week. I started the pills on Friday night, and I slept like a baby the entire following Saturday, thank God. I would have to trade going to work, for sleeping. The pounding and all the sounds were gone.

Almost two days before my next appointment, the sound came back, this time accompanied by a headache and a sense of retaliation. I pressed a pillow into my head. I took more than one relaxant pills per day, which just made me sleep. Even so, I had to wake up every fifteen or thirty minutes with the same pain and the feeling that I needed to puke. Yep! My foe was back to fight with me even harder. This stigma was ravaging my head.

I couldn't have been happier when my appointment date arrived at last. As I waited to see the doctor, I was struck with abominable pain that I couldn't attribute to my usual headache. This time, it was different. The nurse let me lie down on the exam bed. I was freezing and shaking, so she covered me with many paper gowns. The doctor entered, wondering why I was covered like that. He said that the scan looked normal and that there was only an abnormality near my eye. I shook even more from desperation. I was certain that I would be diagnosed with something, that he would find out what the problem was and focus on how to get it treated. "What could it be?" I wondered. I had real and extreme pain that couldn't be in my imagination. My brain didn't have the power to conjure such a profound lie. For my satisfaction, he sent me to have twenty-four hours of digital signals recorded from my scalp, formally known as an EER twenty-four-hour SER. The nurse scheduled me to come back in five days for this test.

The twenty-four-hour digital electroencephalogram was a funny, creepy test. With clean, washed, and dried hair, multiple electrodes were placed onto my scalp with a sort of glue. I drove home with all these cords stuck to me, and lots of drivers stared at me like I was an alien, probably thinking that the ones they saw in movies really existed. It didn't seem to bother other people, though. Perhaps they knew or figured what it was—some kind of funky medical test. I was instructed to continue my normal activities and to press the event button when I went to the bathroom, had a shower, ate something, slept, or engaged in other activities. They gave me a diary so that I could report every movement and each time of the day. The next day, at the same times, I redid the course with all the wires for their removal. They didn't read abnormally. Again, they scheduled me for an MRI result.

That day, he came in and briefly told me that I had a mass by my right orbital, that I'd have to see an eye specialist, and that a letter would be sent to my PCP. He didn't notice anything that could cause a seizure, and all the tests were negative. During both the waking and sleep stages, no lateralization or focal abnormalities were noted through the monitor, nor was any spike/sharp wave. I didn't show true epileptiform activity. He didn't know if my right eye condition could be the reason for my weird sensations because everything else looked normal. He said he'll check on me in two months. What else could I do except continue taking my Neurontin and consider myself to be a special lady with an unusual constellation of symptoms and a negative neurological workup? Sometimes, it's good to hear that we don't have anything to worry about, but I would've preferred to know the cause. I was worried that I wouldn't know until it was too late. Whatever the reason, I could live with it. What annoyed me the most was when I was in pain and didn't know what was causing it.

Months passed, and these head issues continued to persecute me. I decided to see another neurologist. Dr. Harry thought that I might have cephalalgia. This big medical word scared and gave me goosebumps, but I asked him what he was going to do about it. I needed to know exactly what cephalalgia was. He told me that it's a kind of throbbing headache that's caused by tension. It's a psychological effect that affects most people who have chronic diseases. I believed him because my head, neck, and shoulders were heavy and painful much of the time, but I didn't think that he should be throwing around the word *psychology*. I wasn't demented! He prescribed Vioxx, which he said would ease the pain.

I always started new medications on Friday nights. As Friday approached, in addition to the sounds inside my head, I began to experience an intense headache that was ferocious and extreme, like something was stabbing my skull. I didn't have a way to position my head that made it feel better. My painful enemy reared up when I was at work. That day, I made it to the grocery store, then home. It was my obligation to bring home food every Friday for the weekend, and I would never have deprived my children because of my sickness. I took my new drug with a glass of milk. The pain seemed to be saying, "I'm going to kill you before you kill me." (Thinking now about taking Vioxx, it could really have killed me too because according to David Graham this drug had killed some sixty thousand patients.) It was pulled off the market in 2004. Again, I'm not lucky, I was destined to live. After a moment, I fell asleep without knowing why. My husband thought that it was just an excuse to abstain from lovemaking with him. This doubled my headache! Did he think I had an imaginary disease? I tried to ignore the aches all the following week, but come Friday, I couldn't ignore them any longer. The migraine liked to wait for a specific day to freely demonstrate its violence. It was real. I had a factual problem, not a fanciful one, as Sam might've wanted me to believe. He couldn't understand. What else is new? As I said before, men understand only what they want to understand, and that usually makes no sense to women.

Sometimes the side effects can be as bad as the disease itself. I had dizziness and nausea and I couldn't breathe. The test results came back with no significant indication of cardiac arrhythmia. My doctor prescribed melatonin and vitamins and requested that I follow up with him in three months. I didn't understand why doctors kept making follow-up appointments with when they couldn't tell me what was wrong with me in the first place. I took my chances and went instead to a well-known clinic, Bascon Palmer. After more tests, all the doctors there could identify was my orbital varix tumor. "Life goes on," I said. If doctors couldn't determine why I had that bothersome condition, I had to find a way to cope with it. I was determined that one day, the discomfort would disappear as suddenly as it had entered into my head. No sooner said than done, it went away after I battled with it for more than six months.

The frustration and stress I experienced when I had these inexplicable pains that didn't have names made me sick to my stomach. Again and again, I experienced burning in my chest. My insurance now allowed members to go directly to specialists without referrals, so I went straight to a gastro and underwent another upper-endoscopy because I had a history of peptic ulcers. Also, I had a Murphy's sign test in the abdomen that was negative, ensuring that I had no inflammation in my gallbladder. However, the results showed that

I had severe gastritis with *Helicobacter pylori*. I was treated with a combination of Biaxin and Prilosec. This time, I didn't distinguish between the pain in my chest and the pain in my stomach as to not confuse the doctor, who I knew would test my gallbladder for no reason.

It's so funny; when I was young, I used to wear all colors of nail polish, but it suddenly seemed inappropriate. I was allergic to any dirty water, so I couldn't wash dishes or have my fingernails or toenails soak too long in water. A podiatrist had to remove two toenails that were completely covered with fungus. To this day, I must keep them very short to avoid infection, and because of my damaged liver, taking pills isn't an option. It can be very sensitive and painful when the little black spots appear under the nail. I don't do manicures and pedicures at the beauty salon to avoid getting more fungi and of course to avoid spreading it to others, because it's contagious. Also, I have to avoid contact with soil. If I touch a damp mop, for example, I will find out later that my nail has wended from the tip toward the cuticle. At that moment, I need to cut my nails very short to avoid further invasion. I found later that the best treatment is to unction them with coconut oil.

I believe in destiny, so I never asked "Why me?" or "Am I paying the consequences for my progenitors' failures?" or "Do I deserve to be sick?" Illnesses are all simply illnesses. The way I see it, it's just part of life. Each trial is just something I had to encounter during my long voyage from birth to death. I cannot shun or change anything. Why bother trying to understand something that was meant to be, maybe even before my procreation. Who knows! I think that this is a good approach for anyone whose life has been marked by disease, even if they look good on the outside. I turned to dancing to stabilize my mind and avoid going crazy between all the doctors' appointments, tests, medications, work, and family matters. Yes, I danced to Michael Jackson's music almost every day for hours. He was my favorite singer because people with depression understand each other. Dancing was part of my exercise routine and a kind of therapy to work off my tension. The words of his songs were like a wakeup call, a comfort, and a reminder that I wasn't alone. To cope with my burdens, I encrusted in my mind that somewhere in the world, there was a person who, regardless of wealth, race, or country of origin, was grieving something, perhaps a loss in the family, a missing part of their body from a war injury, or an illness. I thought, *There is someone out there waiting for the angel of death to come as a liberator and free them from suffering.* I thought, *There is a patient out there who is suffering with no one by their side to whisper a word of tenderness or courage into their ears.* We are not alone in any circumstance, and I kept repeating this mantra to myself over and over.

I didn't feel sad when I danced. I wanted to be content with my problems so I could properly propel my destiny. My grandmother used to say that a sick person remembers that God exists more often and embraces life more heartily than a healthy person does, and it is so true. I tried to embrace life instead of bitching all the time about what I had. Maybe that's why things seemed acceptable for me, even when I struggled. We are not trees or pieces of wood. We are human beings, and it is normal to feel uncomfortable in our bodies sometimes. The endurance of the pain gave me the strength to purify my soul, to be a better person, to acquire the wisdom, and to pay more attention to others in need. I tried to enjoy everything, every day, just as it was, and to make a pact with life that all would be all right in the end. I don't believe that we should be happy all the time. What would be the real essence of life if everything was perfect? We need to experience the bad and the good moments to know the difference, to make us part of this world; otherwise, we become surrealists. We need to have spice in our lives to give it a sense of purpose. If someone tells me that are glad all the time, I just assume that they're living in a bubble of surrealism. But we can try to bring happiness into our lives as often as we can.

29

The Mistaken Intruder

IN A SENSE, I was in control of my life again. I couldn't stop asking myself "What's next?" or "Is my body producing amazing tricks for my mind?" I wouldn't be disconcerted, even though I felt that my mind was playing evil games with me. To give me the strength that I needed, in front of a mirror in the bathroom, as if my reflection was another person, I loudly recited, "I'm stronger than the diseases are. My soul is strong. I accept what I have." I really thought that God didn't want me to forget about him at all by putting in my way all these burdens." He wanted people to pay more attention to him, to adore him all the time. He really liked to make me feel that way. I wasn't going to pray for healthiness, though. He'd give that to me when he felt like it. Like prayers, I used these words very often. Frighteningly, given all my issues, I screamed with all my force and then laughed after. I thought I might be losing my sanity. Sure, I'm insane to come up with these words. Because I like to sing when I have problems, the Tina Turner song came to my mind: "What does God have to do with it?" Yes! Why was I including him in this? After all, wasn't it absolutely natural? We blame him for everything.

Meanwhile, I was going to the doctors for other relatively insignificant matters that didn't let me rest, such as infections, panic attack, broken teeth, and so on. You name it, I'm related to it. Even when I didn't feel ill and just had to go to the doctor for the result of a test of some kind, they still managed to determine that I was sick with something new. For example, one day, my husband had a flu virus. As you all know, the flu can have terrible, dangerous symptoms. I took him to see Dr. W. After examining Sam, the doctor asked me to open my mouth for some reason. Then he looked me in the eye and said, "You're sicker than your husband is. You're the one who needs the chicken soup." He faxed a note to my workplace notifying them that I'd be on bedrest for three days and gave us two prescriptions, one for me and one for Sam. I didn't feel that sick; my mind was more preoccupied with getting him back on his feet. Is it why they think that women's systems are superior to men's?

As the days passed, I discovered that I had an unusual growth inside my nose, which made breathing uncomfortable. *What can it be?* I wondered. I touched the ball inside my nose and said to myself, "Here we go, another complication. God loves me very much to keep these challenges coming my way." It became very interesting to be consistently under the shadow of diseases. They controlled me. I'm aware enough to know that I can't compare myself to others, but I can't say that for sure. As soon as you notice that something is abnormal in your body, you become worried, even if it is innocuous. It becomes a real, passionate burden.

I went to see a doctor about the ball in my nose. He told me that I had a tumor and that the surgery I needed would be complicated because of where it was localized. He told me to find out if my insurance would cover the cost of cosmetic surgery afterward. He would have to pull some tissue from my jaw, which would need to be aesthetically repaired. I didn't believe that he was telling me the truth, so I decided to get a second opinion. In the time, between when I was diagnosed with the tumor and when I found another doctor (which was very difficult to do with my insurance), I lived in fear, thinking mostly about my disfigurement. For the first time in my life, I totally broke down. Appearance is crucial thing to a woman, and my insurance didn't cover cosmetic surgery. I loved my face, and after the surgery, I'd have a hole inside my mouth that insurance wouldn't pay to fix! Certainly, I would have debt if I went through with it. No way. I wondered, could you really call this "cosmetic" when it was so obviously due to a health problem? As always, I was resolved to find a way to solve my problem. That's why I went for a second opinion. This couldn't be the only way, I thought. I knew that in order for my insurance to pay for the reconstruction of my mouth, I would have to fight for it, a fight that I didn't want to have.

While I was waiting for my appointment with the second doctor, things didn't go smoothly with my appearance, which made me assume the worst. I had the face of a half-human monster. My son, who was a fledging artist, took pictures of my figure. He went to Magnet High School, where he was in a photography course. He rented a professional camera to take my photo for a project. I remember it like it was yesterday. It was a Friday. I woke up with pain, so I didn't go to work. My best friend Irma was coming into town from New York. I couldn't pick her up at the airport, so my husband did. I was going nuts with the pain. Besides the swelling of my face, my head, ears, nose, and teeth were badly hurting me. I also had a sore throat and couldn't swallow. I felt like someone was hammering my head or that bees had nested inside my ears. I had a "teeth-ache," not a toothache, because all of them hurt. Sure, I'd given birth to three children, but there was no possible comparison to the pain I was feeling. Later that night, my husband took me to the emergency room at Baptist Hospital. When I arrived at the ER, I was in so much pain that I was seen by a doctor very quickly. The registration was done while I was in the room. My face was completely deformed and wide. I was unrecognizable. Some tests were done promptly, and the ER doctor said that I was very lucky, because by the next day, without intervention, it could've turned life-threatening. The infection was traveling to my brain. I can't thank God enough for guiding me to the decision to go to the ER and Sam for taking me. That same night, because waiting any longer could've been critical or fatal, I had an intravenous IV drip. As soon it was finished, the pain was almost gone. I was released to go home in the morning with prescriptions for more antibiotics and pain relievers and a note to see my doctor about my nose. He didn't say anything about the inside of my nose or the tumor. All he cared about in the moment was my pain and my infection. He could've admitted me to an ENT doctor later that same morning, but no, he had to move on. He was done with the emergency, so the rest was my job. I guess the dangerous part was taken care of, and that was his obligation. My face took a while to go back to normal. Is it coincidental that bad things always happen to me on Fridays?

As soon I got better, I decided to go through with seeing the second doctor. I didn't want to wait any longer. I called the nurse to schedule an office visit. He was located at Mount Sinai Hospital. While I was driving to the second doctor's office, I didn't consider that there would be any kind of miracle in my diagnosis, but I felt that I should go anyway. I saw a man named Dr. I., who examined me.

"Mrs. G.," he said, "you have a cyst inside your nose. I don't know how you got it, but we will have to remove it."

"How are you going to do that?" I asked hesitantly, remembering what the first doctor had told me.

"This is a simple cyst. I'll just make a little incision inside your nose and pull it out. In two weeks, you will be fine."

I couldn't believe him! There's a big difference between having to remove a tumor through my mouth and having to syphon a cyst from my nose. What to do now? Two doctors with two different diagnoses. I felt relieved because I knew that most of cysts were noncancerous, whereas a tumor is a mass of only-God-knows-what. I never told Dr. I. that I'd came for a second opinion, nor did I mention what the first doctor had told me. I was still hesitant, but I had a few days in front of me to think about it. At least I had more hope. Although I had a reluctant decision to make: do I go with the second diagnosis and have the procedure or do I get third opinion? After thinking about my dilemma for many days and nights, I decided to trust the second doctor. He'd already told me that I'd be able to go home the same day of the surgery and return to work in only two weeks. As an outpatient, I had my surgery. Everything was a success. The cyst was gone, and I returned to my workplace after two weeks, as the doctor had predicted. After this episode, I found myself asking how the first doctor could have a medical license and be so wrong in his diagnosis. He'd created so much needless confusion and worry in my mind. I know that we are all human and that mistakes happen, but this one was an extremely miscalculated error. I don't know what he was looking for. Sometimes it's very good to get a second opinion. If I hadn't, my mouth would be massacred by that fool.

Over the years, I've tried to change my mentality from being offensive to polite and dulcet, but I can still be nettlesome sometimes if you start a fight. Despite my problems, I also added people's issues to mine by listening to their worries. At the same time, I thought of the old saying: when you're too nice, sweet, and good, you die early, and only the bad last forever. So I opted for a half-and-half kind of character. Don't exceed the limit; it's all right to be rude and pleasant at the same time. I was scared to die, of course. In reality, I wasn't deteriorating at a fast rate, but I worried over it because my brain always ran in a thousand wrong directions. "Is my liver okay?" "Will I get worse soon?" "What's next?"

When I went to those group meetings, I'd heard and encountered people whose conditions worsened with the time. Doctors insinuated that I would soon see a declination in my health because it'd been over twenty years since I had the blood transfusion that infected me. Even after years passed, I was anxious, and I still am. It's simply something that I couldn't remove from my mind. Apparently, my face doesn't show the depth of anguish that my soul is in, but I'm always worried. Healthy people wouldn't understand my rule of always making a good impression. When you have chronic health problems, you're always concerned no matter how strong you try to be. At the same time, you try to hide your sorrow so you can look normal and so people won't take you as a liar. Who really wants to look pitiful? After my diagnoses, I didn't sleep much at night because I thought it was a waste of time. I much preferred to monitor my health, to watch like Jesus's disciples at the Garden of Gethsemane, watching for no reason, hoping that I might stumble upon the cause of my worries. I just watched and waited. My thoughts were based on my hypothesis that I could expire at any moment, should my liver degenerate or should the bloody mass behind my eyeball bust or becomes cancerous. I figured that I'd have plenty time to sleep when I inevitably slid into a coma or when I let myself traverse the border separating life and death. I wanted to stay awake most of the time, enjoying everything during the short time I thought I had left. I was convinced that I should audit my time to the utmost limit, even though I knew well that there was nothing I could do to prevent my fatality or my destiny. Time became precious for me, so I figured I shouldn't waste it sleeping. I watched TV, especially documentaries, political news, and history programs. I listened to music of all kinds and remembered the words so I could sing them myself. I submerged myself in good movies that made me forget a little about real life or that made me cry to lighten my own burdens.

I believe that each person has a guiding and protecting angel as a shadow and that it never leaves our sides. When we die, we become an angel, depending on what we have done during our lifetime. I've made some decisions in my life that I don't think I've actually made myself. It had to have been someone else dictating them to me. These decisions were reasonably proper and taken under the influence of a kind of powerful spirit that was clever enough to clear my way of thinking. It was probably my angel who did so, because at those tricky crossroads, I didn't know exactly what to opt for. This is the reason why I'm still standing up and taking my life as it comes, day after day. I'm covered with the love of God and the protection of his angels. I could choose to be sad instead, but what is sadness when you have faith in him? Sadness is merely a moment of weakness, helplessness, and emotional carelessness. We all go through bad stuff in life, but no matter what, someone else out there, maybe even someone close by, is dealing with the same turbulence. I don't believe that life is too hard for me, but sometimes I feel execrated. When I feel the sensation of adversity, I'm not afraid to cry, to scream, and to hysterically screech to let new, fresh air invade my soul. Don't let the madness suffocate you. Try to blow it out and repeat, "I'm not alone, I'm not alone." Repeat it all the time. Do whatever it takes to have a great spirit, which is the key for hope and comfort. I'm sure this changes our lives for the better as time goes on. Also, remember that when things are really good, we should be able to say "Thanks!" to the Creator, set down our complaints, and be grateful for all that the Lord had already done for us. Make every day a challenge, a ceremonial event with honest pleasures and happiness. These are the keys to longevity when your body is conquered by sorrowful diseases.

30

Repossession

As more attacks came my way in the coming months, my battle to survive spiraled out of control, and I struggled to keep my faith in God. My mother became seriously ill and had to be on dialysis, and Sam, after the passing of his father, went back to Haiti to continue the legacy of G. Pottery, a business that he and his dad founded in 1975. He wasn't going to let that legacy crumble. Everybody has their own ambitions, and Sam's blindfolded him to the danger of the decision he was making. Going back to Haiti in that period was ridiculously risky. They still kidnapped and killed people of all kinds, but he didn't care; he was going. That is where his destiny wanted to take him, I suppose.

One afternoon, while I was at work, he called to let me know that he'd quit his job and that he was ready to go back to Haiti. I wasn't surprised. I knew for a fact that this time would come. I didn't protest because I could foresee that it was what he wanted, and I was tired of his hostile behavior anyway. I believed in freedom. I didn't marry him to keep him chained to me. People criticized him for his actions, especially because I was so sick. However, I assented. If this would make him happy, I thought, he should go for it. At that point, it was better to voluntarily agree with his resolution from the beginning than be forced to accept it later. What else could I have done when he had already given his resignation to his employer? Like it or not, I consented, but I didn't know that it would be so fast. People suggested that I should divorce him for doing it. I, however, believed that he should be free to do what he pleased. What would I tell people if I had to cut his head out of our marriage photos? Marriage means compromising with each other, and I didn't think we should look to every little matter or disagreement as justification for legal separation. A relationship between a man and a woman is a very difficult task, and marriage is about acceptance and sacrifice. We were very different, and I didn't want to be a shadow over his life. We shouldn't overwhelm ourselves with finding perfection, which we know doesn't exist.

So I let him take his chances and return to Haiti. I was left by myself to take care of my children and my mother. Rain or sun, it was now my problem. There was no one else to turn to when I needed to ask a question or get help. Sam's phone wasn't on all the time due to the lack of electricity in Haiti. My mother was having a hard time with the dialysis. Like playing a hide-and-seek game, Tita and I were hiding our suffering from each other. My problems became her problems, and hers definitely became mine, but neither of us spoke of our torments. As her only child, I was the only one who could take care of her. The load was heavy to carry. Her jeremiads about the dialysis added to mine. I tried to listen to her as much as possible, but sometimes I simply had other priorities to worry about. The entire house was on my shoulders. Sam left to take over a business, which was as sick as I am. He forgot about my battle to pay the bills. He was following his father's dream, leaving me without financial resources. To keep alive his bequest, he invested all his reserves into the family company, forgetting that I was fighting every day to keep our family—his children—alive and well. I didn't think it was fair, but I was hoping that something might happen to open his eyes and bring him home.

Despite all the troubles in my own life, I continued to take care of my mom. I hid from her that we were broke like she was one of my kids so that she wouldn't stress about my income. She wasn't that stupid, though, and when you are a great mom like she is, there are no secrets. She could see through me even though I didn't want to be seen. She said nothing, though, and kept all these worries inside with the others. To make her forget about her dilemma, I tried to be funny and make her laugh, saying idiotic things to her. We talked all the time like lovers, mostly about her ancestors, which helped her battle her slight memory loss.

She wasn't a diplomatic person at all and she was really concerned about me living without Sam. "When I feel sick," she said tenderly, "you take me to the doctor, but what about you, my daughter? You have nobody with you here to help except for Scott, but he isn't your husband. And you know that I don't know how to drive, but even if I did, I don't have enough strength to help."

It was so true. I felt that she was twisting the knife in the wound. It hurt to hear the truth from her, but I pretended like I was okay. Sometimes, I felt a little heroic that in spite of my health problems, I was able to take care of my mother and my children and go to work at the same time. With the blessing of God, I was there for them. Simultaneously, Sam's family was divided after the death of his father. Each of them wanted to take over of that moribund small business. In the world we are living in, we are eternally unsatisfied. Everybody finds something to complain about, even me; I complain that I should have a brother or sister to help with all my mother's doctor's appointments and her other needs. I forgot about Sam' brothers and sisters, however, who were being so unpleasant to each other over such a minimal acquisition. Each of Sam's many relatives wanted to take over as the boss of G. Pottery, although he was the eldest and the only one who held a diploma in ceramics. Sometimes it's not so good to have many sisters and brothers, take my word for it! The fight among them got stronger and uglier. Plus I had to listen to his lamentations. Who else did he have? My job as a wife was to support him in any circumstance, and I was willing to stand by his side, even though he was abroad. My husband wasn't going to surrender for any reason. Before his father passed away, he had called him and implored him to keep the factory going, especially because ceramics was what Sam liked most. It was what he had a college degree in. He promised his dad that he would continue his work, and knowing him, I was positive that he wouldn't give up.

Sam was a professional in that field. He knew everything about clay. He studied in Haiti, Mexico, and Panama. He used to manage the business when he was in Haiti and while his father was alive. Nonetheless the unfathomable animosity between him and his sisters/brothers made him very irritable. I truly thought that the fact that they have put the second brother as the CEO of the company was unfair to him. His young sister from Canada, moved back to Port-au-Prince to be a pain in his ass as well. During our exasperated period before he left for Haiti, anything I said resulted in a big argument. There was no communication between us. As soon he entered our house—as soon as he crossed the threshold into our doorway—he changed into a wolf. There was no way I could even chat with him. My mother noticed it too, and his malevolent behavior was killing her inside. She suffered in silence because the one time she tried to talk to me about it, it was too hurtful and undignified for me to bear.

I shut her down. "This is between my husband and me," I said, humiliated. "Please don't interfere. We'll be all right. Teeth always bite the tongue, as they say, and yet, they are so close with one another that they always make it up after."

Tita never blamed me for anything. She loved me too much to find a single imperfection in her only daughter. She blamed Sam for all of it. Through it all, I tried to understand what was going on in Sam's life and what he was going through with his siblings. I truly tried to find excuses for his departure that would help me carry on. I figured that in the United States, he had to work a job he disliked very much, so as soon as he had the opportunity to do something exciting and meaningful and to get back to the work that was once his passion, he had to accept it. I too had to accept it.

A few months after his departure to Haiti, my financial situation was dire. Month after month, it got harder to make ends meet. Sam didn't send us anything. I had to play the role of mother, father, and daughter in the house. I lived in a dream situation, pretending that when I woke up, everything would be all right. I kept going every day and did what I had to, including going to my follow-up doctor's appointments, taking my mother to hers, going to work,

THE DAILY BATTLE FOR A NORMAL LIFE

and dealing with my family's daily routine. My youngest son was in college in Detroit, so I had to support him financially and morally. I ignored all the late mortgage payments and final notices because I didn't see a solution. One day, at 7:30 p.m., I had the honor of been visited by a deputy sheriff. I had an FHA loan. Yes, you read that right. The sheriff handed me a certified letter, and I signed it. Before I even opened it, I knew exactly what it was about. The envelope contained court order forms from a mortgage lawyer that confirmed my longtime concerns. I felt like the sky was falling down on my head. I was shaking like a leaf in a windstorm.

The big, sturdy man reassured me with a cold smile. "It's not that bad," he said flatly. "Take care of it as soon as possible. Good night, ma'am."

Although I was in shock, I found the courage to say "thank you" to the man as he left me with my misery. First, I was alarmed to have a sheriff at my front porch, and second, I didn't know how to deal with this type of issue. I tried to get in touch with Sam that night, but I couldn't. I couldn't sleep, and I wanted desperately to talk to him. Electricity in Haiti was unreliable, so my many calls throughout the night were as lost in the darkness as my spirit was.

The next day, I didn't go to work. I was sick but not bedridden. I needed time to think. I had the worst anxiety attack. I felt like I needed to throw up, and my throat couldn't swallow any food. I lay down, fixating on the ceiling and thinking that soon, we would be roofless, that I was the only one who knew and the only one who could help. I went to work the next day and tried to focus on my tasks. I had no one to talk to about my upcoming eviction. I had only ninety days in front of me to pay, or I wouldn't have a house anymore. Would I end up on the streets? I was too ashamed to talk about it to my friends. Plus sometimes friends enjoyed hearing about this type of sad situation, especially in this case. I didn't want to endure their cruelty. Why could I tell them anyway? I thought. They weren't going to help me to find the money, and besides, it was between me and my husband.

When I finally got in touch with Sam, I think that he had the biggest emotional reaction of his life. He didn't talk for a while. He was thinking, I guess. He tried his best to send me part of the money to delay the repossession, but it was too late; they wanted the full amount, which wasn't possible. It was my big secret. I was confident that I'd find a solution, that my angel would guide me through this. But it wasn't a secret for the lawyers and the banks. Two days later, I started receiving letters and ads from all over the country, promoting various quick fixes and refinancing solutions. I can't even tell you how many. I read all of them to understand the process. I made a blanket out of these letters on my bed and prioritized the ones I liked the most. First, one day after work, I went to Fort Lauderdale to see a mortgage agent because I liked his letter best. But seeing and hearing are different things. I didn't like his deal, so I went to another one. The second office was closer to my house, and I felt more certain with that agent.

I was out of time. There was no time to get a third quote or negotiate. My mind was focused entirely on getting this resolved ASAP in order to keep my house. I filled out all the refinancing papers and let Sam know when he'll need to come to Miami for the closing. I was determined that I could save my home. I ended up paying a higher premium for the same principle, but I know that there's always a price to pay when you're in a deep, dirty hole like that one. I stood up and fought like a warrior for my home. I was proud of myself. Hey, who serves well his king only did his duty; that's the way it is in life. I didn't receive any recognition from my husband, of course, but I was happy with the results. Sam had worked very hard on that house after Hurricane Andrew and had done significant customizations. I wasn't about to let our home go to somebody else. I wasn't about to lose it just like that, without a fight.

Through my experiences in life, I've learned that if we persevere, there will always be a solution. With faith and courage, we can triumph over every battle. That. Is. For. Sure. I considered my solution a good one because I'd verifiably accomplished my goal. God always helps when we are in need, but we must show that we're willing to help ourselves first. The manna from sky won't fall like rain, it has to be justified. We have to work hard enough to deserve it. From that point forward, Sam and I promised ourselves and each other that this demon would never come for us again.

31

The Second Treatment

IN 1999, I WAS covered by AVMED insurance. Somewhat haphazardly, I picked a doctor's name in from a book of specialists, Dr. Howard, the doctor who did my first endoscopy. The world is small. I remembered how he'd killed two birds with one stone by removing the polypoid and dilating my narrowing esophagus at the same time. I said to myself, "I'll be in good hands." I called my PCP to send me a referral. He pleased me the moment I met him. He was funny, always sliding a French word into our conversations here and there to show off his vocabulary in my language. He repeated the same phrases every time I went for a visit, "*Bonjour, madame*" and "*Comment allez-vous*" in his American accent. It pleased me very much to see how interested he was in getting to know his patients and treating them humanely. Psychologically, he captured my spirit by welcoming me into his office. My first impression was that he seemed to know a lot about the liver. I uttered to myself, "Here is the one I was looking for." In light of my last endoscopy, I needed another esophagogastroduodenoscopy. The name is so long that it can scare the hell out of people. I had to have it though, because the chest pain wouldn't leave me alone.

I underwent this procedure with him, and in the process, he discovered that I had a small hiatal hernia and gastritis. It wasn't a big deal, he explained, but he still wanted me to have a sigmoidoscopy and barium enema. That was too much. I got tired from having tests after tests. I felt like I was being driven to insanity with all these tests and the boundless uncertainty. If I didn't complain to him, I figured, everything would be all right, and I wouldn't have to endure more procedure. I received a letter about it, they'd found that I had internal hemorrhoids. I didn't have pain, so they didn't give me medication.

At that time, Dr. Howard monitored my high alpha-fetoprotein levels every four months, I had a CT scan every six months, and my liver and other blood tests were done every three months. He put me on Actigall to decrease the chance of cirrhosis. In 2001, scientists released a new trial treatment for HCV, the pegylated interferon, and Dr. Howard's office was looking for volunteer candidates for the trial. He told me that I'm a good one for the trial. I agreed to do it. Per my PCP, it could better off be seen regularly by a hepatologist, but I was interested more in him. Dr. Howard was a gastroenterologist with major knowledge of hep C and liver damage. He promised that he would cure me of HCV, and his assistant scheduled me to see his ARNP to start working on my new treatment. A new CT scan was performed.

I was amazed by the care and the interest that my nurse practitioner, D. B., put into her work. She had an incredible attention to detail and ensured that I knew absolutely everything at every phase of the treatment, even the kind of body lotion I should use when my skin started getting too dry from the medication. She was like a fashion icon in the way she dressed, which I admired about her. Astoundingly, she was a charm to look at, wearing all these custom-made accessories. She said, "They were made by my friend in New York." I was thrilled by her affection and sweetness, though I suppose she was like that to all her patients. She explained that I might lose my hair, be nauseated most of the time, and have fevers—things that I already knew from my previous treatment experience. From my purview as the patient, the new one wasn't all that different from the first one except for its name and its higher chance of curing HCV. D. B. patiently explained to me how to withstand each of the side effects.

"Eat salty crackers or drink ginger tea if you have nausea," she instructed calmly. "Try to always eat something, even if you cannot bear the thought of it. Put hot pepper in your food, which will help." She went on like that as if preparing me for war. She prepared my brain and my body for the eventualities that awaited me. She prescribed Celexa, an antidepressant, which I started three months prior to the treatment. This was to ensure that the same kind of mental depression I'd had during my first treatment wouldn't occur again. I was ready to go. This time, it wasn't a treatment but a trial. I might have better luck than the first time, but it wasn't a guarantee. I took the Celexa as prescribed for two months. Then I received a call from the doctor's assistant, who explained to me that it would no longer be possible to do the treatment with them because they no longer took my medical insurance. It was a trial, so the medication would be free, but my insurance would have to pay for the visits and the tests. They had terminated their contract with them.

There are only three words that describe how I felt: I. Was. Destroyed. I was facing an unexpected dilemma. I don't know how I got home that day. Was my car smart enough to take me home by itself? As soon I got into my house, I went straight to my bed. This was the best place for me to think, to exteriorize my feelings freely, and to liberally empty my eyes of a waterfall of tears. I'd had so much confidence in both Nurse D. B. and Dr. Howard that I couldn't picture myself under the care of another specialist. I was stunned by the news, and my mind was going zillion places at once, searching for an answer to my question: "What do I do now?" Inadvertently, I fell asleep from the pills I took for my headache. The next day, I was more rested and mindful. My brain had been working almost all night to give me a clear answer to my query: "I'm not going to take no for an answer," I grumbled.

The following day, at work, I called the doctor's office and left a message. An assistant called me back later, just to tell me how sorry she was about my turn of fate.

"Things have changed, Mrs. G.," she said, "and I'm not the manager. You probably need to talk to him. I'm so sorry for that."

"Can you give me his name and his direct phone number? When can I contact him?" I spoke with an abrasive tone, not because I wanted to, but because this next crisis was driving me away from my goal.

"Sorry, I don't have that information," she said, as if walking on eggshells, "but if you call the front desk, they will direct your call to him."

I hung up without thanking her. I didn't want to hear her apology, which didn't resolve my problem. How rude I can be sometimes! I was disappointed and frustrated. I called back and asked her if she could, as a favor, allow me to speak to Dr. Howard right away.

"The doctor is with patients now. I will leave him a message to call you back. I'm so sorry about that," she sincerely said.

They shouldn't call us patients, because in a lot of cases, under the stress of medical problems, logistical issues, and inhumane insurance practices, we are not patients at all. At least this was the case for me. I assume that other sick people feel the same way. When you are ill and in pain, patience becomes a lost virtue. What the receptionist didn't know was that I had his personal number from when I was first under his care. During my first treatment, I could call him anytime. I didn't have time to call him, however, but he called me back later in the afternoon.

"Mrs. G., how can I help?"

I explained everything to him, all of which he certainly already knew. I reminded him of his promise.

He calmly told me that he regretted what happened. "I'm so sorry to hear that," he said. "I have nothing to do with it, it's management decision. If there was really something I could do to help, I would." He gave me the name of another doctor to contact, but I refused. I needed him to do my treatment because I had already placed my faith in him.

The next day, I called again, and the receptionist forwarded my call to the manager. I left him a brief message to please call back as soon he received my message. He didn't call that day, so I called the next day and the next, with increasing persistence, demanding that he call me back. I was an angry woman who needed assistance, so finally he did. I was enraged at him for not calling me back sooner and for the problem he and the insurance company had put me through. I lost my control over the phone, especially when he said that there was nothing he could do about it and that I wasn't the only one with the same problem.

"Yes," I told him, "I figured as much. A lot of us are facing the dilemma of leaving a doctor that we like because of administration. Do I care about others now? I'm speaking only for myself." Perseverance is my biggest virtue, and I wasn't going to terminate the telephone conversation without a bargain. I was at work at the time, and everyone in my office was listening, but I really didn't care. I was debating something very important, even more important than my work—my health. I don't know how long I stayed on the phone arguing with him. I didn't want to give up without winning. He signaled many times that he had to end the conversation, but I just kept going and going until he finally agreed to find a way to help. I'd won the battle! I had to apologize at the end of our conversation for my boiling-blood behavior. We made a deal that I'd pay fifty dollars per visit. My prescriptions for the lab tests would be sent to my PCP to order instead of having them done at the same office. I agreed with this, and he switched me over to my doctor's assistant to schedule my next appointment. That confirmed my creed that I had to constantly fight in order to obtain anything. To this day, I always struggle, even with things that are not mentioned in this book.

I believe that for me, if a project is too simple, it's because it's not realizable or I'll be defeated. Everything in my life has been complicated. Fighting to survive became my second nature. Nothing has ever been easy as pie for me, from when I was in my mother's womb to the present day. My life is a perpetual, daily battle, and things that seem effortless for others are complex for me. Fortunately, I don't get discouraged easily, which is an advantage that allows me to walk gracefully through even my most troubled days.

Luckily, before my insurance company cut ties with Dr. Howard's office, I'd had my liver biopsy done. It was very different than the first one, thank goodness. I received anesthesia and didn't feel any pain. During the trial, instructions were sent from the gastro's office to my PCP's office for necessary sonograms or blood tests. They couldn't do anything without the approval of Dr. Joe. The results came back indicating predominantly lymphocytic inflammation of the liver and early focal bridging fibrosis. I had a C-reactive protein level of 1.57, where the normal range is 0.80 mg/dL. Also, the liver biopsy revealed chronic hepatitis with moderate activity and foci consistent with early focal bridging fibrosis, predominantly lymphocytic inflammatory infiltration, and mild focal steatosis. I began the trial with an HCV RNA quantitative of 5,420,000 IU/ml, when the normal range is 50 IU/ml. Some of my levels were low, such as my white cell blood count, my platelet levels, and my absolute neutrophils/lymphocytes, but most others were very high, AST and ALT, to name a few.

Three months into the treatment, my health took a complete turn for the worse. I had flu symptom and nausea all the time. I was tired, but I couldn't sleep too much. While I was undergoing treatment, another chronic disease knocked on my door. I had high blood pressure. The systolic and the diastolic rates of my blood pressure went to 190/110 most of the time, and as such, the migraines worsened. They prescribed atenolol to lower the blood pressure numbers, but nothing seemed to work. This disease was as out of control as the others were. Any contrariety would raise my blood pressure drastically to 200/115. Eventually, I ended up taking three pills to offset that: atenolol, triamterene, and enalapril. That combination finally regulated this bothersome illness. My body didn't belong to me anymore but to these ailments that had taken it captive.

Despite the high blood pressure, I still continued with the pegylated interferon injections plus the ribavirin pills. This time, the care and kindness of Nurse D. B. kept me motivated. I suffered, but I had hope and confidence that the medicine would work. I tried to see my wretchedness and suffering as serving a larger purpose: to free me from hep C. "In a year," I told myself, "this parasite would be gone. I'll remember it as a nightmare that never existed—the demon that lost its battle with me. I'll be proud of my win." I'd been granted a medical leave of absence of two weeks per month per my doctor's request. So I worked only two weeks out of every month, minus the days after each treatment, such as Tuesdays and Thursdays. At this time, my workplace was understanding, and management was considerate. I didn't have to stress about going to work every day, which was a plus, but I was turning into a skeleton. I couldn't eat. My mother, who also had food and sugar restrictions from diabetes and high blood pressure, tried to make me some light food, and to please her, I tried very hard to swallow some of it. Soon after, however, my body rejected everything from my stomach.

I had sparse hair, and you could see portions of my scalp. I weighed only a hundred and five pounds and had to get smaller clothes. I lost thirty pounds in only a few months. At the beginning, I had fevers, but as the treatment progressed, I had fewer of them. I was so fragile that if you blew on me, I would fly away like a piece of paper. I was debilitated. I couldn't walk for very long. I had body aches indeed; the side effects that I'd read about prior to treatment were nothing compared to the real thing. I never imagined that I could travel to hell while I was on earth, alive. I thought that I had to die first. *Am I dead?* I thought to myself. I felt such a lack of vitality. My first treatment lasted only three months, but this time, as the days passed, the side effects became worse, contrary to what was told to me. Strangely, I couldn't even hold my body up.

Six months passed, and hope was the only thing that kept me going. I wasn't despairing and had complete lucidity of mind. The fact that I'd started the antidepressant pills early gave me a large advantage over dealing with the psychological effects. I could be moody sometimes, but it was largely controllable, unlike last time. Every time I had a blood test, there was always good news in the results. My HCV RNA quantitative numbers decreased continuously, which gave me great encouragement. By the time the treatment was completed, the RNA went to 500 IU/ml. It was a success, and I was very happy with it, and my family was as well. The hepatitis wasn't completely gone, but it'd been considerably diminished.

After a year, it was time to stop the treatments. I felt free, like a bird let out of its cage, thinking that I wouldn't have to worry about HCV in the years to come. Even though I knew that I wasn't completely cured, it was a big step in the right direction. I was sure that afterward, if I maintained a careful diet, my blood-count viral level would reduce and eventually reach the normal range. Then HCV would forever leave my body. It will like a bad souvenir. It took me another six months to get rid of all the toxins that were in my body during the healing process. Physically, I looked moribund. It was still hard to talk and excruciatingly tough to go back to my normal routine. I heard that people at work thought that I was going to die. I liked their predilections, to be honest. After all I'd gone through, I considered myself risen from the dead. Thanks to D. B., to Dr. Howard, and to the manager of that office, who made that dream realistic for me.

I went back to work and was soon performing over my capacity. I needed to make up for all the time I was absent. Soon after, I went for a blood test, and surprisingly, my blood-count viral level had significantly increased. Less than a year after the treatment, it was aggressively getting bad again. The viral count had rebounded. Dr. Joe wasn't too happy about it, and I wasn't either, to say the least. More tests were needed to find out exactly what'd happened. Less than two years later, I was back to where I'd begun, and there were no more new options. During one visit to see Dr. Joe, I saw him coming with a thin file folder. I was so used to seeing him hauling around my huge, heavy file. I asked him if they'd thrown away all my records.

"Yes, it was too heavy for my hands!" he said with a seductive smile. After a sparkly moment, he continued. "No, it's not true. They opened a second file because the first had become too thick with all my writing." He paused, laughing. "You are like a sick old lady who has been following with me for a century, now disguised in a beautiful body. Are you a witch? Just kidding!"

I laughed too. He was so funny. "If I was," I said, "I would definitely cure myself, and that would make you a witch doctor as well, like Dr. Bombay in *Bewitched*."

He was determined to find out why the disease has such difficulty leaving my body. He strongly recommended that I see a hepatologist at the University of Miami. Unfortunately, I had to change insurance providers again, and Dr. Joe's office didn't accept the new insurance that was provided by my work. My family and I had been with Dr. Joe for so long. He'd become a real family doctor for us, and sometimes even blamed Sam for leaving me alone during my sick periods. He knew all the good and bad parts of my body. I cried like a child when I left his office for the last time, anticipating that I would never find a PCP like him. Everyone was so benevolent and attentive to me there. I didn't fight this time because I knew I couldn't win. My employer had the right to choose, to change insurance providers whenever it wanted to for its own advantage. To this day, I've never seen him again, but I'll never forget him. Thank you. Dr. Joseph, for your unique kindness and care.

32

Deprivation

I WAS IN THE same scenario again. A new start. Another recommencement. I had to find another PCP, to whom I'd have to give the same explanations and endure the same embarrassment. I tried three PCPs, but none of them met my expectations. Finally, the fourth one seemed to be all right. Dr. A. S. appeared as fine as Dr. Joe was. He was from my country too, and he saw all kinds of patients in his office: Haitians, Spanish, Americans, you name it. He'd have to be bloody good to have so many patients, I thought. He wasn't in hurry, though, and there was always a crowd waiting for him. On my first visit, I had to wait for two hours in the waiting room before the nurse called me in and another thirty minutes in the consultation room before I was seen. He made me feel at ease, though, like I could tell him anything. He was very tall, heavy, and very proportional and had big eyes, and he was smiling and laughing like nothing mattered. Two physician's assistants worked with him, but it seemed like all his patients wanted to see him personally. I wanted to see him too because he knew my native language, meaning that I could describe my conditions to him in Haitian terms, and he could understand it, which not a lot of physicians could. We have words that only Haitians use, and I could speak French or Creole with him. I was very pleased except for the long wait. From then on, I tried to get the latest appointments so I wouldn't lose too much working time.

Less than a year later, another disease attacked my body. I never imagined that someone could have pain all over their body. This is what happened to me. There was no part I could touch without feeling the hurt. Alicia Keys sings, "This girl is on fire," which on that day was about me. I felt like I was actually on fire. I had pain everywhere. I couldn't describe it. After two days of living like that, I called early in the morning to let the office knows that I was coming to see Dr. A. S. "I cannot wait any longer," I told them. They tried to give me an appointment in three days because they were already booked for the day, but my body couldn't take another three days without medication. I had to see somebody and didn't care who. What the receptionist didn't understand was that I didn't ask her to schedule me, I just wanted to let her know that I was coming. I went there crying and sniveling from the pain, my sticky face damp with tears, without makeup. I was in distress, like a sinking boat. I thought that I was at my expiration date on earth, that I would be dead soon. That wasn't like me, going out without makeup. I never thought that it could happen. I guess my desperate visage told them that I needed help immediately. They didn't say anything; I had just to wait until they finished appointments. I wasn't used to this place and had to wait regardless of my health status. It was fair enough, but I was in so much pain. I kept saying to myself, "It's better being here than staying home in pain, and at least I will leave hell and go to purgatory soon." I really assumed I was dying! After thirty minutes, the cold air of the AC and the straight-backed chair making everything worse, I went to the receptionist and complained that my carcass would break into pieces if I don't see somebody right away. I lost my pride and begged to be seen by someone.

At last, they gave me a room to lie down in, and after a while, Roberto, one of the nurse practitioners, entered the exam room. When he touched me, I jumped and screamed like a cow at the slaughterhouse when the butcher is piercing its throat with a knife. He'd caught me by surprise. I told him not to do so again, that my body was demolishing itself. I explained to him that I had pain all over. I couldn't even touch my own legs to put on body lotion. I didn't have a fever, but the body aches had been debilitating for two days. Instantly, Roberto realized that I had a disease called fibromyalgia. He couldn't specify how people got it, but he said that HCV patients are the most affected population. *Really?* I thought. *What kind of devil is hepatitis to encumber me with this awful, insane disease? Is it not enough to be a difficult friend itself? Does it have to give me other diseases to deal with too?* He gave me a prescription of 800 mg of ibuprofen and recommended that I get plenty of rest. It was already Wednesday, so he gave me a note to stay home until the next Monday. Whether the ibuprofen did something or it went away on its own, I don't know, but on the fourth day, I felt much better. After a while, the ibuprofen didn't help too much. When that ailment visited me, it stayed for as long as it pleased, no matter what I drank, took, or did. Almost every ailment I had was due to HCV. Later, Jean, a PA-C, a lovely human being who meticulously watched over my health, replaced Roberto. She turned out to be outstanding, supportive, and professional, the best caregiver of my life. I loved her so much.

How can I explain to my nonbeliever friends all these details about my health? I could be in bed for two or three days, and then I was all right afterward, like nothing happened. Sometimes, I even scared myself. Was I possessed? For sure, I didn't seek much of a quality of life. The power of the diseases claimed my body and dominated it. What kind of bargain could I make with these devilish souls to give me back my health? None! Who wants to be in pain most of the time and have a legion of ailments that attack them, time and time again? I couldn't let myself get overwhelmed. I only did what I could do, what I felt was adequate for my capacity so that I could reserve strength for the next day. I built my journey step by step to accomplish this, and at the same time, always reminded myself that I couldn't do it all. *Impossible* was never a word in my vocabulary when I was younger because I was eager to live well and normal, but it became tougher to keep it out of my lexicon. As a compromise, I decided to try to be moderate in everything. I was getting used to being sick, but it was still an annoying matter and a challenge.

My husband always told me to slow down and do one thing at a time, not to rush to do so many things at once. At the beginning,

THE DAILY BATTLE FOR A NORMAL LIFE

I didn't want to listen to him, thinking that I wasn't disabled, that slowing down wasn't what living was about. I wanted to take risks, to show to myself and especially my family that I could do everything that normal people can. Back then, I usually accomplished everything that I intended to do every day, even if it meant that the next day, I was in multifaceted pain like a creepy old woman, lying in bed with a cynical smile and pride in the thought that I did what I had to do. I somewhat satisfied my eagerness to prove myself. I didn't think that I was ill enough to stop my plans. I thought, *Time is too precious to waste on poppycock!* However, this stress exacerbated my physical conditions. I was living a double life, showing people what I wasn't to avoid further judgments and allegations. People seemed to always say, "You should feel lucky compared to others." They were always ready to tell me a story of someone else they knew who was sicker. Is this what you call lucky? That with audacity, defiance of my destiny, and great effort, and despite my ball and chain, that my life has some bright moments too? What is your expectation? I don't have to die to prove to you that I'm not as well as I might look. If I'm talking to you, it's because you're my friend, and you shouldn't put me on a trial of juxtaposition. I'm not the kind of person who wears a tragic face, blindfolded by my own concerns, who cannot see or understand what we all are going through. I have my moment of torments just like everybody else, regardless the severity of their burdens.

I seek to make spiritual unions with people based on the notion that we should never presume or assume. A person can look healthy today but be gone tomorrow. When someone passes, we often say, "He/she was all right yesterday, so what happened?" It's because you don't usually know what someone else is actually going through. I lose myself in the glory of each day and accept what might come tomorrow, like a cloud in the sky that changes colors depending on the weather. That's how my life is. Comparison is a cruel-hearted, synthetic ego that lowers our integrity.

33

Ravaged by Dementia

"Life continues" became the incantation formula that keep me going. I couldn't change my existence, so I declared that I had to live, to go with the flow of my ailments. However, my mother wasn't coping. Her diseases multiplied, and she wasn't getting better. She was diagnosed with dementia. There is nothing more horrifying than watching your mother lose her memory, and it surprised me just how quickly it ravaged her mind. I remembered one Sunday afternoon when she came to my bedroom asking me what day it was. I looked at her with amusement, wondering what kind of game she was playing with me. Less than five minutes later, she came back, asking the same question again, which appalled me. First, I thought that she was joking because we'd had such a good time the night before, which was the Saturday of Lent. We went to church at St. Louis and had our best mass of the year. She was fine. On our way home, we continued singing and laughing. The very next day, she was asking me what day it was. It had to be some kind of humous game, I thought. She came back within fifteen minutes with a bottle of her medication and gave it to me, stating that it wasn't hers. I told her that her name was on the bottle. She left, and after another fifteen minutes, she came back, asking me the same question. This happened again and again with the same bottle, and right away, I realized that something wasn't right. Sam came to the bedroom, and I told him about what had happened. He advised me to take her to see her doctor the next morning, that it could be the beginning of Alzheimer's. I took her to her doctor on Monday morning. Her PCP examined her, and she concluded that it could be dementia and sent her to see a specialist.

At the specialist's office, while he was testing her, she answered all his questions very well. I was embarrassed. I thought that I must've imagined all of it—that I was the one who needed to get examined! She remembered the day, the date, and even the name of the president. The doctor didn't give her any medication and looked at me like I was lying to him. I felt embarrassed and left the office. As usual, the assistant scheduled a follow-up appointment with her. As the days passed, her memory loss got serious. My mother couldn't remember things, and I wasn't imagining it. It was funny, though, because every time we went to the doctor's office, she was her usual quick-witted self, but at home, she couldn't retain simple things in her memory. What made the situation very hard to understand and deeply broke my heart was to see her unable to recall if she'd already eaten, taken her medications, or even taken her shower. I could understand how that could happen when her sugar was low, but what causes the permanent loss of memory? How can we just become like that, not remembering the most important events in our lives, like a vacuum has swept away everything, leaving only emptiness? Nothingness was replacing her brain.

Despite of all this, her spirit was high, and we sometimes even laughed about her new disease. That is something we had in common: anything could amuse us. We were like two best friends. It was magical to see her unexpectedly remember things from childhood. She could give me the entire story with impeccable details, even though she'd just forgotten what I'd told her a few minutes ago. It's is very difficult to watch a family member, especially your own mother, succumb to dementia/Alzheimer's. I had to strike a delicate balance, trying not to make her embarrassed or frustrated but also ensuring that she was safe, that she didn't touch the oven, for example, when she was cooking. I tried to make everything she might need available in her bedroom in case she needed to use the bathroom in the night. I was afraid she wouldn't remember where it was, so I wanted to give her a plan B. She stayed in that impotent stage for almost five years. Throughout the years, she got worse, worse, and worse. The Lord has a funny way of treating his servants.

In December 2005, I lost my uncle, Tita's brother, who was also my godfather. He denied that he had diabetes, so he never took any medication for that. In addition, his liver was shutting down, but still he repudiated the treatments that could've helped him at the beginning. When he finally accepted his illnesses, it was already too late. My uncle treated me like I was his first child. Even after I was married, he continued to give me money whenever I saw him! You tend to believe that family members are invincible and immortal. That was the case for my uncle too. I never pictured him dying. He was always active. Her daughter called me one morning to give me the terrible news. I was aghast. Despite his bad health, he always went to see his daughters and even visited me and Tita in Miami. I couldn't believe it when my cousin told me that he'd passed away. I was consumed with desolation and a helpless feeling. I hesitated to give the news to my mother and decided to wait for a better time. I was too shocked to find a good way to tell her this bereaved news. I went to his funeral in Haiti. I told my mother that I was going to New York for business. I couldn't find a way to put into words that her only baby brother had died. They were so close that it would break her heart. At the same time, Clara, his niece, was busy burying her own child, who was only two weeks old, in Miami. Her daughter was born with complications and didn't last. I didn't tell my mother about this either. I lied to my mother for her own good. I knew for a fact that she would want to go with me to her brother's funeral, but she was on dialysis three times a week and couldn't miss her treatments. Her health had declined very quickly. Two deaths in the family at the same time. How to explain this to her?

Finally, in January, after insisting that I call her brother in Haiti, complaining that she hadn't heard from him in months and wanting to know why, I had to give her the bad news. I confessed my sin of not telling her the truth before. It was really for her sake, I explained. I knew how poorly she would take it. She loved her brother very much. When I told her, she was shocked and seemed lost. She didn't talk for at least ten minutes. I had to let her know and thought that was the right moment. I think that it took her a moment to process the information. I repeated what I'd told her because I wanted to set down the heavy weight of my lie, but the second time I said it, she exploded into tears. I told myself that because of the dementia, she would soon not remember anything, that I'd have to explain this to her again and again. That is exactly what happened. She tortured me almost every day with the same question, "Why does my brother not come to see me anymore? Is he in Miami or in Haiti?" I answered the last part only because I didn't know what else to tell her and didn't want for her to have that explosion of madness again.

"In Haiti, in the hands of God," I said

"Is he okay, Olivia? The last time I saw him, he was sick!"

Sometimes, I played deaf or left the room without saying a word because tears already falling from my eyes. How the hell could she remember his sickness but not his death? I was trapped in a situation with no end. Every time she asked, I had to repeat the same old thing to her about the two deaths in the family. She always looked confused, like she was in another world. Going over and over was torture to me, to keep breaking her heart. I felt more forlorn for her than I did for the deceased because they were free of feeling, diseases, and fears, leaving the living with grievous afflictions and emotional sorrow.

In February 2006, my mother's health had deeply deteriorated, and I was utterly enervated by it all. I continued to take care of Tita but was also working full-time. Her social worker gave me a letter that allowed me to leave work any time, if needed. Things were difficult. When I left her food in the morning, she would leave it on the kitchen counter, so I changed my tactics. I fixed her a snack, put it on her bag, and called the dialysis office to let them know that there was food there. I asked them to please always make sure that she ate something. They were very kind and they liked her very much. They agreed to help me. My mom was a very kind, respectful woman, so it was easy to fall in love with her. Her days started at 7:00 a.m. She left home on a minibus, NUNI, with other patients, and returned home at 3:00 p.m. I felt bad for her because she looked so exhausted all the time. I could see that she was very uncomfortable in her skin, but I couldn't stay with her. I had to work. I left home at 6:30 a.m. and didn't get back until close to 6:00 p.m. On my days off, I'd pick her up so she wouldn't have to make the tour of dropping everyone else off before she was. My house was further away from the hospital than the others' houses were. Because of my mother's dementia, my caretaking tasks became very difficult. She would say to me that she hadn't eaten anything, even though she'd eaten fifteen minutes ago. In the afternoon, when I got home, I had to open her bag to see if she'd eaten.

Her mind did, however, stay on top of two things: waiting for the bus in the morning and her bag. She wouldn't forget about these two things for any reason, so anything I wanted her to do, I'd write on a note and put on her bag. Sometimes she didn't look inside of it, though, which is how she forgot to eat. Most of the time, she ate lunch but not her snack, which made her sugar go low. She'd became upset and obsessed with the idea that they'd stuck a nail in her arm at the dialysis center. She couldn't distinguish between the big dialysis needle that they used to withdraw the blood and a nail. You couldn't tell her otherwise; she wouldn't understand it. She let anyone know who came over that they were using a nail in her arm and that it hurt terribly. My dear mother had turned into a retarded child, and I couldn't be there all the time to take care of her. It's so unfair to have to turn into a kid at the end of your life on earth. My mother acted like an infant, and this hurt me profoundly. I would've preferred to remember my mother as a strong lady, not a child whom I had to babysit all the time. There was nothing I could do to make her believe that it was simply a big needle. She was determined that it was a nail, period.

Every day, she waited for me by the window to complain about the nail, but tried with reticence, my response notwithstanding, not to bother me too much. When she finally stopped talking for a moment, I profited from the silence to escape to my bedroom, to have some rest after a long day of working. At that time, my son Scott was still living with me, and he was in the medical field. He cared for his grandmother too and was a big help to me. At night, he would check on her. Several times, he was the one who discovered that she was in danger or had lost consciousness. Her blood sugar dropped very low, very often. When that happens, sometimes, she stopped recognizing her grandson. The first time it happened, we didn't know what to do, so we called the emergency room. Over time, we learned exactly what to do and what to give her for different symptom. We kept a bottle of orange juice in the refrigerator to give her when her sugar dropped, and sometimes I'd even mix in extra sugar to help her feel better faster. At night, we always had to stay in the loop of surveillance to oversee her in case she got into some kind of sudden trouble.

34

Valentine's Day

I CANNOT FORGET THE last time that she passed home. I don't intend to forget it. It was February 13, 2006. My mother was complaining about abdominal pain and couldn't sleep. Scott and I stayed up late with her until she fell asleep around 3:00 a.m. We had to work in the morning and needed some sleep. Later, at work, I called the social worker to ensure that she was all right and explained what'd happened the night before. At 1:00 p.m., they called me from the dialysis office and said that they were taking her to Homestead Hospital. Ten minutes later, while I was on my way out of work, the telephone rang again. The Social worker called me again and told me that there had been a change, they were taking her to Baptist Hospital in Kendall instead. I arrived at Baptist at the same time the ambulance did. My mom was so happy to see me and told me that she was so worried about being taken to the hospital without telling me.

"I was afraid you wouldn't know where I was!" she cried.

I reassured her that they would always call to let me know everything about her. She was sitting in a hospital wheelchair.

An old man nearby asked me if he could talk to her. "She is so beautiful," he said.

I told him that she doesn't speak English. He talked to me, and I translated everything he said to her until a nurse came to take him inside. Even though Tita came in an ambulance, she didn't look so bad except for the pain that was hurting her. I made her laugh, joking about her illicit new boyfriend. The pain wasn't severely bothering her like it had been the night before. By experience, I know that sometimes when I have pain, I can't hear anything, but at the same time, watching a good movie on the television can make me forget a little bit about my pain—two hours of relief. So I kept talking about her getting a new boyfriend on Valentine's Day. I was joking about everything, trying to cheer her up and help diminish her pain. I would've done anything to put her at ease.

Meanwhile, they took her to have more tests. Around 4:00 a.m. the next day, she was admitted and never returned home. Existence is so biased toward the humankind. Tita never like hospitals, and while she was there, she asked me many times when she could go back home. I told her that she could go home when all her many doctors released her. I thought that it would be big help to keep her at the hospital for a little while, especially while she was in such bad shape, so she would have nurses to take care of her and could get her dialysis treatments without having to travel. That wasn't the case, however, because in the meantime, she had a stroke. I thought that because she was at the hospital, nothing bad would happen to her. Wrong! Her health worsened rapidly while she was there. The stroke left her completely paralyzed on the left side. She couldn't turn or clean her body by herself. Many times, she told me that she was ready to go home, but "home" was a different place. I didn't understand that the "home" she was so concerned about wasn't my house. She told me that her mother was waiting for her and that "home" was heaven with her parents. *The diseases must be affecting her severely*, I thought. *She is delirious!* As usual, I tried to find humor in it and murmured, "Why choose heaven instead of hell? Is she going to heaven because everybody wants to go to Eden? If everybody goes to paradise, is hell on earth?" I made it a joke because I wasn't ready to believe that my mother was going to die.

Lots of my friends worked at this hospital, so she had visitors all the time. I made sure to stop by at 7:00 a.m. each day before they took her to the dialysis room. I'd walk next to her in the stretch bed and wait until my neighbor, a nurse, came to keep her company before I left. Sometimes, I'd leave her by herself because I had to go to work. I came back in the afternoons at 5:00 p.m. She wouldn't eat her dinner until I got there. I fed her and gave her a wet towel half-bath to keep her feeling fresh before I left. Sometimes, we prayed and sang together. Ironically, she never forgot any religious songs. Sometimes, I had to force her to eat a spoonful or two of food, and perhaps she did it just to please me. In front of my eyes, day after day, my mother's condition took drastic turns for the worse. She got so bad that they had to feed her through a tube. This made her very depressed, and her mind couldn't resist the temptation of darkness. She wanted to die. I didn't ask for medication for her depression because I didn't know much about this type of mental health. I thought that with all these doctors around, maybe one of them had already given her a pill to help with the intense melancholy. I trusted them and I didn't ask for an antidepressant, which was my mistake.

Mental health was still a virgin field for me, one that I didn't explore until later on as I was fighting with my own. Doctors gave me medication for anxiety and depression during my second HCV treatment, but I never paid attention to how they made me feel. However, I expected that the hospital was a place where everyone received good care, no matter of their age, insurance, or ethnicity. I should've seen her depression coming when she wouldn't talk to her sisters in Canada for very long, which was so unlike her. How did I miss it? I don't know! She was an independent person and proud of it. I should've known that she would suffer when other people had to carry out everything for her. I should've known that she wouldn't last long in that state. I'm not excusing myself, but my mind was under constant worry, in continuous fights with my fate. I didn't pay attention to these essential elements. Now, by experience, I've learned that you always must be watching in that type of place. I still feel remorse for not fighting hard enough while she was there. It's so disgraceful. She hallucinated, and not a day has passed that she didn't mention her parents. I didn't exist anymore—it was all about her trip home.

She repeatedly said, "I'm ready to go home to be with my mom and father. Olivia, they're waiting for me."

"What about me?" I asked her.

THE DAILY BATTLE FOR A NORMAL LIFE

"Oli, you know that one day, you will have to bury me, which is the normal way of life. It would be abnormal for a mother to bury her daughter, wouldn't it? You have a good son, Scott, and he will take good care of you as you did me."

These are not the words a daughter wants to hear from her mom. I was afraid, and to give me more control and courage, I had to deny that eventually she might leave me. "I could have a car accident and die before you, Tita," I said, trying to lighten the mood.

She persisted like she didn't hear me. "You're a good daughter." She paused. "Scott is a good son too, and he will take care of you." She continued saying "Look at all the people, look" and pointed out her finger in direction to the door, but I didn't see anyone. She had a recurring hallucination that her siblings were walking through the halls. She often called out to her mother: "Manman, Manman!"

Did she really see those people? At the beginning, Scott would come, carrying her, making her sit down in a wheelchair and pushing her around the hospital, which made her very happy. After the stroke, it wasn't possible anymore, and he'd moved to his own apartment. I'm still trying to understand why, at the hospital, she acted like her morale was totally fine, no sign of dementia at all. She spoke normally, and her conversations made sense to me.

My mother stayed at the hospital for a month and half and celebrated her seventy-fourth birthday there. I ordered her the biggest bouquet that I could afford, but the flowers never reached her! As an excuse, the floral company told me that the delivery person couldn't find the room, but the flowers her sisters sent her from Canada arrived just fine. I was outraged. "What is wrong with me?" I mourned. "Everything always seems to go wrong! Even a simple thing like flowers turn into a complicated issue!" They reimbursed me the money, of course, but my mother never received the bouquet, which would've been the last one she ever received. I couldn't think positively. I was retreating to a hidden, evil place. My spirit was out whack, and likely, so was my mother's. The rest of my body was shutting out the happiness and hope. As usual, I never called God during that despairing episode because I'd fallen to evil side, my head down. I was going into the supernatural world, into an unearthly period, and my mother was moribund. I never asked God to restore her health. I became an atheist who rejected the motto of "In God we trust…so help me God." Day after day, I encased myself into a new perspective of life, one without anticipation, without trust. I felt like I was standing at a four-way crossroads and I don't know which direction might be better to go. There were so many things to do and consider, and I didn't know which one to take on first. Like a robot, I decided to just keep on doing what I was used to doing: going to work, visiting my mother in the hospital, going to my doctor's appointments, and going home.

On our last Friday night together, I was touching her, checking her feet and her body. I was shocked to discover that both of her feet had turned pitch-dark. I called the nurse, and as usual, she told me that this would be reported to the doctor. On Saturday, when I went to the hospital, they had no news about it. Again, I left a message for the doctor to call me on Monday. I passed the weekend thinking about how careless the people at the hospital had been, myself included. I should've caught that earlier. I assumed that no nurse or doctor had ever checked that part of her body, which is very important for people who are diabetic. When I got to the hospital on Monday afternoon, a nurse told me that it was gangrene and that her doctors wanted to schedule a meeting with me the next day. For a moment, I felt like screaming, but the scream just stayed in my jaw. Steam poured from my ears, and my throat swelled with rage. I couldn't utter a single word. A sensation of shakiness aroused my body, something grabbed my thorax, and the space inside my chest became too small for my heart. It was all coming out through my mouth. I thought I might faint, but I told myself that I had to stay strong. *Fainting isn't going to resolve my problem, and there isn't time for that.* I retained myself with extraordinary force. I'd never been so scared in my life. I was inexperienced with dealing with hospital personnel, I stayed silent, the silence of the lamb going to the abattoir. I felt the need to speak up my mind, but at the same time, I didn't want to be too pushy, so they wouldn't mistreat her in my absence. I didn't know what to think or who to talk about it. A year before, I went with her to the podiatrist to cut her nails, as was instructed

THE DAILY BATTLE FOR A NORMAL LIFE

by her physician, and he accidentally cut off a piece of her skin with the nail. Was this the reason for her problem now? Had the wound gotten infected? If that was the case, would the gangrene have manifested in both legs? Why was I asking these questions, but her doctors weren't? What kind of caregivers do we endanger ourselves with?

35

Death, My Enemy

MY MOM KNEW THAT she was leaving me to be with her parents. The same Friday that I found out about her feet, she called my name very loudly as I entered the room to tell me to be brave, that she would be gone home soon. I asked her which home she meant.

"You know—home," she said in a decisive voice, "to be with my mother and my father." She pointed her finger at the door. "Look, look, there are my people walking along the corridor."

I could see no one, but she saw them. Perhaps she saw the angel of death standing by the door, like they show on television, ready to take her away from me and from my children, who loved her infinitely.

"Mommy, Mommy, Mommy," she cried, pointing a finger from her right hand at something, as if she was really seeing my grandmother. She was already in another world, which I was too spiritually immature to share with her.

That same Monday, she asked me to sleep with her. I was too tired to stay with her that night and had a meeting with all the doctors the next morning before work, so I declined her invitation but stayed longer with her at the hospital that night. By 9:30 p.m., she fell asleep, and I escaped to go home. The next day, as usual, I was there at 7:00 a.m. As I kissed her forehead to say good morning, as I was accustomed to doing, her body was cold, and she was mute. Her glossy gaze told me that something bizarre was happening. I called the nurse to find out why she couldn't speak and why she was so cold. They told me that they were waiting for the doctor and that they'd let me know. I got very displeased because they were not taking her to get her dialysis treatment like they usually did in the morning, and they couldn't answer my simple questions. The nurse in charge came to talk to me. In long Aesculapius sentences, she gave me a nonsense explanation, trying to pull the wool over my eyes.

I asked my friend Jessica, an ANP, who happened to be at the hospital for a conference, to come with me to the meeting. I thought that perhaps, I might not understand the big medical words they too often used to explain simple things to patients and families. During the meeting, the doctors told me that they needed to keep her at the hospital instead of sending her to a nursing home but that she didn't have to have dialysis anymore. Her body wasn't responding to it. I asked them about her feet, and they told me that it was impossible to do anything about it—that they would have to cut them off through her groin, and despite it all, it wouldn't resolve the problem. I was more aghast than before, and this time, my mouth froze. I was there to discuss her future, and it seemed like there was no such thing any longer. She was already a thing of the past for the doctors, like any other patient, no big deal. For me, though, she wasn't. She was my mom. Like adding cold water to a boiling pot, they'd instantaneously stopped trying to cure her. I was paralyzed for a while. I'd been joking with her not too long ago, and now she couldn't speak, and the doctors were giving up on her. I felt a bad sensation, as if my blood was turning into hot water in my head.

Finally, I regained myself. I didn't agree with their decision. I wanted them to continue her treatment, but they didn't give me that choice. I kept arguing with them about keeping her on the dialysis, they listened to me respectfully. However, at a point, I was just debating with myself, and soon I realized that I'd already lost the fight. Nothing would be done for her other than keeping her on painkillers so she'd be comfortable until the end. I gave up and left the conference room. I was pissed off at myself for being powerless and at the doctors for their helplessness. They knew that she was dying and that nothing more could realistically be done, but I couldn't see it. I didn't take my mother to the hospital to die but to get better. It seemed that the hospital's floor changed in gravity. I had to walk carefully so that I didn't fall down. My friend tried to make me understand that she was at the end of her life, but I was blinded by grief and strongly denied that fact. I cannot describe the way I was feeling inside—lost, empty, and disconcerted. I was alone with nobody to turn to. I had to decide, but I didn't know how. I was mad at God for the second time.

I called work and told them that I couldn't come in. I went back home to change and to fill a bag with clothes, thinking that I would go back to the hospital and not leave her side. On my way home, I decided to check at funeral homes to see what packages cost. My instinct just told me to do so. There's no way that I could've imagined that Tuesday would be her last day. The first funeral home I went was on US1. The lady who worked there didn't talk to me or even set down the food that was in front of her. I saw her actions as a sign of discrimination. Usually, when you enter a business, someone asks you how they can help you, but she didn't say anything and simply watched me leave. The second funeral home I visited gave me a good deal. The man was very professional and offered me a package that was on sale that day. I could make a payment every month, he explained. I closed the deal and made my first payment. I chose the coffin, which was included in the package, and went back to the hospital. I never thought that I'd be able to be in a room with so many coffins and not feel scared. Surprisingly, I wasn't scared at all; it just felt normal. Where did I get that courage? I don't know. I had to do what no one else could do for me, I suppose. All of this was preparation for the future. When I went back, Jessica helped me realized that my mother was slowly leaving this life. We prayed and sang, as usual. I was still in denial that something like that was about to happen to my mom. *She is invincible,* I thought, *and she will surmount this arduous episode.* Jessica suggested to the nurse in charge that she has to have morphine. She figured that my mother was probably in pain but couldn't speak up about it. Still, I rejected the fact that shortly, I would be in her absence. I remembered that I once watched

THE DAILY BATTLE FOR A NORMAL LIFE

documentary on television that said a person in a coma can still hear what you say, and that it's good to tell them the day, the date, and the news. I talked to her and let her know what day it was—the first day of spring. I told her that if she wanted to go, she may, as she had already said to me many times. I told her that I would be all right.

They were just words, of course, because my heart said otherwise. I didn't want to see her in pain, though, which would break my heart even more. She looked at me and opened her eyes widely as if seeing me for the last time, her only child. We kept praying and singing, and at 6:00 p.m., with one final breath, Tita opened her eyes as if to say *adieu* to me. She was gone for real. My dear friend left me forever. I felt disoriented, and panic enveloped my entire body. I know that death is the accomplishment of our destiny, the last step toward the hereafter, but my heart wasn't ready to see my mother gone so soon. I desperately tried to reason that it was just a dream, a dream that I couldn't get out of. I was alone in that tragedy, without a sister or a brother, without my husband, but I was surrounded by friends, and my friends came right away to the hospital to comfort me and to bid her goodbye.

I called Sam in Haiti, Scott, Steve, and my cousins to let them know. Jessica was still there with me, and she called a few families who were also my good friends. They all arrived so quickly, like they were already in the parking lot. We stayed with her until 9:00 p.m., and then I gave the authorization to the hospital to release the copse to the funeral home. Since 7:30 p.m., the hospital had been after me to order the pick-up, but I'd been warned at the funeral home that they would do that. I knew I had the right to stay with her for three hours after doctor pronounced her dead. They tried twice to help me understand that I had to let her go. I know they needed the room for another moribund person and that they couldn't waste time on her; she was already in the past, like all the others. Hospitals are businesses, after all, and so when one goes, another comes. When I got home, I called her sisters in Canada, my younger son who was in college in Detroit, and her best friend in New York. Then I started planning her last celebration. There was no time for me to sleep, and I couldn't swallow any food or drink. My throat was completely blocked. I was pretty much free of my diseases for those days. I didn't have pain or migraines and felt very energetic, contrary to when I was going to the hospital twice a day. I had a duty to execute and was willing to see it through to the end. People were helping, but all the decisions had to come from me, and there was only one "me." The next day, two friends took me to buy her a dress and accessories. Friends came to stay with me, to clean my house, and because in our culture we serve plenty food at funerals, people brought me many dishes and meals. People even traveled from other states to visit me. It was funny; one of her nephews was a Catholic priest and the other was a Baptist pastor, but they were able to put aside their religious beliefs to arrange together a nice farewell for their Catholic aunt at the funeral home.

I set up a simple funeral for her. The area was so crowded that the mortuary employees had to open the doors to enlarge the room so that more people could come in. I felt like a robot fulfilling a responsibility. I was empty of emotion. Life felt meaningless for me. Whoever we think we are and whatever we're so greedily fighting for every day, one day, we will have to leave it all behind. We became items that the livings can do whatever they want with, at the moment we take our last breaths. My mother never liked the cold, but that night, they took her to the coldest place possible, like she was only a piece of meat that needed to be preserved. I really resented her absence after all the people left. The pain inside, the struggle to make sense of it, and the emptiness were too much for me to bear. Sam stayed for two weeks with me, but then as usual went back to Haiti. I was left by myself with both, my old and new problems. Now that everybody was gone, leaving me at my own mercy, I could scream, yell at God, and yell at myself. There was no reason for my mother's death, I thought. The world didn't make sense to me; being born to die isn't reasonable. I refused to understand this earthly law, that today you're something and tomorrow you're nothing. I was fighting with reality and with my own mind, which was going wacko.

My friends said that I shouldn't feel alone because God was with me. It's easy to say this when you're not in the situation. If I talked to God, I didn't hear any reply. Anyway, I wasn't being friendly to him.

I was mad at him for what he did and mad at everyone who still had a mother. During my moments of meditation, I thought a lot about Sam. I understood more how he must've felt after the death of his parents. Now, we shared the same grief. We were twain orphans. I started calling him Papito and he called me Mamita, an affectionate way to lean on each other's shoulders.

As if they'd been slumbering, as if they'd left me temporarily to ease my grief, all my diseases came back at once. Suddenly, as the dust settled after my mother's passing, melancholy and nostalgia followed me like a shadow. I was bewildered, destroyed, and living with the guilt that I could've done more to save her, that I could've stayed at the hospital with her that night with her. These feelings penetrated deeply under my skin. I was heartbroken. The culpability that I hadn't done enough for her was ravaging my brain. I'd let her down by not standing up more strongly for her at that hospital. How could I have known that they would be so careless? Going to work, visiting her, and going to my specialists overwhelmed me, and I didn't spend enough time with her at the end. Life is so unpredictable. If I'd known she would be gone so fast, I would've taken a leave of absence to be with her 24/7. There was no good reason to think that she wouldn't come back home and live another ten years. I always thought that she was bombproof, that she would never die. The guilt was killing me inside. I was scared in my own house. I heard her steps all the time. I locked my bedroom's door at night but still heard her, whispering my name: "Oli, Oli…" I wouldn't leave my room until daylight. How could I be so afraid of my own dead mother? I was seeing her presence everywhere. I smelled her perfume. I was petrified.

I had to turn on all the lights in the house. As soon it was dark, they lit up and shut off automatically at sunrise. I talked to my aunts in Montreal every week to help me cope with my loss. I cried at work and in the street and screeched at home. She loved me unconditionally, as I loved her. It made it even more horrible to control my guilt and resentment. It was like a horror movie where the bad guy follows their victim everywhere. Sadness became another best friend that was chasing me. I went to a prayer group, but the songs didn't help with my unhappiness, so I gave up. I needed a strong hand to embrace my shoulders and a shoulder to rest on. I decided to see a consultant to explain my deep sorrow and the guilty feeling on my conscience. Quickly, I found out that my place wasn't there. I couldn't let a stranger interfere in my life. How could she assist me if she'd never been in a situation like mine? I stopped going to therapy. She wasn't telling me anything that I didn't know. I know now that it was my own problems that were holding me back. It wasn't working because she was telling me what I didn't want to hear. I did like one book that she advised me to read, though. It helped a little bit, but I still had to work on me, by myself, to get over it. It has taken a long time to repossess my ego.

A year passed, and I was still afraid of the dark and loneliness inside my house. Did I have a choice? If I was in the street and it was getting dark, I had to rush home and barricade myself in my bedroom. That sounds ridiculously crazy, I know, but I spent over two years in that condition. As soon night approached, I filled a tray with water, tea, and bread—everything that I could need for the night—and locked my bedroom door behind me. I got relief only when Sam came to visit for two weeks at a time. One day, I decided to confront my fear. I had a choice to make: live with my fear or help myself. I decided to find out what was making me so frightened. I couldn't sleep, so in the middle of the night, I left my bedroom and walked out of the house, then came back inside. I felt like my heart was going to stop. I needed to throw up. I feared my own shadow, thinking that it must be the shadow of someone else. The silence in my family room, where I sat for a while to brave my nuisances, was agony, but I had to face that enemy who'd made me so miserable in my own nest. I stayed there for the rest of the night. I loudly talked to my mother as if she was sitting in her habitual seat, the brown couch. "Here I am, Tita. You know that I still love you, but I'm too frightened. I cannot continue to live like this, so you have to make it better for me to survive." I repeated that many times. Did I believe that she heard me? At that moment, yes. I'd made a good decision about that situation, because little by little, I recaptured myself. Without me having to pay too much more attention to it, everything went back to normal. Like a flu virus, it went away on its own. My bravery helped me repossess my life, time and time again.

Two years later, I still couldn't pass Baptist Hospital because it reminded me too much of the death of my mother. I wasn't completely cured, that was for sure; I was still angry—furious at this murderer of a building. The questions I kept asking myself were: How come all those LPNs, RNs, and doctors who worked in that big hospital didn't pay more attention to the details of her body? Wasn't there someone who could give patients proper baths and check their bodies? I washed her face at night after giving her food, but during the day, it looked like there was no one to take care of her, especially when she was unable to help herself. If they had, they would've seen that her feet were turning black before it got so aggravated. It's a shame that handicap patients are so often left without proper care. When she had her stroke, I had a big discussion with a nurse who was so hardheaded that she didn't want to call the doctor in right away. It was always a fight. At the hospital, it looked like everybody wanted to relax, even though the diseases weren't taking any breaks. If they'd listened to me, if I'd said more, maybe something could've been done immediately. They waited until Monday for the doctor to read the results of a test that was performed on Saturday. Does Medicare/Medicaid suck to the extent that the hospital can get away with doing the bare minimum for their patients? Even a piece of furniture needs to be cleaned! It should be the same for people. There should be a nurse assigned to this type of duty who checks patients and reports any abnormalities that they see, from head to toe. This policy should be vigorously maintained in all hospitals. Do they intentionally let us die when we reach a certain age or when we've already reached the maximum cost allowed by the insurance per head and per year? I was doing the work of the doctors. After her stroke, I was who discovered that the left side of her body wasn't moving.

The more I thought about it, the angrier I got. I regret that I didn't let the doctors know that I was dissatisfied with the care provided to my mother. I'm the kind of person who forgives people too easily. After this experience, though, I changed. I learned that we should never completely trust our care providers. We need to sometimes do our own research and not blindly accept things without asking for the reasons. Sometimes, we have to get a second opinion if we don't agree with the first. I'm grateful to the doctors and nurses who have a real interest in health, who aren't just in it for the money but because they love the profession and care about people. I blamed many doctors and nurses for their roles in the lack of care they provided to my mom. Their implications in a patient's life should be greater than that. You're not God, that's a fact, but he has given you the knowledge to do a better job. If you cannot fight for us, especially against the biased policies of hospital management, if you cannot defend your patients, your place isn't in the medical field. Taking care of patients is a vocation and a responsibility. If you find it awkward to do so, become a businessperson instead. Also, a patient's family should be more involved, should feel comfortable enough to ask questions if you don't understand medical buzzwords, to show interest when they want to know more. Doctors should write daily notes about all the updates and changes in the health of your loved one. I was the daughter who dealt with the grief of seeing my energetic mother reduced to a vegetable, unable to care for herself because they didn't care enough, probably because of her age or her insufficient insurance. I was the provider who had to work full-time to pay bills while also checking on her and attending to my own appointments. Obviously, I couldn't stay at the hospital all the time to check on what should've been checked by hospital employees. At my job, a leave of absence for loved ones was without pay. I think the government should allow paid time off in the cases of sick children, spouses, mothers, and fathers.

After her death, I checked on her medicines and saw that she'd been given nothing for depression. Depression can truly harm people and makes everything worse. Through that experience, I learned my lesson to always ask, even if our request doesn't make sense, to look at every detail, and to fight for what I believe is important. It took them more than forty-eight hours to realize that my mother had an overnight stroke and to have a test done to confirm what I'd said. Me, who knew zero about medicine. Her feet were not checked until I decided check on them. Still, I cannot explain this to anybody or even tell you exactly what illness killed her. She was seventy-four years old, but the negligence of the hospital staff contributed to her dying too soon. Six years passed, and the more I thought about it, the more I was convinced that something bad had happened to her at the hospital. I was willing to find out so that others wouldn't have to go to the same process. I was afraid, though, afraid that the truth would affect me more than I was prepared to handle. I didn't want to reopen the wound, to revisit something that I was forcing myself to forget. I preferred to live in denial, convincing myself that her death was God's wish. To witness her passing from this life to the hereafter was such an emotional moment, and I cherish it a lot. First, I feel privileged to have experienced something like that, to be at her side during her last moment. To be an eyewitness to her departure from earth by standing near her so that she could see me for the last time—it's spiritual beyond my reckoning, beyond my imagination. It's a terrible picture, of course, but it's a souvenir that I want to keep alive in my mind for the rest of my life. Strange reality—one moment she could respire, and next, she couldn't breathe at all. What a big difference!

We often ask for daily bread, but we forget about the most important thing, the spiritual bread of life. After her passing, I often lay on my bed and let my mind floats, attempting to find peace, thinking that she was probably in a better place with her parents. At the end, her face turned toward me, and her eyes were wide open, looking at me as if to say, "I'll be fine where I'm going. Take care of yourself, my dear daughter." I found myself doing that same movement again and again, recreating that peaceful moment.

After her death, I missed my husband even more than before. Before she passed on, at least I had my mother to talk to, even though she rarely could remember even half of our conversations. I didn't care. She was my dear friend who always took pleasure in listening to my stupid jokes, dramatic news, and goofy stories. I missed her deeply. However, focusing on the fact that she was at peace helped me create a future where I could live without her and heal myself over time.

I lost devotion to going to church and became a nonpracticing nonbeliever. I didn't accept the fact that I had to fight to get what I needed. I never prayed for her recovery because I thought that God would know what I wanted. God knows our thoughts, the present, and the future, so why should I always have to ask? I'm the same person he created. I don't like to have to ask. He knew that I didn't want my mother to die, but he expired her life anyway. That's why I blame him. I blamed everybody and everything for my solace. When Tita first moved in with me, my marriage was crumbling. I was intensely loved by two extraordinary people living under the same roof, which scared me a lot. My husband and my mother both wanted me to themselves. There was never a familiar conversation between them. If Tita had chosen who I would marry, I don't think she would've chosen Sam, and he knew that. Her unconditional love could make her ambitiously blind. Because of her experiences with her own husband, she overworried about me and was reticent of accepting that Sam could be a good husband. She wanted a son-in-law with more steady, standard accomplishments. As she used to say, "Art does not give bread." She was a conservative mother, and she wanted the best for her daughter. I understood that, but I loved an artist and thought that she should be all right with my decision. They were very distant with each other. I did all I could to get them to become closer, but never found any real success. For example, when I was sick, my mother would wake up early to prepare me breakfast, but Sam didn't know she'd done so, so when he got up to make coffee, he'd prepare my breakfast as well. Both breakfasts would end up in my bedroom, and I'd have to taste both so I wouldn't disappoint either of them. I made excuses for what happened like I was the guilty one!

"He should know that I was preparing your breakfast," my mother would say. "He saw me in the kitchen."

"Doesn't she know that is my responsibility to give you breakfast when you're sick?" he whined.

What would you do in a situation like that? Sometimes, they'd both complain to me about the other's attitude. If I tried to explain the reason why the other was acting or feeling a certain way without putting anybody down, they'd assume that I was taking a side. So on many occasions, I stayed silent.

They made it very hard for me to please everybody, and some harsh remarks came out of Sam's mouth. "I didn't know that I married two women at the same time, two women to please," he said.

Should I listen to that blast concerning my mother? No, but still, he didn't deserve an answer. Before she got sick, she was so helpful around the house. She did all the laundry and cleaned up after all of us during the week. Honestly, I didn't really think that I should pay attention to his quips and remarks at her expense, and so I ignored him completely. Once, when we were all in the car together, Sam was talking to me. My mother didn't say anything, but I could hear her breath in the back sit, and we both knew what that meant. I was her only child, and there was nowhere else for her to go. In Haiti, I could rent her a house in her city, close to her sister, but when I moved here to America, I couldn't leave her behind. It would've broken both her heart and mine. I decided to have her with me all the time, thinking that I could take care of her. Also, I figured that having her around would be like having a friend, that she could keep me company when Sam was out spending his Saturday nights carousing with friends. I would have my mom with me instead of holing up by myself in my bedroom. So they'd have to just learn to deal with each other, I decided. But believe me, it got worse and worse. Eventually, Tita accepted Sam for who he was, but he rejected her sentiment like a punishment, as if inflicting cruel revenge. I suffered from their bad behavior, but they both seemed to ignore my feelings. What was incomprehensible to me, and still is to this day, is that they were both very kind to everyone except each other.

36

Another Invisible Disorder

SOON AFTER MY MOTHER's death, I developed a disease called solitude, which dragged me into a deep and desolate depression. Nostalgia became another unwanted friend who followed me around. The aerosol of our relationship fumigated all the remaining good inside of me, leaving me with only the spectral of an empty soul. I was starting to degrade myself and close the door on almost everything I used to enjoy. I would lock my bedroom door and watch television for an entire weekend like there was nothing else to do. When I say I was watching TV, I don't mean it; if you'd asked me later what movies or shows were on, I probably wouldn't have been capable of answering. It was more like the TV was watching me. I didn't hear any of the words and didn't see anything on the screen. I went thoughtless, and my mind went blank, like I had swallowed and rejected my own spirit. I was very disconcerted by my surroundings, and a ghostly expression veiled my appearance. I felt like a secluded prisoner in jail.

    I didn't even answer telephone calls, just sat there in my harrowing cage. My husband would call me from Haiti again and again, desperate to get in touch with me. The phone was within a step from me, but I couldn't touch it. I didn't want to—I didn't want to hear anybody. The silence was too precious for me to lose by talking to someone. Sometimes, I even had to turn off the television. I didn't want to perceive sounds or voices. I just wanted total silence and muteness, staring at the ceiling. Physically, I was there, but the most important parts of me had transitioned to a deserted zone full of sand, one hundred degrees and ever-increasing, like the fires of hell. I had to just keep moving through it without knowing where I was going. I was so thirsty for happiness and companionship. I wasn't a solitary person by nature, but I became one by circumstance. I became desensitized to anything and everything.

My son called, but I didn't answer. I was taking my family down with me into that ferocious tsunami, which I'd selfishly created. I had the right to be mad at Sam for leaving me alone and my mother for leaving earth too early, but I had no right to make my son responsible for those disasters. He was too sensitive to let me go on being miserable without interfering. The wars of bad health and lonesomeness made me extremely antisocial. As soon I got home from work, I hid in my room like a captive. Was that any way to live? I thought about it a lot and decided to pray. I'd lost my faith after the death of my mother, but during a brief moment when I'd regained my lucidity, I felt the necessity to renew my pact with God. I watch the EWTN channel on TV a lot. I didn't have to look at the screen, I could just listen. Thus, I realized that there was light even after the door closed. Darkness is a pollution of mind that I needed to stay away from. It was frustrating to feel as if I had to move on from grief very quickly. I had to stop myself from getting too used to it and pulling away from my loved ones. The word *impossible* only exists in life if you do nothing. I kept repeating to myself, liberally and loudly, "It's going to get better," even though I didn't know exactly how or what to do to make it so. In life, we shouldn't get discouraged by the difficulties that fall into our paths. There is always light and hope waiting for us somewhere if we search for it. So that is what I decided to do—to forcefully look for that light, which I knew would appear someday again.

It wasn't an easy fight. I was already completely transported into a world of solitariness. I needed someone to hug me, kiss me, and perhaps make love to me, to console me and make me forget about my unfortunate circumstances. My three children lived away from home, Tita was gone, and Sam wasn't there to help me with my needs. He was nowhere to be found during that wicked moment. I felt neglected. Like baby birds need their mother's wings to warm them up, I needed his shoulder to lean my head on, to find comfort, for his body to embrace mine and make me feel safe. Unbelievably, I searched for this in the pornographic channel on TV, thinking that I could do it myself, right, but it didn't work. I didn't understand. Some people can do it themselves, I suppose, but in my case, I preferred a living human being. I was trapped in my misery. I wanted to hate that man as much as I had when I'd first agreed that he could go back to Haiti. Why, I wondered, was I so attached to a man who was so seldom there for me? Calling three to five times a day wasn't the solution.

In September of the same year, my cousin's cousin died from pancreatic cancer in New York. He was only fifty-five years old. He wasn't only Clara's cousin but also mine by extension. We weren't blood-related, but we lived like family. I cried because I'd lost so many people in such a short period of time. He was the cousin who all those years ago took me to school that day I got in trouble. That was the fourth death in the family within a year. Johnny, I miss you.

Loneliness, sadness, and madness invaded my soul after all those events. Then another ailment started consuming my mental health—depression. I cried for no apparent reason, I was irritable, I had more pain than ever, and my mind went to multiple places at once. I felt that like the world was ending. I was already in another universe; the world of animosity, malice, and despair. I didn't want to let my doctor know about it because of the reputation of that sickness—I was embarrassed. This time, I felt powerless and didn't think that I could resolve it on my own. So I decided to speak up a bit about my mental sensations to Jean, my PA-C. Right away, she understood and gave me an antidepressant prescription, Cymbalta, which just made me sleep all the time. I felt more powerless, the medication demoralizing me even more. An atmosphere of nullity reigned me. I didn't want to do anything anymore. I was close to giving up on life. In that lethargy, I found no meaning in life. I thought that I should never have been born. Why put people on earth if they have to go through so many hindrances? If I didn't exist, my children wouldn't have been born either. What did I do—give them lives where they had to constantly struggle to have balance, to weigh the pros and the cons of everything just to survive? The worst part about depression is that at a certain point, you develop a taste for your state of mind—you begin to cherish it, in a certain sense.

We shouldn't undermine people who have severe mental illnesses because it's as real as any disease is. There was no clarity or luminosity for me. I was swimming in dark water, and there was no island in sight, not as far as my eye could see. I couldn't see what was beyond the dark mass that I was living in. I felt like I was floating in subterranean water, my boat having sunk. I was at the mercy of the sharks, who were willing to make a feast of me. I struggled to find the strength to defend or protect myself. I thought I should simply give up on the struggle by traveling beyond the universe to finally find peace. I never thought that I could be Janus-faced in that sense. I'd always liked my life. At times, though, when I was deep in my depression, I was completely ready to travel to that horizon of no return. It wasn't my nature but my subconscious that motivated me to have thoughts like that. I didn't feel that I could kill myself, but if something happened and I died, I thought that it would be deliverance. I would welcome it, in fact. I could be driving to work and realize that I didn't care if I had an accident. Some days, I even hoped that it would happen, even though I knew I might not be the only victim of my carelessness. I changed lanes like I was driving in my backyard, not paying attention to the other cars. *I'm alone on earth*, I thought. I was ready to go find my mother. I wasn't afraid of death. I knew I had plenty of family in the beyond. Everything irritated me so much that I would hilariously cry for no reason, without the ability to stop.

It's Friday afternoon, my chronic headaches hadn't spared me. I drove back home under the influence of my ailments, happy only when I get to my house. I had no one living with me anymore, to give me reason to pass at the supermarket, so I went straight home. I took three butalbital pills instead of one to make me sleep until Monday. The devil atrociously attacked me.

Saturday morning, I woke up completely intoxicated by that high dosage. I was walking in slow motion. I felt great, relaxing. After eating something, I went back to bed to continue my sleeping beauty until Sunday. Here comes Sunday night, I am there in my pitch-dark bedroom, crouched in a ball in one corner of my big empty bed. My head was slightly bent and my legs were crooked, trying to touch my forehead, like one was trying to console the other, like my body was trying to squeeze out the intruder that'd invaded my common sense. Increasingly, the disease was taking control of my body. Serving as my only supporters, my arms tightly embraced both of my legs. This was the position I used to press my body, to crush the pain into crumbs, hoping that in little pieces, the gnawing devil inside of me would be less powerful. I tried to protect my carcass from falling into a river full of rapids. Wildly alone, like a wounded animal left by itself in a deep forest, its force abandoned, incapable of enjoying the beauty of nature and the cooling breeze, I was letting my soul tumble into the wickedness. I couldn't govern my mind to collect any positive thoughts in the darkness. Fears completely blocked my lucidity, as if I'd been thrown into a bizarre, frightening, and unnatural way of life. My body was infused with solitude, ailments, and madness. I was on the topmost mountain, standing on the rock. I didn't know how to get down, how to leave that igneous spot and find a safer, more gratifying place. I was so miserable, vulnerable, terrified, anguished, and in a lot of pain. My loneliness was deep, and I was immensely appalled by the silence of my wide room, which was occupied by a king-sized bed, which was too big for one person, a chest, and an armoire—my sole friends to talk to. They were my only allies, always there for me night and day, benevolently listening to my distressing exaltations. Next to the bed, on either side, two nightstands sat stonily, holding two golden lamps, each steadily waiting for me to light them up so they could reverse and brighten the darkness. I needed this light for sure, but I stayed in the dark, which seemed more appropriate to the condition of my spirit. I felt completely empty and wondered if my blood had turned into water. "Am I dead yet?" I asked myself. Toward the evening, my eyes roamed from right to left and vice versa, like I was expecting a visitor to come at any moment. I transitioned into a blackout of time, which suppressed me from reality. I was immersing myself deeper and deeper into this indescribable, deep, dirty water without much expectation that I could ever come back to the surface.

Fortunately, I had a tiny bit of subconscious left, which alerted me of my lunacy. "I can stop it," I mumbled to myself. I kept repeating the words, "Please, God, give me the strength to end this difficult occurrence." I whispered them over and over. Suddenly, a heavy weight was oppressing my chest, then that weight raced through my throat to suffocate me. I had to do something fast. I tried to inhale and exhale. I needed air, and it started becoming difficult to catch my breath. My pain became so invasive that I swore my heart was having trouble handling its normal functions. Like a baby at the time of birth, I screamed—a scream of infinite desolation—a scream to move the fixed celestial stars from their immovable places, a scream for help. I behooved assistance from beyond. I hysterically screeched to release the devil who was sitting across my gullet, which seemed to have no desire to go away on its own. I have to confess that I was so confused that I couldn't distinguish which of my illnesses was kicking me down like this. The pain monopolized my entire body. I really couldn't tell. In a thundering, breaking voice, trying to catch my breath, I pleaded to whatever deity could hear my supplication and asked that they intervene, that they master my environment for me. I desperately tried to connect my thoughts to all the good spirits that encircled me, suspended above my head. I even caught myself saying a few words out loud.

This all might sounds ridiculously senseless, whimsical, and ominously strange, but I was in a state of trance. I watched heavy dark-gray smoke fill the room. I was coughing—a dry cough—and I couldn't stop. I don't know how long it lasted. My eyes were wide open, gaping with exuberance at this incredible scene. I was completely lost in the spiritualism of that moment that I couldn't even blink my eyes, or perhaps they forgot to blink because they were too preoccupied with the magical, psychological images around me. My face got wet with teardrops, but I couldn't tell why I was crying. The tears flowed more abundantly down onto my face, my nighty, and my pillows. Was it because of the pain I was in or the emotional significance of that holy instant? I don't know. I just remember that

I was in tears while the fumes softly floated around me. Slowly, the smoke dissipated, leaving me feeling like I was in a dream. I gently stood up, both of my feet planted on the square tile, and watched the dark cloud dispersing. I didn't want it to leave me, but no words would come out my mouth, nor could I move. I couldn't hold onto the spectacle any longer. I suddenly lost my voice. Immobile like a Greek statue, I was somewhere else, in another place where there was no ache, no misery. I couldn't feel myself. I was lifeless, or more likely, still in a trance. I have no idea how long I stayed in that catalepsy, but afterward, I did find some relief. My pain disappeared little by little, and I regained my lucidity and force. Suddenly, in an explosion of faith, I said to myself, "I can make it well again."

I hadn't seen a vision of my mother in that dancing smoke, but I'm convinced that she visited me in spirit that day. It was real; her smell was all over the room. Afterward, I felt like a person who had smoked pounds of marijuana. My eyes were getting heavy, and I fell into a soporific lethargy, probably a result of all the painkiller pills that I'd been taken. To recover from my tormented night, I called work at 4:00 a.m. and left a message, informing them that I wouldn't be coming in. I calmly slumbered through almost the entire afternoon. The next day, I was ready for my normal activities like nothing had happened the night before.

This is a type of invisible sickness that many people face daily, people who we all interact with every day. I hope that my storytelling gives you a better outstanding of what people with chronic diseases and tormented lives often deal with. Because of their normal, seemingly stable outward appearances, people tend not to believe them. "Is he/she really sick?" they ask. What you see isn't always what's real. The time we are living is wrought with false impressions of reality. Medications offer us the stamina that help us tolerate our diseases, but they don't go away. I think it is awful to lie about your health conditions, but sometimes, it's better and easier to always say "I'm well" even when you're not. We don't always know who is struggling to live a normal life.

Having depression is a serious disease, not a bogus or voluntary ailment. It means moments of malfunction in the brain that go and come and make victims totally blind about what is wrong and what is right. No one is exempt. Depression attacks by surprise and populates the whole organism, operating in your mind for a long time before it rears its head to ravage you. It's never too late to take action, though. You need to confront it like it is, an invisible enemy, and tell your doctor about those symptoms. It's embarrassing, I know, and it has bad reputation, but you can keep it between yourself and your psychologist or psychiatrist, so long as you are getting help. You can't do it alone. You might not be able to completely cure it, but you might find a way to manage it. Mental health is another reason you need to understand and know your body well. Even if you think that something is normal, it might not be.

I believe that if your mind is strong and you intend to achieve something, there is no way your brain will refuse. Your body will work accordingly, fulfilling a very important role in recovery. A positive attitude is always the best way to live. For many years, I've brainwashed myself with the desire to prove things to others. I didn't take into consideration that my body was really unwell and needed to be protected from hurt. The same thing happens when you are at the hospital; when you have visitors, for a moment, you forget about your sickness and pain. Why? Because your mind is so bemused by the talking, the laughing, the presence of your loved ones, that for a few minutes, it becomes disconnected from your painful reality. It doesn't mean that your agony has gone away, of course, but your nerve cells are preoccupied. In a sense, the positive sensations overpower the negative ones. Visitors inadvertently help you control your emotions. I'm not a doctor or scientist, but from experience, I can say that emotions play a big role in our lives, both good emotions (laughter, thunderous exaltations, getting excited, new adventures, and positive events) as well as bad emotions (sadness, receiving bad news, not feeling good, adversity). Therefore, as much I can, try to distract my mind with laughter and relaxation.

Meditation is good for everybody; try to live for a moment in an imaginary bubble that cuts you off from actuality. It's beneficial for that short period of time even though it doesn't cure the mind or the body. Depending on what we have, we need to cure both the body and the mind. Like going somewhere on vacation to get peace of mind, you might falsely assume that when you get back, everything that stressed you before will be gone, that you will come back restored, that all your bills will be paid. Of course, no matter how good the vacation was, you can't really run away from your life, and your troubles will be there waiting for your return. So instead, when you get back, you feel as if you never left. Perhaps that doesn't mean that you shouldn't go at all, because you get the benefit of having a break from reality, but that logic doesn't work well for me. Unsuccessfully, I have tried meditation programs, most of which ask you to silent your mind and be free of your problems for at least an hour every day. I have a busy mind, so it never works for me. I cannot stop myself from thinking about myself, my family, what is going in the world, and what I could be doing instead. I find it difficult to go to that "Eden of the mind" where I can close my eyes and discover myself floating in the clouds, playing Cassandra like there is no other existence. It is hard for me to penetrate into that ecstasy of forgetting things that really exist. My mind is too possessed with my life to find serenity in meditation. I remember that when I was pregnant with my first child, I went to a prenatal class where they taught me how to breath to relieve the pain of contractions. They told me that breathing would help a lot with the dolor. It's good to do in the classroom with your husband holding you from behind when there isn't pain yet. When the real moment of delivery came, however, I was in so much pain. I commenced inhaling and exhaling like they'd prepared me to, but I realized that it wasn't helping. I couldn't keep up with that classic style. I needed to vociferate like a normal human being giving birth to a child. By the way, Sam was such a chicken that he didn't ever stay in the delivery room while I brought our sons into the world.

I jolly well enjoy a moment of relaxation, for sure—lying down on the mat, listening to soundscape music—but I cannot call it meditation. I like to use those moments of downtime to plan what I have to do later.

37

The Third Treatment

A FEW MONTHS LATER, I finally decided to see a hepatologist at the University of Miami, Center for Liver Diseases. Long ago, Dr. Joe recommended that I give it a shot. In reality, I didn't decide to go myself, but received a letter from Dr. Howard about research that was being done there. They had the reputation of being the best of the best. Dr. H. was no longer doing HCV treatments. He'd joined a group of physicians and care providers to campaign against liver disease. The letter he sent me was officially signed by about fourteen specialists who were seeking cures at Schiff Liver Institute. Dr. Schiff was referred to as "one of the world's most-renowned liver disease researchers." They were asking my permission to provide my name and address to the Jackson Memorial Foundation and suggesting that I call the vice president of the institute. I thought it was very nice that they'd given me the number of such an important person. Who was I? I remembered all the trouble I went through with my eye, though, so I didn't call him. I did, however, call to schedule an appointment to see Dr. Schiff. I could get in with him within a month. I was so excited to meet him. His name had been in my fellow patients' mouths in every group meeting I'd ever attended, and he was all over the news and magazines related to hepatitis. The center was designated as "the world's first independent division of hepatology dedicated solely to the treatment of the liver." When people talked about Dr. Schiff, they referred to him as the savior of the hep C community, God's healer for the liver. I wanted to meet him because I was convinced that he had the power to save me from that bloodsucker.

During our first appointment, he didn't say too much. He ordered a laparoscopy biopsy of the liver that was processed by Dr. Jeff. I signed a consent form that gave the university the right to do the next steps, a fibro-scan and blood test. Without realizing it, I'd signed up to be part of a study. The majority of the labs were done at the university—an ultrasound, blood tests, and so on. I had more tests every time they scheduled me for a visit. They determined that my liver didn't look too bad—stage 2, borderline 3—but a lot of my levels were "out of whack," such as the alpha-fetoprotein tumor marker, AST/ALT, carbon dioxide, the bun/creatinine ratio, a very low platelet count, and absolute neutrophils. I thought that my next visit would be with him again and that he would tell me more because I'd had all these tests, but another hepatology specialist, with whom Dr. Schiff had left some notes, consulted me, read the results, and sent me to have another sonogram and blood test. The new doctor prescribed Actos as medication for my glucose, which was also a little high. That was it. I never saw Dr. Shift again. I concluded that he probably only saw patients once and then left them in the hands of somebody else. Or else, my case wasn't severe enough for his attention. What did I expect? He was a professor, a scientist, and a savant who was studying different kinds of liver damage. With all that said, I didn't feel good about it. I thought that he had duped me. I went there to have him as my doctor. I know that I was lucky to be able to see him and that many people might not have that chance. At UM, doctors don't stick around long enough for you to get used to them. They come and go. They're often from elsewhere, young doctors who just finished school and are there for training. When you visit, the specialist is usually accompanied by one or two students. For example, by my third visit, the second hepatologist I'd seen had moved to another city and left me in the hands of an ARNP. She was very knowledgeable about the liver and eager to help patients with this type of virus, which is what she was trained for.

I have to admit, all the women caregivers I've had have been very nice and professional. She was one of them. She even told me how much I should weigh to help with my fatty liver. Again, by my fifth appointment, she moved out of Miami and left me with another doctor, Dr. Leo. With my consent, the new doctor decided to repeat the last treatment, which would be the same, he explained, but would go on longer. Dr. Leo told me that the last treatment would be more efficient if it was elongated for another six months. After my trial, researchers discovered that this was more effective than the short-term treatment period was. The duration would be around eighteen months, give or take. For patients like me, it would definitely help, he explained. I like when doctors say "help" instead of "cure" because it meant that they were not sure of the results and really that was the case there. This seems more honest, and it doesn't matter to me whether I'm cured or not. As long I'm breathing, I will try anything, again and again. There is hope when you take a risk, but there is no chance of hope when you give up. This hope gives me the courage to continue my health battle. Hope is my faithful comrade, just like when I bought a quick-pick lottery ticket. I kept the ticket in my bag for almost two months with the hope that maybe I was the winner and just didn't know it yet. So I wasn't afraid to go back on that adventure. I figured that after so many twists and turns, I could someday find a cure for my HCV. Destiny has a big place in my body's core; what has to happen will happen no matter what. We are all routing a specific itinerary on earth, which is basically the same, but each person takes their own direction to attain the same destination. That won't ever change.

It was soon time to start the third treatment, and I was ready. The treatment was done through my hepatology doctor at the Sylvester University of Miami. The quantitative count of my blood units was high, so the doctor decided to increase the dosage. I agreed and started my medicine. I declared war on that SOB, HCV. I definitely wanted to rescue my blood from that bloody viral disease. I craved giving blood like a normal person does, helping others like they had for me in 1984. Unfortunately, per my specialists, I would never be able to. Even if one day I was completely cured from that virus, they said that it would be wise for me to not to hope. They told me that even if I stayed cured forever, my liver would still be damaged. I could live with that, I thought. I had good intentions, but you can't often force the unfeasible to be feasible.

Once the treatment started, I was taking more units and higher dosages of ribavirin. I was doing well, but something inside my body was going wrong. I don't know what it was, exactly, but I had an overwhelming sense of dread. I was going to die and didn't know why. I needed somebody to help me get even from my bed to my bathroom. I was very weak and fragile. I was still living by myself. Every day, I got a little bit worse than I was the day before. I had double fibromyalgia: body aches, nausea, shortness of breath, fatigue, chills, fevers, dizziness, you name it. I went to work every two days despite my wickedness. It became very hard for me to drive my two-hour roundtrip, depending on the traffic, and to hold a job for eight hours. My bosses understood me, but I was there to work. They tried to give me simple and easy tasks, but my body was already endangered. I was losing weight quickly. Sam kept asking me if he had to come back sooner. I would've liked that because I couldn't really take care of myself. I needed assistance, but the fact that he had to ask made me into a rebel. As usual, I tried to be stronger than I thought I was capable of. I said, "No, you come as scheduled." It wasn't what I would've preferred, but I let him decide what his priority was. Of course, he didn't get it. He would've been my salvation if he'd decided to come on his own. He came as scheduled, one week later. He helped me go to the bathroom and he fed me. I couldn't eat too much. I was losing pounds like crazy. I couldn't go to work at all. One morning, I felt that I was in the last stage of my life. I sent an email to the nurse in charge of my treatment to call me as soon as possible. They gave me a 24/7 telephone number to call in case of needs. I tried to reach her through the telephone in vain. She called me back the same day in the afternoon and told me to go to the nearest emergency room right away. Soon after, she called me again to ask if I could find someone to take me to UMH instead. My husband was home, and I told him to take me there. God does this thing that even when we feel like we are the border of a flooding river, the water coming

THE DAILY BATTLE FOR A NORMAL LIFE

fast—even when you feel like there is no time to run away—if you trust him enough, he will send a savior. Sam was my savior because by myself, I wouldn't have been able to drive the thirty miles from my house to the hospital. At the emergency room, I underwent a wide variety of tests. They put tubes in my nose for oxygen and took my blood every two hours. I had three-arterial blood, which was very painful. I was sent for respiratory therapy, or EKG. All in the same night. Instead of easing my pain, it seemed like that they wanted to exacerbate it with all these labs. I was so drained that I couldn't talk. Sam was very nervous. He kept looking at the monitor to ensure that oxygen was flowing, especially when they told him that my blood platelet is too low. He came and went, calling friends to tell them about my health issues. By 8:00 p.m., the doctor came to tell me that I'd been admitted. He explained why, but we couldn't understand it, something wasn't clear to us. My husband kept asking questions. Yes, you heard well; this time, he asked too many questions, but all his questions were answered with incomprehensible responses in heavy medical jargon. On my way to the room, at 10:00 p.m., they told Sam that he couldn't go behind the door because I was going the CCU (critical care unit). He was as shocked as I was. It sounded serious. I wondered, "Am I going to die?" He kissed me hopelessly and with sadness said goodbye. "I'll be here early tomorrow," he said. I could see the concern on Sam's face. He was scared. He didn't want to leave me, but he didn't have a choice. A nurse was watching me through a window. I was checked on often and had many blood tests. I can't even say how many.

They gave me steroids to keep me awake all night. By eleven the next day, Sam was able to see me. The nurse told him that they have given a shot this morning and she has another one to be given to me. As she said, those types of shots were given to people who were very sick, and they were very expensive. Thanks to my insurance, I didn't have to worry about the bills. I was covered 100 percent. I had a rally of doctors and students coming to visit me every hour. My PCP at the hospital, fortunately, was a friend who I hadn't seen since he became a doctor. He originally studied in Washington, DC, and I was glad to see him again. Coincidentally, he was in charge of my health. He told me that he just picked up the file at the top and saw my name. Miracles happen every day in people's lives, we just have to recognize them for what they are. I hadn't seen him in ten years, and there he was at such a crucial moment in my life. Why did that person, who I hadn't seen for such a long time, just appear in my life and in that circumstance, at the very moment when I needed a trustful doctor? Not only did I have the opportunity to see him, I felt very confident that I was in good hands. They kept me at the hospital for a full week, and after many meetings between my hepatology doctor and the other specialists, they decided to totally remove me from the treatment. I felt crushed, disappointed, and incapacitated. I wasn't born with this infirmity that restrained me from doing what I wanted. It looked like I was going to die with it, for sure. Many people get a lasting cure from that disease, but it seemed to me that this was a pipedream I couldn't ever achieve. I never realized how scary a CCU room can look when you are extremely sick, with all the tubes and wires attached to different parts of your body, machinery suspended above of your head, a table next to you full of medical accessories, shining and ready in case of a code-blue. Code-black, code-red, whatever. Who knows? To me, this room resembled a torture room like the ones I saw in horror movies. It was frightening. But the good news is that these rooms exist to save lives, not to kill, no matter how scary and imprisoning they look.

    I got better. After a few weeks, I went back to work. On the first day back, I got sick again, right while everybody was saying, "Welcome back." They were so happy to see me. Suddenly, I couldn't breathe. My malady didn't like work anymore. Two coworkers took me back to the hospital in the company truck, which created a lot of controversy for my supervisor. The problem wasn't too bad, but I was still convalescing. I'd gone back to work too early. I stayed at the hospital for another week, which was a good thing, because at home, there was nobody to take care of me. Sam had already departed to Haiti. I needed more time to clear away all the interferon toxins from my body. People said that I should've dug to find out what went wrong during the treatment, to determine what'd nearly killed me. The important thing to me was that I was alive, and that was sufficient for me. It wouldn't stop me, I decided, from having another treatment in the future, should the opportunity arise. I was a warrior, and the fight to survive didn't stop there.

Two months after, I lost a tooth that I didn't think was normal. I didn't have pain nothing remarkable to oblige me to go to the dentist to prevent it. I was driving home, and I felt something in my mouth. I spat it in a piece of Kleenex tissue and it was my tooth scattered in fragments. What happen now? I save the pieces for proof that it was real and the next day I called the dentist for an explanation. She told me that happens sometimes when people took steroids, it's one of the multiple side effects.

After the treatment, I'd seen Dr. Leo twice, then a new doctor replaced him. I had a hard time pronouncing his name. He looked like he was of Indian origin and was so very young that I couldn't resist asking for his age. He laughed, and we conversed. He seemed to admire the way I was living with chronic illnesses and told me that if I was feeling all right with what I was doing, I should just continue doing it. *Age quod agis*; do what you are doing. He complimented me for my bravery and my strength, and I loved these hurrahs! That was a new thing for me. Doctors always push you to accomplish things that they likely wouldn't dare themselves, and they often use one patient as an example for another, as if to say, "One of my other patients made it through, so you should be able to make it as well." Doctors have to discreetly push their patients to do things that our lazy, sick bodies don't want to do, even though they know that we might not be able to meet their expectations. I, however, tended to challenge myself before my doctors had the chance to. I was always eager to try something new, even if it was hard. I resented the fact that doctors also made these comparisons, even when it comes from an intelligent mind. Comparison hurts and kills.

My doctors gave me the impression that they were proud of the work that they'd accomplished with me. They pragmatically gave me the right medications most of the time, but often, they made me so sick that I had to stop taking them by the next follow-up. So is that good care or bad care? I have no doubt that they had good intentions—they wanted me to get better—it's just those pills and their unpleasant side effects.

My philosophy was to let my specialists believe that they were doing a fine job, especially if I didn't want to pass on the next round of experimental pills. We all know that if you say to a doctor "This pill didn't do much good" or "It gave me lots of problems afterward," they will give you another drug or the same drug under a different brand. That's the Hippocrates law, to care, "to always consider the benefits of the patients before all." I'm not blaming the rule or the doctors. They're doing humongous jobs. I think you need to have a divine conscience and enormous aspirations to be a doctor. You shouldn't go into that field if you're just in it for the title or the money. I'm asking for doctors to read carefully about new medicines and find out about their ingredients before putting them to use. Their oath also states that they "should not voluntarily give deadly medicine to patients." Are you aware that some of the medications are pseudo-killers? I want you to understand my point. I would like doctors to say to manufacturers and agencies, "I'm not giving this medication to my patients because it will hurt them." Read all the ingredients before you prescribe something to us. Be our caregivers as well as our protectors. I'm saying this by experience. (You will find out what has happened to me in this regard as you keep reading this book.) I don't like when doctors say, "Let try this one, it's new on the market." What am I, a guinea pig?

On many of these occasions, I acted like a dumb dude, saying, "I feel good," referring to the James Brown song. I didn't want them to give me something worse, so I fibbed. I guess they let us do the task of reading the ingredients ourselves, which doesn't make sense to me. I don't have medical knowledge! Did my doctors always believe me when I said I was all right? I don't think so. I could often see the vexation in their eyes, especially when they'd given me samples of new medications. They expected me to report reactions. Sorry—somebody else can tell you the truth, not me. I didn't want to be the lab rat for new medications that would give me more problems than I had before. I read about their ingredients and looked up the medical words I didn't understand before I gave any prescription to the pharmacist or took my drugs. If I had samples to try, I would throw them in the garbage. It was hard to keep track of it all. I had so many pills from many specialists, all of which had different names, colors, and shapes. They all came with bad side effects that obliged me to act like that when I reported back. I couldn't risk accruing more ailments, so the lies continued. What else could I tell them? That were wasting their time with me, but that was too bad. I was saving my life in my own way. Too many chemicals for one body to absorb. I wanted to see if living with my chronic illness, untreated, as is, would make me feel better than dealing with all the side effects of my many medications. My poor health turned me into an addictive and compulsive liar. I lied to people about my daily feelings and to doctors when I didn't want to experiment with new remedies. It's shameful that I had to use this strategy to control my well-being. For me, it wasn't a big deal because I knew that those medicines wouldn't change or cure my unremitting diseases but would only endow me with temporary relief.

I have no doubts about how much doctors care, nor do I doubt their obligations to alleviate my troubles and restore my health, if possible. This is what they are charged to do. This is the reason we go to a doctor, but it is also our right to say no when we feel uncomfortable with something. Trust is a part of the healing process also, so if you don't trust your doctor, leave and find another. If you don't trust a medication, don't take it. The same way my doctors feel sorry when they cannot find the proper cure to give me, I feel sorry too for the trouble my problems cause them. That is why I preferred to tell them that all was well. I could always feel their discontentment, see that my load had become part of their loads as well. My PA-C and my hepatology doctors sometimes give me a "What more can I do?" kind of look. I know it's not their fault—and it isn't mine either! This is definitely the drug manufacturer's fault, rushing to produce more and more without taking time to seriously analyze the products and their subsequent side effects. It is the FDA's responsibility to approve the products, and as such, take into consideration the problems it might cause to future patients. All the time, we see manufacturers on television recalling drugs because of their grave side effects, as well as lawyers offering to sue for the same reason. It shouldn't be like that. After numerous patients trustfully and blindly take these medications and then find out that they're not suitable—come on—that's a disaster. Does medication really help when it gives you other diseases that are similar to or even worse than your original ailment? After the manufacturers make enough money, they recall the drugs. That's the cycle. Or a competitor creates a version of the same drug under a different name to create a mirage for their customers. "This one will be better," they say. From my experience, we need to be cautious of individuals and companies that see their pockets first and then see patient's welfare. Maybe that's why, in addition to what the drug agents tell doctors, doctors are always so eager to hear what effects new products have on the first patients who use them. Hell no, it's not going to be me. I don't want to be the Good Samaritan in that case. Those drugs are capable of eventually bringing instant relief to humanity, I have no doubt, but for what price? Who must be sacrificed? They might cure one thing but add multiples others, which isn't what you'd call the search for health! It's like washing your dirty hands and drying them with a dirty towel! Think about it. All I know is that I didn't want to be a trial patient for new medicines, except in the case of extreme sickness. If I had critical or deadly symptoms, which could appear without warning, I thought that I didn't really have a choice. Either way, I figured, I'd die, so I'd take the chance in that case only. I would already be on my deathbed, so why not try to get lucky? Still, I should be able to do what my heart dictates, even if it isn't in harmony with my doctor. Some of the doctors get extremely upset when you tell them no. They say they can't be your doctor if you don't take the medication. That makes sense in a way, but I should be able to discuss the medication with my doctor, and they should at least try to accept my opinion. I chose my doctors very carefully and meticulously and stuck with them forever when I found good ones, depending on insurance, of course. I can't neglect this part. We need good care, and I agree that researchers should keep producing inventions, finding new treatments, and manufacturing pills that could help people. My fear about some medications, which are full of bad side effects, tells me recuse myself from this process, though; a drug might be good for one problem but bring on more complications. I need adequate care, but I also need peace of mind.

I had plenty of reasons to be obsessed with cures. It's not because I was scared of dying. Rather I wanted to be free of all my diseases, especially HCV, which was an illness that made me worried. If I injured myself at work and drew blood, nobody could help me without wearing a glove for prevention. I always keep one in my handbag and in a drawer at work, just in case. But this Good Samaritan might not be aware of my disease, so I'm always concerned about spreading my virus. The nurses touched me when they were trying to find a vein, of course, but even though the virus isn't horribly easy to pass on given that it has to be blood-to-blood contact specifically, I was very preventative. When they couldn't find my vein, or it slid out from under their finger, they would remove one of their gloves to assist them. I would remind them not to do that with me. My emotions were stronger than I was, and I couldn't help me but try to help them. They would smile and let me know that they would be all right. I worried about my husband when he kissed me, anxious that I had a bleeding gum and didn't realize it. I also worried about cooking and took extreme precautions not get any kind of cut so that my blood wouldn't end up in the food. I cannot donate blood or be an organ donor. I would like so much to help someone out there who needed donations, but I'm completely restricted from doing so.

These factors made me eager to try anything that might eliminate the sickness from my body. I needed to rid that SOB from my life. My desire was to repeat and continue that treatment as advised by the doctor, gavel to gavel. I would restart it and continue it through the end.

Doctor K. R. B. sent me to have an anti-smooth-muscle antibody and an IGG test. Actin antibodies are found in 52 percent of patients with chronic, active hepatitis, and mine was reactive. He explained the results to me, I'm sure, but I don't recall anything. I had my third liver biopsy, which wasn't at all like the others. They didn't have to keep me for the twenty-four hours of observation. I was sent home two hours afterward. I was so concerned that the young doctor didn't know what he was doing. I kept arguing with him over the phone that the doctors before him had never let me go home so fast. He kept stating that the type of the biopsy he'd done was better and more efficient than the ones before were. I heard about someone who died from a simple biopsy because they bled internally. That change in the process scared me.

Sam was annoyed with me when I complained about it to him. "Just do the biopsy, Oli," he said.

I went to the hospital the morning the biopsy was scheduled. After a moment of hesitation, I called the nurse into the room and asked her to let my doctor know that I was canceling everything. But at that instant, the doctor arrived and gave me all kinds of updated intellectual explanations about the procedure. As they were pushing me into the operating room, I kept thinking, "How can it be so simple?" Finally, I slumbered. Nothing bad happened, though, and I didn't have any problems after. He was probably right, I decided. I was so grateful to the scientists who'd made the tests and treatments more manageable for patients. My second biopsy was better than the first, and respectively, the third and the fourth were better too. They were all painless procedures. They sedated me with some kind of twilight anesthesia, and when I woke up, it was so cool. I could be laughing with the devil without knowing it. I had to touch myself to be sure that the procedure was done. That's the way improvements should be made in the medical field across the board—for the betterment and comfort of patients.

38

Too Much to Handle

IN ADDITION TO EVERYTHING else, I had to fight for my survival at work. Nineteen virtuous years working for the same company isn't nineteen months, but life can be so unfair. Despite my illnesses, during my annual review, my supervisor and manager blamed me for not performing well enough that year. They put me on probation for three months. I almost died, and they were charging me in a closed-door trial. "Justice for some," if you ask me. It was flagrant that my health was bad and that it was the reason I wasn't working as hard as other people were. They saw how hard it was for me to even come to work while I was having treatments, and their verdict was I deserved to be punished. What kind of snakes in the grass were they? Sometimes, they'd been the ones who decided I should stay home. My review was an N, meaning "needs improvement." How could I have done better? I was on Pegasys ribavirin for two months and had spent two weeks at the hospital and only one month at home. Also, I didn't get a raise I was owed because I hadn't worked enough that year. What kind of hypocrisy is this? I thought. I shouldn't be penalized for something I didn't have any control over.

It was the first time I was dealing with something like that. *Is the new manager after me?* I wondered. She didn't like me, that's a fact, but she had to be fair to me. I had to do something. I thought I should go to the human resources department and complain. I'd already fought and won many battles with my ailments, so I knew I could fight for the additional fifty or seventy cents per hour that I was eligible for. I rarely made mistakes in my work. I took a lot of pride in doing my job well. I simply couldn't let them deprive me like that. Human resources made my boss change my review to G, meaning "good," but she and her assistant still secretly monitored me for three months. I wasn't aware that I could use FMLA forms when I went to the doctor for tests and so forth because nobody had ever mentioned that to me. I had lots of sick time. I thought that the form was only necessary when requesting a leave of absence. I resented the fact that I didn't know about this. Given all my diseases, I should've been informed that there was a form I could fill out. I'd never filled it out before, so it was new to me. They told me there was nothing in my file about my chronic illnesses. It was a bluff. I was trapped. (They didn't like the word *trap*.) But I knew that I had many doctors' letters in my file regarding my health. Before starting the treatment, the hepatologist filled out another form to let them know about my restrictions and the side effects I would be facing. They explained that I would be very sick and wouldn't be able to go to work. The most recent treatment was my third I'd undergone while working for that company. They were very diplomatic about my probation period.

I was coached by my supervisors and was under lot of stress. Sometimes, I had to laugh at all of it. Despite this, I was willing to dance the tango, so to speak, as if nothing was happening. I smiled to dissimulate my frustration. Few people knew what I was going through. I shared my problems with my best friend, T-C, who was a believer in praying.

"God will resolve this matter," she said. "Don't worry, Oli. Leave everything in his hands. He will take good care of it. I'm praying for you."

Did I have a choice? On days when I had a test or doctor's appointment, I took only thirty minutes for meals and stayed late the next day, even after I clocked out. I was trying to make up for my time off. My supervisor always asked me "Did you have lunch?" or "Are you sure that you can stay tonight?" Are these a bluff? She doesn't defend me in front of her manager. I can't tell who was worse—my sneaky supervisor or my manager. I couldn't trust her. I'm not sure that my supervisor had any choice in the matter because she was an employee, like I was, who worked under the same vampire. The manager had trained her to be tough and to be a pretender. I excused her in that case because I thought that inside, she was a good person. "If you don't feel good, go home," she said again and again. Like a Good Samaritan, she cared at that moment but didn't care enough to mention in my review that I was a sick person or to discuss the FMLA forms with me. Plus I had to provide doctors' copayment receipts each time I had an appointment and had to submit copies of my lab tests. I busted my buttocks to complete my work and achieve a higher performance rate so there would be no more bad reviews. It was the first time in my life that I got a bad review on anything, so I was stunned. *This shouldn't stop me from achieving my goals*, I thought. That bias didn't slow me down at all. I got involved in so many things—planning birthday celebrations, holidays parties, fundraising, meetings, all on top of my own duties. None of my colleagues did these things. I was trying to prove to them what I could do when I was well, but later, I dealt with the consequences.

I often asked myself if stress played a big role in worsening my liver conditions. After my second treatment, the virus was almost gone. I believed professor Blair J. when he said "Disease is a response to stress" and "Stress is defined as an imbalance between what we are willing to acknowledge to ourselves and what actually exists [and between], what we deny and what actually exists." People with chronic illness tend to ignore this fact from time to time, but our emotions torment us. Every time I ever heard a word about a life-threatening illness, I felt something in my body—an anxiety. I wasn't scared of death but of the agony of dying, especially from HCV, which often kills brutally and without warning. Things can get worse and even fatal for no evident reason. Those of us with chronic illnesses are often as stressed as people with terminal diseases are. The difference is we are outsiders waiting to get inside, waiting to hear our verdicts, whereas the others are inside already, aware of their death sentences. We are counting the hours, standing on the outside waiting to be called, and we are also fully aware that we might not be called at all. I'm so thankful to God for letting me wake up every morning and find out that everything is still stable. I've never been diagnosed with cancer or liver failure and probably won't ever be, but I have to prepare myself corporally and spiritually for this eventuality. Some don't have the privilege to prepare themselves and to thank God. I'm grateful for that blessing. I'm not certain that it's luck, as some might think. I'm just following my inescapable fate. Those of us who live with chronic diseases should allow ourselves the necessary time to appreciate life, to live in a positive manner. We shouldn't ignore that our pathways are unknown.

39

My Misery Is Mine

ANOTHER EPISODE WAS OVER. I was content with my many prognosis. I regained my energy, which had been deprived from me for long time. I found a good way to make things very simple. I started telling people that I was fine, which was untrue. For a while, this mantra really worked. By repeating "I'm fine, I'm fine," my brain got used to this idea, and so did my body. Like I said, it worked for a while. I believed my own shibboleth so completely that even when I went to bed in pain, I took my pills and said to myself, "You have nothing, Oli. Everyone is in some kind of pain. You're just a coward, so be strong." But over time, my body finally rejected this lie. My body needed real help. I had moderate pain in my neck, shoulders, back, and hips. Even sitting for eight hours in front of the computer became unbearable. This pain was a different kind, a burning sensation in the posterior of my anatomy that ran from my neck to my lumbar. It was a constant pain that spread up my back like my muscles were ripping and burning up. That was another challenge I was facing. A few years ago, my PCP had sent me to rehab for physical therapy. They were very nice people. I had an x-ray, and right away, the physical therapist came back to give me his assessment: in his opinion, I had arthritic pain and the possibility of spondylitis of the lumbar spine. *"Why did he say "possibility?"* I wondered. *Did the radi-*

ography reveal something or not? He affirmed that he'd treat me. It's so easy to say, but it's so difficult to accomplish.

My insurance allowed me twelve visits, which wasn't enough time to reach our goal. After eight visits, the pain and the muscle spasms decreased, but the time allowed wasn't sufficient. He said that he was going to request a longer time span, which must've been denied because I never heard from him after that last week. Soon, however, my pain regained ground, so I decided to see a chiropractor. It was expensive, and I had to pay out-of-pocket, but I decided to invest in my welfare. I ate less to pay for the copayments of $40 per visit every week. I started, and it got more painful. I went home with a sour body, but I was all right the next day. The funny part was that when I stopped going, all the pain galloped back to the same places. The chiropractor explained to me that people needed to check their bones every year and that it like going to the dentist to check for cavities. A chiropractor's duty is to prevent or help with bone deformation. I restarted going three times a week. He asked me to come to therapy four times a week and said that my spine was taking too long to properly align. I couldn't afford to pay more for these sessions. I'd missed three months already. I had so many other doctors I went to for various reasons. I couldn't go for three months. What made it worse was that whenever I stopped my therapy, the pain came back. I opined on my own that I wasn't going to pay that kind of money for temporary relief. By the way, I don't think that the chiropractor should've used the dentist as an example, because I dislike dentist; you go without pain to a dental office but come back home in a lot of pain, depending on the treatment you have. I stopped going to the sessions completely. My pain multiplied. I had it all over my body almost all the time. Fibromyalgia was bad enough on its own. I didn't want another ailment. I could easily tell the difference between the different kinds of pain because the sensations were not all alike. Sometimes, I had both kinds of pain at the same time. I couldn't bluff anymore.

In the meantime, I was seeing a dentist to remove my bad teeth, get crown bridges, etc. I tried to stay away from the dentist, but bad teeth made me change my conception of them. Between work and

THE DAILY BATTLE FOR A NORMAL LIFE

doctor's offices, I was immersed in the shadow of a health-related revolutionary war. I might see two doctors in a week, plus all the labs and tests. They always found something in my body, but there was never a permanent solution. Most of us have a simple mammogram every year, but I needed two or three. If I have one, it's always accompanied by an ultrasound, because there's always something irregular in my results that needs to be monitored: "There is residual nodular fibro-glandular tissue or spiculate tissue." "Your mammography shows an area that we believe isn't cancer but requires a follow-up mammogram in six months." "Your mammogram is abnormal, and a PRN breast U/S is needed." An annual Pap smear is never normal for me either, even though I had a complete hysterectomy. My gynecologist always finds something wrong with me: the pelvic area is abnormal, the epithelial cell is abnormal, a human papillomavirus effect is present, cellular changes associated with inflammation are present, there are low-grade squamous intraepithelial lesions, and so on. I never get over these encumbrances. The same pattern, every year or every six months, overwhelmed me with panic. I took pills for temporary relief, but I never totally cured any of my diseases. They always continued.

It was very embarrassing to leave work early or come in late two or three times a week because of my health. My gynecologist also found that I had osteopenia, which later became osteoporosis, despite the Actonel pills I took once a week. Later on, he put me on Boniva once a month, but it didn't get better. Now, I'm on alendronate 70 mg, and my last bone density test revealed "a high risk of fracture in the spine and in the left hip, severe osteoporosis left side. Repeat Dexa in 18 months to assess for further bone-mineral loss."

My faith left me again. Some days, I was close to giving up on my health journey and living out my life without medication, without going to the doctor's office. I felt that swallowing all my drugs was a colossal waste of time. I wanted to live completely naturally, without these chemicals, but the pain wouldn't let me achieve this resolution. Before I left one clinic, I was already scheduled to see another specialist. My wellness was in jeopardy, and I felt helpless. Desolation and disappointment blinded my spiritual conviction. I couldn't see that I was hurting myself with my deficiency in hope. I was in disarray, in need of some clarity about what my life had become. Pain doesn't make people think straight. I had many sorrowful illnesses, which weren't normal for me. It was hard and frustrating. I needed an invisible force of nature to help me stay focused and guide me during these dark times. I went outside and stood under clear moonlight. I talked to my friend, nature, like it could save me from my anguish. I screamed at God to help me transcend my adversity and loneliness. I felt that my mother was trying to communicate spiritually with me, but I didn't know how to respond.

Sometimes, in the middle of the night, I had to get out of bed because I could feel the spirits who wanted me to live. I wasn't in the same realm that I'd been in prior to getting sick. It was as if I was going back and forth, as if I received a command to lurk into death. None of my ailments had ever been healed, and I was going along without hope of better days or any idea of how I would reach my destination. The road gets prolonged and strewn with more problems: arthritis in my neck, pain in my shoulder and lower back, osteoporosis, chronic migraines, liver damage, the orbital varix, high blood pressure, and fibromyalgia. My body became a sanctuary for pains and illnesses. Given all these complications, some days were very hard for me to even wake up. Did I complain? Yes, I did. In fact, I had to talk about it to ease my suffering. I was scared of becoming disabled. Already, I was unable to wear certain type of shoes that I used to like so much. It was a hard-knock lifestyle for someone who liked to wear high-heeled shoes. I changed my garb and started wearing platform shoes instead. I wasn't happy with it, but at least I had a compromise.

It took me twenty-nine years to realize that I wouldn't be able to prove that I was 100 percent normal. I couldn't deny it any longer. I didn't regret that I used to see it differently, but I could better handle myself if I wasn't blindly focusing on proving the opposite. The scarf had been lifted, and my mind had been cleared up. I felt so frightened. I watched my mother die from diabetes, my friends and family members pass away from liver failure and stroke from high blood pressure, and people croak from arthritis and muscle-bound illnesses. And so on and so on. My tenacity left me with the notion that it could be me at any minute. I selected to stay healthy with a good diet, which for me meant eating small quantities of food of any kind. I always fought to stay a normal size and be fit. I'm not sure if my desire to stay undernourished was for health purposes or to maintain the cosmetic shape of my body. To this day, I still maintain my weight, which is puts less fat on my vulnerable liver. Whatever the real reason is for this, I'm very content with it.

My work atmosphere changed a lot. It became something of a competition between employees. Everyone vied to file the most works per day, and that became the rule of law. We needed to report every day, at four o'clock, what we'd done during the eight hours we were there. It didn't matter how much time I took time off for tests and doctor's appointments, I had to work as much I could to keep up with my coworkers, which was fair enough. This wasn't my fault or the company's. Sam continued to visit every six to eight weeks for two weeks at a time. Yearly, I had to fill out a FMLA form that gave me authorization to go to the doctors or to the lab—everything related to my health care except the dentist. Given the changes at the company, I managed to pass three years without accumulating any sick times. The annual twenty-one days of allowed sick time that I used to have wasn't in effect anymore. With the new company policy, we can only accrue a few hours every paycheck. Thankfully, I accumulated many of these hours over the years. I had to reduce my cache of sick time to sixty-four hours or fewer before I could restart the accumulation. This meant that it didn't matter how long you'd been at the company, everyone got only eight paid sick days per calendar year. Being a loyal, long-term employee wasn't lucrative anymore. The new company was only interested in what benefitted the employer, not the employees. It was very clever to me what they had done. For example, if an employee had to have a surgery and stay home for a month, the company wouldn't pay for all their sick time. Sixty-four hours is less than even one working week. Afterward, the employee would only receive 60 percent of their salary on short-term disability. Were they purposefully pressuring the middle class, the average people? They say that all workplaces drifted toward that nonsense. It's amazing how often the law works against the hard worker.

For younger, healthy folks, the system might work, but for older, unhealthy people, it's insanity. All the old policies were changed in favor of the company.

If worse comes to worst, we think, at least we have a job, but companies are so inhumane. All they dream about is greed, the desire to have more and to lead employees to accept lower, unreasonable sources of income. Thank goodness that there is still a law that says you can't work free, because if you could, companies would ask for one day free in every salary year so they could reach their avaricious goals faster. If I had to go to the dentist, I stayed late at work the next day, trying to accomplish my work. Dental wasn't covered by FMLA. Graciously, my supervisor would send emails to remind me that I needed to submit receipts for my doctors' visits to keep them on file, as if I would lie about my health for a few hours off work! No way. I still had a scar from a beating I received from Tita in my childhood for lies I told when I was nine years old. Since then, I don't lie often. She'd beaten me for a good reason too. My mother could afford to buy me school supplies, but some of the other students' parents couldn't, so I had to share my pencils, pens, erasers, and so on. Unfortunately, they never returned my stuff. How could I explain something like that to my mom? How could she understand it? I only saw her once in a while, anyway. So every time she asked, I told her that I'd lost them. That was the lie for which she'd beaten me.

Anyway, God only knows how tired I was, between going to work and running to doctors' office to get relief from diseases that were rooted in my body. Likewise, these ailments aged my body like I was in the workforce. I could miss work several times a month, but when I returned, I had to perform over my capacity to make up for the missing time. I felt like a modern slave. They even treated me poorly, even if it was subtle, and made me work hard no matter how unwell I felt. Despite my soreness from eyes to toes, I was willing to work. I needed to make money and stay active. My superiors seemed to understand this, but what could they do? They had to do their jobs, and the company had a right to enforce its own policy. My life was in limbo. It was clear to me that I was a missionary of God to have all these burdens and still live! I smiled and laughed to thwart these inflictions. I was okay with my condemned life. I carried a cross, a cross that for others might seem light, but for me was quite weighty.

40

The Scare

MY SUBMISSION TO LIFE wasn't well-understood by most of my colleagues. I challenged my ailments, wearing high-heeled shoes when my feet ached, wearing more makeup when I felt bad and hadn't slept well due to my orbital varix pain, dressing in red when depression wanted to take my soul. No one knew my strategy to survive. I hurt myself more than the disease hurt me so I could proclaim "freedom" over these annoyances. I was searching for freedom—the freedom of nature that even meteorologists can't predict. I deserved that freedom of movement, of thinking, of not plunging into desolation. "What is my reason on earth?" I wondered. I didn't know. What was the reason I had to take on so many execrable encumberments? I kept asking that question but never got a proper answer back. What answer? The answer is that no one is exempt from some kind of burden. I regained my faith, and with a refreshed mind, was convinced that I had to fulfill my destiny judiciously. I had to just hope that someday, something would change.

My happiness soon faded when my gynecologist called to tell me that my Pap test result revealed an abnormally in the pelvis and that he needed to see me ASAP to have a colposcopy. My heart unwillingly started pounding. I wanted to stay calm, but I couldn't. I didn't want to talk about it, but I called a friend anyway, too scared to keep it to myself. I thought that once you had a complete hysterectomy, you didn't have to worry about this kind of thing anymore. The gynecologist's office scheduled me to see the doctor in three days. Usually, I Googled any disease that I was diagnosed with, but the doctor didn't tell me what it was called. Reading online about abnormal Pap results made me have a stroke before I even knew what was wrong with me! So I avoided doing so and tried to think positively. By experience, I knew a lot about searching about health on the internet. I did it all the time. But for the first time, I wanted to skip this step in my ordinary process. I was impatient and didn't want to stress myself out even more. That day, I left work one hour prior to my scheduled time. I couldn't focus on my job any longer.

When I got to the office, I didn't go straight into the exam room as usual but to the doctor's personal office. Given this solemn entrance, I knew that it was serious. After he told me about the results and the little procedure he was going to do, I asked him the question that had been burning on my lips for three days: "How come I have an abnormal pelvis? I had a complete hysterectomy. I should be worry-free regarding pelvic cancer, no?" He explained to me that the pelvis had nothing to do with the ovary and the uterus. It wasn't the time to try to understand, though. Already, I was shaking like a leaf. You could hear my teeth clattering like a windchime. I was scared about the little procedure when I saw all the surgical instruments. I was cold. Like a normal female gynecology exam, I was laid on the gurney, a speculum instrument was inserted into me to dilate the walls of the vagina, and the doctor placed the colposcope to look inside. It's always an embarrassing position. Males have done everything in their power to embarrass females. Lying on a stretcher with both legs open and heels resting on either side of the table—what could be more graceless for a woman? That time, however, I was too frightened to care about it. Here comes the best part. A piece of tissue from that sensitive area had to be cut off and sent to the lab. I felt cramps, numbness in the lower part of my body, and a sudden bad headache. That process reminded me a little of my first biopsy. After that, a potion that smelled like white vinegar was injected inside me. The pain worsened for a few seconds and then was gone as quickly as it came. The doctor comforted me. He didn't see anything harmful, he explained, but he was going to send the piece of tissue to the lab and would call me in two weeks with the results. By the time I got dressed, all the pain was gone. I was left only with the anxiety of waiting for another two weeks. The nurse called me with the good news—the result came back negative. I didn't have to go back. She scheduled me to have it checked again in six months.

I wondered what'd happened at the laboratory with my abnormal Pap test. Did they confuse my name with somebody else's? Was my sample switched with someone's who was really sick? I hoped not. I hoped that the other woman didn't hear, "Your tests came back all right, and there isn't anything to worry about," then when she found out in a year that she was ill, it would be too late. I was seriously worried that someone had mistaken my test results with someone else's. I concluded that I was fine, and that's what mattered to me. I kept thinking about that other person for six months until I returned to the doctor to ask him about what really happened with my first test.

His response wasn't too convincing. "That happens sometimes, and we have to make sure that there isn't anything growing there."

He wasn't going to tell me the truth because he probably had nothing to do with the mistake, but I had to ask anyway. I tried to forget about it because there was nothing else I could do. *L'erreur est humaine*—to err is human, I suppose.

Most of the time, I pretended to be happy, but how could I be? I only saw my husband every six or eight weeks, and only for two-week spells. We'd have a couple of good conversations for the first three days, but after that, our *tête-à-tête* was all about economy. We fought constantly. I asked him why he kept coming back if he was just going to argue with me most of the time. I always supported myself, and when he was around, he suddenly wanted to manage my finances. I felt trapped with him telling me what I should do with a paycheck that I worked very hard for. First, shouldn't his place be next to me during the good and bad times? There wasn't even anyone around to make me a cup of tea when I was sick. When I left work early because I didn't feel well, before I went into my bedroom, no matter how bad I felt, I had to prepare a tray with everything I needed: water, tea, food, etc., so I could rest in peace. I was singlehanded most of the time. I drove myself to the emergency room and I drove back home, no matter what kind of sedative I was on. I lied, telling the nurse that someone was waiting for me, trying to be brave. "I don't need a chair. I can walk," I said. I lied so that she wouldn't see that I was alone. But then, hospital policy changed, and they wanted to see the person who was accompany you before they'd release you.

I woke up that Friday with my ritual headache. I had my shower trying to make it to the workplace. My head was pounding, I finally got to work. After a few hours, I'd to stop working, my eyes couldn't take the glare of the computer. I sent an email to my supervisor to let her know that I'll be leaving soon because I'm not feeling well. On my way home, I had to stop by the supermarket myself to buy something to eat before I could take the Fioricet pills. One tablet didn't do the job anymore. I had to take two because my head was too full of crap to get relief for the headache. By 7:00 p.m., I went to the emergency room to relieve my pain, and they injected a painkiller through an IV. When I woke up to go home, I felt like the entire building was moving with me. After I finished signing the release papers, I escaped. I'd disappeared so they won't ask me to call the person I was with because there was no one. I drove home through the rain that day, my eyes closing every few minutes. Thank God, my house was only fifteen minutes from Homestead Hospital. I braved that danger many times in my life. I didn't like to ask friends for favors unless it was strongly necessary. It would be inappropriate to ask a friend who was going to work the next day to stay with me until 3:00 a.m. at the ER. Come on, I would never importune someone with that. This should've been Sam's responsibility, but he failed to accomplish it many times. You might think that such an absence wouldn't be a big deal, but it hurt me because it wasn't normal. Anything that isn't normal can hurt

People often told me that I had to pray. Pray for what? Does God have anything better to do than involve himself in something so banal? Banal for God, depressive for me. Sam wasn't coming back, so I needed to accommodate accordingly, to live my life without him. My prayer was that if I died while he's overseas he would feel the guilt of abandoning me when I needed him the most. I knew that this was a devilish hope, but I was desperate. If I had to die before him, I thought, that was my wish; let him carry the stamp of guilt for a while. I let everybody know that I was better off without him, but it was just a lie. I liked his company and genuinely missed him. I felt confident when he was around. Despite our frequent fighting and our often-emotional discussions, I still thought that he was a charming *hombre* and loved him very much. He loved me very much too in his own way.

41

Confirmation

A FEW YEARS BEFORE, my PCP told me that I had borderline high blood sugar. I was put on glimepiride for prevention at the time, hoping that it wouldn't ever get higher to be on insulin like my mother was. I didn't want to have another untreatable disease. I controlled my weight and exercised by dancing at home four times a week. I only had a little sugar at night before sleeping, like a sleeping pill. I thought that all these preventative measures exempted me from ever getting that big nuisance of a disease. When I was on the glimepiride pills, I didn't feel like a diabetic. When I'd heard about sugar diabetes, I always associated it with insulin, not pills. If you're on insulin, I thought, you have the real thing. So I took it very lightly. During a visit to my PCP's office, Jean gave me a copy of my blood tests to take to an endocrinologist. It stated that my A1C rose to 8.1. This time, I felt like I really needed to pray to change my shady course. I forced myself to exercise. I danced while I was on the pills, along with other drastic measures. I suddenly had to carefully watch everything that I ate. I liked sweets, though. What horrible news for someone with my taste!

I was lost. *This illness isn't for me*, I thought. I tried so hard to keep that evil away from me, but it was already ravaging my existence. I'd never heard about blood test A1C, even from my mother. I didn't remember her ever having that test. Later, I found out that it was just an additional pathology lab. I was a novice when it came to those medical codes. I was shocked and didn't have the desire to talk too much about it at the doctor's office. Jean's explanation about the A1C must've entered into one of my ears and out the other. I was more focused on how I'd let this happen to me. Suddenly, I felt truly confused. I couldn't remember one word that Jean had said. I didn't understand anything. I was living in a mysterious world of ignorance. I'm sure that she gave me more details, but my mind was far away. I already envisioned my fate: kidney failure, dialysis, stroke, and paralysis for the rest of my life. I needed some fresh air to think, some privacy to curse at the enemy. The adversary that I had struggled with for so long had won, I thought. It was already inside of my house, waiting silently to harm me as it had harmed Tita. I left the office feeling like I had been condemned to death. I rushed home to consult the internet about the medical language and my real health hostage, high blood sugar. The next day, at work, I told my supervisor about my new unwanted friend and showed her the results of my test. She shared that she also had high blood sugar but that her AIC had never been that high. She tried to give me some clues about it. I listened, but there was no use explaining it to me. The night before, I spent most of my sleeping hours searching for everything related to diabetes. In less than twenty-four hours, I was already an expert. I read a lot about it and what people experimented with to try to cure it. This helped me confront my new disease with confidence.

 I saw an endocrinologist, Dr. Ken. The first thing he did was he stop me from taking glimepiride pills, which he claimed were doing nothing for me anymore. Instead, he put me on Humalog 75/25 twice a day. I didn't like the fact on being on insulin, I asked if he could just double my previous pills instead. He showed me the test results that my PCP had sent to him from January to July; my A1C had gone from 6.1, to 6.2, 7.8, 6.1, and 8.1 respectively. Also, he explained to me that my triglycerides was 267 mg/dL, my glucose/plasma was 149 mg/dL, and my T4 and cholesterol levels were high. He said that we needed to get all these under control. He referred me to a two-day class at South Miami Hospital that would teach me how to deal with my new comrade, such as what to eat and how to control my glucose. It was funny to see that most of the people there cared so much about food. They were mostly focused on how many slices of bacon, eggs, slices of bread, rice, milk, meat, poultry, fish, fruit, etc., they could guzzle. They never mentioned vegetables in their menus. When the nutritionist tried to help us understand that raw or steamed vegetables were best for people with diabetes, we were all silent. I figured that I wasn't the only one with an aversion to vegetables. Who really likes them?

For my good health, I desperately threw myself into exercise, yoga, and a strict diet. I went to a fitness place that Scott paid for to avoid any future catastrophes. Many times, when I drove home, I felt like I needed to faint. At the beginning, I thought that I should have a snack before going to the gym. I did, but there was no change. My son told me that I should drink more water. I'm like goat; I don't drink water too much or even juice. It's continuously like that, and I get dizzy, close to passing out. One time, I hardly made it home. I had palpitations and was out of breath, so I stopped going to the fitness center completely. Anyway, I didn't like the tiredness that I always felt when I got home. Also, I didn't like to walk by myself in the street or in the park, like a confused, crazy woman I continued to dance as exercise in the heart of my own bedroom. Incredibly, I had been thrown to the ocean many times, and the tide always brought me back to the wrong port. I scathingly murmured to myself, "This credo in my family won't affect me. I will end it. My next blood test will show that everything is normal, like everyone else." I put my body on a stern six-day diet. On Sundays, I let myself eat what I wanted without restrictions. Being on a diet wasn't difficult for me, in a way. I was never a big eater, which made Sundays like normal eating days for me. I didn't like vegetables and green salads, but I tried to eat them sometimes. I wasn't obese, but in my family, this illness was quite common. I tried to control the onset of diabetes as much as I could, like I had done the previous three years.

Over the following months, my blood sugar got lower and stayed like that for almost a year. I don't know what I'd done differently. After a while, that SOB wasn't going to give up the battle. My A1C went to 8.5, and my endocrinologist increased my insulin to three times a day and told me to prick my finger before each injection. The high blood sugar was troubling me again. That thing wasn't satisfied. It was mad at me for fending it off for all those years, and it wanted me to fight harder. I was working, though, and didn't have enough time or the convenience of puncturing my fingers and belly at work. The doctor agreed to let me continue with the insulin twice a day, so long as I promised to exercise harder and stay completely away from sweets. I practically had to beg him. Given the amount of work I had to do each day at my job, I didn't see how I could leave my desk to go to the bathroom in the middle of the day. I promised that if it didn't work, I would go for the thrice-daily plan, of course. I would take a fifteen-minute break just for that and a forty-five-minute break for lunch. He gave me an insulin adjustment scale to know how much to take depending on my blood tests.

I hated that disease for killing my mother, and now it was after me. Could I deviate my destiny or deactivate that gene in my body? I was stressing at work, plus I had to take care of all my incurable diseases. What life offered me in terms of health issues was engrossing. I had so many bad memories from my mother's illness, and now I was following in her steps. *Does God want me to pray for good health?* I wondered. I declined to do so. I thought that he should be able to provide good health without my having to ask. We call him Father, but as my husband used to say, he's more like our Master, and we're only his servants. That doesn't make us nonbelievers in any way, but I think of myself as being more of a subordinate than a child. I put everything in his hands to decide.

I often went to hospitals for lab tests, if not Quest, it's Lab Corp depending of my insurance and to the emergency room. I had blood tests for sugar diabetes and hep C. The two illnesses were competing. With my new friend, I always had to remember to bring a snack with me wherever I went. My glucose was uncontrollable, sometimes high, sometimes low. I was babysitting my illnesses more than anything else in my life. I danced more, crazy dances, to any kind of music I heard on television or the radio. I cried, laughed, talked to myself, and answered my own questions. I walked back and forth. I saw raccoons on my roof. I was scared and played with my fear. I ran to go nowhere. The telephone rang. It was one of my neighbors calling. He saw the raccoons too, and it was getting dark. There were two sitting on the roof by my bedroom window, likely a male and a female. *What about me?* I thought. I was alone and frightened of them. I looked at their romance and wished that I could find a soul-brother too. I wished to be dead, not because of the ailments that monopolized my body, but because of the deep silence that encircled my house, the loneliness, the boredom that I slept with and awakened with, and the nostalgia for children, who grew up too fast and left the house. I also had to fight with the raccoons that invaded my property. There was a hole in the roof, so they got into the attic. *Maybe they're happy together*, I thought, but I wasn't. I was sad and nervous, and I couldn't sleep. There I was, looking for company in the company of raccoons. I was short of breath, and my imagination made me think that I could smell their odor from where I was in my bedroom. Depression made me having delusion. I wanted to kill myself, but I wasn't sure how. Did I really want to do that? I wondered. Let me double the dosage of my painkillers and drink them with a cup of Rhum Barbancourt (Haitian rum). I was conscious of what was happening, I thought that I would just sleep for two or three days straight and that afterward everything would be all right. Even though I didn't want to kill myself, but I would've been okay if I died. Does that make sense? Well, for me it does.

    My doctors always told me that I carried the diseases of four people. I'm very blessed to be the porter of these maladies because they've helped me improve myself, be a better person, and better appreciate my good, healthy days. People kept saying that I had to pray to God to heal me, but did I have to tell God what he already knew? Nothing was a surprise to him. A positive mind can help alleviate our burdens, I think. I'm confident that if he wanted to change anything in my life, it would already be done, or else that he would act according to his plan for me. I'm human. Sometimes, I got stressed out and felt depressed that I couldn't do my work at 100 percent anymore, or that I felt physically weak, tired, and lonely. Most of the time, my soul was filled with positive thoughts. Truthfully, I'd rather look for how I could energetically deal with what I had in a constructive manner rather than beg for health. Inside, I knew that this was my destiny. God exists, and we are rationally here for his use. I also knew that behind the dark cloud, the sun was still rising, and that after the rain, the good weather always came back even nicer. As such, after death, there was another world waiting for each of us. These are the words that I expressed when I woke up and needed to put myself in a better state of mind. One moment, I could be down, and the next, I would be okay. I embraced my good moments with gratitude, thinking, *It could be worse!* We need to have faith in the Lord that one day, we will meet him, and plausibly we'll be able to receive responses about so many inquiries that were mysteries to us on earth.

Life goes on, and so I tried to live a normal life. It was so difficult to do so, and I prayed for strength and good morale. My migraines became more severe, and my PCP was very concerned about that. My blood pressure escalated through the roof. I had to take two medications, atenolol and triamterene, to control my tension. Sometimes, it was very difficult to move and walk, and I couldn't go to work as usual. Five days a week on the job overwhelmed me with pain. My PCP had already diagnosed it as fibromyalgia, but it was increasing in magnitude. I was taking more and more ibuprofen and butalbital to stay active. I couldn't pinpoint a specific place that hurt when I had a crisis. My entire carcass was in pain. It could last for two or three days, and after that, it would be partially gone. Then it would come back whenever it felt like it. In those days, living by myself was problematic. I had to manage getting food in my stomach without help of any kind. I called it my unexpected visitor. I had to find a way to survive during those episodes if I didn't want to die from starvation instead of my diseases. So resting every three steps or so, I fed myself. I thought about the old times when no doctors existed to give people medications, and sick or not, people did everything themselves. I said to myself, "If they could do it, I can too." It's always good to find an example to copy when life seems pugnacious.

We have the tendency to portray people with hepatitis C as being on recreational drugs, or as being bad. Don't assume this, because it's not always the case. We need to teach everybody that despite our bad reputation, we are still human beings of God's creation and deserve fairness. HCV kills as many people as cancer does, if not more. A heart attack, liver cancer, and liver failure can directly related to HCV. How worthy is your life when you're trying to hide your ailments from society? Why are you not curious about your body? Why not find out if you're a carrier of this virus so you can be cautious and preventive? Why should you be ashamed of something you didn't want, and even if you did, it's a disease that needs to be treated. Hepatitis C needs more campaigns. Don't be a hidden, anonymous victim. Find out before it's too late—the sleeping killer could already be inside of you, and you just don't know it yet.

42

The Catastrophic Day

On January 11, 2010, I took Sam to Miami International Airport for his regular trip back to Haiti. As soon he arrived, as usual, he called to let me know that he was all right. The next day, like I was accustomed to, we talked on the phone from 6:30 a.m. until I arrived to work. It was a way for him to keep me company while I was driving so I wouldn't fall asleep. I was on so many medications that made me sleepy most of the time. My work schedule was from 7:30 a.m. to 4:30 p.m., but one of my coworkers finished at 4:00 p.m. By the time I got home, she'd already been home for two hours. My home was farther from the office than hers was. I was at the entrance of my house when my residential phone rang. I rushed to get pick it up. It was my colleague, asking me if I'd seen the news.

"What news?" I asked her. We'd talked a lot about politics in the past, so I thought it was about President Obama, of whom she wasn't a fan.

"There has been a terrible earthquake in Haiti, and they are saying that a lot of people have died and lost their houses. It's on CNN."

I'd known Caroline for twenty years. She was a very strong woman, and so the groan in her voice made me realize that it had to be a very significant disaster. My first reaction was to call my husband and then turn on the TV. I got no answer from Sam. I didn't know the severity of the catastrophe, but when I sat down to listen to the news, I was horrified. My children, his brothers and sisters, his cousins, my aunts, and our friends began calling from everywhere, asking, "Where is he, in Haiti or Miami?"

I told them that one day prior, he'd returned to Haiti. The question "Where is he now?" became harder for me to answer. I didn't know what to say. I didn't know where he was either. I was trying to figure out why he wasn't responding my calls, and I was interrogating myself with the same question: "Where could he be?" I couldn't leave my seat, worried that I might miss something on the news. I was glued to my chair and didn't remove my work clothes for many hours. I called him every five to fifteen minutes, at least, without getting any answer. At this point, I lost control of my mind and blew up in tears. The more people who called, the more I despaired. I needed to hear him tell me that he was all right, as he had said to me when he landed. I felt building anger in my chest. I was mad at myself for taking him to the airport just prior to the disastrous day. My heart was beating with a hectic rhythm, about to fall out of my mouth. I was totally submerged in the same feelings of culpability I had after my mother's death. I blamed myself to the point at which I couldn't breathe anymore. Panic attacked my entire body. I kept asking myself, "What I'm going to do?" I was feeble, vulnerable to the worst thoughts. "Is he dead? Has he left me completely on my own?"

At a moment like that, a person can be very selfish. All I cared about was finding him, knowing that he was alive, and I was ignoring the rest. The rest wasn't important to me, only he was. At a certain moment, my brain became less focused on the news. I wasn't even particularly concerned about the other victims. All my thoughts were concentrated on Sam. I feared that he might be lifeless somewhere at any moment. I was worried that he was stuck somewhere under the debris, helpless and waiting for the divine hand to tend to him, to walk him to the door of no return. I must hear his voice, I thought, telling me again, "I'm all right." I passed the night anxious, crying, agonizing, thinking, and already picturing him in a coffin. I couldn't get that image out of my head. I didn't want to imagine something so repulsive, but I couldn't help it, and this made me more furious and devastated. I couldn't sleep. My eyes were congealed on CNN.

I ignored the other facts. I counted the hours. I was losing hope. Twenty hours passed without any news of him. I didn't know if I was mad at God or at him—maybe both. I invented a good reason to be mad at Sam, thinking that if he were here with me, I wouldn't have to fret so much about him. Why did he have to go to Haiti that specific time? God, why? How could he not prevent this devilish catastrophe? I didn't go to work. I stayed home, praying for a miracle. I felt hopeless.

"God, is your wish against mine?" I pleaded. "I'm not going to pray anymore. I'm putting everything in your hands now." With an upturned face to the sky, I released my last postulation to God. "Let your will be done, not mine."

It's not that I was giving up, but I was losing a portion of my soul. I was so lost. The negativity was mastering my spirit. I was already planning to travel to PAP to look for him. I planned on booking a flight to Santo Domingo because there were no planes that went directly to Port-au-Prince. That was my resolution, I decided. I was leaving. Friends were trying to do the same, flying to Santo Domingo and then taking the bus. A few minutes passed, and the phone rang.

I heard a soft voice on the other end. "Oli, hi. I'm okay."

I didn't believe what I heard. I thought that my brain was playing tricks on me. I was too far gone in my grief and worry to expect something like that. My sanguine expectations left me with pessimistic thoughts. In my mind, he was already dead. I stayed silent until I realized that it was really Sam on the phone.

He continued. "I don't have too many minutes, but I'll call you again. I'm okay."

I said one word: "Okay."

I hung up the phone before he did, essentially hanging up on him! When I realized what I'd done, it was too late. I tried to call him back to apologize for my innocent gesture, but there was no connection. All I wanted was to hear him, I guess. I was exalted in my joy, repeating a song from church over and over: "Alle-Alle-Alle-Alleluia. Amen!" My heart opened up as if it were the first time I'd ever talked to him on the telephone. I was relieved from my torment. I thanked the Lord and cried of happiness. The next day, my husband called again and told me that he was okay, but that he gotten hurt by a flying concrete block that had come from his bakery. He'd opened that bakery only three months prior. He also explained that part of his business was gone. When the disaster happened, he'd been at the bakery with his workers and some customers. The second round of sellers were coming to replenish their stock of bread. He could feel that something wasn't quite right in the air. Intermittently, he heard light cracking sounds and felt some shaking in the room. Items quivered on the counter. Instinctively, he started asking people to leave the place. A few minutes after, he went outside and could see that the two-story building that was adjacent to where he stood was bending in slow motion, toward him and then forward. So he went back inside and requested that everybody evacuate right away. I knew that he was smart and predictable, but the fact that he'd had the common sense to check outside and evacuate everyone at that very moment made him the savior of these people. As I see it, his angel told him to do so. Certainly, he couldn't have done that sitting in Miami. He had to be present in Haiti to save those people's lives. A moment after everyone left, the stone building crumbled. Everybody was safe by the grace of God, and he was safe as well. He made sure that no one was left behind before leaving the business, and that's how he got injured. Afterward, he couldn't use his cell phone because there was no signal the day of the disaster. There was no electricity either, but he charged his cell phone in his car. There were so many aftershocks that it wasn't prudent to go out for the next three days.

 Immediately after the disaster, the American government sent a Boeing to evacuate all the Americans. I was concerned about Sam's wound and wanted him to come home right away. He categorically objected because his neighbors and the people around him needed his help. He told me that he was building a tent in front of the factory with sheets, everything he could possibly find. It would take them a while before they'd be able to find their way back home into the rubble. He was feeding his neighbors with bread he'd found under the debris and some groceries that he'd had in his refrigerator. It wasn't safe for him to go upstairs to his residence, but he managed to get water and some other important things for them to use. He told me that he had a bandage on his wound, that he was hunky-dory. I was scared that the destroyed roof might fall on him while he was playing the hero. After God granted him a second chance at life, he wanted to jeopardize it! On Friday afternoon, he called me at work to let me know that he would be landing in Miami at 11:00 p.m. He said that I needed to pick him up at the military air base, which was four to five miles from my house. It was so strange to be at the military airbase because I was used to going to the international airport. When I saw him, it was like I'd never seen him before. He didn't have luggage and wasn't too enthusiastic to be there. That night, we didn't talk much about the events at hand. The confusion on his face was telling me to be patient, to let him talk about it when he wanted to. The next day, on Saturday, I told him that he should go to the emergency room to find out if the wound on his forehead was serious. He told me that so many people had been seriously injured in that disaster and that they didn't have medication. He said that compared to them, his problem was nothing.

He proceeded with profound sadness. "You should see the dead bodies…bodies mutilated…the smoke and dust…desperate people searching for their loved ones in the streets. Olivia…" He paused. "My neighbors lost it all and don't know when and how they will be able to rebuild. People are walking in the streets, shuddering with fear, covered with debris and dirt, looking like the zombies you see in horror movies. They don't know where to go or where to stay. The scenes that I witnessed looked like animated cartoons, like surrealism. Corpses missing parts of their bodies and corpses with their parts lying by their sides are everywhere. The carcasses of some dead people were completely nude, and people didn't care. They just saw them as dead bodies! Some had been lucky enough to be covered with dirty sheets of plastic by their parents or whoever. On my way to the airport, I saw decomposing corpses pulled by truck tractors. Some of the bodies were being torn apart like garbage, trailing the repugnant smell of spoiled meat left out in the sun for days. I saw flies making a feast of human bodies. It's the apocalypse in Port-au-Prince." He took a deep breath to help him continue the conversation. "What you have seen on TV isn't the real thing. What I saw there is completely different and far more disheartening."

Even when Sam lost both parents, I'd never seen him so distressed, so troubled, and so demoralized. The gloominess in his eyes and the sorrow in his voice made my initial happiness at his return diminish quickly. He stayed at the window most of the time, staring out with a vague gaze. In the afternoons, he described to me in detail what he's seen there, reminding me that what was on TV was nothing in comparison to the real picture. He often had nightmares and woke up at night, sweating. He kept asking himself if he was dreaming. He couldn't believe what he'd gone through in only three days. Well, I was wrong. God sent him to Haiti at the right time to save people and be a helping hand to these in need. I realized that I shouldn't let my ego blinded me to the point that I didn't care about anyone else. His trip to Haiti a day before the tragedy had a purpose, a reason. I was so proud of him.

He was happy to see me, but I could see that he was very preoccupied. I could see that soon, he'd need to go back to Haiti because his soul was still there. After a week, he'd already planned his return so he could get some peace of mind. He'd helped many people during the initial disaster, and he needed to go back. He told me that he didn't tell anybody that he was leaving because he felt culpable. He was upset with himself for leaving them without any resources on which to live. He'd come back just to assure me that he was all right. He stared out the window, looking at I-don't-know-what. I told him to seek a psychologist, but he refused and said that he was fine. As soon as the planes started flying into Haiti again, he went back to secure what was left of his business and to help others a little. This time, he stayed there just for three weeks.

Finally, I had him back for a while. As usual, he had to move. This was part of his life. He went to New York to try to make a living. After we spent our money to open the bakery in addition to the ceramic factory, we were broke. After two months in New York, he came back to Miami with a plan to buy a taxicab medallion. He complained every day about working hard for such little money. We couldn't pay our bills, so we filed for chapter 7 to discharge our credit card debt. We weren't proud of our actions and were ashamed to talk about it. At the end of December 2010, Sam decided to go back Port-au-Prince to rebuild. Once again, I didn't try to retain him. How could I? We couldn't live on only my salary and some hazard money from the taxicab. Sam worked twelve hours a day, four times a week, and then he gave the car to another driver. There was nothing left in our bank account after we paid our lease. I was worried about the future.

"Things are already tough here," I told him. "What will you do in Haiti? How will the business survive? The people there are more focused on repairing their houses than buying decorative ceramic pieces."

He answered me philosophically. "If we cannot do much for ourselves with what we have, it's because our needs are too big. However, we can always help others with little things. Perhaps all we need for now is a blessing from God, and good fortune will follow later." He continued the conversation with poise that I'd never witnessed from him before. "Imagine how hard it is for us to live with only our minimal resources. It's arduous for my employees who don't have anything now, some of them had worked for more than twenty-five years in the business. I cannot let them down. Believe me, Oli, I'm their only hope, and for better or for worse, I'm going back to give them a lift. I promised them that I'd be back. If the barge must sink, it's going to sink with me onboard."

I dreamed of being again together, as mister and missus living under the same roof, but that hope vanished into nothingness. What could I say? What could I do other than let him go? On January 10, 2011, I drove my husband back to Haiti, just like I had done the Monday before the earthquake.

43

More Ailments

AFTER I TOOK HIM to the airport, I went to work, feeling discouraged. My coworkers couldn't believe that he'd left again. They didn't say too much, but their eyes said it all, and I clearly understood them. This added to my stress, and I fell into a deep depression, so bad that you can't even envision it. I had high stress circulating through my bloodstream every day. When I got home from work each day, I felt exhausted and I was nauseated most of the time. I took too many painkillers to kill the pain, I had upset stomach. Every day was a repetition of the same scenario: work, pills, and sleep. My heart pounded all the time like I had received bad news. Sometimes, it was so bad that I swore that the big one, the big stroke, would hit me at any moment. I always kept a sachet of sea salt in my bag to put under my tongue when I got an unsettled stomach. I was dizzy all the time and drowsy like I was on some kind of leisure drugs. This made it very hard for me to drive to work. I mentioned once to my PCP that I felt sleepy while driving, and he threatened to prohibit my right to drive if it continued. He told me that it was very dangerous to do so and to tell him if it worsened. One of his patients had a problem like that, he said, and he almost died from a car accident. He wasn't going to let this happen again. I know, dude. I was conscious that one day I might have an accident, but what else could I do? I had to work and needed my pills to keep going. When I had to change highway lanes, I couldn't focus enough to see that another car was coming. All I could hear was the horn or shout from the other drivers, but did I have an option? I didn't want to kill myself this time, I just couldn't focus on the road. The choice was very difficult for me. I couldn't get rides from other people because first of all, none of my coworkers lived nearby, and second, I needed my car with me at work to get to my appointments or to go home if I was unable to finish the workday. The doctor gave me pills to keep me awake, but this made it even harder because I always felt nauseated. As soon I got home, the sleepiness was gone, and my eyes stayed open at night. I didn't sleep at night anymore, but I was sleepy during the day. It was a very controversial situation, and I didn't see a solution in sight.

Nevertheless, when I got my paycheck, I forgot my troubles for a while. I had the power to buy whatever I needed. Blindly, I entered into the magic world of depression. I became hypnotized by the simplicity of a world that told me to give up on myself. I was under depression's charm and had no power to get rid of it on my own. Many times, my PCP recommended that I see a psychologist or a psychiatrist, but I answered that I wasn't crazy enough for that, just overloaded. Deeply inside, I thought that I probably need one, though, because suddenly, I didn't care anymore if I had to cry in front of people. I became shameless, reckless, skeptical, and fragile. Nobody could talk to me without interpreting the conversation my way. Between my health, work, and loneliness, I was going kaput! I couldn't function. I was putting so much effort into accomplishing so little and merely showing my friends that I was normal. I was drained by my fear of not making it through to the end, fear that soon, I might not be able to perform my duties at work or pursue things that I used to do with great pleasure. I wanted to stay the same perfectionist of a person that I used to be, the one who'd been working for so many years with perfect scores, errorless and accurate. I used to be so proud of my work, but that was slowing coming to an end. Did I enter this world illegally, or did my roughshod destiny decide to drive me into the darkness before I reached old age?

Despite my refusal to see mental health specialists, my PA-C prescribed me Xanax, Cymbalta, and Savella for depression and anxiety, which I took only on weekends because of the side effects. Xanax was my preferred one. It works faster than the other ones. As advised, I also kept a brown paper bag in my handbag to blow in if I had a panic attack crisis. I knew for sure that I wasn't well, but I still kept pretending. I needed to cling onto that little pride to walk with my head held high and cope with my burdens.

In 2011, my PCP sent me to see a pulmonologist and a cardiologist. I couldn't breathe properly and had a dry cough that made my chest less resistance to activities, plus my blood pressure was rising to the sky. I had to stay calm and live in a serene environment. This time, the more I slept, the more tired I felt. I was miserable and didn't know what to do, and neither did my PCP. After any activities, I had to stop and get some fresh air. I drove to work or home with my eyes half-closed, waiting for a red light to snap. I had no control over my life with the panic attacks and anxiety. I always carried a bottle of Xanax with me always, which I took at work, while I was driving—anywhere I felt it coming. First, the specialist, Dr. C. C. told me in his Cuban accent that it could be an early stage of dementia. I thought that my symptoms had nothing to do with loss of memory, but I said to myself, "Maybe he's right." My mother had dementia, so maybe I was following in her footsteps. I was thrilled with Dr. C. C., and he wanted to help me. He had a heavy accent that made it difficult to understand him, and he couldn't understand mine well either. We made a good old couple, unable to understand one another. He told me that the problem was allergies and the beginning of asthma. He prescribed Singulair and gave me samples of inhalers and sprays to try, many of which Jean had already given me, only different brands. Our incompatibility of understanding one another was so advanced. I told him that I had Angina once to help him on his search of finding what I had, but he thought otherwise. Also, he was concerned about my sleepy driving. He thought that at night, I didn't sleep deeply enough. He sent me to have a sleeping test at Mercy Hospital.

I booked an appointment with them the following Friday at 8:00 p.m. Because there wasn't work the next day, I didn't have to miss any work. The day of, I left home with a little bag and went straight to the hospital. I wasn't alone. Many people were waiting for the same exam. We talked and exchanged feelings. Thirty minutes later, someone showed up to assign each of us a room. Then after a short wait, a technician entered with a tray of two ham sandwiches and a little can of juice. They let me know that I could put my pajamas on and that he'd be back before nine to prepare me for the test. I drank the juice but left the sandwich because I don't eat meat on Fridays. As he said, at nine o'clock, he came back and started wiring me. I had to tell him what time I wanted to go to bed so he could come back to connect the wires to the monitor. I didn't want him to come back, so I told him that I was going to sleep immediately. Why wait, I thought. I had nothing else to do. No TV, even. I couldn't watch it while my wires were connected. I didn't want to make any movements, thinking that those wires were glued to my scalp, and that if they got torn out, my hair and skin might be pulled out too. The results came back, demonstrating that I was awake, turning right and left most of the night, which wasn't too bad, but that I should be able to sleep better.

"During the non-REM," they explained, "you had seven obstructive apneas with a maximum duration of twenty seconds. There is was one obstructive hypopnea with a duration of eighteen seconds, for a total of eight apneas and hypopneas. The apnea/hypopnea index is two, and you slept nonsupine. However, there were twenty-six respiratory-effort-related arousals, for a respiratory effort-related arousal index of five. You have a respiratory disturbance index of seven. Sinus rhythm was noted."

I thought, *How could I sleep well with so many ropes stuck to my head and plugged into a monitor?* It was the stupidest test I'd done in my life. Dr. C. C. wasn't impressed by the test results, convinced that I had a sleeping disorder. He sent me for a second overnight sleeping test. I hated that incomprehensible test. They woke me at 5:00 a.m. to get ready to leave the premises at 6:00 a.m., without breakfast. Don't they know that 5:00 a.m. on a Saturday is when sleep is so good and for me that haven't slept well through the night, it's when I was finally taken away to the magic garden by my angels. What a blasted test!

After the second test, the doctor declared that I had sleep apnea. I had two choices: use a CPAP machine to sleep at night or have my tonsils enlarged. I opted to have the machine. I had other tests done at his office such as a pulmonary function laboratory that showed mild obstruction of the lungs. I was given Flonase, Flovent, and Proair. Also, I was diagnosed with chronic dyspnea due to the difficulty I had with breathing. I didn't try to understand more because it was too complicated. To tell the truth, I wasn't convinced that I had all these disorders, but I wasn't feeling well. It seemed like I didn't have any internal body secrets anymore. I'd had so many tests to reveal everything inside of me. In a way, I thought, it was good. At least I knew enough to help prevent it from getting worse in the future.

    A company called me within three days to have the machine delivered and to explain to me how it worked. They were very fast. I'd forgotten all about it until they called. It wasn't an urgent matter. I had worse things than that to remember. They had to remind me of the reason for the phone call. I completely lost track of that new ailment. Did I believe that I had sleep apnea? Not really! I wanted to rid my mind of my minor ailments so that I could focus only on the big ones. The doctor had enforced it with other medications such as Advair and gave me samples to use right away. I didn't see big improvements, but I was slightly better. Religiously, I utilized the machine every night, until one night, I woke up with the idea that a snake was around my neck. I was in sweats, and with no hesitation, I pulled the cord from my nose. That same weekend, my aunt in Canada telephoned to let me know that she'd heard on the news about someone who was electrocuted overnight from that machine because he'd used an extension to plug in it. Thus, I had two good reasons for not using it anymore. My PCP was persuaded that I would have an asthma crisis, and so he prescribed me Flovent and Fluticasone, a nasal spray to inhale for the shortness of breath. I diagnosed myself with sinus problems instead. I still believed that I just had sinusitis and allergies. I had so many medications to help me with that issue. I felt very blessed: *viva* America and *viva* insurance. In my country, I don't know if I would've lasted that long. I had something different ailing me every two to three months. My PCP scheduled me to see her every three months, but I never reach that before I had to return to the office with something new. Over time, everything went back to being more sustainable. I still used the machine occasionally, when I had difficulty sleeping at night or when I really felt like my heart was coming out of my chest. I don't know if it helped me relax a little bit or opened my lungs so that I could breathe better, but for the peace of my mind, I used it until those two inconveniences stopped me.

I'd essentially become my own doctor. I could tell what was bothering me and take the right medication for it. I have a drawer full of medicine. I went to my referral cardiologist. I had an EKG test following many other tests, and none revealed that I had a problem with my heart. That was a good sign, but the chest pain persisted and got worse, so he kept monitoring me. One day at the cardiologist's office, I felt like I was spinning like a whirligig. The entire building was turning like it had when I'd had vertigo a long time ago, but this time, my heart wasn't complying with its normal rate. I was hot, feeling faint, like I needed to throw up. The doctor's office was on the fourth floor, so I went to the window to dupe my brain, as if it would see the open window as a signal to breathe normally. That only aggravated the situation. A patient asked me if I was okay, and I said no, so she called the receptionist. They took me to a separate room to do more tests. I can't tell you names of these tests because I was empty and insusceptible to everything going on around me. They took me to the emergency room, which was in the same building. I stayed there, all alone. I could've called my son, but I didn't want to alarm him. Nothing was found in any of the tests. I was released and sent home to rest. Was it a game my brain was playing on me? If yes, I thought, I was for sure crazy.

A long time ago, while I was with my PCP's first surrogate, he told me that I had arthritis in my neck per an MRI test that I'd had done. The pain was tolerable. Over the years, parts of my body started to rust, and I began having more pain in my neck, back, left hand, left foot, and hips. Sitting for eight hours at work could be painful and trouble me a lot. I ended up seeing a rheumatologist, not for first time. I underwent another MRI scan of the soft tissue of my hand, which was giving me an electrical shock. The result showed that I had a tiny midline bulge with an underlying annular tear, but that the disc canal and foramina were normal. There was no subluxation, bone marrow signal abnormality, spinal cord lesion, craniovertebral junction abnormality, or prevertebral soft tissue abnormality, but small anterior spurs were probably present. My blood test also confirmed elevated rheumatoid arthritis. I had an x-ray done of my cervical spine and my right shoulder, which indicated a rotator cuff tear and a slight elevation of the humeral. In my left foot, there was a left-heel inferior osteophyte. To conclude, my lumbar spine showed that I had a scoliosis convex to the right and that there was calcification of the abdominal aorta but no aneurysms. There were so many minor details that I got lost when he tried to explain it to me. Maybe, I thought, my bony craniovertebral was already split into two components. Because he never asked for other tests, I stayed mute. I was too tired from going from one lab to another. The only thing that I memorized and forced myself to live by was, "if he didn't refer me to have more tests done, it is because the symptoms aren't grave." I kept repeating the mantra, "It's not serious." That doctor blamed all the musculoskeletal pain I was having and the positive rheumatoid factors on the hepatitis C.

Because I had that disease, most doctors made HCV responsible for all my problems, especially if I complained about something that they couldn't see. It was nearly as frustrating to them as it was for me. Once, the doctor tried to move my right arm up, but it was so sore that I screamed, and tears dimmed my vision. I could barely see him with the salt water flooding my face. He was shocked by my inadvertent reaction. That shoulder was on fire! He called the nurse right away to bring him some medical accessories. He explained that he would give me a shot, and with an extremely emaciated look in his eyes, he excused himself and told me that he didn't know that it was so bad. What he didn't know was that I was so embarrassed for screaming that I couldn't even look at him. I gave birth to three children without yelling, and for this shoulder to make me behave so inappropriately was unacceptable. He treated me with a local injection for the left shoulder joint. I couldn't understand why my left shoulder was hurting more than the right, but the medical way he moved that shoulder made me think that none of both of my shoulders were better than any others. He chose to touch the right arm instead of the left, which was the one that I told him was hurting me like hell. Possibly, he saw something that I couldn't, or perhaps I didn't know my right from my left anymore! Doctors do things to mortify you. I had local injections in my right shoulder joint and had my supraspinatus tendon sheath treated with Xylocaine to numb the skin, as well as 80 mg of Kenalog, 40 mg in each. On my concerning side, from the left cervical muscle to the trapezius muscle and the splenius capitis muscles, I was also injected with the same amounts of Xylocaine and Kenalog. These relieved my pain immediately, as if it never existed.

I went every month to get my shots and listen to Dr. W. tells me how the pills he had given me were working successfully. I wasn't on cocaine, but the name of the injection and the after-sensation made me think that perhaps they were linked. The effect was very rapid. Dr. W. advised the company I worked for to change my chair and my phone at work, due to the fact that my neck and my back were giving me so many problems. They did so three months after I presented them with the prescription. The doctor was able to put my pain to sleep, but as soon as it woke up, it was back as if it had never left. Furthermore, I didn't know why he hadn't requested physical therapy instead of these shots. I had my hands full with problems and wasn't ready to add more. I thought, *Let's leave it like that, because who knows, miracles occur every day in my existence.* I was condemned to live with unfixed, insignificant illnesses. I had to find ways to stop going to the doctor all the time. It wasn't easy to accomplish, God only knows, but I tried. I often sang this song "I Will Survive," and I did survive.

In November 2011, I had another bone density test that revealed severe osteopenia and mild osteoporosis, a T-score in the right femoral neck of −2.5, in the left femoral neck of 2.4, and in the lumbar spine of −1.9. To treat this condition, which had increased from osteopenia to osteoporosis, my PCP put me on Boniva, 150 mg monthly, and a calcium and vitamin D pill once a week. The one thing that stayed healthy was my hair. I even had problems with my nails and toes. I couldn't wear nail polish or wash the dishes without gloves and couldn't stay in the pool too long or allow dirt to get anywhere near my toes. Any of these things could result in a fungal infection. Believe me, black mold under the nail can make it very uncomfortable to touch. It came and went any time I paid less attention to it. I could spend months free from it if I soaked the ugly monster in a solution of baking soda and apple cider in the morning and coconut oil at night. I sometimes used garlic when my mind really thought it was a monster. I didn't care if was helping or not, but I was always sure to cut my nails very short to stop the spread of the disease or further damage the nails. I've battled with this for my entire adult life and still do to this day. People with this ailment never get a permanent cure. It comes be back when we least expect it. The oral medication for this syndrome wasn't recommended for me because it could affect my already-damaged liver. You've probably never paid attention to it, on television, when ads finish with "Not recommended for people with liver damage." What a big celebrity my liver became!

My abnormal eye also became a perpetual persecution for me, especially at night. I couldn't tell anybody about it because by 9:00 or 10:00 a.m., all the discomfort went away. People thought that I was lying about that disease. My eye would look normal a few minutes after I left bed, but the uneasiness would be present all morning. My husband and I were the only ones who knew that the eye problem persisted. Imagine having pain in one eye so bad that you can't sleep! I didn't see an eye specialist for long time because I know there was nothing they could do for me. At my doctor's advice, I decided to go to Bascon Palmer, a well-known hospital for eye diseases, thinking that they might have discovered a cure for this annoying illness. I submitted myself to the usual number of tests, bending up and down. The results showed the same mass behind the eye, but as the prior doctors said, there wasn't a treatment available. They noted a cluster of several cotton-wools in the retina, possible associated with hypertension, meaning that my blood pressure had been elevated for a while, which I already knew. They were all curious to see the phenomenon themselves. One doctor invited in another and another to witness it.

Anyway, my PCP wasn't satisfied after six months of hearing my complaints. She referred me to another eye doctor, Dr. M. I believed that the new doctor was bloody scared of anything he'd never encountered before and discombobulated after he saw the images of my eye in his test results. By looking at his face, I could tell that he had seen Satan in the daylight, he was extremely confused and concerned. He became pale, as if he was in the presence of a surreal nonhuman being. I asked him if he ever saw somebody like me.

"Yes, but not like yours," he said, unable to hold back his emotions. When you came in, I couldn't tell that you had an issue with your eye. It looked to me so natural." He paused. "You are a pretty young woman, so don't let this disturb you. It might never get worsen."

It was easy for him to say. He didn't know how many nights I spent with that f——ing eyeball stinging in my skull. Many nights, I half-sat in the dark with my swollen eye in my hand to prevent it of falling out—or at least that's what it felt like. I couldn't change positions. Lying on the left side, on my back, or facedown on the bed would make it hurt even more. He washed his hands of me like Pontius Pilate washed his hands at the trial of Jesus and sent me to see another ophthalmologist, who coincidentally happened to be the first doctor that I visited in 1995 for this problem. Dr. H. remembered me very well. Who could forget a woman who was fashionably dressed, covered in makeup, with a wild, sneaky eye? But he couldn't remember that my eye didn't get just get red when I bent over but swelled for hours and hours in the night. Many doctors don't listen to their patients, just assume what first comes to their minds. I left him for the first time in 1995 for being careless and left him again in 2012 for the same reason. He even sent the wrong ombudsman's report to my PCP.

44

Side Effects

DESPITE IT ALL, I still considered myself to be encircled by the spirit of God, even during my difficult moments. For example, I always caught my illnesses early by going to the doctor's office so frequently. The Lord embraced my soul and made me a real, living person, with good and bad moments. I wondered what my life would be like if I didn't have so many inconveniences. I might forget about him and sin every moment! I wouldn't understand that people go through life with difficult conditions, some worse than and some similar to mine. He blessed me by making me aware of my illnesses in their early stages so that I could cope with them. I was fortunate to have great medical insurance through both companies I worked for in Haiti and in Miami and to meet great doctors on my path. God gave me courage to deal with it all, no matter what.

In January 2012, I went to Haiti with the committee Hand-in-Hand for Haiti to see the progress of the schools that a few companies—Starboard, DFS, Onboard Media, and Estee Lauder—were collecting funds to build in Haiti. My company was one of the participants, and that made me very proud. I was an active member and a fundraiser. I was very excited to be part of this humongous project. In reality, it wasn't a project anymore, because we had already 250 students enrolled. We still called it a project, though, because we had a bigger vision to build near the city of St. Marc. The program would provide students with good education, food twice a day, supplies, uniforms, and spaces for sports, among other things. It brought me such joy to be part of it, and I would have done anything to contribute to its success. The main reasons that I left my country in the first place were to give my children a safe environment and a good education during the revolution. Now, I was giving back to the impoverished kids. I was giving them some of what America had given to my family. I was so thrilled with the mission that I tried the impossible —approaching people after work for donations, despite my health conditions. The immensity of the construction site astounded me. The garden was already growing vegetables and fruits, a medical nursery was erected to give the children care, and a playground was built to offer them exercise, fun, and fresh air. It was amazing to see the happiness in the eyes of the children there, playing and learning like they owned the place!

I felt really blessed to be able to help and support the organization. I went to Haiti with some of the other members and our company's CEO, listening to his encouraging words, his plans for future steps, and his good, insightful intentions. Typically, he came to our workplace only twice a year. When we knew he was coming, we cleaned the place from top to bottom, and only high-level employees such as the president, vice presidents, and some directors were lucky enough to meet him. And there I was, hugging him and eating with him. Rich, huh? What blew me away the most was to be around the Haitian children who kissed and embraced us as if they really understood what we were doing for them. I wouldn't give away that feeling of freedom for anything—of doing something so special at my job. Going to meetings, events, and fundraisers at work put me in another dimension of my life. I projected inward with a sparking, bright light like I was in a dream, overwhelmed by my surroundings, by things that I enjoyed doing. My group stayed in Haiti for only twenty-four hours, but I needed to see the damage caused by the earthquake, so I decided to stay two days longer. After the other members boarded their plane, I hung out with my husband.

It was Friday afternoon. I visited Sam's new boutique in Petionville and promised myself that I'd see the city the next day because I was already so tired. I woke up that Saturday with a migraine, nausea, dizziness, and sensitivity to light and sun. I couldn't do anything with my body. It was stuck in bed with no strength. My head was too heavy to drive my body out into the hot, sunny streets. I was so disappointed. I stayed in bed the entire day, my head close to exploding. I assumed that the emotions of seeing the town so ravaged caused my raging headache. I took my butalbital pills, but nothing seemed to change. Something was endlessly pounding inside my head. I managed to return to Miami on Sunday because I had to return to work on Monday. I went back with that infernal headache hammering my scalp. I left my car in a pay parking lot hotel for three days during the trip. Their shuttle bus took me to the airport. After the trip, as I was waiting at the airport for the shuttle to come to take me to my car, the migraine was hard to bear in and of itself. I held my head in both hands, feeling like I could screech, like my skull was too heavy for one neck to carry. When finally I reached home, it was a relief. I was more than happy to have made it the thirty miles from the airport to my house. I had a shower and took another pill with a cup of milk, then I went straight to bed. The next day, I went to work. The headache wasn't too bad in the morning, but as time passed, the pain intensified. I couldn't work with that uncongenial headache. My eyes were highly sensitive to the light above my desk, and a colleague kept talking and talking, his words hammering into my head. I turned all the lights off that I could. I couldn't eat anything, just a few saltine crackers to help with the nausea. I had a plastic bag ready in my garbage can, in case. People who passed my desk looked at me with a grim, resentful faces, probably thinking that I'd been lucky to go on a trip at the company expense, and there I was, playing sick. That suspicion I had about my coworkers made it all even worse. The pain had conquered my head, and now it was taking possession of my mind. I wanted to work so there would be no complaining from the higher-ups, but that migraine was unwilling to let me do so. I felt like I had an infected wound that was going to burst inside my head, like my skull bones were cracking, like there was an erupting volcano in my brain, especially around the sphenoid osseous tissue behind my right eye. The orbital plate of my frontal bone seemed be separating from the parietal coronal suture, and my temporal bone couldn't support my face any longer. My jaw and my ears were also part of the dance. I wasn't capable of doing anything to get rid of that ogre in my head. I drove home with only one hand, my left hand pressing my cranium. I had the impression that the pain was behind my eyes, hidden in my forehead and taking residence in my crossbones. Even though I wore very dark sunglasses, the pain powered through my face, making it hypersensitive to the light. The appearance of my nose, my jaw, and my cheeks even seemed to be wider than usual. After a few days with that unceasing headache, I decided to see a neurologist. With my new insurance, thank goodness, I didn't need referral.

Dr. B. worked in the same office that I went in 2008 to see one his colleagues, Dr. A. (The medical world is comprised of small circles of doctors; there is no way around it.) He wasn't friendly at all. He looked more like a businessman than a doctor, impeccable in his starched white shirt. His face showed that he didn't give a damn about what I had or how I was feeling; he was just doing his job. He sat in a chair near the door with a little pulpit for his small fancy laptop. My chair was all the way across the room. He was tall and handsome. He had all the advantages; he was young, healthy, happy to be who he was, and clearly not bothered too much by his patients' problems. When he entered that room, it looked like nobody existed except for him. He sat down without a "Good morning" or a "How do you feel?" He just sat down, set up his computer, and asked for the reason of my visit. His manners made me think that I'd perturbed his sacred environment. I explained that I'd had an unusual headache for two weeks. He sent me to have an MRI test done. The test came back with no evidence of abnormal brain signals, and an evaluation of the orbit revealed the presence of right-side proptosis with an intra-orbital mass. The mass characteristics were most consistent with a cavernous hemangioma, which I already knew about. My brain was unremarkably normal except for that mass, my hysterical eye, of course. That was good news, of course, but I wanted to find out what had given me so much pain in my head. He took me off the butalbital that I'd been on since 1998 and prescribed me Topamax.

Despite his weird attitude, I was satisfied with the new prescription, which I thought might end my misery. It was a very strange headache that I'd never had before. It went from mild to very painful in the span of one day. Sometimes I asked myself if I was going to have a seizure. I'm trying to explain that wild sensation, but there are no specific words I can use to describe it. It could be graciously moderate in the morning, but any kind of exhaustion would change its course to severe at night. "What is it?" I wondered.

In the meantime, the hepatology doctor suggested that it was in my best interest to have another HCV treatment immediately. I declined his advice and told him that I would wait until 2013. I wanted to do so much for the school in Haiti. I had a bigger responsibility that year. Two weeks later, the headache was completely gone, but I started feeling another sort of reaction. It was as if my brain was being drained from my head. It felt like I didn't have a brain anymore, that the space in my head where it used to be was just empty. I couldn't focus on anything, and my work was paying the consequences. I was sure that I was getting dementia like my dear mother had. I couldn't remember a thing, sometimes even whether I'd taken my pills already. At work, I started forgotten the process I needed to do when customs didn't release the merchandise, where to call, how to initiate the FDA process, etc. It took me longer to do a simple task. I was confused with the new customs regulations. Even driving to work was unbearable. My blood sugar jumped higher and higher to 259, and there was no way to get it controlled. It didn't matter how many units of insulin I took in the morning and at night, glucose was always traveling into my blood cells at an incredible speed. I had a terrible taste and smell in my mouth and couldn't sleep at night.

I thought that these side effects would go away after a month, so I refilled the prescription. Instead of getting better, however, the side effects became exacerbated. I had disturbances with my vision, and my face got puffy as if I had lupus. Suddenly, I had many bruises on my stomach and on my legs, but I hadn't gotten hurt. I couldn't eat either. After a while, I realized that something was definitely wrong with me. *Could the topiramate be the cause of all of it?* I wondered. I was tenaciously taking the pills to avoid having my longtime, torturing friend of a headache anymore. I enthusiastically wanted to challenge it because I badly needed to get rid of that phantomlike head pain, which was disturbing my life. I was so dazzled by the thought I could withstand it and change the course of my chronic headaches that I couldn't see that I was getting sicker, even if I didn't have the cephalalgia anymore. After having thrown myself so deeply into this blindfolded surrealism, I became conscious that I was going to die. Physically, I looked like a zombie without much meat on my bones. I couldn't control my movements even when I was writing. My hands trembled, and I couldn't follow the lines on the paper, so my words went astray on the page. I couldn't type as fast as I used to either because I had to check almost every word carefully for missing letters. I had a dry cough, and I couldn't breathe properly. I soon started seeing bald patches in my hair. My vocabulary became so limited that during a normal conversation, I had to venture deeply into my memory to find the right words to say. I was losing weight very fast. Finally, because I was feeling so weak and tired, I decided to go to ER. Later, I was admitted to the hospital without knowing exactly what was wrong with me.

One week before, I'd had bronchitis, which was diagnosed by an outpatient doctor from another ER hospital. I don't know how I got it. I had all kinds of tests at that hospital, and my hexose was still going through the roof. I couldn't sleep with all the nurses testing my blood every two hours. They were like vampires, sucking my blood with needles for tests, even when I told them that my fingers were sensitive. They wouldn't stop, like vampires searching for blood. My fingers became very delicate to all the pricks, so to be sure that they got the blood they needed, the lancet is inserted very deep. I tried to explain that the topiramate was the cause of my sickness and that the corticosteroid drugs administered to me for the bronchitis was not helping my blood sugar decrease, but they still gave it to me because the only neurologist could stop it. At the end of it all, I was so tired of all the tests that I had to beg them to let me go home. I needed to have a complete night of sleep without disturbance. I was dead tired, and the sugar refused to collaborate with my body. They released me on Saturday afternoon after I signed all kinds of papers stating that I had requested my own discharge. As soon I got home, a nurse called, saying that she would come over later to control my blood sugar and give me insulin. Even at home, I didn't have the peace I was looking for. The next day, she came over once at 7:00 a.m. and again between 5:00 or 6:00 p.m. After a week at home, I was able to slow down my sugar count. I couldn't wait to tell the nurse that I could manage by myself and to please stop coming. I didn't like the name of the company that sent her, Angel Home Care, which made me think that I was really in hell. I was on so many medications: prednisone, Tessalon Perles, Cipro, Phenergan with codeine, ibuprofen, Ventolin, and Proventil, in addition to all the sequences that I already had. It took me about two months to feel a little better.

At length, my PCP told me to take half of the Topamax pills and see the neurologist as soon as possible to completely stop them. My husband drove me to his office. There, I realized that the neurologist didn't totally believe that this medication could harm me at all. He tested me with a simple math question. I couldn't find the solution, and I felt so embarrassed. I wasn't bad in math at school, so how come I couldn't find the solution to a simple problem of arithmetic? I felt humiliated, like he was going to think that I wasn't as educated I looked. But when I started to feel better, during the following visit, he asked me the same question, and I answered it well.

"This is the same question I asked you during your last visit," he said, a mix of surprise, sarcasm, and humor in his voice. "You couldn't answer it then, so what happened now?" Shaking his head, he continued. "At least you feel better now, after taking the topiramate. You don't have your daily headache." I think he said that to preserve his reputation. He didn't want to admit that he'd prescribed me a murderer's medication.

"No," I simply replied. It was true. I hadn't had the headache for almost two months, but some other major illnesses replaced the migraine. There was no comparison. I was very sick for as long I was on these immoral pills. I'm very sure that I would've died if I had stayed on Topamax for any longer.

Silently, I said, "Your medicine almost damaged my entire functional system, so don't be fresh and proud of yourself." Finally, he came to his senses and took me totally off the drug. Little by little, I regained my normal life, but I never completely recovered. Some of the aftereffects lasted for a long time, and some never left my body at all, even to this day. I went back to work, working half a day for two weeks as was advised by my doctor. I couldn't even have a long conversation without having shortness of breath. I was a ninety-year-old woman in a fifty-seven-year old's body. Dr. B. never admitted that the side effects of that medicine were very serious. I'm sure that I wasn't the only one complaining to him about this drug. He did what he thought was good for me, I understand that, but the fact is that this pill is a real killer of the human immune system. I wrote a letter to the manufacturer without mentioning the doctor's name, asking them to recall the medicine. I went on the internet and read almost all the accounts of people taking this medicine. They had similar same side effects, and in some case, it had badly affected their pregnancies. I also read that the company had been sued, but the FDA allowed them to continue selling the product, regardless. The manufacturer sent me a form to fill out and send back, which I did, but I never heard from them again. I was going to send a copy to the FDA also, but over time, as I got sicker and sicker, I lost my confidence in fighting to recall the drug from the market. Considering that some people already filed lawsuits against the manufacturer, per what I read throughout the internet, I consciously chose to focus more on my own improvement. You have to pick your battles sometimes.

My health took a drastic turn for the worse. In September 2012, I went on a medical leave of absence as was advised by my psychologist and PCP. I couldn't manage going to work any longer, especially if I wanted to fend off my symptoms. I wasn't the same individual anymore. "This isn't the kind of experience I should go through," I thought, "on the journey for better health." It was like half of me was gone, leaving only the other half of me alive. I was missing a part of my brain for sure, that's the kind of feeling I was dealing with. Each medicament I was taken has its own side effects and I was taken a lot. We, as patients, seek to enhance our health, but most of the time, incredibly, we end up with more issues than we had before. I know that some treatments have lots of side effects. I'm familiar with that because I went through three hep C treatments. But this one had just been pills for migraines, which shouldn't have had so many terrible, life-altering side effects. I think that reckless behavior on the part of drug manufacturers and many others in that industry is unacceptable. These pills shouldn't have made me feel like I was on chemotherapy. That is so wrong! Manufacturers can do a better job than treating patients like experimental subjects and looking only for profitable ways to make revenue.

I'm still alive today because the agent of death didn't come to our rendezvous. I became a skeleton with brittle bones. If you blew on me, all the bones in my body would be dislocated. Sometimes, I asked myself if they really cared about patients or if they just wanted to make money out of our misery. We trust our doctors, and they shouldn't use their patients as guinea pig, or *cobaye*, as we say in French. Medications should be used to cure diseases, not to add more. Of course, that drug didn't affect everyone like it did me, but my many chronic afflictions made it more difficult for me to handle. Lately, on television, I see many ads for pills. It seems to me that their side effects often hurt more than the diseases they're meant to cure! Is it normal to advertise these drugs despite the severe side effect warnings? I don't understand the credo that makes the drug makers so coldhearted and insensible. I appreciate that scientists are willing to find new, advanced cures for so many diseases, but can't they improve their trustworthiness and credentials further by studying and nullifying the side effects? Drugs shouldn't be only a commercial industry, but an industry that pays attention to the safety, care, and concerns of its users. What price must a patient pay to restore their health? From experience, I can say that sometimes, the benefits are not even worth it if the drug adds other diseases to the ones our doctors are already endeavoring to treat.

I've since learned that there are many more severe side effects of Topamax than those that I had. I'll let you search for "Topamax" or "topiramate" yourself, the hitman's pill that can send you to hell before it sends you to death. I was on that medicine for a mere headache, and I almost passed from life to mortality. Does that seem right to you, scientists? My advice to everyone who takes medication is to read the instructions and the drug components well, including all the side effects, and research what you're about to put in your stomach. Be sure that you feel confident with it beforehand. If you're not confident with your doctors or with a prescribed medication, it's okay to pass on them.

I believe that when manufacturers send these drugs to the FDA for approval, the humane process would be to go over them, study them, test them, make some changes and restrictions to offset side effects if need be, and return them for changes in ingredients. We can't live in a society where we are afraid to take our medicines. Often, however, we don't feel like we have a choice in this matter, even if we know that a drug will kill us soon or later. It's like we are washing our hands and then drying them on a dirty floor. Doctors should pay more attention to what they give to their patients that might have bad consequences and refuse to accept any crap from agencies. Know and protect your patients against these "get rich quick" pharmaceutical companies. Even if I want to sign for a trial, you need to explain clearly all the potential side effects before we begin. It's not okay to prescribe something with elevated secondary effects without warning the patient, nor is it okay to put the patient's life in needless jeopardy for the sake of "trying." My neurologist thought that he'd given me the right medication, the miracle one, and I have no doubt that he wanted to help me. In that regard, I don't want to blame him. He definitely wanted me to be free of that chronic migraine, and he accomplished that for a while, which is what I'd asked him to do. But was it his only duty to provide me with relief regardless of what might come after? It's a good philosophy, but I doubt that it's the right one in the medical field, especially given the seriousness of some side effects.

I decided that I preferred to cope with my head pain instead of going back into the hellhole of Topamax. I know that sometimes, it's a combination of insurance, the FDA, and doctors, but do we have to beg to get better care? Sometimes, caregivers don't even believe you until many people report the same side effects. Doctors need to recognize that what is good for some is not always good for all. Your patients aren't always delusional, so listen to them! Your patients are humans seeking better, more comfortable lives. They are searching for your help. In many cases, I dropped my referred doctors because of their attitudes. I'm allergic to the kind of doctors whose first question is "What's wrong?" while standing by the door to show me that their time is chronometrically precious. If I knew what was wrong with me, why would I be at your office? I can only explain my symptoms. Change your aggressive language to a softer one, put your patients at ease, and don't be rude because you have the power to cure. Patients need support from their loved ones as well from their doctors. Find a better way to communicate. I like doctor who treat me as a patient, not as another case, or an item to get experience with. I know that your time is limited and that lots of patients are waiting for only one doctor, but don't have an attitude of "I don't have much time for you" or "Time is money, so the more patients I see, the more money I have in my bank account." I pay for a doctor's visit like everyone else does, so if my presence is a disturbance to you, you are in the wrong career. Take time to listen and to understand.

The question is, why does the FDA let its savants use us, the patients, as test subjects for some of its crazy, chemical, ambitious ideas? It is inexcusable when we know that they're aware of the ingredients and they don't try to correct the dilemma. I'm not blaming only the FDA for approving these chemical killers too quickly without paying more attention to the products, but also the producers, who should take more time to analyze the products before sending them out for approval. In addition, the government needs to do a better job improving the quality of everything that goes inside the human body. Does anybody give a damn about the consequences? What's the purpose of seeking cures when we have to worry about the consequences? Sometimes, we discover these dangers too late, when our bones are already rotten with all kinds of ailments due to the side effects of our previous medications.

I can't understand why a drug that I'm taking to relieve my depression lists anxiety, panic attacks, impulsive actions, and hostile/angry feelings as some of its side effects. My medication for vertigo lists dizziness as one of its side effects. My muscle relaxant tablets for pain/muscle spasms list agitation as a common side effect, as well as muscle breakdown. What is muscle breakdown? Isn't that contradictory to the point? The key thing for anyone who takes medication is to read every detail before starting a new prescription. They say that the road to heaven is usually thorny and prickly, but when we get there, there is no suffering. Let's use this analogy for our health. When we get cured, we should be able to live comfortably within that "cure," not deal with another disease, sometimes as significant as the "cured" one was, adding more sorrow to our lives. We need to carefully and watchfully investigate these symptoms ahead of taking any medicinal drug. Whenever we start taking medicine, we risk messing up our health with bad chemicals or combinations of chemicals that don't collaborate. Are those drugs really helping, or are our brains so damaged that we cannot see the danger clearly?

Sometimes, we say, "What the heck, all drugs have bad side effects," but this is not the moment to preclude the worst. Is this the way a sick person should always perceive life? Hell no! To prevent a disease from getting worse, I shouldn't have to add another one to my list. We are often so eager and willing to get cured that we skip reading the side effects of our medications, trusting instead that the doctors will know what might go wrong. This is the wrong way of doing things, so always read and be careful. When you get a new prescription, ask yourself, is this drug worth taking? Does the government really care about our health when it lets people accrue more diseases by consuming bad combinations of ingredients? I would prefer to live with some non-life-threatening diseases than cure one but add three more! The FDA needs to watch this matter more carefully before approving a predator medication that will be prescribed for a simple illness.

45

Insane Behavior

Jean and my PCP were getting serious about me seeing a psychologist. I took their recommendations the wrong way. They said that my health issues were starting to really attack my emotional system, which was making it all harder on me. They explained this to me in detail, of course, but I thought that my behavior wasn't so crazy that I needed to see a psychologist. Crazy people don't know when they turn ridiculously demented! They might think that the people around them are the crazy ones, not them. For example, I thought that my doctors were going insane to oblige me to see a counselor. *They must be really tired of me*, I thought. I couldn't stop crying because it felt like my world was changing very fast, at a speed that I couldn't apprehend. I found myself turning things over and over in my mind and returning to the same places where I began. I felt that earth had become a whirlwind and that I was deep inside it, spinning and spinning. I cried for any or no reason at all. A simple word that Sam said would exasperate me and him also before I even responded. *We should both see a psychologist*, I thought. *Why only me?* He wasn't helping. I felt like he wasn't supporting me because instead of being gentle, he liked to fight with me. He couldn't see that his wife was having bad moments. Men with their brains in a bubble are so limited in their ways of doing things.

Nothing was registering positively in my brain. If my brain didn't understand something, even something seeming insignificant, I would cry. I was losing my sanity but couldn't see that I needed help. I kept thinking and looking at myself in the mirror, trying very hard to discover if there was a new me. Everything seemed to be normal except that I was aging considerably faster and getting even sicker than before. I stopped taking the Xanax pills, but I couldn't pause the painkillers. I took them for pain and to help me sleep. Did I look crazy to my PCP and Jean? So crazy that they'd advised me to try something like therapy? They tried to make me understand that I had a lot on my hands, that I needed therapy to deal with all my emotions surrounding my health conditions. After two months of hearing the same suggestion, I decided to see one. I called my insurance to provide me with the name of a good psychologist. It was embarrassing for me. I made jokes about it so my mind could accept this new challenge. People mostly don't mention it when they are seeing this type of doctor, not even to friends or family, but I was so out of it that I told everybody in a humorous manner about my plan.

Convinced, I finally called the doctor to schedule my first appointment, and a tape recorder answered to let me know that he wasn't available to take my call. I hated those machines. I reacted like it was the first time something like that had ever happened to me. I was furious. The demoniac darkness had already invaded my knowledge and my emotions. I called again later and left a message. I waited the entire day for him to call me back, my eyes on the telephone screen every time I heard it ring. Nothing. As usual, I was impatient with this type of thing. I had a newfound willingness and drive to find out how it would work and how he could help me. I wasn't able to get in contact with him as soon as I'd wanted to, though. Two days passed without a return phone call, so I decided to act. I thought I might be able to use my new emotional disease as a pawn to reach him. *They think that I'm crazy*, I thought, *so why not use that to make him call me back faster?*

Thus, I called again and left another message: "Dr. J., I have called you several times to schedule an appointment without success. I can see your insouciance toward your patients. You've really shown me that you don't care about us at all, so if you don't call me within a short period of time, I will search for another psychologist. Goodbye."

They had truly created a monster. At that point, all the anodynes in my brain were probably disordered. I didn't feel any remorse for leaving him such a hash message without even meeting him. I was mad at my situation, at myself, at everyone. I had to empty and release my chest, which was inflamed with anger and frustration of all kinds. I was proud of my immodest language, to be honest, and pleased that I could use my psychological credulity and distress to be rude to him. Later, I had to apologize for that and explain the reason why I was so mean over the phone. At that fraction in time, I saw in him an enemy who would humiliate me again and again with his pertinent questions. Someone who would go on a deep search inside of me to find a reason for "I don't know why," another ailment to fight with. Also, I was practicing my role of being crazy. It worked, and the doctor called me the same day from his house at 8:00 p.m. He explained why he hadn't called me back earlier, and despite it all, we bonded over the phone right away.

My psychologist was appropriate, patient, and discreet. I don't think I would say what I said to him to any other kind of doctor. Prior to my first appointment, I arrived ten minutes earlier. The door was still locked, and someone showed me to the waiting room. He didn't have an assistant, just the neighbor next door. I sat alone in the tiny waiting room. I felt even more ashamed when I saw him face-to-face. Tall, skinny, and smiling, he opened the door for me and courteously offered that I sit or to lie down on the couch. The bag he held contained his computer, where he registered my name. He could see the reticence on my face. He knew that he wasn't going to get a lot from me right away, so he helped me with a few questions.

On my first visit, I didn't want to open my entire life to him, and he seemed to understand that. "Take your time," he said. "Maybe next time, you'll say more about what's been bothering you." I interpreted that as "I'm patient. I'll give you more and more sessions until I'm aware of all your deep secrets." Accordingly, he scheduled me for appointment every fifteen days. During the second time, without resistance, I told him more about me because he was pleasant to talk with. I was scared he might confirm my fears, that I was being silly by seeing him, but he didn't. Who knows what he was thinking inside? I wondered. It was like he knew people like me very well, like my case wasn't new to him. I visited him every two weeks so I could rid my chest of some secrets I had previously been resigned to take with me to my grave. I talked, of course, about my semi-separation with Sam and how it affected me, and about the stress I was under at work when I was sick. After a few sessions, he recommended that I not work at all, that it was too much to handle with so many ailments. He wasn't the first to say that to me, but he completely rejected that I should work even part-time. He sent a note about that to my PCP.

I don't know exactly what he said in that written report. Surely, I thought to myself, he diagnosed me with a manic disorder that would enforce Jean's opinion that I really needed to seek help. Are they sending me, next, to a psychiatrist to make me believe that I have a mental illness? Am I in denial? In the moment, I'm thinking, *How far will this sickness go before I finally realize that I truly needed assistance?* Jean was in charge of my health. She told me that she had been reviewing my file again with my PCP and that they both thought that it would be good for me to have another emotional support provider in addition to the psychologist, a psychiatrist as I assumed. I knew that I talked a lot about loneliness when I didn't feel well, but I didn't think that it made me a psychopath who needs to see a psychiatrist. It's true that I had considerable issues with my health, but I'd maintained my relationships with friends who had been supportive for years. I looked reasonably all right on the outside. After much consideration, I decided to follow her instructions. I booked an appointment with the psychiatrist she referred me to.

On my first visit, Dr. N. E. diagnosed me with the following: "Sad-looking, appears wary, distracted and tense, axis of major depressive disorder." I can't recall how many times he said that to me on that introductory visit, but it was a lot. Of course, I was unhappy and glum! I had too many doctors and illnesses, and now he was playing with my mind. I couldn't hold back the tears from running down my face when I told him about all my diseases. I cried because I didn't know what to do with my life, which felt upside down. It wasn't sadness, just a natural way for me to discharge my distress. Is that not what a normal person would do in a similar circumstance? I was giving him information regarding my private life, and he was asking me weird questions, questions that I'd never thought about. I was baffled by the mess I was in, and I was thinking that I'd probably never find my way to a normal life. I kept stating that I wasn't depressive, that it was just a moment of wickedness that soon would go away. He didn't want to hear my defense. As much I wanted him to hear my appeal of "I'm not sad as you think I'm!" the more he did the deaf-hearing thing. He was dogmatically sticking to his pinpointed, analytical egotism and was ignoring my persistent pleas. I was ashamed, superfluously thinking that it wasn't necessary to add more doctors to my collection. I cried for all the problems I had, and because I was telling a complete stranger, for the second time, of my surreptitious battles. With him, it was a one-way street. He thought that only his opinions counted. Finally, I came up with the thought that if my PCP had sent me to him, it's because I really needed help. He jumped to that conclusion assuming that all his clients have a similar diagnosis. Did I really need his help? Ostensibly, it was like when you're in jail; it doesn't matter why you're there—you are as guilty as the others are, innocent or not, and they have to treat you in an equivocal manner. He didn't care about all my gimcrack defenses. I was in his office because I was brain-sick. Period.

"Do you have suicidal thoughts?" he asked.

"No," I answered.

"Do you have family members with psychiatric disorders, like your mother or father?"

"My mother had dementia, that's all."

"Have any of your closely related family members received treatment for substance abuse?" That was too much to ask, and my blood broiled in my veins. I tried to stay calm. I took some deep breaths.

"Not as far as I know," I said in a nonchalant voice. He wasn't in rush; he was taking his time. I always thought that doctors didn't give enough time to their patients, but this time, I was impatient to leave.

He kept carrying on his acerbic verbal research. "You have the hepatitis C virus." He paused. I waited. "How did you get it?" He took the time to ask me the same question that dozens and dozens of doctors had asked in the past and no doubt had noted in my referral files.

I breathed deeply again. "From a blood transfusion."

How did I survive the ordeal of his interrogation? I couldn't tell you. Soon, after many questions, there was a spell of silence. He was recording himself. When he was finished, it was a relief. He prescribed me bupropion and clonazepam to make me euphorically happy, and on my way to the exit door, he tapped on my shoulder.

"You will laugh again—you'll see," he said. "I'll make you laugh. Feel better."

I whispered a thank you to him, not so that he would hear it but because of my second nature, the decency I was accustomed to. I had to retain the dignity of being polite, if only for myself. Satisfied or not, I thought, life should never get in the way of showing your good manners to people.

Dr. N. E. was a somewhat old, conservative Cuban who was not willing to put the past behind him. Electronic modernization was not for him, so everything in his office looked aged from too much use. During our long conversation, he was writing, questioning, listening, and writing some more. There was nothing modern in his office, just an old heavy wooden desk full of wretched papers, obliquely facing the window. The large, heavy shades were half-closed, faded by the ultraviolet light of the sun, which brought no light into the room. To complete the dull atmosphere of the area, a musty smell mixed with the scent cleaning powder, probably used to vacuum the carpet, hung in the air. Dr. N. E. personally came to the sitting room and called my name to let me into his office. The door of his office was connected to the narrow waiting room, and if he was straight behind his desk, I could only see his back. To talk to me, he moved his chair to be in front of me, like he was interviewing someone on TV. He was a funky old man who really believed in science and thought that what he was doing would certainly save humanity. Like I said before, if you're sent to him, it's because you're as guilty as the others are. He wasn't there to hear my gibberish but to give me medications as needed. Still, I was resistant to spend my money on the chemical substances that he ordered me to take, but my PCP persisted and wanted me to give it a try.

My friends were very funny people. They made me laugh, and they were my therapists, so I thought that I didn't need that supplement. When I was around them, I forget about all my burdens. We could get together for no specific reason just to have fun. These were friends that I considered to be members of my family who were always there for me. That said, I was still going to please Jean and buy these medications. At that point, I seriously started thinking that most of the time, crazy people don't know that they're crazy, which was perhaps my situation. I started my performance, acting like a mad woman around my husband, then around a few other people. Truly, it was fun. I was testing myself to see if my brain was truly damaged. I wasn't totally deranged, so I based my impressions on the notion that I could recognize my own wrong behaviors. Soon after, I realized that my conduct didn't fit my character. I decided that I should stop pretending to have a cognitive impairment. What really impressed me in all this is five years later, another doctor who wasn't aware that I took bupropion before prescribed it to me again. Perhaps behind my exposed face of rapture, there was the real me, full of sad thoughts that only professionals could unmask. Fake glee doesn't cure the mind of its longtime wounds.

46

Imminent Departure

I DIDN'T BECOME A fitter person right off the bat. I stayed on emotional distress drugs from many different brands, and this was always changing depending on what was new on the market and which doctors I saw. I realized that I'd been on mental health pills for almost forty years, starting with Valium, which I thought was for my ritual headaches. Unfortunately, when you're in, you're in for life. Medicines help to control your behavior. You shouldn't take the chance of stopping this type of therapy. Keep in mind that they don't make these kinds of drugs to cure people, but to harm patients more by ushering them into long-term abuse. When you've taken these kinds of pills before, doctors will continue to prescribe them "to be on the safe side." I found out that through the eyes of all my doctors, these pills gave me a permanent title of "mentally deranged." I became stuck in that system. There was no exit from my wretchedness. The system doesn't permit you to pause or stop. If you do, you will have affair with society, which will judge you for what you have become and for what you have done. Can you blame society? No.

Walking a few blocks made me so worn-out. I couldn't even dance as exercise anymore without having shortness of breath. I had more bad days than good. I wanted to return to work on a part-time basis, but my company refused to accommodate that. Isn't that absurd? You tell me. After twenty-two years of working for this company, it categorically refused me the right to work part-time; was it either full-time or nothing? I wasn't ready to retire, and I needed my job to keep me alive. SCSI denied me the right of doing so because all they were after was money, not retaining a handicap person who would ruin their production. Presumably, I was going to impair their value if they let me work three days a week. I battled for so long with my diseases, and I was simply too tired to start a new one with my workplace. Working part-time was my idea. I insisted to my doctor that it would be best. I said to her that I would try part-time work first, and if I couldn't manage that, I would definitely go on full disability. I needed to keep my insurance and the biweekly paycheck, at least something to pay my bills. But no! Part-time was not allowed at my company, which was shameful. I went to work, and they sent me back home. Human resources called to stop me from working and stated that when I was able to work full-time, I could come back. Three days before, when I'd sent the letter, it wasn't a problem for them, but when I showed up, they sent me home. After all those years there, I was with a difficult choice to make. My conditions weren't getting better, and I needed someone to help me decide what was best for me. Despite the note from my psychologist stating that I shouldn't work at all, I wanted to keep that job. I knew that job stress had affected me greatly given my health conditions, but without a job, I wondered, what would I do with my life? I thought that I had to keep moving.

I was engaged in a battle of understanding my body, which had to come before understanding my work. I became sicker and woke up almost every morning with a foggy, lagging body and mind, close to being crushed by desolation and all kinds of bad thoughts. I was more anxious than before. That was rock bottom for me, in a sense, and the incident that proved to me that I needed my psychologist more than I did before. I'd been thrown into deep water, swimming near the border of an overhanging cascade, hoping that I'd have enough strength to pull myself out before I got projected beyond the precipice. Every little contrariety I encountered, on a daily basis, was a big problem for me. I always found an excuse to cry. The more I cried, the more difficult and incomprehensible it all seemed to be. I became very sensitive to everything. I didn't want to live anymore.

As usual, when thing got bad, I took a few sleeping pills with a half glass of rum. My objective wasn't to kill myself but to sleep for a long time, to rest my brain, and to eliminate the evil spirits that were speaking inside my head. I would sleep for an entire day and the day after, and when I woke up, I would feel even drowsier and dizzier than ever. My body was so used to the painkillers that I would have to take the entire bottle with a whole bottle of whiskey to really kill myself. Thank God that was never my intention, but if an accident happened, I thought, I was ready to be with my mom in the afterlife. How was that so? My mind was split fifty-fifty, one side saying, "Get killed!" and the other fighting to stay alive. I didn't have the courage to end my life. As a fervent Catholic, I believed that I wouldn't go to heaven if I committed suicide, so I wouldn't be with my mother. I deeply believed in that Catholic nonsense. So sleeping was the only way I could get relief. I wanted to be numb to everything around me, knocked out from feeling any pain, in a trance that allowed me to forget that I was taking a big step that I didn't want to take. I thought that I was too young to give up on working, but my doctors insisted on it. If I persisted, they explained, and kept going to work, everything could become worse. I could feel it too. I stayed home against my wishes, for the sake of my health conditions. I remained cloistered in my bedroom, and my son stayed in his, unaware of what was going on with me. (By the way, Steven came back home after he has broken up with his girlfriend.) If I passed out, I figured, nobody would find me until it was too late. Sam kept telephoning me from Haiti, which was his way of offering his support. Sometimes, however, I got tired of hearing his voice and chose not to answer his phone calls. I stayed for a long time in that sluggish state of mind, which I feared would be permanent.

It was either one or the other: I could sleep too much or couldn't sleep at all. At 2:00 a.m. on September 30, 2012, I tossed and turned all over my bed, right to left, up and down, searching for the sopor that refused to come. I'd stopped my abusive cycle of drinking alcohol and taking the pills together, and my brain was running out of steam. I needed Morpheus's arms to embrace my soul so I could have a little bit of tranquility for a while, forget about my existence for a few hours, dream of something wonderfully different than what I was enduring, metamorphose into a surreal peace of mind. Where was sleep when I called for it, when my condition necessitated it the most?

The calm around the house was so profound that it turned into a kind of a burial place. I was the deceased, left behind in a too-narrow coffin after my funeral. I was so uncomfortable in my own body. The fuel in my body was running low, which made it so that my brain couldn't communicate well or remain positive. I knew that optimistic thoughts wouldn't change the facts of the matter, but at least they would make me feel better and help me cope. I felt like I had to throw up, anxiety arousing in my stomach. I didn't feel right, didn't feel well at all. My mind was full of bad things that may overflow within a short period of time if I don't do anything to control them. *What to do?* I thought. I was witnessing my torso going up and down, alarming me that something was wrong. I was looking for a liberator who could free me from my twilight zone. I was smothering a sensation that was always there during my dark times. I was out of breath, my heart palpated, and the pain invaded me from head to toe. I was cold, so I pulled up my heavy wool blanket over my body, and soon after, a sensation of hot flashes seized my body, and so I removed it with rage. I was moving my legs, constantly fending off the bizarre sensation of insect bites inside of me. It was like having a Norwegian omelet, half of it hot and half of it covered with cold cream. I didn't know how to eat such wild food. Did I taste the hottest part first or the cooler side?

"Am I already dead?" I wondered. I didn't feel any aesthesis. I was numb, like they had injected local anesthesia through my whole body. I was frozen. No words would come out of my mouth, but I wasn't sleeping. Afterward, I had vertigo. Everything around me was rotating, first slowly, then very quickly, like a carrousel turning in the air. I wasn't moving, so where was that sensation coming from? I was spinning without moving at all! I wasn't crazy, just bewildered by everything that was going on in my head. I wanted someone to hug me, to kiss me, and to tell me that everything would be all right. Alas, I was wholly alone, only in the presence of my own reflection in the mirror. Silence reigned in the house—silence, utter silence. A feeling of psychological hurt possessed my body. I decided to get up and walk around the house, holding my head in my hands for protection, talking to myself like a fool, using my shadow as a friend, and finally having a glass of strong alcohol despite the painkillers, despite my resolution to not do that anymore. I couldn't keep that promise to myself any longer. The river always came back to its original place. I had to do it. I couldn't take it anymore. When I walked, every step hammered in my head. I had a migraine for two days, and my blood pressure escalated through the roof. I didn't care anymore about the side effects of combining drugs and alcohol, I just wanted my headache to go away. After the potation, slowly, my eyes fell half-closed, and my body was transported to a peaceful world of serenity. Soon after, at almost 5:00 a.m., I finally slumbered. I knew that drinking was a bad prescription for my insomnia, but I didn't have a clear mind. The front lobe of my brain wasn't working properly and couldn't distinguish what was wrong and what was right. I just wanted to sleep. I wanted to cast out the devil. I was morally and physically tired. My pain was like a vampire, sucking out my health at night. This type of crisis wasn't new for me, but this time, depression and anxiety were guests at the party.

After all that trauma, in the privacy of my bedroom, the discomfort in my body vanished the same way it appeared, making me look like a liar. This is that sort of invisible sickness that can't be seen by outsiders without medical knowledge, but it's there anyway, laughing at its victims. I had wanted to find out why people always assumed that because I looked well on the outside, there was no way I could be a sick person. After I slept for an entire day, when I went out, there was no way you could see the illness on my face. I think it's understandable. They are right, in a sense. I always looked good, so who would think that I'd had a hard time the night before? As a rule, the discomfort from my illnesses always appeared at night. This hypocritical devil distressed me most nights, leaving no trace the next day except the tiredness from lack of sleep and the drowsiness from the pills and alcohol abuse. My diseases were no excuse to appear trashy and neglected when I went out, I thought. I kept repeating,

"It's all appearance." Is there a difference between having illnesses and being sick? Yes. My ailments made me truly ill periodically, mostly at night when there was nobody to witness my tribulations.

When you see me in the street, it's likely during a good moment, so if I'm well at the time, I figure that there is no reason for me to pretend or talk about it. You wouldn't believe me anyway. When I'm feeling well, all I can do is melt into the joy of the present, to continue of fulfilling my tasks, being happy. Happiness is a curative process for my brain, a therapeutic way to forget about yesterday and to be ready for tomorrow. It loads my system with a lot of energy that I need to fill up my days. Thee, why not use my jovial character to feed my spirit instead of doubting me? Stop judging, prejudicing, and incriminating when you don't know the truth. I'm burning up inside with pain, anxiety, and nagging worries that you cannot see. I fooled myself and others with my lies, telling people that I was well when I wasn't, wearing all the fashion brands that I was obsessed with. Clothes served as a cover to fend off the curious from obtruding upon my clannish life. Clothes made me feel good, and why shouldn't they? I liked fashion, which was one of the things that kept me going. My clothes made others believe that everything was all right with me. They signaled "Don't ask questions" and "I will survive." I thought that complaining was a sign of weakness, like I'd be searching for pity from people who didn't give a damn about my feelings. Why should I give them that satisfaction? It was my problem, not theirs. I seldom bellyached to people, and when I did, I only told people who I knew would understand. I'm a human being, aren't I? We all need to complain sometimes. My best friends really helped, especially when it came to therapeutic shopping and dancing. I always found an excuse to shop, thinking that a good new pair of shoes or an up-to-date dress would help me cope with my silent burdens. Inside, I was mentally and physically in a lot of pain. Do you know how many times I shed tears for your lack of understanding? Practically, I liked to hide my emotions so there'd be nothing to explain to others. I didn't want to parade my life to the world. It was a private affair, and I didn't want to expose myself to the curiosity of people who wouldn't hesitate to judge me behind my back. If you weren't so judgmental, you would know by now that I was trying to live my life as normally as possible despite all my problems. It wasn't easy. I had colleagues and friends who genuinely thought that my diseases were all bogus. But how could I imagine these things and make them appear in my test results? That magic is impossible. I'm not that good!

My husband, who always told me to quit my job for the sake of my health, seemed very shocked when it abruptly happened. I was susceptible to every conversation we had and to any gesture he made. I watched his face and his movements with my eyes. I used to be responsible for myself, paying all my bills myself, and didn't ever have to ask him for money. However, I found out that he'd changed and now had a devilish face all the time that often discouraged me from accepting my newfound unemployment. I could understand why he was afraid of having too many responsibilities. He wasn't used to taking care of me, and I always earned as much money as he did. But he was my spouse, and although he wasn't going to have to babysit me, he had to take over most of my bills. With everything that was going through my head, I would've preferred someone who paid attention to me and left the rest for later, not a frustrated man who screamed at me in the street and yelled at me in front of the house like a fool. Women take pills to control our emotions so that we don't embarrass ourselves, but men don't. Still, his miserable comportment wasn't justified. He needed more time to adjust to the circumstances, I understood that. But he denied the realities and got more upset when I told him what I thought was the reason behind his bad behavior.

Still a spoiled child at heart, my mind went back to my mother, thinking that if she was still there, she would've accepted all my problems with kindness—my mood disorder, my discontentment over things that I couldn't do anymore, and my unhappiness. I couldn't sleep at all, night or day. I was awake, thinking about what might be the best thing to do: ignore him or leave him. I refused to take the medicine the psychiatrist gave me for "happiness." I didn't want to get addicted to those drugs. I was cracking down. The more medication I was on, the worse I became. I could see the "sorry" on the visage of my PCP and his assistant, as well as the "I don't know what else to do." Poor Jean. I think that she was as stressed as I was. Well, doctors are not gods and cannot change what God intends to do with us on earth. In her mind, she was thinking "What can I do for her?" She was so sad because she couldn't find a specific medication that would cure me from all my calamities. She was so sensitively affectionate to her patients and very knowledgeable about health care. "I understand," I said to her to make her feel at ease, but what I really meant was that she couldn't change my destiny.

Soon, I developed another pain in my ribs, on the right side. First, I thought that my liver had worsened. At the supermarket, I always looked at the livers in the meat area, thinking about how mine might look: a putrefying black organ, some kind of gummy, sticky gelatin that would come out of my stomach like the alien in the movies on television. Oh no! I should say instead that my liver is a piece of hard meat that gets lazy doing its normal job. Does this make sense to you? I hope not, but it did to me at the time. I thought that my liver was greatly infected like an infected wound would be. The pain that I had was like somebody was stabbing me with a knife. Great, I thought, another thing to prevent me from sleeping at night. Generally, I have all kinds of pain, but on my right side, the pain was dreadful. My PCP sent me for an ultrasound, which demonstrated that my liver was the same and that there were no other abnormalities or signs that it was getting worst. They said the pain might last a day or two unless I took some ibuprofen. As usual, I had an appointment with Dr. B., the gastro-ARNP. While I was still under the coverage of my work's insurance, I tried to see all my doctors without delay. She did a very deep, thorough consultation. She pressed somewhere by my ribcage, and I jumped. She realized that I had costochondritis, which is inflammation of the ribs that can be cured with ibuprofen taken daily for a month. She said that this would clear up that matter, which is what I was already doing to ease the pain, anyway. My sonogram revealed no abnormality other than my fatty liver, but the CT scan showed that something else was cooking. To repeat exactly what they have written in the lab results: "a tiny punctate in the bilateral renal calculi, its location somewhere between the nephron-calcinosis, tiny collecting system calculi, abnormal left paraaortic, 2 cm soft tissue density with rapid opacification of draining veins mid-portion left renal vein, and azygos/hemiazygos veins consistent with arteriovenous fistula." She they told me that I would've to see a urologist. Unluckily, by the time I'd made my appointment to have an MRI, I was uninsured. The AFP abnormally, which was high at 105, wouldn't be monitored like the physician was expecting. I learned that I'd have to wait for Obamacare in 2014 for a follow-up. The insurance referred by my ex-employer was too expensive for Sam and me at $800/month. That's a lot! I decided that I'd take my chances with the public clinic for emergencies or things that required immediate attention. That how goes life. It can brutally change for anyone at any moment. No one is exempt from this kind of challenge. One day, you're content, and the next day, you can find yourself in a position where you need to make a hard choice.

I was more stressed than ever. I didn't have insurance, but I was still sick with the orbital varix tumor, arthritis, asthma, depression, diabetes, fibromyalgia, hepatitis C (and fatty liver), hypertension, chronic migraines, osteoporosis, and sleep apnea. I needed medications for almost all of it, including atenolol, enalapril, triamterene, ergocalciferol (i.e., vitamin D2), Flovent Diskus, Humalog insulin, Librax, Savella, Ventolin, Fioricet as needed, and ibuprofen. It was scary, and I needed good faith in God to prevent me from going totally mad. If you never had insurance or you don't have these ailments, it might be okay, but when you're aware of all these troubles and there's nothing you're able to do to get help, it's discouraging and frightening. I decided to develop a monomania to get used to the reality of death. I repeated the mantra "Dying will happen sooner or later, there is no escape from the laws of the nature." I studied the "before" and the "after" of death on the internet. In every Catholic pamphlet, they talked about death and resurrection. I encrusted in my mind that I would be with my mother, repeating the same things that she did before dying. After a while, death became a friend, not an enemy. I even planned my obsequies. It's easy; everything you log in your mind goes to your brain and is put into practice. With all that said, I was ready for heaven. Like all normal people, I didn't want to go to hell. I dreamed in fear about my workplace every Sunday night and probably two to three additional times a week. Even in that moment of conflict with myself, my job still haunted me. Very often, I had to say, "Girl, you won't be going to work anymore, so take care of yourself now."

It was an intense and emotional time for me. I played, replayed, and played again Michael's song "This Is It" to assure myself that it was real, that I really had stopped working. Henceforth, I took all my depression pills. I finish the bottles of bupropion and clonazepam and reconciled with my leftovers, Xanax, Paxil, Prozac, and my best one, Lexapro. I hadn't been able to take them while working due to their side effects— drowsiness, dizziness, and oversleeping, but I could now. Some of the bottles were still sealed. Seeing me in the street, I looked damn good. I figured out that exercise and dance couldn't save me by themselves. I needed chemical balance also. I needed a psychologist and mental health pills more than ever to avoid the worst. My neighbor Pat told me that I should start a twenty-one-day meditation program titled Perfect Health from Deepak Chopra and Oprah. I tried it, but I wasn't assiduous about it. I couldn't remember which day I'd already done, and I got lost. It wasn't the program for me. I'm not going to lie, while I was practicing yoga, I have tried meditation many times, and it just didn't work for me. I know that for many people with anxiety, depression, and other mental health disorders, yoga/meditation helps lower the gamma-aminobutyric acid in the brain, but nonchalantly, I can say that it doesn't work for me. I've never being able to concentrate on the present moment during a session of meditation. Instead, my mind captures everything and flies everywhere. Many thoughts are always floating in the air, and unfortunately, I intercept everything around me, even when I'm supposed to be emptying my mind. I've even asked myself, while meditating, about what I was going to eat later on, what was on TV that night—even little things like preoccupy me all too easily. However, the sound of the soft music in the silence of the room were golden benefits to me. I liked the sensation of staying in my bedroom doing nothing, listening to music. I did the deep breathing to stimulate the parasympathetic rhythms of my nervous system, especially when my head was pounding with a heavy migraine. I was very pleased with it. I got relaxed, but the magic of being "in the clouds" that so many people seem to get from yoga and meditation never happened to me.

I had to find an acceptable way to understand death. Dealing with a combination of diseases put me on death row. I don't mean to claim that I was dying, but I was at higher risk than a normal, healthy person is. I used this touchstone to test my life, wondering what life would be without any troubles: completely dull, I suppose. It wasn't that I was unhappy with what I had, but I was trying to cope with my new life with fearlessness. I started to go deeper into my learning, marveling about the afterlife. Is it possible that we never really die? I wondered. Is mortality a recycling cycle? For me, earth has always been a transition place where we stay between one point and another. It's like going on vacation to a different country; at the end, we have to come back home to where we started. The invisible cosmos should be considered home for everybody. Our souls will immigrate to different families, countries, and races after death. In a way, we never really die. I came up with that school of thought to help me deal with life as it came. Sometimes, we have tendency to stay stuck in the past, but that gives us insufficient time to enjoy the present. Living like that can really shorten our existence. The present should be what we care most about because it is the most important thing. We cannot jump from the past to the future without being transited in the present. The present is the main moment that joins the past and future together. We can fix reality if we take time to correct the past in the present, and by doing so, we can make the future brighter. If we cannot do so, we have to keep trying anyway. I would say that sometimes it's better to slow down on materialism and let spiritualism elucidate our souls to reduce the acceleration of the gravity of our fears. The body dies, but the spirit remains intact. We need to preserve our bodies from our thinking and speculation.

I remembered a young, beautiful, popular girl who died in a car accident while traveling to another city in Haiti. People in her hometown swore that at the time of her death, even though she was more than one hundred miles away, they saw her walking normally in the street. Some of them even said that they spoke to her. Can all those people have lied? What would be the reason for such big lie? I think that they mysteriously saw her double, the errant spirit looking for another body to occupy. I couldn't understand because I was a child when it happened, but I remembered her; she was visible to their eyes! They believed that every month, at the same time, day, and place, they saw her passing in the street like when she was alive. I don't know how long it went on like that. I left town about a year later go to school in another city. When I remember this true story, I believe that our spirits never die, that they are reincarnated into other bodies. We can call it the recyclability of the soul. Take care of your soul so that when it finds another body, it can be gracefully strong.

That said, despite my soul-searching and medications, I was driving myself to nothingness. I couldn't accommodate my new life. I took more pills than ever to clear my mind and get used to reality. I was in a funk about myself. I didn't think that I existed anymore. There was no way out of my misery. Another kind of stress was loaded into my mind, which gave my body another rational motive to be in pain. I didn't understand it. I thought that I should feel great because I didn't have to work, but I didn't. Depression is a tricky condition that isn't easy to get rid of. There's always a reason for this psychoanalytical disorder to be present in our lives. As soon it gets comfortably installed, it's very difficult to take off. To an extent, my lies continued. I said that I was okay to everyone who asked. Yes, I was physically a little bit better, but mentally, I was destroyed. I thought that with time, it would get better, but that mental disease had already eaten most of my brain, and what was left couldn't fight my negative thoughts that unpredictably drowned everything else. I was trying to fit into my new personality despite the smog I felt around my existence. Now that I had time in my favor, I couldn't get adapted to it. Such is the irony of life. I did things exactly the same way I did while I was still going to work, for example, rushing to overdo everything on Sundays, which would leave me short of breath and nauseated, not from compunction but from doing so much, so quickly. I thought about that compulsive style of living and uttered to myself, "Take it easy, lady, you don't have to worry about Mondays. You're home now, so there's no work anymore for you."

I didn't find it amusing. It was a sad situation because it wasn't my plan. I had to instruct my brain not to worry about work and to be agreeable and at ease. I could stay in bed whenever I didn't feel good, but truthfully, it wasn't easy. Sometimes, I went days without seeing anyone, without talking face-to-face to a human being, so I created an imaginary bosom friend. I used both of my names, Rosette and Olivia, to make dialogue.

"What's your name?" I asked.

"I'm Olivia," I answered.

"Aren't Olivia and Rosette the same person?"

"Perhaps. I don't know anymore. It's all confused in my memory."

"What happened with your life?"

"It's a disagreement of everything. Nothing seems to be coordinated."

"Do you feel rejected, abused, abandoned, and lonely?"

"Yes."

This the type of conversation I had with my friend. I can't tell who of the two answered this or that question, I just played the game to keep my own mind company.

47

Understanding Chronic Disease

In March 2013, I went to see a friend who'd had neck surgery. I traveled with another longtime friend. We had wonderful time together. I was truly happy, except for the intermittent, hush-hush pain I felt in my feet. I hid it to enjoy the moment. My blood sugar was lowering in glucose, so I ate a piece of candy to restock the sweetness in my organ. It was a long day, for sure, but I had so much fun. Later, at night, once I got home, I started to have all kinds of pain. Sam called, but I couldn't talk to him because I was in so much pain all over my body: chills, a fever, and an extreme headache. I couldn't concentrate enough to have a long conversation. My left hand was also at the party, driving me crazy with that electrical shock feeling, and my right shoulder was a real mess. My brain was simply not responding to my body. I couldn't focus and share in Sam's happiness, even though he'd had such a good business day. He'd sold lots of ceramic sculptures at the annual fair. I had to excuse myself and hang up the phone. He didn't understand and kept calling, again and again. I couldn't answer, not because I didn't want to, but because I couldn't articulate a single word. It was a weird sensation of distress—palpitations, a dry cough, and fatigue, all at once. I tried to stay calm after taking all the medications I knew might help, accompanied by a good, alcoholic drink. Finally, I finally fell asleep at 3:35 a.m. I knew the exact time because I was counting the seconds, minutes, and hours.

I woke up the next day feeling like a hurricane had devastated my carcass in the night. My legs were sore and my body was too heavy to hold up my feet. Three days later, most of the pain was slowly disappearing the same way it had entered my body two nights before. If my friends had called me, there's no way that I would've told them about the perturbations I had right when I got home, because they wouldn't believe me. I was fine around them, acting as if there was nothing wrong with me, but just a few hours after I left, I wasn't the same. What kind of phenomenal thing can trigger me to be well one moment and sick the next, so sick that I feel like of all my vital functions are languidly breaking down? Am I the kind of creature that changes in the night? Sometimes, it's really difficult to understand the paranoid effects of the human body, especially mine.

As usual, Sam came home for the Easter holiday. I was eager to enjoy his company. Despite his presence in the house, I still couldn't sleep, and passing an entire night without sleeping didn't even make me sleep during the day. Contrarily, I was okay with it mentally, but my body was deprived of energy. To sleep for a few hours, I had to take pills, and when the pills couldn't give me the effect I was looking for, I unfortunately had to add some magic; the drink. I was not an alcoholic, but I used alcohol for pain and peace of mind. It wasn't even a daily thing. My metabolism didn't react the same way to it anymore. Sleep was not a welcome visitor, neither at night nor during the day. But for Sam, it was so easy to fall asleep. He passed most of his free time in that lethargy. His snore was so loud that he would wake up any ghost in the cemetery, but my eyelids were divided, refusing to attach. Selfishly, as usual, I needed him to give me a little of his time when he was home, but this wasn't a priority of his at all. He didn't share his sleep with anyone, and he could catnap anywhere in the house, most often while watching TV. He seemed to want to avoid any kind of conversation with me. Often, he went to another room, leaving me alone and wishing he'd snap out of it. This kind of thoughtless behavior made me furious. His attitude made me more depressed, to the point that I needed to go somewhere for a while where nobody would be able to reach me. The plan seemed very appealing. At that point, I didn't care if I had to use all my reserved cash to go to a retreat village. The only obstacle was my children, who would be worried if I vanished. I'd have to tell them, and telling them would be similar to telling their father. I was trapped, unsure about how I could escape from my burning cage. I certainly thought that it would be appropriate to make him worry a little bit, but that plan was aborted because of my concern for the kids.

Sam's presence didn't support me. He threw himself into sleepiness so that he didn't have to think about anything. I stayed upstairs, and he stayed downstairs. His presence wasn't different from his absence. We seem to be disturbed and phantasmagorical, both of us adjusting to our new stressful dynamic. He didn't tell me, but I knew him very well and realized that he was maladjusted. *He just needs time*, I thought. I respected his muteness, hoping that time would help him with his adaptation. At any rate, the fact that he was with me brought me serenity somehow. It wasn't much, but it was something.

When Sam went back to Haiti, I had to do something with my life. Was that the kind of life I wanted to live for the rest of my existence? I became less talkative to him because I was searching for the road to my destiny. Did I have to leave him? I wondered. I was so unhappy with my life. I felt it more because I wasn't working and had more time to think about it. I didn't have anyone to talk to about it, not a single word, and even when Sam was there, I was the invisible wife that he wasn't used to anymore. I was trying to challenge my pitiful life. I called on God to show me the way to end our nuptial vows or the way to get our relationship out of its hellhole. I wanted to drag myself off a cliff, and not for the first time. I tried to reconcile with reality. I held my body responsible for its incapacity for doing many things. I mourned the days when I could say yes to lots of deeds. I was pretty much demented. The queerest part is that I would wash my hair and do everything that I used to do, as if I was going to work the next day. I couldn't update my brain with the fact that I was unemployed. I fixed a section in my patio to be my office, and sometimes, I got dressed, put on makeup, and did anything I could to make it seem like nothing had changed. I had to have a purpose to stay alive. Although I was telling people "I'm well, I'm well," I was fighting inside. I started writing about my struggles with life, thinking that even if people might not understand me, my voice could be heard through my writing. It was hard to dig out my past, but I enjoyed some of my recollections. It wasn't in my calendar to stop working so early in my life. As a matter of fact, my soul still refused to accept this, even after two years.

I would pass days without talking to anyone except T. C., my best friend who made it an obligation to call me almost every day on her way back home from work. It was a benefit for both of us: she got home quicker, ignoring the length of the distance, and I had someone to talk to for at least forty-five minutes. I felt good after even a nonsense conversation with her. We laughed and understood each other. Something about her gave me comfort when she called, I don't know why. It became difficult for me to converse with anyone, as if my tongue was too heavy to lift in my mouth, but with her, it was different. She listened to all my complaints without putting me down and laughed at my stupid jokes. I couldn't work anymore, but at the same time, I couldn't stand staying at home, sick and helpless. It was a dilemma. I was wholly out of brainpower. I watched Pastor Joel Osteen on TV every Sunday and listened to his sermons. I thought that he was speaking just to me. I liked his viewpoint, that by repeating "All is well" all the time with a positive attitude, I could eliminate bad thoughts from my mind and prompt things to change for the better.

Of course, all wasn't well for me. In fact, I was more dreadful than ever. I had a splash of mud all over my body, which I believed only water could clean. Anyway, I kept repeating the pastor's motto, "All is well." I needed more than this, though, someone to offer his shoulder for me to lay my head on. My melancholy was too profound. I couldn't contradict it any further, no matter my positive attitude. I persisted, saying, "All is well, all is well," but it didn't resolve the dilemma that I was in. It was just a parade—the real thing was deeper. My problematic issues were there. I laughed at myself and my life's ironic, queer patterns. The tussle was there, pitiless, ruining my life like an enemy following me step by step, wishing that I might succumb to misery forever so it could gloriously howl, "Oh, victory!"

Preposterously, I thought that I must know my enemy in order to win this battle; otherwise, it wouldn't let me encompass the range of peace that I desperately needed. Through this very hard time, I was disposed to mend all the broken pieces of my brain into one strong state of mind. Once again, I engaged myself in a fight that I wasn't sure I could win.

    I drew up my survival plan. First, I decided to go to San Francisco for a retreat to refine my mental behavior and free my brain from its rough, gaudy thoughts, so that when I returned, I could be a refreshed, new person. I stayed there for three weeks. I tried to center my psyche less on my actual life. When I got home, I went out more often with my baby-cake son, and when I stayed home, I focused my thinking on the TV show, *Dexter*, which my son has graciously put on TV for me. From the first to the final season, eight seasons and ninety-six episodes, I watched all of it over the course of two weeks, day and night. I made myself busy with the show, no time to think about my miserableness—especially when I was around young people like my husband's nieces and my son's friends. I felt rejuvenated. "All is well" was the purpose of my plan, and it worked well while I was on vacation. However, when I landed at the Fort Lauderdale airport, all my problems came back to haunt me even more. This time, however, I was more confident and wouldn't let them poison my life. "Everything is okay," I hummed to myself. What was the purpose of complaining, I thought, when pain had become my natural way of living? I woke up like a decrepit woman and carried on with my occupations like my body didn't exist anymore. If the pain worsened, I took two ibuprofen tablets and went back to bed. I'm not sure that there has been a day when I have woken without pain since 2011. The important thing was to adjust my everyday life to cope with what I had and to laugh at it when I could, like it was any other funny thing: the creepy-crawly woman! I made a pact with myself to be strong, not to be a crybaby, and to strike back at that maddening distress.

    It can be very hard to understand people with chronic diseases because they seem so unrealistic and incomprehensible; one day, they're good, and the next day, they're bad. People mostly make assumptions based on appearances (e.g., "You look good, so you're not sick"). We often don't pass judgment on what we cannot see. We are all traversing moments of disappointment and intolerable episodes of pain land in our pathways. We all have unpleasant, immovable, hard journeys, filled with too many unwanted incidents, but at the same time, we all want our problems to remain private. Would you believe me if I told you about my quandaries? No! Because I look well on the outside! On the contrary, inside, all I have left is a crumbling remainder of my life.

48

The Walk-In

It wasn't as easy to feel better than I thought it would be. The depression was having fun with me. I was back from my retreat, and my alter ego was back too to persecute me day and night. "What is wrong with my house?" I wondered. Was there a ghost possessing me from time to time? I returned to the same position I was in before. I wasn't crying anymore, but I was screaming at anything, at anyone, for any reason. I couldn't watch Lifetime TV anymore because I saw my untoward life in all the movies. Theoretically, I was living on another planet, in a one-way world where there was no returning to normal. I was concerned. It wasn't that I couldn't see what was around me or that I wasn't aware of my conduct, I just couldn't deactivate the fuses that were triggering my abnormal emotions and unreasonable actions. I was immensely distressed for the third time in my life. I felt utterly incapable of continuing this battle, and I implored to God to take my life away. The good thing was that I was too chicken to consider taking it away myself. I was on pause, unsure of how to continue. It was an awful time. I needed to assert my spirit with the confidence that I won't do anything hurt to myself. "I have to live, I have to live," I repeated to myself.

The madness was everywhere in my house, in my bed, walking beside me like an inseparable friend. I was lost, the dolefulness marking my face. I didn't know whether to let it be or prolong my war against my desperation. I felt guilty over ceasing working so soon, guilty of putting all the responsibility on one shoulder, and helpless for not being able to fit into the workplace anymore. *I deserted my camp, so I deserve to be punished, and depression is my punishment*, I thought. I couldn't even properly mourn my sudden termination. It really was impressive, now that I think about it, that I could felicitously pretend that everything was all right in the presence of my friends and family. Except for Scott, of course. I couldn't bluff with him. My son had the power to look deeply inside of me and find the truth. Steven got depressed from seeing me like that, and he tried in his way to make it better. I felt bad about that too. At the same time, I was saying to people that I was okay because it was easier for everyone that way. It was better for my health too, but for my morale, it was a disaster. I was seeing a counselor and a psychiatrist at the same time. The main problem of my disarray was a secret that I couldn't express in addition with all the rest. What really kept me going was motherhood. I wanted to live to see my children's accomplishments in life. It seemed to me like my torment occurred mostly inside my home. I had to leave that horrible house. I was smothered and couldn't breathe properly. Madness gained on my spirit. Finally, I decided to go for the weekend to see my sunshine son on Biscayne Boulevard without telling anybody where I would be. We talked and had fun together, a little distraction for the well-being and fitness of my brain.

Like a Catholic family who doesn't believe in contraceptive pills, who puts as many children on earth that God would give them, my body did the same; the cavalcade of illnesses was always triumphant inside me. Without insurance, I communed with myself, trying not to have any cause to go to the emergency room. It would've been another load to add to the ailments I already had. Paying bills became a promise that I couldn't keep every month. With firm conviction, I tried to keep myself from being sick. I rested as much as possible. With the depression pills I was on, I could sleep for ten hours at a time, something that I could never do before. I woke up by 9:30 or 10:00 a.m. and always ate the same healthy food. I programmed my days so that they would go quietly. In the morning, I had to determine how I would balance my eating habits and provide my body with the necessary nutrition. Strangely, I still allowed myself the time to read during the day. I kept my television turned off in the mornings, which was a big sacrifice for me. I liked TV. As a substitute, I listened to all kinds of music and wrote. At 5:30 p.m., I would devotedly garden for one hour, then I would start the fun—my dance exercise, yoga, and meditation relaxation until 7:30 p.m. Afterward, it was time for me to watch TV until I fell asleep. Was this a good accommodation? I guess so! The time passed so quickly that it always surprised me when my clock showed the time at the beginning of my workouts. My body seemed to like my plan. My unsatisfied friends were still not happy with my new routine, because my feet swelled up and were badly hurting me. My left hand often made it impossible for me to rest at night, maybe because I spent so much time digging in the dirt. It wasn't new to me, but it was going downhill. I couldn't use it to do yoga movements in addition to all the positions I couldn't do because of my orbital varix. One night, I didn't sleep at all, regardless of the depression drugs I took before going to bed. The pain was horrible. I made it through to the daytime and felt slightly better. To help me with my pain the next night, I had to strongly bandage my foot and hand. It was the third night that I couldn't sleep with that disagreeable dolor. I whispered to myself, "Girl, you need to drive your body to an emergency care facility and find out what's cooking now." Contrary to my wishes, I resisted that irresistible thought until I stepped on a nail that pierced my right foot.

The curse was still after me, despite all the precautions I'd taken to stay away from doctors and hospitals. I planted my foot on a nail attached to a piece of wood outside. I was so frightened when I saw the blood leaking onto the concrete. My first reaction was to go to ER because I was diabetic, but how could I do that with my foot pumping blood? My son had taken my car to work, so I wouldn't be able to drive there anyway. *Should I call 9-1-1?* I wondered. *No, it's not that bad, let me call my neighbor instead.* Then I got worried. *Oh no*, I thought. *I'll alarm people for no reason. I will take care of it myself.* All these notions appeared in my mind within a split second. I went upstairs to clean the foot with peroxide, put on some antibiotic ointment, and took an antibiotic pill that they'd given to me for a vaginal infection. I always saved two or three in case my infections came back, and now I was using it for my foot. Who knows? I figure. Maybe it would help with something. I showered and cleaned all the blood from the floor, which had leaked from my foot when I walked from the yard, to the patio, to the kitchen, to the living room, up the stairs, and to the bathroom. Lots of blood splashed onto the floor. I was very anxious and egocentric about blood because two of my ailments were blood-related. I went to bed and elevated the wrapped foot on a big pillow. The next day, my neighbor saw that my foot was wrapped with tissue. He asked me what happened and I told him. He said that he would take me to the emergency room right away. I refused and promised that I'd go myself. I didn't want him spending hours waiting with me. In the afternoon, my friend T. C. called as usual. I told her what happened. She had the same reaction, asking me to go to the ER without further delay.

"It's almost seven at night, let me wait for tomorrow," I answered.

In the morning, I went to a public urgent care facility, Community Health of South Florida Inc. It seemed impossible to locate the right department. Astonishing myself, I went straight to the information desk, telling her that I was there to see a doctor.

"Are you a walk-in patient, or do you have appointment with a specific doctor?" she asked.

"I need the emergency room, please," I politely replied.

"Are you in pain?"

"Yes," I said, showing her my foot.

"What happened?"

I explained that a nail had punctured my foot.

"*Madre de Dios*," she said. "When did this happen?"

"Two days ago."

"You should've come here the day of to get a tetanus shot." She pointed me in the direction of the emergency department. "Explain everything to the nurse," she said with sadness in her voice.

"Thanks," I said, surprising myself with my own politeness.

It was like being in another world. I was amazed to see so many people in one place going in different directions, like there was no other program for them. I heard many languages: Spanish, English, slang English, and Creole. It was all so loud that it was almost difficult to hear and understand what the receptionist was telling me. At the emergency room, the receptionist, who happened to be a Haitian like me, wasn't friendly at all. Probably the way I dressed and composed myself made her wonder *What she is doing here?* or *What has life done to her that has brought her to a place like this?* Without apologizing, she gestured at a chair, suggesting that I should sit in front of her. I did, and she proceeded to talk to a coworker for more than ten minutes, like I was invisible. She could see in my face that I was pissed off by her lack of professionalism, but she kept going with her personal conversation, clearly just trying to irritate me. I realized that and changed my attitude. I was here like anybody else was, so I decided to be patient and play the game. I tried to include myself in the conversation so I could relax.

"Do you have an appointment?" she finally said, looking at me straight in the eyes as if to disfigure me. She glared at me through squinted eyes, which were framed by long, artificial eyebrows.

"No," I said. "Isn't that why they call it a 'walk-in' clinic? Isn't it for people like me who don't have appointments? I would like to see a doctor, please." As I spoke, my eyes filled with tears, tears that I didn't want her to see. But the tears kept coming out bravely, wetting my face. She tried to defeat me.

"Ma'am," she said, "we also receive people for follow-ups." She clearly saw my hidden crying. "Are you in pain?" she asked me with a strong voice.

"Yeah," I answered. I wasn't crying because of the pain but because of the pity I had for everyone there. It saddened me that when they needed care, they had to talk to some rowdy character like this Wiccan! Already, I hated that place. People everywhere were talking, yelling on their cell phones like they were there for fun, and babies were crying, their mothers tired of trying to soothe them. It was clear that many patients knew almost all the employees in that facility, they stopped to tell a story. I got lost in such big area with all sorts of doctors: dental, behavioral health, maternity, pharmacy, labs, etc. All on the same floor! Time seemed to stop right there. The line wasn't moving. The same crowd that sat in the waiting room when I arrived was still there when I left.

What am I doing here? I asked myself, half-expecting an answer. *Is it what life has reserved for me?* a Bob Marley song came to my mind, "No Woman, No Cry." As I sat there waiting for my turn, I tried to make my bad fortune feels like good fortune. I had the possibility of being seen today, and for something I judged wasn't really a big deal. I remembered what the woman in Haiti had told me and I wanted to put it in practice: "How could I be so ungrateful while so many people in the world were dying from a lack of care, from all kinds of diseases, without the ability to even be seen by a nurse?" They eventually called me in for registration, which removed me from my deep thoughts. The medical assistant questioned me about everything in my personal life, even my annual income, to find out how much my copayment would be. Then I was sent back to wait in the same place until I was called again. Another nurse arrived and called me to go inside with her. She closed her door, took my weight and my temperature, and started her probe. Nothing was left out; she put absolutely everything into her computer for the doctor. I knew she would eventually want to find out how I got HCV. I was prepared for that eventuality. She asked for the names of all my diseases and my medications. When I said hep C, however, she seemed embarrassed to pop the question.

"You said hepatitis C?" she said incredulously.

"Yes."

"Do you drink, smoke, or do drugs"

I understood the kind of drug she was referring to with her questions, but I wanted to play with her mind. "A lot, ma'am," I said.

She was confused and looked at me disquietingly, trying to understand how someone like me could be on recreational drugs. I let her write that note in the computer, but her reaction made me decide to clarify.

"I hope that you didn't write drugs as in marijuana or cocaine."

"Is that not what you just said?" she replied.

Stupid b———, I thought. *You have nothing in your mind! Why do you want to pierce into my private life to find a reason for the hep C? It* really wasn't any of her business, nor was it the hospital's. *Does that have anything to do with my visit today?* I wondered. *Am I going to be treated for my foot or for HCV?* I thought it was wise to promptly tell her the truth before she put something wrong in my file.

"No, I was talking about medicine prescribed by doctors, also called *drugs*," I said, without displaying any regret for my repulsive actions.

"Of course. That's true," she replied with a big smile of relief. But she wasn't finished. "You have hepatitis C. How did you get it, *mamacita*? From a blood transfusion?"

"Yes."

"How long ago? I have to write all this for the doctor because you're a new patient."

"I understand," I said. "You're not the first person who had asked me these questions. It happened when I gave birth to my youngest son, twenty-nine years ago. Are you satisfied now?"

"Okay, I think we're ready. Please have a seat outside until you are called."

"Okay, thanks," I said, trying to be courteous. It was always funny to me that when I went to the doctor, they were almost always more concerned about my hepatitis than they were about my real reason for being there.

Shortly after, she came to take me to another room to wait for the doctor. He was very short and unpleasant, rushing after everything like the place was on fire. While he was in the room with me, he was also on the phone giving orders. He didn't touch me at all, as if I was contagious, quietly reading the notes the nurse had written.

"Do you have asthma?" he asked suddenly.

"How did you find out?" I responded stupidly.

"On your list of medications, there's an inhaler and a spray, both of which are medicines for asthma." He paused, making a note. "Next time something like this happens, you need to go to the ER right away, especially because you are diabetic."

In a rough, brusque voice, he told me that he would send me to have an x-ray of my right foot to find out if it was infected. "That will be done here in the clinic," he explained. "I will wait for the pictures and come back with them." Also, he sent a referral for MRI to Jackson South Hospital so that I could get my hand and left foot scanned. Without stopping writing, he complained that the nurse hadn't notes everything.

"Be sure to get a Jackson South Hospital card before going in for these tests," he said on his way out, putting my file back on the door. I didn't know if he was finished with me or not. I stayed there until the nurse came back to show me where to go for the x-ray. It was done very quickly. I came back with two pictures of my foot, and she put me in a room to wait for him again. The doctor didn't come back, and after a while, the nurse told me that the foot wasn't infected and gave me a prescription to take twice a day for seven days. She asked me to return in a week for a follow-up. I felt sorry for her because she had to work under such wild, unreasonable person.

"Mrs. G., please have a seat over there," she said courteously. "I'll call you when I'm finished with your release."

"Okay," I gently said. I had to wait again—what torture! I murmured to myself, "Here you are, girl, this is your new life. Be calm and let yourself experience what regular people with small incomes or no medical insurance have to go through all the time."

I wondered, were all the people around me are thinking the same thing? Maybe they'd never been to a private doctor, so they might not know the difference. I promised myself that I would be in the first round to sign up for health care under the health care reform. The nurse soon called me back to her office, where she had a little heater going to warm her cold feet, I suppose due to the blasting A/C. I thought about how I used to do the same thing. I had one under my desk at my job. I used to get very cold to the point that my fingers turned wrinkly. Just to make conversation, I asked her why she had a heater going.

"Oh, for my feet," she dolefully said. "It's so cold here. Today might be the last day I can use it, actually. They just sent a letter to all the employees here explaining that they couldn't afford to pay for more electricity. Effective today, I won't be able to use it anymore. Isn't that monstrous?"

"Don't they know that if an employee is not comfortable in their skin, they can't perform properly?" I said.

"They don't care," she said, silver-tongued.

My big mouth, I thought. I'd done it again. It shouldn't have been my business, but I made it mine, thinking of my ex-workplace. I was really upset by the lack of consideration from the higher-ups toward their employees. *Oops*, I thought. I put my hand on my mouth and said to myself, *Shut the f——— up, girl!*

She told me that the prescription for both MRIs would be mailed to me along with the appointment for the test and repeated the same words of warning. "Try to get a Jackson's card before scheduling your appointment. We'll send you a referral through the mail so you can take it with you when you apply for the card. Otherwise, you'll pay too much for your copay."

I waited for an eternity, about two months, before this precious piece of mail found my mailbox. I called Jackson South Hospital to make an appointment to get a card. The first day, no one answered. I thought that maybe it was lunchtime. After two days, I called again, and someone scheduled me for an appointment in a month. She told me everything that I needed to bring in order to process the card. I needed to know how much the two MRIs would cost, but they couldn't tell me exactly. They said that I had to apply for a card first, and then they'd be able to determine my copayment. Finally, I went to apply for my card, the office was no longer at the hospital but at a new address, which they gave to me. When I got there, many people were already waiting to do the same thing, and the waiting was very discouraging.

A man finally called me to follow him inside. He asked me a few questions and found out that I was missing some paperwork. He told me something different than the person on the telephone had. Notary letters from anyone that was helping me with bills had to be provided in order to put me into a certain category. Because I didn't have that, he couldn't proceed with the application for the card. I had to come back and he scheduled me to be there in a week. "It's the only way they can tell you how much money your deductible will be," he said. He explained that this card would work wherever I went in that hospital for lab tests or admission. I went back home without any more knowledge than I'd had before. By the way, my appointment was at 7:30 a.m. that day, I almost fainted while I was there, my sugar went low, and thank goodness, I had candies in my purse. It's was complicated. I had a prescription that I couldn't have filled because of the logistical crap. It wasn't easy to get all those letters; Sam was in Haiti, one was in San Francisco, and one was living in Miami, which made it impossible to get it done as quickly as I wanted to. Heartily, though, they all found a way to send the notarized letters to me in a timely manner. I went to my second appointment, but still, something was missing that he thought I'd forgotten to bring. He was sure that he'd requested it from me, but I had the list with me that he'd written himself, and that item wasn't on the list.

He came up with an excuse with his audacious sense of humor. "I know that as we age, we have tendency to forget, and it happens to me often, like it happens to everyone, probably you too," he said in his Jamaican accent.

I didn't have anything to be sorry for, but he had the nerve to blame my brain for the error, even after he recognized that it wasn't my fault but his. I didn't have an alternative, so I had to swallow that discomfiture without saying anything. Again, I went back home without that damn card. It was a Friday, so he told me to just call him when I had the proper document. Sam came in that Friday evening, so he was able to drive me there on the following Tuesday. Fortunately, once I got there, he realized that I needed Sam to sign something. Luckily, he was waiting for me in the parking lot, so I went outside and gave him the paper to sign. When I returned with the signed paper, he told me that I was a lucky woman, that my husband was there when I needed him. I thought that he was being bloody honest, not realizing that he was just testing the veracity of that signature.

"Without his signature on that paper, it wouldn't be possible for me to issue the card," he said. Happily, I had my Jackson Hospital card and was ready to leave, when suddenly, the man asked me to wait. He didn't trust the sudden appearance of Sam, so he told me that he would go with me to the parking lot, to salute my husband. "What the heck is this?" I wondered. Did he just want to see with his own eyes that I didn't forge my husband's signature? I'd worked for so long to get the paperwork filed, and now that man didn't trust my credibility. Just to get a goddamn health card! Of course, he didn't know me, but it was too much for me. Anyway, I didn't receive yet the other letter for my appointment. That hospital didn't schedule over the phone but through the mail. In that in-between period, I received the appointment for my MRI test, but the date of my test had already passed, not because of the come-and-go problem but because the postmarked date on the envelope was June 5, 2013, and my appointment was on June 5, 2013, as well. That hospital had mailed it the same day as the designated test date. I received the appointment slip on June 10. I had to go to Jackson to change the date to June 17, which was the coming Monday. This is how they play with the minds of impoverished people. This is what you have to do when you don't have health insurance in this powerful country.

On June 17, I went to have my test done, and I had to pay for each MRI separately, $50 each. The technician called me, and as I was going to the room, I asked him if he was going to do both MRIs while I was there. He looked at me with surprise and told me that they weren't both scheduled for that day. I tried to make him understand that I'd already paid for two MRIs. He wouldn't listen and was rude—rude, I said—totally rejecting what I was saying. He told me that my payments weren't his business and that the only thing he knew was that he was supposed to process the MRI for the foot only. I kept arguing.

"Why do you think I had to pay for two MRIs?" I asked. "At registration, they told me that I'd have two tests done today." Frustrated, I kept repeating this over.

He completely ignored my *palabras*. "Ma'am," he rudely said. "I'm very busy. I cannot keep talking to you now."

I shut my mouth and let him do what he had to do. I was too mad to give up so easily, though. After he finished, I requested to speak to the manager, and he took me to a nurse. I showed her the receipt that proved I'd paid for both MRIs, and she said that if I could wait a little bit longer, they'd certainly accommodate me and get my second MRI for my hand processed. My husband was in the visitors' room waiting for me. I explained the situation to him, and he agreed with my decision to wait. It wasn't really my decision; they'd made a mistake and didn't want to take responsibility for it. Was it the plan of my life to have so many difficult moments, or did I always flare complicated situations onto my own path? Nothing seemed to be simple for me. After both tests were done, as scheduled, I went to the clinic for the results. I paid the requested fees for visit and waited, as usual, to be called. At the last moment, as the nurse was checking my pulse and weight, she found out that the proper results hadn't been sent to them yet. This is after two hours of waiting. I couldn't see the nurse practitioner at the ER to whom the doctor had referred me. I was sent to the record department to sign a form, giving them authorization to acquire the results from Jackson Hospital. I guess the technician wanted to punish me for what I did, for going over his head to have both tests done the same day. I didn't know what to think because it was their responsibility to send the results to the doctor.

Another fifteen days passed before I was able to see the nurse again. So much time was lost, and so many people got involved in what should've been a simple thing. I didn't get it. Administrators make it so difficult for average people to survive in their world. The nurse could've called Jackson and had them fax the results, but no, we little people have to do all the work ourselves. Imagine everything that I went through for a simple test to find out what was wrong with me. If I'd had a life-threatening illness, would they have treated me the same way? Do you know how much of a screw-up you feel like when you don't have the leisure of insurance or money? Those who take it for granted probably don't understand what other people have to endure all the time. We all have the same blood circulating in our veins, and we all need to be taken care of in the same way. The results about my foot revealed an effusion in the ankle. How could that be the only problem when I'd spent months in pain, pain so bad that I couldn't sleep in peace? Everything else looked normal such as the anterior and posterior tibiofibular ligaments, the calcaneofibular ligaments, and the flexor tendons. In my hand, there was a small tear in the ulnar side of the triangular fibrocartilage, and there was a small amount of fluid along the hypothenar aspect of the TFCC, representing a small, post-injury cyst.

"Is it possible these little things periodically can become very painful?" I questioned the nurse.

"Yes, with HCV, you will always have variable pain," she said, batting away my annoying questions. She listened to my chest and sent me to have lots of blood tests, advising me to check with the lab department prior to the procedure to see how much I'd have to pay. She didn't check my liver or anything else. I had to ask her to do so.

My husband was such a believer in Jean's methods. He told me that I should go to see her with the results, and so I did. I was happy to see everybody there, especially my Jean, and vice versa. I'd never gone such a long period without seeing my practitioner. Seven months had passed. She was always a real pro. She checked every detail, checked my foot for numbness, and checked my wounds, things that even my endocrinologist had never done for me. She is the only provider I ever had who paid such close attention to her patients. God bless you, Jean. She not only checked everything in my file and in my body but also sent me for more types of blood tests, such as my alpha-fetoprotein and vitamin D levels. The former was high, and the latter was low. She wanted me to have an ultrasound of the liver, which I hadn't had in seven months. Because of my chronic illnesses, I was supposed to have my liver checked every six months.

49

Grace

Through all my trials, I discovered that there are three levels in each social class. I'm a woman in the middle class. It's the same with diseases; everything is related. In the middle class, there are three stages. Stage 1: people who are barely making it, who cross the border into poverty and have no way to climb further. Stage 2: people who are intermittently pulled down and up, who struggle to climb because of competition with the bottom and oppression from the top. Stage 3: people who manage to cross the border to the top. When one is in the second category, thing don't often go smoothly. We need to always watch our step so that we don't trip; one stumble could take us back all too easily to stage 1. We frequently deny reality, living in the bubble of ignorance and overdoing things because we feel like we have something to prove. We're often worried about tomorrow, because unpredictable, bad things can happen in an instant, returning us to level one.

This is the same for people with chronic diseases. We superfluously worry, sleep with one eye closed, and stay awake at all times, waiting for the worst to strike. Best or worst, good or bad, we need to be ready. Sometimes, it's wiser for us to put our faith in God, who has the power and had already decided what is best for us. I know that it's not easy to paint this portrait. I'm one of these people. I asked the Creator of the universe, from time to time, to help me bear my cross when I felt that it was too heavy for my shoulders. I prayed to him, even though I knew that God's covenant would give me the right challenges. I called on him to help lift my burdens so that I could continue on my journey.

My left hand became such a distraction to me. The shocking electrical pain that I had in my palm became a field mark of my life. I dropped dishes if I unexpectedly touched them to the sensitive area on my hand. Doctors believed that the soreness and sensitivity was not from the cyst in the palm of my hand, which was located between my thumb and index finger, but from nerve damage caused by the fibromyalgia. It ran in the family, the liver damage caused the fibromyalgia, and so on. The removal of the cyst wouldn't bring too much relief, they said. Also, my right shoulder was so delicate that I couldn't even stretch it. Any movement made the pain so ravaging that it went to my neck. I couldn't reach the light on my nightstand or do anything else with my arm. My foot also hurt very badly. *Un seul Dieu en trois persons*, meaning "the oneness of God, in whom there are three persons." I was one body with three different kind of pains—my hands, my feet, and my shoulders—which made me so unbalanced.

As such, I was among the first group of patients to get Obamacare insurance. I needed to be able to get back to my doctors. On the first working day of January 2014, I went to see the doctor that was assigned to me by Preferred Insurance. It wasn't the name on my insurance card, but when I called the office to schedule my visit, they appointed me to him, Dr. F. I didn't care as long I could be seen by a doctor. That was the goal. That said, I got the cheapest coverage, and trust me, I paid the consequences. The entire clinic was handled by family members, and the TV was always playing Fox. Maybe they had interest in that channel. They were business-doctors who lived by the mantra that time is money. I went from one brother to another and to another. I mostly worked with Dr. J. F., who was a PCP for critical care. I'd never heard of that title except at the hospital when they had to put me in the critical care unit. Still, I didn't care much him.

I sat in the waiting room with Sam. It was full of brand-new patients, all of whom were filling out forms. The first week of

Obamacare—imagine! We were happily waiting. After a long time without insurance, what could be better? Two nurses called us at about the same time, and we each went to an exam room to be checked, to review our medications, and get our blood pressure and temperatures taken. They sent us to separate examination rooms. Dr. F. saw me first. His appeared for no more than fifteen minutes, and he was on the phone for ten of that. That gave me five minutes. I daresay that he wasn't even with me for a quarter of an hour. He apologized for receiving the call, then took a look at my brief file and sent me to have an x-ray and a blood test. Everything was done right there in his office. The hall was a cavalcade full of patients, nurses, and doctors passing through. Sitting along the wall, my head went from right to left, from left to right. After the tests were done, the tech sent me back to the hall to wait, but this time, there wasn't a vacant seat. I stood, and Sam came to keep me company. I was close to fainting, and my blood sugar was low. Sam went to buy cookies and juice for me. Meanwhile, a man saw my distress and offered me his seat. I was grateful, which I'm sure he also saw on my face. After about thirty minutes, the same nurse came and told me that I could go to the reception area, that they'd give me my prescriptions and schedule me to have another visit in fifteen days. The man didn't examine me or Sam. On my second visit, I was seen by a PCP critical care doctor instead of him.

That didn't please me at all. "What?" I said. "Am I going to be seen by a different doctor every time?"

The nurse responded my question with an idiotic answer. "I don't know," she said. "Maybe your case is different. You're not the only one."

I still didn't care much, though, I was just glad to be seeing a doctor. Sam continued to see the doctor too every two months when he came to Miami. Everything that I said to these doctors meant a referral to a specialist, to whom I had to pay additional copayments. They wouldn't take any responsibility for anything on their own. The third time I came, I saw another doctor because Dr. J. F. was absent. They never touched me with a stethoscope, not even once, in the whole year I spent with them, averaging one visit a month. They

THE DAILY BATTLE FOR A NORMAL LIFE

all had the same attitude. They would stand by the door and ask me for the reason of my visit, even though for follow-ups, and the same happened with my husband. It was like they weren't obligated to do anything. It really disappointed me to see how quickly the doctor treated me during my visit. On my way to the parking lot, after I left the office, I saw him outside, slowly walking his dog. That didn't happen just once but many times!

For some reason, I thought that my place wasn't there, especially because the nurse assistants and the other employees didn't understand any English. They gave me the look, as if saying, "If you can't speak the language, why are you here?" The patients did the same when I sat next to them and they asked for something in Spanish. When I answered in English, they looked disappointed. Like I was, they were taking advantage of the health insurance marketplace. They all had the same cheap insurance and were here to see their allotted doctors. One day, I asked the critical care doctor, one of the siblings, to send me for a bone density test because I hadn't had one in almost two years and because I didn't have any medicine left. I explained that I had osteopenia on one side and osteoporosis on the other. I told him that I used to be on Boniva, but I hadn't taken that kind of drug for a long time. He grunted at me and said that he'd never give medicine me for that and that I need to walk more in the sun.

Emptyhanded, I left the office feeling that he was churlish and careless. I was confused, taunting myself about why, for all those years, I had been taking that remedy. I called my friend T. C. who had the same disease to let her know the good news, that we didn't have to take Boniva anymore. "Is it a new fashion?" we asked each other. I wasn't too sure about this, but my friend never stopped taking hers, and she never mentioned it to me again. I wasn't pleased with this office at all, so later on, I decided to see an affiliate, Dr. C., who wasn't related to that first family of doctors. He was much better, more patient, and older, but he complained that he wasn't taking new patients any longer. He had so many patients already that it gave him anxiety. He told me that after my first visit, I'd have to go back to the F. brothers. Dr. C. was completely the opposite; he took the time to explain everything and was sure that I understood everything he said. Still, he didn't want me to be his patient until I showed his name on my insurance card, where my PCP was listed. He asked me why I'd originally gone to the brother doctors. I explained that the assistant had just assigned me to them because he was already overbooked. Dr. C. was very grumpy about that. He was a kvetch every time I went in. In the end, I stayed with him, and he scheduled me for more visits. He complained and complained that he couldn't take it at all. I never saw too many people at his office—four to five other people entered with me every time I showed up. It seemed like the anxiety made him kind of paranoid around his patients.

Unfortunately, in 2015, my new PCP found out that I had severe osteoporosis with a high fracture risk, which he wrote in my file in capital letters. They put me on alendronate, calcium, and vitamin D. I had to see three specialists who were referred to me by the brothers. The doctor who was caring for my hand gave me a prescription for ibuprofen and sent me to have therapy, which didn't work. He promised that he'd take care of it, though. For my shoulder, the specialist asked me if I used to get injections for pain in my neck. I affirmed that in order to function, my arthritis doctor gave me shots every month for more than seven months in 2011. The pain back then was unbearable. She told me that as a result of this, the tendons were damaged. She prescribed Gabapentin, Meloxicam, and Voltaren gel for the painful sensations. Also, she sent me for therapy, which actually helped a lot. My feet were giving me lots of problems too, and so, with the results of the MRI, I went to see a very nice orthopedic doctor who worked in the same building that the brothers did. Everyone there showed me kindness. They were easygoing, nice people. I saw Dr. Tracy once. For my follow-ups, other doctors and students treated me. All the nurses were very skillful and gracious. I started with pills and then shots in the foot, and they also sent me for therapy. That worked a little bit, but it didn't resolve the problem. Unfortunately, the following year, I had to change my insurance and they weren't participants in that group. It is a dilemma when you find good doctors but have to leave them because of changes in insurance. At that point, my only choice was to switch because the premium overwhelmed my financial limitations.

50

The Precious Call

THE PREMIUM FOR MY supposedly cheap insurance, Preferred Medicare, had increased sixfold. I couldn't afford it and didn't know really what to do. *Do I have to file another application with the marketplace?* I wondered. I found out later that like all insurance providers, you had to renew your plan every year. It's so annoying, but at least they provided something. It was like God had answered me when the phone rang and an agent from Molina Insurance asked me if I was insured. Usually, I don't answer the phone when I don't recognize the number, but this time, it was different. I don't know why I wanted to pick up the phone, but this was the type of call that I needed to get. When God did his business, it was incredible—an invisible hand forces you to follow his wishes. The agent was very kind from the beginning. I could've hung up, but I patiently listened to her. She helped me fill out the renewal forms over the phone, and so I vaingloriously said goodbye to Preferred and welcomed Molina. As usual, things weren't simple for me, and I had so many problems with that process. It required all kinds of paperwork, but the result was good in the end. Both Sam and I got covered. Everything happens for a rational reason, and sometimes, bad things turn out to be for the best. For example, my first insurance premium increased considerably, but it led me to my new provider, which was a little more expensive but still affordable. Of course, I had to change all my doctors again, which I was going to do anyway because I wasn't happy with my primary physician's office. I found good caregivers at an office called American Care, which was close to my home. At that point in my life, I wasn't going for the best—good enough was all right. I was just happy that I had insurance. To date, I'm still with them.

In January 2015, Sam and I went to that clinic. We saw Dr. B. L., who refilled the medications that we'd been given by our previous doctors. He also sent us to have blood tests done. I believe that Sam had an x-ray as well. We were happy with him. We went back home happily, glorifying in the new insurance and national the health reform. The second visit wasn't what we expected, though. Mine was first because Sam went back to Haiti, and I had more health issues. Our files were transferred to two different nurse practitioners. I was blissful with my new nurse, but Sam wasn't, so he asked for another NP. He was looking for a man. He said he would be more confident with a man—"*Mano to mano*," he said, man with man, but I know that this was because of his gender bias. I told him to go see mine, and after a great deal of convincing, he finally accepted, but he was unsatisfied with her too. *How could he be?* I wondered. I'd liked Yody, my NP from the first time I met her. She reminded me of my Jean, who we both used to like very much. She was very thorough and went over all my diseases and pills. Nothing was left unnoticed, and she deduced that my ailments hadn't really changed, nor had my depression.

Downstairs in the same building was the emergency unit, which was open from 8:00 a.m. to 11:00 p.m., Monday through Friday. There were three units assigned based on patients' insurance: Medicare/Care Plus, Medicaid, or Molina. There was also a cafeteria where they served coffee, tea, soup, sandwiches, and juice for free. It was largely open to people on Medicaid and Medicare, who were most of their patients. Yody went over my blood test results and sent me to see legions of specialists, including a psychiatrist. I didn't think that I'd gotten crazier, but I needed medication to keep me going. Otherwise, I'd cry over nothing and feel anxious all the time. So as directed, I went to see another psychiatrist who accepted my insurance plan. This is the cool part of insurance coverage for normal people; you can only go to see doctors who they allow. Period. I couldn't go back to the providers I'd seen while I was working. I had United Health Care that time and then now Molina. There's a big difference between the two. I could only go to the walk-in clinic for services. You remember the place I went before the emergency room? It was always packed in the mornings. There were big signs that gave directions to the right departments now. Mine stated Mental Behavior, a very long sign compared to others: Pharmacy, Maternity, Dental, Emergency, Lab. All the signs were small plaques, but mine was longer, across the wall and very flashy. Even a blind person could see it! I used to go to a closer circuit where everyone in the sitting room was there for the same reason. At the clinic, however, we all sat in the same big hall, regardless of our illnesses. I felt really embarrassed to be there. Before I went to the half-open window to write my name, I looked to the right, left, in front of me, and gently behind me to make sure that I didn't recognize someone. I had a few friends working there. While writing my name, someone asked which doctor I'd come to see. Believe me, they treat you as you are, as if you are mentally debilitated, they treat you with pity and roughness at the same time. Looking back, I can see why the employees had to be so brash and rude. I checked in, and they sent me to wait in the long hallway with the people who were waiting for the pharmacist to fill their prescriptions, people waiting for dental care, and others. A man in a suit appeared in another window and called me to register and pay my copayment. Unlike my previous insurance, I didn't pay anything, which was very good. It had gone from $30 per visit to zero. Then I was sent to sit down and wait to be called. Like it was when I went to the emergency room, the long wait time never changed, despite all the renovations that had been made to the building. I was looking at the scenes around me, forgetting that I had a cell phone and that I could be cleaning out all the junk they'd sent me the day before. I was lost in the scenery, like I was waiting for St. Peter. A very tall, beautiful girl walked back-and-forth from one extremity to the other, never sitting down and never getting tired of doing that same motion. Another man, many times, tried to open the locked door and get inside where the doctors and employees were positioned.

He was very pissed off because he'd been denied access and cursed at everyone and everything. Some people were calm like I was, and others were doing gestures with their heads.

As I kept looking around with a dull expression, marveling at the metamorphosis of the human spirit, I uttered to myself, "Lord, what have you done to us?" I felt like I had been left in a forgotten world where no one understands anyone else. It's like I don't see you, you don't see me, but I exist. How did I arrive there, so close to the culmination point? I wasn't myself anymore, just the ghost emerging from the deep obscurity of the grave. There was no light. A nurse on the speaker called someone, which woke me up from my trance. Two teardrops ran down each of my cheeks, wetting my pants. I wiped the water with the back of my hand and looked beside me to see if my weakness was seen by anyone. Suddenly, I realized that I'd been seated in the same place for over three hours. My appointment was at 9:00 a.m., and I arrived at 8:30 a.m. I'd only eaten a slice of bread, a piece of cheese, and half cup of coffee as breakfast. Then it was 12:00 p.m., and I was still waiting. Paula, the psychiatric nurse practitioner, had appeared around 11:00 a.m. I knew her, so I went to ask how much longer it would be. She explained that there were two people in front of me in line. When I finally entered her sanctuary, it was after 1:00 p.m. I was hungry and felt like my sugar was getting low. I hadn't brought anything to eat and didn't have any change to buy something from the vending machine. The cafeteria was under renovation and closed to the public. Paula apologized for the inconvenience and gave me a cookie from her full drawer. She called someone to buy me an apple juice, which was very sweet of her, but she was the one responsible for my ravenous condition. *Madre de Dios*, she wasn't in rush at all. Because she was late, one after another, people interrupted her with all kinds of issues, and she had to leave the room again and again to solve their problems. Meanwhile, I was there waiting. She even ordered her lunch in because someone came to let her know that she was going out. Her brother called to let her know about a sick parent in Jamaica. Again, she excused herself and took the call. I was still there waiting. She did all her personal business at her desk! Nipping my lips, I thought about what else I could be doing instead of waiting. After taking my medical info, she asked me if I'd filed for social disability, and I said yes. An assistant entered the room like a tornado, without apologizing, and started talking to her like I was invisible. After she left, Paula apologized for the intrusion. I didn't say anything, but my blood was boiling in my veins. She continued writing her notes like she wasn't expecting a word from me.

"After a few sessions," she said, "if they didn't approve you, we should still be able to help you refill. Depression is a big issue."

I didn't say anything. I could've told her that I'd already been denied twice by Social Disability, but I stayed mute. I was looking at her, but my mind was elsewhere. All these complications made me so tired. I simply wanted to go home. Paula prescribed me fluoxetine and clonazepam (Klonopin). She escorted me to an assistant to schedule another visit with her in a month and referred me to a counselor in the same building. Fifteen days after, I went back to the clinic for my first visit with the counselor. Flor was really nice. She was on time, and we walked together to her office. She closed the door after her and told me I could lie or sit down on the couch. I chose to sit down. I wanted to keep my pride because I knew that I wasn't a lost cause, even though they wanted me to believe I was, as was evidenced by all the medicine they'd prescribed. Anyway, fools don't know when they're fools.

"How are you?" she said.

"I don't know," I answered, my voice close to exploding into tears. "I'm here to find out."

"Okay. Let me rephrase my question. How do you feel exactly today?"

"Anxious and nervous."

"Is this the first time you're seeing a counselor?"

"No."

"Tell me anything that you want to talk about," she said vaguely.

I wasn't sure where to start, what to tell her. "Should I invent something?" I wondered. No. I was only there for my benefits. I explained my mood changes and my problems with palpitations when I had to go out. My heart raced like someone who had received bad news. I felt nauseated, overwhelmed, and dizzy. A weird sensation filled me with heat, like the heater in the house was on. I wasn't afraid, but I felt so disquiet that I preferred to stay home all the time, whenever possible. I explained all this to her.

"Is this happening each time you decide to go out?" she asked.

I shook my head first, but then said, "Yes." I thought to myself, *I don't decide to go out. I go out of necessity, like today.* I said, "Even when my friends invite me to a party, I can prepare what I'll wear, but I can't prepare my mind."

"Are you worried about something?" She asked.

"Always," I answered.

"About what?"

"About everything," I said. I paused. Annoyingly, she waited for more explanation. "It's my nature to always worry," I explained. "The present doesn't exist for me. I'm always leaning into and preparing for the future."

"You like perfection."

"Yes, at work, they used to call me Martha Stewart."

She told me to take a piece of paper and write down everything that I had to do each day and each week. "Don't exceed the maximum, and stay with on itinerary," she strictly added. She didn't give me any medical diagnosis like my previous psychologist had. What really deceived me was that while I was talking, my eyes were already full of teardrops. She handed me few Kleenexes and then the whole box because my fingers were bloody wet. The more I wiped my tears, the more they flowed over my face. She was patient, waiting and looking at her watch. By the time I'd calmed down, the hour was already up. She told me to go to another window and schedule more appointments with her. She returned to her computer to update her calendar. I was scheduled for two appointments with her every month, plus one with the psychiatrist assistant.

On my second visit, I told her little more about my diseases and my family, she told me that if I was not happy with that kind of sporadic separation between Sam and me, I should opt for a permanent separation. She gave me a solution that didn't make sense to me because I wasn't looking for the extreme. I tried to forget about it. I visited Flor for nearly a year, twice a month, without any problems.

THE DAILY BATTLE FOR A NORMAL LIFE

She knew almost everything about me. Some of her advice I kept and some I rejected, until one day, she made me wait for three hours. I became a madwoman that day. I couldn't control my temper. It felt like a deception, and I was very disappointed. I didn't want to see her anymore. I'd already paid for the counselor's visit, so I made them reimburse me my copayment, and I left her and never went back. In the meantime, I left Paula as well after four sessions. I requested an alternative doctor, a real doctor. The doctor, Dr. Gracia, was on time but didn't give me enough time to say anything. His only goal was to give me medicine and get out of there. No matter what I said, he found something to prescribe me and left in a rush. I saw him three times, and that was it. I wasn't a fool and didn't intend to become one. I realized that I'd have to work by myself to wake up from that trance. All the counselors told me that everything in my past had caused an anxiety disorder: the sexual assaults, constantly moving, chronic and intermittent sicknesses, Sam's departure, etc. But there was something else that I never told them, a secret that I will reveal soon.

Depression has always been my companion. In my twenties, I was on Valium for a long time. I don't have to say too much for doctors to find a reason to put me on that lethargy pill. After just a little conversation with them, I'd end up on some kind of magical, relaxation drug. I seemed like I was carrying the world's problem on my back. My troubles left me with so many onuses that abraded me like rat bites. It wasn't easy. I was too "thin-skinned" to live in this universe. In reality, my illnesses weren't the only causes of my burdens. Rather it was a combination of all of life's irregularities that accrued over time. My family thought that I was strong, but I wasn't, I only had the audacity to play make-believe. Nightfall was my accomplice during my times of wickedness. When I laid my head on my pillows, I felt free of frustrations and sorrows. In daylight, a masquerade of smiling covered my face, so that people I crossed paths with assumed I was all right. It was like I was two different people in one body, and it became automatic by practice. Sertraline, Prozac, Celexa, Lexapro, Fluoxetine, bupropion, Xanax, Neurontin, clonazepam, alprazolam, Buspar, Valium, buspirone, Cymbalta, Paxil, gabapentin, Trazodone, clorazepate, amitriptyline—I took them all. I had the generic versions as well as the brand-name versions. They did alleviate my symptoms, but they didn't cure the problems. I figured that maybe I didn't have to be cured because mental disorders were a part of my living. Their side effects made me sicker. If people believe that they can deviate from their destiny, they can't. Mine has walls that border me in, preventing me from taking another path.

Over the years, I learned to enjoy my good days like the bad days don't even exist. This doesn't mean that I forget about my troubles, but good days are so special for me because I don't wake up painless very often. I don't say anything anymore. I don't complain. I simply accept my life as it is. I know that for each person on earth, the dance of life doesn't always have the perfect cadence, so we have to adjust the rhythm of our music from time to time to continue enjoying the party.

51

Find Happiness Again

IN A SENSE, I do feel lucky, not like those people who some of my friends, family, and acquaintances want to compare me to, of course, but I feel like I'm one of the luckiest people on earth. I'm able to experience all these burdens and still maintain an exciting life. From my bad times to my good times, I think that I went through a lot. I'm lucky because I always find a way out of my encumbrances, which I call a blessing. I don't even like the word "lucky" in this type of circumstance. I began to cultivate faith in myself, thinking "I can do better" instead of lamenting. During my good days, I gardened in my backyard to take away my gloominess. That was one of my life's butterflies. I didn't know that cultivating a garden could be so peaceful. The smell and the touch of the humid soil gave me a sensation of tranquility and clairvoyance. I started to see the light of hope that I'd lost for a while. Like in my childhood, I took time to look at nature again. I listened to the wilderness howling, the crickets chirping, and even searched for the insects themselves, feeling a real need to see them singing. I saw frogs everywhere, in damp vases or behind an abandoned plant, which made me jump and laugh at myself. At night, if I went to the patio. I heard a concert of them singing in the empty pool, wet from rainfall. I enjoyed looking at the birds simply digging in the ground to find food or drinking water from a wet leaf, a container filled with water by chance. I saw birds that I didn't think I even had in my backyard because I was too busy in the mornings to get to work and too tired in the afternoons to pay any attention. Like a good Christian does to praise the Lord, for each crawling earthworm they swallowed or each drop of water they drank, the birds waved their heads toward the sky to say thanks to God. I chased away my neighbor's cat, who preferred to poop in my backyard just to upset me.

All these fun discoveries were very precious to me. I breathed the fresh air of the wind in the morning, which came and went, leaving me with enough time to catch the moment between inhalation and exhalation. That air was so pure and innocent. It wasn't the same as the air in my car or from the air conditioner at work. Time was finally on my side. I was less stressed, in heaven with my new decisions. I felt fortunate to be still part of the universe, to witness the change in generations, the evolution of the mundane world. Most of all, I was so grateful for innovation in medicine, which despite all the side effects, managed to bring greater benefits to patients. Just in my lifetime, scientists had achieved and discovered so much in terms of bettering drugs, treatments, and therapies. I experienced these significant changes, which were made over such short periods of time. From the peginterferon and ribavirin treatments, for which I took five pills a day and three shots per week for a year, and which came with all kinds of side effects, to the latest treatment, Harvoni, which is a once-daily pill that cures 96–99 percent of hep C patients in twenty-four weeks without almost any side effects.

My doctor agreed to put me in Harvoni for five months instead of the usual duration but my insurance wouldn't pay for. It's very expenses $1,000/pill a day. I'm waiting for my Social Disability to be approved so I could mark my fourth treatment attempt. I can't afford to pay that amount per pill per day for five months? Health is a luxury in our country.

A liver biopsy used to be excruciating painful. They pulled out a piece of the liver under local anesthesia while you were awake! Then after so many medical advances, with the general, light anesthesia, I woke up asking myself if anything had been done because I didn't feel anything. My heart was lifted with the ecstasy of this immense emancipation. If the manufacturers could take just a little more time to make drugs a little more pleasant and offset their side effects, life would be less abominable for those of us who take them.

In my exploration of how I could find happiness despite my troublesome issues, I lost myself in the mystery of understanding my body. I asked myself, "What will make it as comfy as humanly possible?" I had plenty time ahead to do things I couldn't do when I was working. When you have no one to talk to, you can really become frenzied. I inculcated myself into the love of gardening during the day when I felt less unwell. I did what I used to do a half century ago, staring at the nature around me. Regretfully, I didn't have the leisure of having an ocean in front of my house, and I could easily count the number of trees I had in my backyard—one, two, three. But I made do with what I had, envisioning the majestic, panoramic view I had in my adolescence but also enjoying my new surroundings. As a habit, I went outside in the mornings to water my garden and freely snort the cool breeze before it got too hot, thinking of the old maxim "Make habits as a routine as brushing your teeth." *Why not?* I thought. I never forget to brush my teeth, so I could make anything part of my daily routine as well. I made an accord with myself to continue doing what was enjoyable and conducive to my desires. Nature gives us so many chances to play, either for a healing process or for joy. In our busy lives, we should stop sometimes and look around us to find a green field. Let nature inspire you; it can offer great gifts to all of us, regardless of our encumbrances, and it can especially help with peace of mind. I'm sure that if each of us dedicated some time to this great pleasure, the world would be less angry. Even when I don't feel well or when my sleeping angel is late to our rendezvous, I nag myself outside at two or three o'clock in the morning to savor the odor of the rosemary or mint, or of a rose that's just timidly opening up to become a beautiful flower. I go outside and force myself to feel the ground sprinkled by the wetness of the night. I often pick some soursop leaves for my tea to help me fall asleep. I go into my little garden, cradling myself in my rocking chair to look at the infinity of the sky with all its luminous stars, to listen to the water cascading into my pool, and to thank God for being an omniscient God. He knows all the details that can please us.

No one can monitor our lives better than we can. By not working, I discharged my doctors from their responsibilities and became an active caregiver of myself. I took ownership over my life and am happy with the results. The energy that I used to split between my job and my health is now dedicated to only one thing, my health. My life makes me heedful to anything around me and very appreciative and thankful for the things I'm still able to accomplish every day. It made me a better servant to my family and friends. Some people who crossed my life only once left permanent effects on me. I'm not perfect, none of us are, but sometimes it's good to show our gratitude to God for each day he lets us breathe on earth.

While I was working, I was seeing lots of doctors and had more bad developments with my health. The hep C had made a deal with the devil to destroy my liver. I had severe liver fibrosis and then cirrhosis. My kidney was being attacked, and my cholesterol was going up. It was a test of my faithfulness in God. I decided that I had to go to church more often to break the curse of being sick. "No," I said, arguing with myself. I didn't believe that going to church all the time would solve the problem. "God is everywhere," I reasoned. "I can do exactly the same worshipping at home, and perhaps even do it better." I believed that a miracle would soon happen. I had no hope that I would be approved for that very expensive treatment, but I realized that God would provide a way if he wanted me to be cured of hep C. I repeated this almost every day. To avoid the costs, lots of insurance companies made it very complicated to approve patients for the Harvoni treatment. There was no way that my little insurance company would pay the $1,000 per pill per day, which I'd need to take every day for months. After having gone through three failed treatments, though, that was my only hope. Hope or no hope, I needed a miracle. I had more tests and waited to be approval for a fibro-scan, which the insurance requested. It took forever to get it authorized. Now I have heart murmur. It's not too bad, as said words to words in the result of my test "the mitral regurgitation test showed evidence of mild aortic regurgitation. My left ventricular ejection fraction rate only 55 percent". Thank God there was no mass found there. Despite the explanation given to me by the doctor I still don't understand. My heart beat so hard sometimes, like it was going to explode. I could even hear the pulsations from my chest. I didn't need to do anything to trigger the chest-squeezing or chest-pressing, they just happened, and they were as bad as those of someone in terrible emotional distress. Nothing helped, not standing up, sitting down, or lying in bed. Spontaneously, the suffering would start without notice. I had palpitations and the feeling that I needed to throw up. It came to tell me that my demon's shadow was around. For me, the worst feeling is when you're not feeling well but can't even explain what is hurting or what is making you sick. I just couldn't describe it, even to myself. It was an unfathomable situation with no end. My new ailments weren't severe, but they compounded when added to the others. My cirrhosis, however, was bad, and they told me that to offset it, I had to take care of my HCV in a matter of six months. This made me feel ill at ease, like I was going to pass away despite the fact that my prognosis was pretty good.

We all know that life will end somehow, in some way, one day. So as much we take medication to make it easy on our bodies, we need to prepare our souls too. Nobody wants to die, including me. We know where we are but we don't know where we are going. It's very comprehensible, but being saddled with diseases for so long can make you feel invincible. As I forced myself to understand life, I got the advantage of seeing things differently, and I made time to prepare my soul for this eventuality. As Oprah said, "Our body is the vehicle of our soul." I like this *beaucoup* (very much). I repeatedly say the mantra "My body is the sanctuary of Lord. I need to take good care of it and keep it clean for my soul to rest." This is why we should mindfully pay attention to our bodies just as much as we do our spirituality. They go together; if the body breaks down, we can guarantee that the soul won't respond well and vagabond around.

When we are diseased, our thoughts aren't often clear enough to recognize what is wrong or bad. Hurts in the body create divisions of spiritualism, and sicknesses produce madness. Always be proud of what you have accomplished in your life and never look back and say, "If I knew, I would've…" Instead, let it go. Leave it to the past and happily allow yourself to continue on your journey without remorse.

That's the way it should be. Belief is paramount to existence. When the time comes, we must say that we completed our missions, whatever they are, with no regrets. We can be good examples for others by always accepting the fact that we were not made equal. We are different like the fingers are in length. Bad or good, our lives are all tragedies, but these tragedies manifest differently for different people. Don't get intimidated by the troubles you encounter on your trajectory. Every day, I feel like Jesus is still carrying the cross for us. If not, many people would succumb to despair every hour! This cross is heavier for some, but without his help, we would never make it through. In my solitude, I rediscovered the love of God, the love of people around me, and especially the love of my family that never let me down. Love cannot cure our malignant diseases, but it can alleviate our pain. I'm typing these words with great pain in my left hand, but I know that if I strongly pray and hand over my suffering to God, for a while, I will truly feel relief. That little moment of being free from pain is so important for me. By reveling in it, I've regained strength, stability, and trust in myself. Don't be afraid to solicit divine help. It can take time to reach out and be understood, but be persistent and patient. Help might be a step away from ringing your doorbell.

Our thoughts play predominant roles in our lives. They can distract or amuse us, depending on how positively or negatively we see things. Our conscience is also a big trigger that makes us believe that death is a bad thing when it might not be. A baby's conscience is not as developed as an adult's is. What happens if both are thrown into a pool but neither knows how to swim? The adult panics and will surely drown, but the baby will simply act amused, and as such, there is a good chance that the baby will stay alive until someone comes to the rescue. It's the same for sick people; the more we are worried, the less chance we have to survive. If we give ourselves the opportunity to see things differently, as it is supposed to be, we can have a better understanding of life. I see life as a piece of abstract art that everybody is trying to make sense of. If we ask about what the artist envisioned to make such an incomprehensible piece of art, we won't get our question answered. The Lord is the artist and the Creator of life, and life relies on what we make of it. No matter what we deem to be the final meaning of life, if you have faith in miracles, they will happen in your life. Miracles happens every day for believers, we just cannot always recognize them. We believe in the crazes that are palpable or that we can visualize, so why not miracles? Our thoughts are typically too preoccupied by other things that are less important, or we are too blind by materialism to consider that everything that happens to us is simply normal.

When I stopped working, did it resolve my medical problems? No, not at all. All my diseases remained onboard because most of them are chronic. However, when I was in pain, I finally had the luxury to stay in bed without worrying about a load of work waiting for me or how I'd even drive to work. I finally had more time to deal with my diseases. To this day, I spend my nonworking time getting in better shape despite my unhappy moments. I repeatedly say to myself that I'm not going to be rich, so I should stop worrying about my former workplace and thank God instead for the blessing of being alive. I believe that if my destiny is to be wealthy, I will be. It won't ever be too late, no matter of what. I can pass days without talking to someone face-to-face, which is very lonesome and depressing, but we don't always get everything we want in life.

My migraines still bother me almost every other day. I take fewer butalbital pills because when the pain is acceptable, I can rest. I take my mind off the uncomfortableness of my condition. I booze my system with more water and add a square of the dark chocolate, which is said so good for the body. I use Palma Christi oil for my headaches, which is a natural vegetable oil made from castor beans. It's good for sore throats, fevers, and coughs. I also use it as conditioner for my hair instead of one on the market. It's even better than the real stuff and helps me maintain a full head of healthy hair. An American nurse told me to dampen a cloth in this miracle oil and place it over my liver, which would supposedly ease the pain from my scar tissue. I believe her, but I never do it, I don't know why. To boost my energy and for vitamin supplements, I drink the leaves of moringa, the miracle tree, every day. I grew the tree myself at the edge of my house. If you cannot find fresh leaves, you can buy the teabags. It is a native, natal plant from Africa and Asia, which they often plant in Haiti for nutrition. It's a multipurpose plant full of benefits. I also use the semi-contra herb, which they call the tea of life, to clean my liver from toxins, which also has multiple health benefits. The smell is not that great though. I don't like raw salad, so I use lots of herbs in my food, which I pick fresh from my garden. I raise them without insecticide or chemicals. My herbs were just raised and grown by nature. I have to say, it's not an easy task to grow plants without any chemical substances. Additionally, I use the power of mint for my aches. I like using organic, peppermint castile soap to soak my feet, along with a warm infusion of natural mint from my garden steamed in a lot of boiled water. In the summer, I try to infuse the mint in sunny, warm water to add more goodness. I don't know what works, but I always try. I'm sure that I can get the natural vitamin D from the sun to make it more beneficial. For my depression, I go to my garden and start digging, planting anything I find in my kitchen or that my neighbor has given to me. If the plants die, I don't get upset, I just put in something else or try another kind. It's fun. Death should be a normal phenomenon for people like it is for plants. For my eyes, I use a cold compress and stay with it for hours, lying down on my back, half-sitting in bed. This is my husband's remedy, not mine. It doesn't always help when the pain is out of control, but it does relax me.

I learned to brush my teeth longer because I don't have dental insurance. I use baking soda sometimes like my grandfather and my grandmother used to do, with salt or with lime juice to keep them white. They used a kind of root along with the baking soda, but I can't remember what it was, so I pass on it. To sleep and relax at night, I drink the soursop tea leaves. I have a big tree in my backyard that I paid no mind to before. Soursop is an herbaceous plant that produces a sweet fruit. I make my favorite juice with it. It's so flavored by itself, so I just add water, vanilla, milk, and sugar (optional), and it makes the most tasteful juice in the world. Try and let me know. It's also called *graviola*. It's not proven yet, but the tea of the leaves is known to cure cancer and many other things. I use rosemary herbs from my garden ground with salt and brown sugar to scrub my face.

People tell me that my skin glows, a result of this natural process. Of course, for my blood sugar, I add sticks of cinnamon to my morning tea and sprinkle lots of cinnamon powder in my homemade baked goods. In several studies, researchers found that including cinnamon in our daily menus can help controlling our glucose levels, plus it's good for lot of other illnesses. These are not fast relievers or curatives, but I'm a big believer in natural medicines that pay off over time. These are some tips you might find very helpful if you want to go green. I don't say that I've stopped taking my medication, but I've tried to take fewer, especially pain killers.

That said, I still have frequent anxiety and feel my spirit breaking down. When you have unlimited contact with incurable diseases and wake up most mornings with ailments, you can't be completely satisfied. I always expect the worst to happen. Leaving the workforce didn't cure my afflictions, but it greatly helped me cope with overcoming my mental and physical disabilities. It's hard to live with limitations. By suppressing my ego and my "need" to work, I took better care of my health and put less of a burden on my body than I used to, when I dragged myself out of bed despite it all. Generally, people are stubborn and refuse to see what is good for us. God sends us light and friction, signs and warnings, to open our eyes to what might come next. Many times, we don't realize what is meaningful. I still don't know how I used to deal with both my work life and my illnesses.

52

The Heavy Secret

HONESTLY, I CAN'T END this book without talking about my main surreptitious struggle, with which I have battled for a long period of time. I want to open the gate to free my mind and leave behind the world of judgmental people. Beyond this gate, I see the light that tells me, "Only God is our judge," and what Pope Francis once said to an Italian journalist, "Who am I to judge?" I always say, "Who are you people to judge, the Lord's our Savior's creation?" Believe it or not, we all come from the same Creator, no matter what you call him.

Seven years ago, my life was torn apart by an erupting volcano that almost ran over me and almost burned me alive. The dense fire really got to me. I was deeply hurt because I was ignorant. My core felt the burning sensation to a degree that I didn't think I could survive it. I had nowhere to escape to from such eruptive and devastating news: two of my three sons declared that they were not straight. I always thought that being horribly sick all the time was a normal life process, but I couldn't reconcile that two of my children were sexually attracted to the same sex. On one hand, I could see it coming, but on the other hand, I denied it many times, thinking that I must be spreading false accusations in my own mind. A maternal instinct never lies, but I simply rejected the possibility that something like that could happen in my family. I wasn't necessarily "against" this particular, natural behavior, but I was afraid of the embarrassment that it would bring to the family. I was living for what other people would say, what they would think, which I realized later was a failure on my part.

When one of my sons told me that he was bisexual, I said, "At least I have two other normal ones!" In our society, what we call "normal" is the priority, no matter of what is wrong or right. The shock took me by surprise, and I wanted to talk to someone about it. These words burned in my ears. They went dolorously under my skin like an arrow piercing my heart. I repeated these three words over and over: "He cannot be, he cannot be." I didn't know if I should cry or laugh at this joke. *It had to be a dream,* I thought, *and when I wake up, the sensation will be gone! It's just a nightmare I'm having, and it will end as soon I'm awake!* The unchaste universe that I made so powerful was being torn down. Pathologically speaking, I had a big problem swallowing this fact. I told myself, "It's an acute disease, and it will go away with the time. Others can be gay, but not my son." I felt so many churning emotions at once, like the world around my family, which I'd carefully designed and built, was going to be ruined. I had other plans for him. I wanted him to give me grandchildren from my blood.

I called my other son to vent some of my emotions, but it only got worse from there. He didn't hesitate to let me know that he wasn't any different from his brother, that he was also same-sex orientated. I couldn't say anything to my elder son because I knew for a fact he was a Casanova. I'd seen a file of women coming in and out of my house. The sky and all the planets fell down on my head, without any stars to illuminate me. The load was too heavy for me in that darkness. I still thought that I was dreaming, that it couldn't be real. *It will go away,* I thought, *because it's in my imagination.*

"Let's not think about it," I said. The more I tried to remove it from my mind, the more the stain grew. I was fighting with something that I never thought would happen to me, a dilemma that I couldn't change. I couldn't believe what I'd heard and couldn't understand it either. This time, I had to question God about what I'd ever done to him to deserve this albatross. Despite all the burdens I'd had in my life, I also had to endure this? I cursed at St. Joseph even more than ever. Instead of a girl, I got not one homosexual but two! I couldn't sleep before, but after the news, it became agony every night to catch some Zs. There was a buzz in my head, asking all these questions: "Why? Why me? What did I do wrong? What did I miss? What kind of education did I fail to give them? What should I do to repair this damage? Why? Why, Lord? Will their minds change? I hope! Does this make me a lesbian too? No, I cannot be, that last question disgusts me! But one of us, Sam or I, must have the homosexual gene to procreate two homosexuals!

I was devastated inside. The question "why" was after me. I was screaming "why" everywhere, the homosexual drone following me everywhere like another shadow. In my torment, my only piece of resistance was that Sam shouldn't know about it, and no one else should either. I decided to take full responsibility of my progenitors. They were my babies, and I was willing and ready to be blamed. Every night, I spent hours on the internet searching for answers to my questions but didn't get very far. The one I was looking for was, "Can it be cured?"

Days and then months passed, and I regained a little lucidity. Instead of searching to answer that unreasonable question, I decided to do better: find out where I could meet other parents who were facing similar stumbling blocks. I went to a group meeting at Coral Gables, where I met some other LGBT individuals and their parents—mothers and fathers who were asking the same questions that I was. It was the only place I felt free to talk about it because all of us were there for the same reason: searching for answers and learning how to cope with it. Every conversation was about LGBT issues, but the hours we spent talking about it didn't even seem to be enough. We voiced lots of queries, in reality, we were just asking the same questions over and over, in different ways, because the answers didn't land where they were supposed to. The answers were never satisfactory for us. It was like my heart was shut off to all the replies to my inquiries. I wanted to ask, but I didn't want to hear an answer. There was no good explanation for this phenomenal, uncontrollable situation. For some, the father came instead of the mother, but it wasn't any different; we were thinking the same thing. After more than four months, I concluded that homosexuality was not imaginary and that my situation wasn't a dream. I knew that I needed to accept it but how? I had to be supportive, so they didn't feel depressed like I was. I wanted my children to be happy with who they were.

I became certain that if my children could be homosexual, this phenomenon must be real. I was scared that they might think otherwise. They were God's willing children, and I never honored anything other than Him. I was scared that they'd feel like humanity had rejected them. I was scared that they'd hurt themselves. I didn't want to show any disappointment, but it was there, and I was fighting with that nonsense emotion. I had my heart broken, and this was not what I was expecting from my kids, but what could I do? Every time I said "This is what God wants," I found myself feeling jilted. I couldn't apply that same notion that I'd used to reconcile my diseases to this situation. I couldn't say it anymore because it hurt too much. Everything that I constructed had been demolished. I was hurting badly, and my mind kept rejecting the reality. I was sicker than ever before, trying to hide my feelings. With a spirit like that, the arms of Morpheus stayed closed to me for a long time. I couldn't sleep anymore from the physical hurt that had increased considerably due to the constant emotional distress. I thought all day and all night about one thing: homosexuality and why it existed. With closed eyes and open eyes, I just pictured my sons with male companions. I was terribly wounded by this infernal arrow and underwent a sensation of wanting to die. It fluctuated every day depending on how much negativity was in my soul. It was a cancerous mass in my chest that was only there to kill me. I felt like my brain was narrowing all good thoughts and expanding the bad ones.

This time, I had to pray for myself. It was the only solution. I didn't often use prayers written by others. I liked to use my own words for each specific occasion. I don't recall ever requesting something for myself from Him, but this time, it was different. I had to pray for God to clear my mind. I just wanted to place a "help me, God" order! Over time, I reminded him that I was waiting for my shipment and that I knew that he had a lot to fulfill but to remember my prayers too. One day, as if by accident, I felt that the load of the firmament over my head had lifted a little. I was happy to get a little relief. Soon after, though, that heavy load came back, and it felt like the earth was crumbling under my feet. Everywhere I stepped, I fell into a crack, sinking deeper and deeper. Like I said, I never prayed for myself because I believed in destiny, but to me, this wasn't destiny's course but a curse. I don't know exactly where it had come from, but it was there. I felt pain in the core of my heart like I never had before. I always asked, "Who is responsible for this, Sam or me?" When Sam came home, I looked at him innocently sleeping while I was awake with my deep secret and lies. I felt disgraced, ashamed for not telling him anything about his children, ashamed of myself for giving them an unruly life, and ashamed for the lies I told him when I had to go to a group meeting. Over time, I stopped crying. Finally, I profoundly accepted that it couldn't be otherwise, that this was the way that God created them, so I had to accommodate myself accordingly. *If this is what he wants to add to my family story*, I thought, *so be it*. I started to believe in sex orientation. I kept the secret from Sam and Steven for several years. I showed happiness, even when I felt weak. I tried to clandestinely be their supportive psychotherapist by showing them my happiness, my comprehension. *If I don't*, I thought, *who will?*

One time, I had a couple staying with us for New Year. We were sitting at my dining table, drinking our cultural pumpkin soup like we always do to celebrate our Independence Day. We talked about everything, and the conversation meandered to couples of the same gender. All three of my children, Sam, and everybody at the table seemed accustomed to talking about it. Through the conversation, the man of our two houseguests spoke of homosexuals with all sorts of derogatory names, such as *faggot* and *queer*. That was the first time in my life that I'd heard those words. I couldn't have been more vexed! I tried to reason with him, but he just kept going on about homosexuals, using pejorative words like *sissy*. My sons were probably hurt by that. I always believed that same-sex orientation was an involuntarily choice, people are born that way, but regardless of what I said, I couldn't make him shut up. I was like Mother Goose protecting her babies, coming up with all kinds of arguments to make him understand that homosexuality wasn't new and wasn't a matter of choice. I was also hoping that because the man had a heavy accent, my children didn't pick up on everything he said. Every word goaded my body as if he was beating me with a whip. My children were very polite about it, and it was our secret. That day, I recognized how people can be so blind and ignorant in certain situations. It's so unfortunate that some people in society can be so cruel without even realizing that they're hurting people's feelings with their sharp mouths. Your best friend can become your worst enemy if you don't share the same ideology, or if one of the parties is not humble enough to let it go. This husband and wife are still my good friends and still don't know anything about how that conversation made me feel.

As time passed, I thought about my son's sexual identities only when they were around. No matter what, I decided, they were my only loving children, my protegees. Everything around me went back to its normal shape. I was still working at the time but forced myself to forget about it at my workplace and during my alone time. I put into practice the expression, "Out of sight, out of mind." Although I was coming to terms with it, Steven wasn't. He'd found out from a friend that Scott had been at South Beach with a man. He entered my bedroom like a hurricane to let me know what I'd already known for years. He was out of control, raving, using all the bad words he could find in his brain. I understood that it wasn't going to be easy for him, so I thought, *Let's kill two birds with one stone.* I let him know that his other brother was also homosexual. That was the drop of water that made the vase overflow, as they say. He became very angry and said that he didn't want to talk to his siblings anymore.

I reasoned with him a little and told him that for their sake, we both had to lie. "Don't ever agree with people who say that your brothers are gay," I told him. "Defend them instead." From that point on, that became our familial law. "They're your brothers, and they'll always be your brothers. Don't ever forget that."

He was furious and reasoned that he liked women so much, probably because he was the firstborn son. He figured that he'd taken all the male chromosomes, leaving none for them. I didn't know where he found that big medical word. He went back to his bedroom without saying another word. Now, all my children were having issues, so I have to be strong for them. I paid closer attention to Steven because I knew what anger could provoke in men, especially in a case like this one. He was mad, and I understood him. Every occasion I got, I said something funny about it to him, just to put him at ease. Over time, I began to see signs of acceptances in him—acceptance of the inevitable, ironic tour of life. I never really knew what Sam thought about homosexuality. He never talked about it, like it didn't exist. Even during that conversation at the dinner table, he didn't say a word. Sam doesn't talk about what he cannot understand. When I told him about our sons' sexualities, he only said that he could've guessed it about Scott because he never brought a girl home. He was too quiet to be a straight man, he said. But for Sam Jr., he reckoned, it would never catch. He was always around girls. Was that just to hide the truth? I didn't say a word. We didn't talk for long about it. It was like he was saying, "Thanks for letting me know, but I'm not interested in knowing more." We both stayed on the *qui-vive*, and he never acknowledged anything else about it. Even when they talked about it on television, for example the coming out of many gay people, he seemed insensitive to it. He never said anything when their boyfriends were around either. He played the "invisible man." Perhaps he wasn't concerned, or perhaps he felt too manly to talk about it.

I met with my very best friends each month for some kind of event, and when I saw all their sons with girlfriends, I said to myself, "God, what happened to mine?" I couldn't say anything to my friends about it because I was frightened of their reactions. I didn't know who my real friends were in that circumstance. What would they say about my children behind my back? How would they take it? I didn't want to cause any hate toward my children. They always asked me when I would be a grandmother, and what could I say? I joked by telling them that they were gay, but they didn't believe it, assuming that I was kidding as usual. The situation made me nervous. We're living in a world of antagonism and cruelty, a world of oppression against humanity. A world that says that if you're different in any way, you shouldn't exist. That increases my anxiety and my days of bleakness. I worry when they go on vacation, when they are in the street, at a club. It's a continual anxiety, which is more suffocating than the uncomfortableness of being sick. This drove me blindly toward the darkness more than all my diseases together ever had, but I didn't want to show it to them. There's no one I trusted in whom I could confide my secret. I kept it for myself. What I knew for a fact was that I would always be there for my children. After weeping, I reconnected myself with the idea that my children were healthy and that they were some of the best children in the world: polite, respectful, caring toward others, what else did I need? It was just a matter of sexual orientation, and they certainly weren't alone in that. Were those logical enough reasons to secure my fears? No! It was only superfluous.

I continued my research and found out that homosexuality is formed while the baby is still in the womb due to epigenetic or epi-marks influences and that it is a natural process you can find in humans, nonhumans, and even in plants. It's simply natural. People don't choose to be LGBT like some believe they do. They're born like that, period. Who would voluntary allow himself or herself to be on the wrong side of discriminatory controversy? When I went deeper and analyzed the mythology of homoerotism or cisgender-ism, I found a great deal of information that has existed in our world for centuries.

Biologically

Studies have shown that "too little testosterone can make a genetical male fetus more feminine and vice-versa. […] If an epi-mark that kept a mother from getting exposed to high testosterone during development gets passed on to her son—the opposite sex—it could desensitize him to testosterone, contributing to his sexual preference for men."

There is no confirmation of what I just quoted from a scientist named Dr. Rice, but I believe that it might be the cause in my sons' cases. One of us probably had hypogonadal, I figured, which is caused by low testosterone, we just didn't know it. That can explain a child being gay or lesbian. It is a deficiency or elevation of testosterone in the parents' blood. The progeny isn't in any way responsible. This is an abnormality, like someone who is born with an infirmity or another unwelcome prenatal ailment. Would you deprive that person the right to have a normal life? The only crime in it is that these scientists don't talk enough about it for the public to better understand. They prefer to turn deaf ears, letting the public scourge homosexuals. Even though we're still at beginning of this research, they should at least release something about it. Anyway, it should be normal to consider a human as a human, regardless of their ethnicity, sex orientation, etc. It astonished me to hear a political neurosurgeon talking on television about homosexuality like an illiterate would, using blah-blah words like he never went to medical school, and citing, for example, how male prisoners chose male partners in prison when they don't have another choice. "It's a choice," he reasoned. That was the worst example ever, in my opinion. If I ever have to choose a neurosurgeon, he'd be last on my list. It's already hard enough for homosexuals to live normal lives in this nonsense world, so why make it harder? If I want to go further from a cultural standpoint, we should all conclude that LGBT people are born like that and are genetically incapable of loving anyone other than those of the same sex. Period. Why do you have antipathy for them? They've struggled as much as you have to understand it. The universe was created for everyone to find their place and to be happy.

Historically

Homosexuality has always been part of the world since the world was created. Ancient Greeks and Romans are reputed as having large homosexual populations. Many dominant figures had wives for the purpose of appearances only, but this was only to hide who they really were. They would go clandestinely to homosexual clubs and enjoy same-sex intercourse. During the Middle Ages, many historical, enigmatic figures have had attributed to be gay or bisexual. Less is known about gay women because men had more autonomy at that time. Males being with other males is very common and always has been. Our existence is full of hypocrites! We impose on each other about how to live and what we call morality, but who's really a moral philosopher? No one! You create the law and you transgress it beyond the limits. Too often, we want project notions of what is immoral into other people's mind, for example, that marriage has to be between a man and a woman. This is a disrespectful recognition. We're all human, and we're all different. We all should be responsible for our own lives without others passing so much judgment. We create false movements and ideologies to empower our deep discrimination, as if to say, "If you're not exactly like me, you're automatically my antagonist." You might not like it, but who are you to determine what is normal or abnormal in other people's live? What do you know that the Lord himself doesn't know? People say that homosexuality is a sin, so what do you call what you do in secret behind your wife's back or with multiple people? We should respect each other and leave each other alone other regardless of what we call atypical or sinful.

It surprises me how often the story of Sodom and Gomorrah is used to condemn homosexuals. It's so wrong. The story in the Bible is only about ill will. They're punished because they commit incest and want to rape the messengers of God, not because they are two men. It's all about inhospitality, but antigay people use it as propaganda and to inflame the hearts of people with hate. We're so quick to talk about immorality that we can't see that we're throwing cold water on everything to obtain self-satisfaction. People shouldn't have to hide their love for someone else. Society condemns the union of two persons of the same gender who are in love, and all the while, animals and plants couldn't care less about it. Because of civilization, humanity has become a dictatorial system where those in power can tell everyone which way to go and who to love. I'm not sure I understand the doctrine that says that human power contradicts natural law. The most honest, pure thing—the best part of existence—is loving somebody. We haven't evolved past this ruthlessness. I also don't understand why those same antigay protestors stay quiet about polygamy. (Unfaithfulness to your spouse is also called bigamy.)

Theologically

Christian clergy largely ignored homosexuality until the eleventh century, when it was actually digested by the church very well. Probably, the church considered it to be low-stakes immorality, all things concerned, and didn't rally against it. It was tolerated and allowed between members of the highest autocracy under the veil of secrecy. Again, homosexuality is not a recent development—it has always existed. Monks were doing it among themselves and with adolescents, as well. To deviate from society's rules, some men went to the monastery to camouflage their feelings toward the same sex. Pederasty used to be a secret affair among members of high society, the unanimous and anonymous clan. They kept it among themselves and blamed the lower class if their protection was ever threatened. Humans make laws for things they cannot understand, so same-sex love and intercourse take the hit. In this era, anyone who didn't follow the law became guilty, whereas the philosophers who operated under the same laws and broke those laws went free, even though they were acting against of their own regulations.

In our century, marriage shouldn't reflect an obligation to procreate. Marriage is the union between two souls, which is not the case for the polygamist. Wedlock didn't even exist before we create that nonsense to legalize law. There's nothing in the Bible about this except in the Canaan, which only explains the miracle of changing water into wine during the ceremony of marriage. God doesn't care about this social law we made to control society. As long as there's love between two persons and they consent to living together, we should consider it normal. I'm pretty sure that if God wanted it to be otherwise, he wouldn't have made LGBT people. It's only immoral because people have constructed it as being abnormal, even though it's normal for animals and plants. Is your human brain less evolved than that of a flower or leaf? We inflict universal laws, but they don't mean anything in real life. We create rules like we're God because each of us has the tendency to define how all we live. All laws are not reflections of God's morality, and we all know it. In the third and sixth commandments, it says, "You shall not take the name of the

Lord, your God, in vain. [...] You shall not murder." But what have you done? You hate and kill in the name of God, and that's a sin, per the ninth commandment: "You shall not bear false witness against your neighbor." People look for any reason to be against LGBT people and then call themselves Christian. True immorality is when you search for uniformity among people, which doesn't exist in nature.

Same-sex behavior is not unusual or unnatural. It's all natural. Parents are responsible for that phenomenon, not the children. If there is someone to blame for that condition, it's parents. If scientists like Dr. Rice would talk more about it, many lives would be saved. If they tried to inform the public about that change in metabolism, many progenitors would get tested for testosterone levels so they can get treatments before procreating. If they acknowledge to the public about what they've found in their research—that homosexuality it's not a person's fault but rather a bodily failure to produce or overproduce hormones, they would save many lives. LGBT people wouldn't get as depressed and rush into the void so regularly. I understand that we all have the freedom and rights to believe whatever we want and to be suspicious about other people's choices in life, even choices that are independent of their wishes. But don't you ever ask yourselves, "If it was me, what would I do? How would I react to peoples' opinions?" What you think is insignificant and easy in life might be a huge problem for LGBT people at all times.

Theologians, commentators, translators, and writers are like us in that they can make you believe their own schools of thought. I believe that everyone knows someone who is in the closet, even if they don't know it yet. I'm sure that God doesn't love them any less than he loves straight people. If you took time to learn about LGBT people, you would know that they don't hate you. They are the nicest people in the world. They accept, with faith, who they are and how they were born, and this is a big quality. If everybody was gay in that world, we would be so much better off. The planet would be a better place to live in, and we would all be at peace. Who starts the violence? You do, with your false convictions. They are as normal as we are, even cleverer, kinder, and more respectful. Stop discriminating. They are who they are. Every time malevolence gets to you, sing Bob

Marley's song, "Let's Get Together and Be Alright." It's just a simple act of comprehension, and you need to change your heart. It's amazing to find out in this day and age just how many people still live in fear. Homosexuality is no longer a concern for me, and I feel so free. I got over it and hope you do too. My children are lovely the way they are. I couldn't be prouder of them.

53

An Unpredictable Life

GROWING UP, I DIDN'T know that life would be so limited for me. Life is full of promise that might not come to fruition. I suppose that we're all born to accomplish great things, to be healthy, and to go toward our final destinations with minimum complications. This is what life should always be, but unfortunately, it's not always the case. For some people, this may be realistic, but for others, if they are blessed enough to last, they need to work hard to attain this level of glorification. Whatever your lifestyle is, be respectful and loving to yourself and your neighbors first if you want to be respected and loved by others.

What people might not know is that as I've gotten older, I've become more susceptible and sensitive to every word and gesture due to the increase in the severity of my ailments. I feel deeply any mistaken interpretation from my family and friends. I can feel it when people ask me "How do you feel?" just to satisfy their curiosity or as a way to start a conversation. Sometimes, I talk to you because I'm feeling a little bit seedy and need a little attention from you to warm up my frigid heart. Sometimes, even when I'm talking to you, I'm consumed with angst, asking myself, "When the worst will happen?" Even when my face is covered by the mask of happiness, I'm still worried for my health. Also, don't put me down with your propaganda of "I'm sorry." What in the world are you sorry for? You're in no way the cause of my bad health. When I share my story with you, I only want to share my sorrow, so can you just listen? Don't say meaninglessly "I know how you feel." How could you? What do you know about my feelings? You're not standing in my shoes or sharing my footpath. Have you had these maladies before? Are you an expect of chronic diseases? I'm not blaming anyone who has an easier life than I do. I'm just telling you my state of mind because you asked, and as such, I need your comprehension *vis-à-vis* my fear to make it an easygoing interaction for me. With your incomprehension, you became part of the cause that makes me plunge, every so often, into deep distress, where I have no chance of being well at all. Families need families, and friends need friends in circumstances like mine.

The same way we don't choose our family, our gender, our sexual orientation, or our time of birth, people don't choose to have one or more chronic diseases. Why would we ever consciously decide to be perpetually sick? It's a fact that we can choose our friends, our career, where to live, and so on—these are the accessories of the human being—but our genuine lives can't be altered even though we might desperately want them to be. I would love, for just for a moment, to trade my unhealthy life for a healthy person's life, to experience the awareness of such comfort. However, I can't. I would love to experience in my body the phenomena of being healthy, that which I've been deprived of my whole life. I would also love to switch my life, for one day, only one simple day, with someone who is disease-free so that I can feel their sensations and have the pleasure of saying "I'm feeling 100 percent well today!" Of course, this isn't a possibility, and it is what it is. Do I get mad? On occasion, yes, but quite often, no. I believe that we hold what we are meant to hold and that we have no choice. If, by hazard, we fall down during the course of our march through life and cannot stand up anymore, it's not because we made a choice; it's because of destiny.

My dominant thought, the one that always graced in my head, was "I'm fine," and apparently, I was. Everything seemed to be so beautifully normal at the beginning of my life. As I became older, I realized that my cry at my birth was a warning that my life was going to be in the hemisphere of survival. I'm not saying that it is as such for everybody, that crying at birth always means bad fortune and bad health, but it depends on what life brings to you. Some children are born holding a golden spoon, with a nice and fair life waiting for them. Others are born with swords hanging over their heads, and others with the sword of Damocles, retained only by a single hairy thread, making any move fatal. Mine is likely the last one, where everything becomes a problem. My mother was certain that my existence would be overwhelmed with difficulty due to the fact that I was born from a complicated pregnancy. However, she didn't know, nor could she anticipate the degree of sicknesses that I would later bear. We live in a society where ill health, except for things like cancer, is not seen as being serious. Our burdens are often seen as being "nothing" in comparison to those who are deemed "terminally ill." In their eyes, they can only see the surface of the person under which the sickness hides. They don't think that challenges or worries exist under there. We're all right, they say. We're not ill, so we shouldn't be complaining. Or, we must be pretending! The fact is that we're not always bedridden, and that makes it complicated for outsiders to understand.

People tend to ignore that we live among imposters, imposters who have taken our bodies hostage and have avowed to slowly destroy us. How are we supposed to not worry? Worrying is part of our existence, something like a second nature, inherent in our evolution. In modern life, everyone lives with worry, no matter the cause. Such callousness can make me very sensitive to people's hurtful opinions, which is a form of ignorance. Ignorant people refuse to see the invisible through their healthy eyes. Does their opinion really matter? I say yes sometimes and no sometimes, depending on my relationship to a person. The closer you are to my heart, the more it matters to me, and I think we're all the same in that sense. People can be so cold to others with their unfair, competitive ways of thinking. They say to my face with deleterious gazes, "At least you're still alive! Some people don't make it to the age you are now." Some don't make it; yes, that's true. But I'm still a living human. I have feelings and deserve the kindness of consideration, sympathy, and respect. Comparison has never helped. It doesn't help us feel connected or that we can share our sorrows. Instead, it demolishes the support you're trying to give me as well as my trust in you. People often don't realize that their behavior harms others. We're humans with hindrances that they don't have. My sickness is a very real problem, regardless of how minimal you think it might be. Do you ever think about how I might feel after staying up all night with pain, a pounding heart, going nuts about life, being cold and hot over my negative thoughts, having an empty soul that cannot reply to my innermost inquiries, unable to focus even on the least significant things, my carcass full of rotten insiders? You might say, "Oh yes, I understand you very well," but have you ever experienced any weird sensations like mine? I have to believe that your spirit isn't cognizant of your snide remarks. You're completely cut off from the normal comprehension of what is to be a human being and setting your mind on the fact that I'm just delusional. How could you be so blindly incapable of seeing that I'm trying to spare myself from a curse? This is the mystery of my torment—the torment that has been held captive for so long behind my mask of a good appearance.

    I'm not searching for pity or for anybody to feel gloomy because of me. My intention is simply to let you know that when you see people in the street, regardless of how they might look, they're not always what you think they are: happy, healthy, or living ideal lives. A face's appearance is a tricky stage because the mind doesn't always reflect the body. If you have no medical knowledge, most of the time, you can't assess whether someone else is ill. Laughing doesn't always express happiness, sometimes it just gives the impression of it. Anyway, what would life be if nobody struggled and we all always reached our ideal goals? Boring! Selfishness and laziness would invade our world even more than they already do. Would we be able to tell difference between anything? I can hide my situation perfectly with a fake face to make believe that everything is normal. My families and friends are not always aware of my secrets and the painful feelings that I've lived with for a long time. I was surely sentenced to die at birth, but God changed his plan and said, "No, she shall live." I still don't know why and for what purpose. Perhaps I have a duty on earth to carry through, but the fact is, I'm well and alive and will fight to stay in good spirits. We all know that wherever people are rejoicing, elsewhere people are grieving over a fatality, eventuality, or adversity in life. After reading this memoir, I hope that you'll have a better and more sympathetic view of people living with chronic diseases and their daily struggles and accommodations.

For me, traveling offers a kind of fullness of information about other cultures and things that we would otherwise never imagine. Also, traveling allows me to disappear into a world of forgetfulness. When I go on vacation, I have to count on the fact that some days, I will surely be sick and unable to go out. Still, vacation is temporarily healing for me. For the duration of that period, I can pretend to be a woman who is mostly free of pain and liberated from illnesses. My soul becomes totally separated from the physical actions of my miserable body and floats to an immaculate white cloud floating over a garden of happiness. The joys I encounter by a simple change of landscape and by enjoying other people's cultures are so relevant to my spirit that they seem, for a moment, to take orders from my morale only. My ailments disappear for a while. Sometimes, during a vacation, I have to spend one or two days in bed to recuperate from the overdoing it the day before. I try to forget who I am and what I have, but the diseases never forget me at all. I like to experiment with new traditions and meet new civilians. If your body can handle the aplomb of traveling, just do it for a moment of relief.

At the end, what is life for me? Life is a string of perpetual, hazardous, chance occurrences. Certainly, life has a different meaning for each person, but we all began existence with the same mission—to reach the end point. No matter what path we follow, the sole goal is and always will be the same. Life is a special race in that you can't determine where it will begin or where it will end. My life is comparable to nature: sunny today, rainy tomorrow, and stormy the day after. But isn't nature beautiful despite all of this? This is how we should always see life. Like the plants, which grow, bloom, and eventually fall down, our lives take the same trajectory. The insects make holes in the leaves, bad weather cracks the tree branches, and so do diseases to the human body. Some plants are pest-repelling, antiparasitic, and weather-resistant, and they just fall down without ever being attacked, and so it goes for healthy people who just die from old age. It's not that these plants have been lucky, it's because that's just the way they are. Some of us have more burdens than others do, but we all must finish at the same destination. I can't say that I've loved my life every day, but as of the present time, I can say that I've adjusted to it as a way to accept and live my life with a soul full of love.

Despite of all, I'm so grateful for many blessings: My eyes are still good. I can see my face in a mirror. I can talk, and my tongue is still doing its original movements in my mouth. I'm still breathing on my own (by the grace of God, considering that the night before writing this, I had such shortness of breath and I swore I wouldn't breathe normally anymore). I can still touch myself and feel it. I can walk despite the pain that threatens to take away my mobility. I'm able to smell the wet soil after a drizzle of rain throughout the night, which is my favorite natural scent. I'm able to look at the crystalline dew on the stem of a plant and smile at the firmament for all the details it created. And I can witness the rising of the sun as it shyly brightens the sky and earth.

I believe that my maladies are a double blessing from God. I'm still able to observe the magnificence of all these things and the magnitude of some of my own parts, which have stayed loyal to my body. I call it a blessing, not luck. Why? I was created to live longer. I'm one of the millions of warriors who battle every day for a good health and seek to be victoriously rewarded. I doubly thank him for these glorious gifts of life. Many times, I've been near death, but I survived because it wasn't my time yet.

54

Lifetime Friendship

NATURE HAS REMAINED A mystery in my life. All I know is that it marked me forever with indelible ink. The hours I spent throughout my life carefully watching all of nature's details have been very beneficial to me. I use it to make examples and comparisons during my moments of exasperation in life, when I've had to reconcile my two selves: happiness and madness. The close associations among the ocean, the sky, and the sun still take my breath away any time I have the leisure of facing them together. They give me the opportunity to appreciate the universe for all its wonders and rejoice that they're available to my view. Nature gives me the perspective on life that everything shouldn't always be the same. It's good, sometimes, to have some clusters of challenge in life. They help us jog our memories and recall that we haven't being thankful enough to God for all his creations and his blessings. My life has been defined by so many enigmatic occurrences that I wonder about myself: who am I to have such an exceptional existence, where uncanny, unfortunate, illuminating things happen one after another? I believe that the emotions running through my blood give me my beliefs, the spiritual power of faith that makes me always think that tomorrow will be better. I feel the pillars that encircle my essence, which kept me as rigid as a rock and allow me to absorb the annoyances of life with dignity.

I feel like the butterfly, beautiful to look at and fragile to the touch. I feel like the horse, strong and brave, able to carry the world on my back, which isn't always dependable. I feel, sometimes, like a monster, living under the dark thumb of fear. I wonder when the bright light will come to take away my pitiful soul. I feel like the flower seed, which germinates, grows, blossoms, fades, and dies after all. I feel like the bird, using its wings to freely reach all its desired places without restraint. I feel like there is a sad part in my body that you cannot see. I feel like the sun, rising down and up like a human being with chronic disabilities does: one day up and one day down. I feel the urge to scream, to scream about the wonder inside of me, which is similar to that of others. I feel like I'm in the middle of the ocean, and there is a big hole in my canoe. I have no safety ring and I can't swim, so only God's hands can rescue me from the inevitable, perilous water. I feel like the lamb, silently waiting for the sacrifice with fear of a certain death but acceptance of being the chosen one. I feel that I have been baptized again, that the spiritual dove flew out of my body to reveal to others that I'm free of bad episodes and persecutions. What I feel doesn't seem so imperative anymore. Now, all I need to do is survive all my tribulations. My life has been a controversy in motion, and I need peace.

I've seen a lot and gone through a lot in my life. I've dealt with many burdens, both insignificant and significant, that have made me believe in destiny. Every day, I wake up and brag about the blessings that surround me. I could be dispirited, unhappy, and ungrateful all the time, but I endeavor to be the opposite. I want to think about the thorns in a branch of roses; as much as you want to grab a beautiful flower, you should expect to get lacerated many times as well. Likewise, a storm never lasts because it's just the reverse of good weather. When the sky turns pitch-dark, and the flashes of lightning take possession of the battle that is about to start, and the clouds hide somewhere to allow passage to the rain, I know that after all is over, the sun will rise, shinier and without shame. This is nature's law, and as such, everything has a reason to be. Don't you sometimes want to know what is behind the silence of the nature? Does the forest stop talking while you're there, or is it talking to us despite our disinterest?

THE DAILY BATTLE FOR A NORMAL LIFE

What's beyond my contemplation? What's behind the scenery? My eyes are so eager to find out the secret. Only the heart can profoundly feel the limitless elation beneath the muteness of nature.

Acknowledgements

BEFORE I END MY story, I want to thank all the people who have been compassionate and concerned toward me, and especially to those who, to this day, have never abandoned me.

To Jean PHC, Darlene ARNP, and particularly, my first PCP, Dr. Joe, thank you for your generous care, your cautious advice, and your all-ears listening. I'm proud of having you in my life, and you should always be proud of your good work. God put you in the medical field to make a difference, and for me, you went above and beyond. I deeply appreciate your kindness as well. May he bless you always.

I truly appreciate the academic pursuit of better health, and I have to thank all the researchers in the field, especially my dear Dr. Howard S., for your efforts in researching treatments for HCV, HIV, cancer, and many other ailments.

I'm tremendously thankful for my neighbors, B. P. and Pat, for their help and support during my many bouts of sickness and for caring about me to this day. You always noticed when my car was in my driveway during the workday and called to ask if I was on vacation or sick, and how you might be of assistance to me. B. P., you always fixed my broken things during my husband's absences, and, Pat, you brought me groceries when my body was too lazy to go out on its own. You warmed me up when my heart was cold and dashed by my multiple afflictions. You talked to me when I didn't have anyone else to talk to. I cherish these moments, which were very beneficial for my health.

I started writing this book over five years ago. I wrote about three paragraphs and left it untouched, thinking that I wouldn't be able to achieve this objective. Truthfully, I didn't think I would write more than these few paragraphs. Pat, my dear friend, came to see me in August 2012, which was a very sick time in my life. She chatted with me for a moment about female topics, and she told me that I should write a book about my life and endurance. She didn't even realize how complicated my life really was! She didn't know too much about me, but she could see that my ailments suggested that there was more under the surface. She believed that my life would make an interesting story. I told her that I'd started a book in 2007 after the death of my mother, but that I couldn't continue. She assured me that I could and showed strong confidence in me.

From that moment on, I felt the urge and desire to write about my journey with chronic diseases and demonstrate that people don't always recognize the suffering of others. I wanted to let people know that they're not alone in their daily spiritual battles and that, together, we can hold hands and march to providence. I wanted to say, don't be afraid to use the shoulder of a friend or a family member to search for commiseration when you feel defenseless. We all own candles that aren't always lit up, so we need to make efforts to light them during moments of exasperation. Do this so that you can clearly see the way to the promised land. Pat gave me the buoyancy and the courage that I was looking for. I went back to those three paragraphs and began to write this book. Like the slogan for Obama's 2018 campaign said, "Yes I can." Pat and her husband weren't only my neighbors but my guardian angels, my benefactors, and my caregivers. I won't ever forget everything that you've done for me. Thank you, my friends. I love you.

What would life be without a best friend? That was who T. C. was for me. T. C. listened to me without putting her priorities first. Sometimes, I promised myself that when she called, I would let her talk for once! I knew that friendship shouldn't go one way, but inevitably, the moment I said "Hello," I became selfish and immediately forgot about my resolution. She asked me, "How was your day?" and I just kept going and going. She called me on her way home almost every day, and we talked about everything. I always expected and waited for her call. We never got bored with our daily conversations. This is how we knew that we were born to be friend-sisters. We like and dislike the same things, except that she is more religious than I am. She prays and brings me blessed water and image of Notre Dame and every religious article in which she believes, thinking that she might advocate for my prayers in front of God. Notwithstanding, I don't pray for myself because I have faith in my destiny. I don't have to, though, because she prays on a quotidian basis for everyone in the world! Like a doctor takes care of our health, T. C. takes care of our souls. Monthly, she unites people at her house just to pray. I love you my dear friend, my sister in God. Thank you for your listening, your patience, and your continued support.

My love goes to Clara, who always taught me by example that "it's never too late to do well." "*Nininne* Oli" (meaning "Godmother Oli"), she said, "you can do it." She believed, like me, that nothing is impossible when your heart is deeply in it. She doesn't let a week pass without inquiring about my condition. I love you like a daughter, dear godchild.

I'm so grateful to my son Scott for his support. He was sure that I could write this book from the moment I told him about it. "You will find plenty to talk about," Scott told me. "You went through so much drama and so many burdens in your life." They exclaimed with extreme conviction in my abilities that I could write a book.

Scott is the one with a strong character, so he can pass as the oldest. He knows almost all about my burdens. I can talk to him, and he'll advise me. One day, I was in great pain and didn't feel like talking to anyone. I wouldn't answer the phone, no matter who called. Sam is the kind of man who never gives up and will make it everybody's problem until he gets his way. When he didn't hear from me when he was in Haiti, he kept calling my cousins, my friends, and Scott to find out what was going on with me. He was probably worried, but I didn't care about other people's feelings. Mine had been hurting for a long time. That day, I was immunized completely to people's daily repetition of "How are you today?" I didn't want to hear it, especially over a long-distance telephone call, so I resolved to not answer my phone. This was one of those days when I couldn't control my emotions. All I wanted was golden silence around me. The silence of the lamb that doesn't make one screech, even when the big knife is careening toward her throat. So having failed to reach me, my husband called Scott, and Scott called as well. I didn't answer.

That day, my son drove seventy miles round-trip to come to my house to find out if the Jolly Roger flag was planted in front of my house as a sign of death. He came at 11:30 p.m. and wasn't home until 2:00 a.m. He had to go to work the next day at 6:00 a.m. He was more concerned and scared for me than anyone else was. He couldn't sleep without hearing from me. He was and is always there for me. I regretted that I'd caused him sadness and worry. I'd wanted to punish Sam, not my poor son. Scott was the husband, the son, and the friend. Throughout my many treatments, all the responsibility fell on his shoulders. At work, they used to call him my second husband, and he was. He picked me up at work so many times, and his name is still on all my medical papers to be called in case of an emergency. He has that gifted kind of personality that makes me smile as soon I see him. I love you, sunshine. Thank you for everything.

I have to brag about my oldest son too. He moved back home at just the right moment when I needed help. By Jove, in February 2012, he called me and told me that he would be back home soon. This was after he hadn't talked to me in almost a year. They always say that children return to the thumb of their mothers when they feel abandoned. That is exactly what happened to my son, Steven, when he left his fiancée. I was glad to hear from him, especially that he'd be back home. Everything happens for a reason, they say, and he was back at a time that I really needed help from close family. From July to November, he was the one who chaperoned me to the doctors for tests, took me to the emergency room, accompanied me to the market, etc. He also kept me company during the day and at night when I had to stay at the hospital.

"You see, Mommy," he proudly said to me many times when I was sick, "I've never been back here. I never thought that I'd be back living with you again, but God has a purpose for me, a mission, which was to be there for you at the right time."

He's a good talker. He can easily get to your sentimental core and make you blush, this son of mine. It's true—he's so lovely. There is no doubt that God didn't want me to be alone at that crucial time.

THE DAILY BATTLE FOR A NORMAL LIFE

I don't know what I would've done if he hadn't been there. I would've had to take risks in the streets or to tell the truth about my health when people asked me if I needed help. It would've been impossible for me to drive myself anywhere. I don't want to think about the real reason he came back. All I knew is he came back at the opportune time. He had a hard time with me because I tested him in so many ways. I needed to know that when I called him, in less than two minutes, he would be able to find out if I'm okay. My sugar went too low many times when I seriously thought I wouldn't make it. I trained him to be in my bedroom less than two minutes from the moment I called him, in case I had something very serious. Without any complaining, he passed the test. He was a radical child, always excluding himself from the family, but when he returned home, he and I became so close. I could see his loving, caring side, and to be honest, it shocked me to discover that in him. Thanks for everything. I love you, sweetie pie.

My younger son is an absentee. He left home right after high school. After college in Detroit, he moved to San Francisco and came home every December to be with us for the holidays. Unless there was an event requiring his presence in Miami, he only stayed for a week or two. I never liked to bother him with my health problems. I thought that being away and far from his family were enough challenges for him. I kept him out of my troubles. I manage to find the best voice when I talked to him on the phone and was sick. He calls every week, but he also calls to tell me when he wants to check on me, or to tell me that he's working on a background video for a celebrity, which he knew always makes me excited. Sometimes, I don't even mention that I don't feel good. When he was a child and I was at the hospital, everybody came to visit me except him. When I asked him the reason that he didn't come, he told me that he didn't want to see me sick. I knew how hard it would be for him if he knew of my trials, especially because he was far away, so I kept them from him. When the earthquake smashed Haiti and we didn't have any news from his father, I could hear him crying over the phone. He's very sensitive, the type of person who rejects the fact that it's normal for their mother to be sick sometimes. He came in January instead of December that year, when I told him about my biggest disease and how I got the HCV. He kind of said, *mea culpa, mea maxima culpa*—it's my fault. He didn't say too much because that was already too much for him to bear. He just gave me a long hug. I'd never told him about it before, but he was finally old enough to know about it. He was very enthusiastic about me writing a book too. Thank you for believing in me and that I was able to write a book, even though you know English is not my mother language. I love you, baby cake.

In addition, many thanks are owed to my husband, Sam, for his extraordinary support. Sometimes, my views are different than his, and often I blame him for not being present enough. Even though he calls four to five times a day, it never replaces the shoulders he could offer during my moments of sickness and weakness. He certainly loaded his obligations on someone else. However, I have to confess that his physical presence notwithstanding, he won't sleep without hearing from me first. His first thought in the morning is about me too. I know that because he often calls at 5:00 a.m., then 6:00 a.m., then 7:00 a.m., every hour until I pick up and say that I'm all right. Plain and simple, he is my friend. Sometimes, while he is overseas, we talk on the phone and watch the same programs on TV, as if to simulate being in bed together. He plans this to remind me that although he is far away, his soul is always with me. I truly love you, Sam.

To everybody who has being a pioneer in my life, I say **thank you**. To those who I encountered only once on my route but who had an impact on my life in one way or another, I say **thank you**. To my dearest friends, who have supported me with a smile, a word of encouragement, or a crazy story to make me laugh during my tribulations, I say a heartfelt **thank you.** To those whose bad comments have inadvertently pierced my heart and put me on the defensive, I also say **thank you** for trying to talk to me as your way of showing support. Moreover, to those who can barely express themselves because of pain and desperation, I say, let me hold your hands in mine so we can walk together down this thorny road of ours. **Thank you** for walking with me. Furthermore, to those who keep their heads straight with dignity and faith despite their trials, **thank you**—you have been a model of courage, perseverance, and joy for me. I salute victims of diseases, heroes of illnesses, and survivors of life's many battles. **I love you all.**

About the Author

The author, Lorette Gay, truly believes that it isn't by hazard that bad or good things happen to us. We're here on earth with a predeterminate assignment and with a plan that was designed for each of us. We don't make our destiny; we're born with it. Born in Haiti and married, she's the mother of three lovely, handsome children. At the age of ten, she traveled to Canada with her mother, then returned to her origin country two years later to complete her residence. Oddly, her mother refused to go back. In 1987, after the presidential overthrow, she and her family established their lives in the United States. She thought that it wasn't meant for her to become Haitian Canadian but a Haitian American. She never had the good fortune to meet her father, even once in her life. She was left to live with her grandparents. Deprived of her mother's presence, and as the only child in her grandparents' house, aloneness didn't take long to invade her young soul. She took refuge in reading books, especially good French literature books—Victor Hugo, Pierre de Ronsard, Jean de LaFontaine, etc.—and Haitian literacy classics of Oswald Durand, Etzer Vilaire, and Massillon Coicou, to cite a few. She also took real pleasure to observe the folkloric panorama of the nature. Nature, which has become her best friend. Through her journeys, she has encountered various up and downs that didn't let her any lull. She doesn't let all this dishearten her because of her belief—that burdens are part of our life to deal with, no one is exempted, and our destiny is unchangeable. Life can be crueler to some, but the cruelness of life should not be defined as a punishment or comeuppance but as a preordained path to follow through.

CPSIA information can be obtained
at www.ICGtesting.com
Printed in the USA
FFHW022203110619
52954608-58553FF

9 781644 249253